God,
Scepticism
and
Modernity

Ϙ PHILOSOPHICA

40

God, Scepticism and Modernity

KAI NIELSEN

University of Ottawa Press
Ottawa • London • Paris

© University of Ottawa Press, 1989
Printed and bound in Canada
ISBN 0-7766-0241-1

Canadian Cataloguing in Publication Data

Nielsen, Kai
God, scepticism and modernity

(Collection Philosophica ; 40)
Includes bibliographical references.
ISBN 0-7766-0241-1

1. Atheism.   2. God — Proof.   3. Natural theology.
I. Title.   II. Series.

BL2775.2.N43 1989   211'.8   C89-090249-6

UNIVERSITÉ   UNIVERSITY
D'OTTAWA   OF OTTAWA

The University of Ottawa Press wishes to thank the University
of Calgary for its support in the preparation and publication
of this book.

**The Philosophica series
is sponsored by the
Department of Philosophy
at the University of Ottawa.**

General Editor: Guy Lafrance

For Hendrik Hart and Béla Szabados
who disagree with much of it

Contents

Permission to publish the essays in this volume has been granted by the following:

Alba House, Staten Island, New York
  (Chapter 2)
Idealistic Studies, Clark University Press, Worcester, Massachusetts
  (Chapter 9)
The *International Journal for Philosophy of Religion*, Martinus Nijhoff
  Publishers, Dordrecht, Holland
  (Chapters 1 and 3)
The *Journal of Religion*, University of Chicago Press
  (Chapter 13)
The Philosophical Forum, Baruch College, the City University of New York
  (Chapter 5)
Philosophical Investigations, Basil Blackwell, Oxford, England
  (Chapter 11)
D. Reidel Publishing Company, Dordrecht, The Netherlands
  (Chapter 7)
Religious Studies, Cambridge University Press
  (Chapters 10 and 12)
The *Scottish Journal of Theology*, Scottish Academic Press Ltd.,
  Edinburgh, Scotland
  (Chapter 4)
Sophia, Deakin University, Victoria, Australia
  (Chapter 6)
The Thomist, Washington, D.C.
  (Chapter 14)
University of Notre Dame Press, Notre Dame, Indiana
  (Chapters 8 and 15)

Introduction

I

NATURAL THEOLOGY ONCE PLAYED A VITAL ROLE in the defence of religion, and there are those today who believe that, if religion is to have anything like an adequate defence, at least the minimal claims of natural theology must be sustained.[1] What did natural theology try to achieve? It tried to show that the core cosmological commitment of the believer, namely the belief that God exists, could be rationally sustained by showing that from information believers and unbelievers both agree on, utilizing standards of inquiry they both share, they could establish that God exists or that at least such a belief was rationally justified, i.e., more likely to be true than its denial.

For natural theology, where it is in the service of Judaism, Christianity or Islam, to sustain its core claims, it would have to show that it was irrational for at least a reasonably knowledgeable unbeliever not to shift to being a believer and that it would be irrational, in such circumstances, not to believe that God exists, that God created the world and all the beings in it and that God providentially governs the world. To argue the case successfully, the natural theologian would have to show that the unbeliever ought to believe those things on pain of being inconsistent with his own overall belief-system and on pain of violating his own criteria of rationality. He cannot, if a natural theology succeeds in establishing its case, fail to believe in God without being irrational. This is, of course, a very strong claim. Still, it is the claim that natural theology has always made.[2]

Classically Augustine, Aquinas, Scotus and Ockham developed elaborate metaphysical systems in an attempt to make the case for natural theology. With the Enlightenment, and particularly with the work of Hume and Kant (the latter himself a pietistic believer), it came to be widely believed, in intellectual circles, that natural theology had been undermined, not only in the sense that the claims of certain natural theologians had been refuted, but that the very idea of a natural theology had been shown to be misconceived. The counter-Enlightenment, where it took a religious turn, did not try to restore natural theology but accepted the Enlightenment's critique of natural theology and took a fideist turn. (Georg Hamann and Søren Kierkegaard are key figures here.)

Sometimes (to use Terence Penelhum's terminology) this has taken the form of a conformist fideism and sometimes the form of an evangelical fideism.[3] The former consists in the belief that scepticism establishes that it is reasonable to follow the habits of ordinary life without accepting metaphysical claims about a reality behind appearances. We can, and indeed should, follow the religious practices of our faith without much attention to the cognitive creedal claims of religion. Bayle and Hamann are historical examples and D.Z. Phillips and Ilham Dilman contemporary examples. Evangelical fideism, by contrast, believes that scepticism has established that it is not unreasonable to believe in a reality behind appearances in ordinary life even though that belief is groundless, and similarly it is not unreasonable for the believer to believe in God and to follow the requirements of that faith even though no justification can be given for the belief. Pascal and Kierkegaard are historical examples and Alvin Plantinga and Nicholas Walterstorff are contemporary examples.

In this volume I seek to further the Enlightenment project of showing that neither can we have nor do we need a natural theology, neither theoretically nor humanly, and that the fideist options are also not genuine options. I argue that it is not merely the case that there are no sound arguments for the existence of God and that the claims of religious experience give us no good evidential grounds for belief in God but that no such arguments or evidencings could do anything of the sort, for the very concept of God, where "God" is construed non-anthropomorphically, is incoherent. The problematicity of the concept of God in developed forms of Judaism, Christianity and Islam is so deep that it is irrational for someone to believe in God who is fully aware of that problematicity. There are, of course, anthropomorphic conceptions of God—Zeus-like conceptions of God—that are coherent, but, while being coherent, it is little more than a superstition to believe that such a God exists. We do not know what would have to be true for it to be the case that the non-anthropomorphic God of developed forms of Judaism, Christianity or Islam actually exists, and we do not understand what "God" on such a conception refers to. By contrast, when we operate with a Zeus-like conception of God, we know what "God", on such a conception, refers to and we also have the very best of reasons for believing that it is false that such a God exists.

The first chapter of this book tries in a general way to make that case. Then, in chapters 2, 3, 4, I examine various attempts in the tradition of natural theology to rebut such claims and to establish the intelligibility and rationality of the God-talk of Judaism, Christianity and Islam. Chapter 14, while linking with the chapters that immediately precede it, should also be seen as a return, though now from a new angle, to an examination of the feasibility of this general project of natural theology.

In the middle sections of this book, I turn to modernist or perhaps post-modernist conceptions, conceptions which do indeed take—indeed normally just assume—natural theology to be an impossible task. First, I seek, against another kind of atheism—the "Wittgensteinian" atheism of Alasdair MacIntyre—to (a) meet its critique of what it would take to be the "positivist" atheism argued for in this volume and (b) to critique MacIntyre's own form of rather religiose atheism. (This, of course, refers to MacIntyre's views before he took his Catholic turn.) Then, in Chapters 6 through 11, I return to a central and abiding concern of mine, namely to what I have dubbed Wittgensteinian fideism, the most powerful of the contemporary articulations of conformist fideism.[4] After giving it its full run, revealing its plain appeal and power in answering to the concerns of the religious life, I subject it to a sustained critique in its strongest forms, namely as it occurs in the writings of Stuart Brown, D.Z. Phillips, Ilham Dilman and Norman Malcolm.

In Chapters 12 and 13, I critically examine and then argue for setting aside two other forms of Christian revisionism, namely the cautious revisionism of Terence Penelhum and the starkly reductionist revisionism of Richard Braithwaite and R.M. Hare. Finally, in chapters 15 and 16, I return again in more general terms to arguments for the incoherence of God-talk. There I specify more exactly what is at stake, make carefully qualified and what I hope are nuanced arguments for the irrationality of religious belief, delineate carefully the senses in which my account is a form of atheism, and examine and respond to a series of searching criticisms of my defence of atheism.

It is the underlying thrust of my argument in this book to raise fundamental questions about the reference and the meaning of the concept of God in Judeo-Christian-Islamic religions. Arguments are given to establish that that very concept is so problematic that its very coherence is in doubt. With that I argue the rather startling thesis, and what some may well find to be the offensive thesis, that belief in God in our times is irrational for someone who has both a good philosophical and a good scientific education. However, it is important to realize that this claim is doubly hypothetical for it comes to this: if natural theology has been shown to be a nonstarter and if arguments of the sort I shall make about the incoherence of God-talk are correct (partially explaining why natural theology is a nonstarter), then, for the philosophically and scientifically trained who are in a position readily to recognize this, it is unreasonable to believe in God.

However, some will resist this, claiming that the unbeliever has, and unavoidably so, his groundless beliefs as well and that the believer, being in the same boat as the unbeliever, is not being irrational in continuing to believe in God. This parity argument, as it has been called, was not in the forefront of discussion when I wrote most of these essays. However, it has since come into prominence and, if it is well taken, it would deflect some of the central theses argued for in this book. So I shall in the next section of this Introduction first state it and show its rationale and then, in the following sections, argue that it does not shield the believer from the charge of irrationality or from the wolves of disbelief.

II

Natural theologians, to come first indirectly at what is involved in the parity argument, tried to show that it is irrational not to be a religious believer. They sought to establish either that, in some tolerably latitudinarian sense, God's existence could be proved, or that there are probative revelatory phenomena attesting to his reality. Their stance was not the defensive one that without such assurance religious belief would be shown to be irrational but they were concerned with the task of showing that unbelief is irrational.[5] Philosophical argument and the persistent thrust of modernization have changed things here. There is a broad consensus among people (principally theologians and philosophers) who have studied such things that the task of giving some refurbished proof or providing probative revelatory phenomena is hopeless. Perhaps, not unsurprisingly, we have no sound a priori proof that there can be no such proof of God's existence, but we have very good inductive reasons for thinking such religious assurances will not be forthcoming, given the long history of failures and the character of the arguments deployed against such assurances. Natural theology is a research program that has been thoroughly tried and has not panned out.

The contemporary heirs of natural theology (including those philosophers who have been dubbed "reformed epistemologists") have become much more modest than natural theologians of old. They have taken up the less demanding defensive task of defeating the arguments, emanating from the Enlightenment, of sceptics over religion. They have tried to show that sceptics are not justified in claiming that religious beliefs are irrational. The religious believer, they contend, is both intellectually and morally within his rights to remain faithful to his religious traditions. A key argument here is the one, mentioned in the previous section, that has been dubbed the *parity argument*. Crudely expressed, as a first approximation, the parity argument goes like this: suppose, for the sake of the argument at least, that the sceptical arguments against natural theology are well-taken and that we have no proofs, including proofs of probative revelatory phenomena, for the existence of God; and suppose further that sceptical arguments such as Hume's are also well-taken concerning our basic commonsense convictions, e.g., the reliability of our sense impressions, our belief in induction, our belief in other minds, the reality of the past and the like, such that they are revealed to be mere *natural* beliefs, bits of animal faith, as devoid as are our religious beliefs of rational justification. Then, if this really is our situation, the unbeliever (the atheist or agnostic) can hardly be justified in claiming that there is anything irrational about the believer's continuing to believe in God and Divine Providence when the unbeliever also accepts many groundless beliefs (beliefs for which there is no rational justification) which are seen to be fundamental. Indeed, the unbeliever may even be caught up in an inconsistency of sorts in making secular commitments without grounds while refusing to make groundless religious commitments, commitments which would also be central for a properly human life.

There is, as is in effect suggested above, a stronger and a weaker form of the parity argument. On the stronger form the unbeliever is said to be in some, not very clear, sense inconsistent in adopting groundless commonsense beliefs and rejecting groundless religious beliefs. There is, however, a weaker, more permissive version of the parity argument which does not try to convict the unbeliever of inconsistency but contends that the believer and unbeliever are in the same boat, that both must accept groundless beliefs such that the unbeliever cannot, while accepting the groundless beliefs of common sense, justifiably accuse the believer of irrationality for accepting religious beliefs purely on faith.

I shall be concerned here exclusively with the weaker permissive version of the parity argument. It is an argument that has considerable support, at least among the Anglo-American community of philosophers of religion. Defenders of reformed epistemology such as Alvin Plantinga have accepted it, as has Norman Malcolm among the Wittgensteinian fideists, and as has such a modest and cautious Christian philosopher as Terence Penelhum.

The stronger form has little plausibility and has been reasonably set aside. My argument shall be that the weaker, more permissive, purely defensive version is, when carefully inspected, also without merit. It will not provide a sound basis for setting aside the challenge to religion which emerged from the Enlightenment.[6]

III

The parity argument, in its most general form, has at its core the claim that, epistemologically speaking, religious beliefs are no worse off than the beliefs of common sense and science, since all these beliefs rest on assumptions that cannot be rationally justified. We cannot, they claim, rationally justify our belief in the past, in other minds, in the general regularity of nature, or in the reality of even the most stable and precious of our moral beliefs. We are not justified in accepting these beliefs as rational or reasonable to believe without proof while at the same time rejecting equally central religious beliefs as groundless or irrational. Both sets of beliefs are groundless and since it is not unreasonable even in the face of philosophical scepticism to accept the groundless commonsense and scientific beliefs, it cannot then, by parity of reasoning, be reasonable or justifiable to claim the groundless religious beliefs are irrational.

I want first to argue that it is only a severe foundationalism—a foundationalism of the classic sort—that gives the parity argument much force. Without assuming such a foundationalism we have no good reasons for believing the different sets of belief are actually in the same boat. By "classical foundationalism" I mean a philosophical account that holds that the only beliefs that are properly basic are beliefs which are self-evident, or are incorrigible reports of experience, or are evident to the senses. These, and only these, are foundational and thus properly basic beliefs on such an account. All other beliefs are rational if and only if supported either deductively or inductively by properly basic beliefs. However, on the basis of this classical foundationalism it is not only religious and theological beliefs that are neither properly basic nor supported by properly basic beliefs but the same thing obtains for our familiar basic commonsense beliefs such as beliefs in other minds, the reality of the past, and the like. Indeed, none of the things we want and need to know, or even the things among them that we should be confident we could really know, could be known or justifiably believed if we accept classical foundationalism. Indeed classical foundationalism itself would be self-refuting, for that very belief itself is not self-evident, evident to the senses, nor an incorrigible report of experience, and we cannot deduce it from any such propositions or inductively justify it on such a basis. If it provides a correct criterion of rationality it is itself irrational.

However, and be that as it may, the whole thrust of the development of contemporary philosophy cuts against foundationalism. Most notably, if there is anything at all to the work of the pragmatists and such powerful anti-foundationalists as W.V. Quine, Wilfrid Sellars, Richard Rorty and Donald Davidson, such foundationalism is, to understate it, very implausible indeed. There are no beliefs which are foundational in that strong sense and, except in a very pragmatic sense, we should not take any beliefs at all to be foundational. Rather we have, with a thorough-going fallibilism, a web of belief in which all beliefs can, at least in principle, be questioned, and none is taken to be self-evident or certain or beyond the very possibility of being questioned. The beliefs in a web of belief get mutual support from each other in patterns of coherence with some being more central than others in the system and thus, if you will, pragmatically basic, but none is permanently immune from revision and perhaps even rejection and none is basic to all the rest such that if it falls the rest will all come down. (That does not mean, in practice, that there is even the slightest reason to be sceptical about some of the central, most deeply embedded, commonsense beliefs in the system.)

Classical foundationalism yields, in a way that is utterly fantastic to someone not hooked on philosophy, pervasive scepticism where it is accepted as a litmus test for not only religious and scientific beliefs but even for those commonsense beliefs of which we are the most confident, such as: Canada participated in World War II; it is colder in December in New Hampshire than it is in July; people require sleep; they are sometimes in pain; and the like.

The parity argument found its rationale, such as it is, in the claim that religious belief is no worse off epistemologically than the beliefs of common sense and science, since all such beliefs—that is both religious and non-religious beliefs—rest after all on assumptions that cannot be justified. They are all, that is, ungrounded beliefs. But that belief itself—that strong claim about ungroundedness—requires for its justification the acceptance of classical foundationalism, a belief which is at worst self-refuting and at best arbitrary. Classical foundationalism is arbitrary because: (a) its merely stipulated criteria for what is justified and what is not are so severe that none of our beliefs (even our commonsensically firmest beliefs) could possibly be justified if we accepted such criteria; and (b) it does not at all give us grounds for not accepting instead a fallibilistic coherentist model of justification which does plausibly sort out our justified from our unjustified beliefs in a way that roughly squares with our firmly intuitive but still reflective sense of which beliefs are justified and which are not and which enables us in turn to correct our commonsensically intuitive beliefs when they clash and correct the practices of practical justification when in their very workings they get into difficulties. There are in that fallibilistic model no absolute presuppositions which just must be accepted nor any use of assumptions which cannot possibly be rationally justified. This is a model plainly alternative to foundationalism which squares better with our common sense and scientific understanding of the world, but no reason has been given for accepting the more arcane criteria of foundationalism rather than the more commonsensical criteria of fallibilism. This being so, it is more reasonable to stick with fallibilism.

Many of our commonsense beliefs and scientific beliefs can be shown to be justified on such a coherentist basis. We can know, as we bloody well ought, that the Earth has existed for many years past and that cats do not grow on trees, while still having very good reasons for being sceptical of religious beliefs such as that God speaks to us, God created us, God shows providential care for us and, indeed, that God exists. Defenders of the parity argument take the classical epistemological tradition entirely too seriously. They should take to heart Richard Rorty's and Charles Taylor's attack on the tradition.[7]

Our basic commonsense beliefs—beliefs philosophers such as G.E. Moore took to be commonsense beliefs—and our religious beliefs are not on parity. They are perhaps on parity where classical foundationalism or something very like it is accepted, but there are very good reasons indeed for rejecting classical foundationalism as well as any of its near cousins.

IV

The parity argument was designed at the very minimum to show that in important respects, with respect to the justifiability of their beliefs, believers and non-believers alike are, if classical foundationalism is true, in the same boat and that as a result non-believers cannot justifiably accuse believers of irrationality. Whatever we want to say about the justifiability of that general accusation about irrationality, the parity argument, if my above argument is near to the mark, cannot be deployed to protect the believer.

Perhaps a more modest foundationalism could be used to shore up the parity argument. Suppose this foundationalism claims that a belief is properly basic if and only if it is either self-evident, fundamental, evident to the senses, to memory, or defensible by argument, careful deliberation or inquiry. A belief is correctly said to be fundamental if it is unavoidably part of the noetic structure of every human being and could not be abandoned without causing havoc to that structure. I have in mind beliefs like

"The sun comes up in the morning", "The Earth has existed for many years past", "Human beings need food and sleep", "Dogs cannot fly", and the like.

However, I am not inclined to believe that we should accept even this modest foundationalism, but should continue instead to work with a non-foundationalist coherentist model such as the one described above. But suppose for the sake of continuing the argument, we accept this modest, rather commonsensical, foundationalism. My argument will be that even if we do it will not help the parity argument in the least, for on such a basis many of our commonsense beliefs would be shown to be properly basic, in being fundamental or evident to the senses, and many of our scientific beliefs would be defensible by argument and inquiry but, with the collapse of natural theology under the onslaught of the Enlightenment, and most particularly because of the criticisms of Hume and Kant and their contemporary heirs, religious beliefs cannot be so justified even if we do accept a modest foundationalism. They are not in the same boat with commonsense and scientific beliefs.

Religious beliefs are not fundamental in the way we have just characterized them with our modest foundationalism. And, with the failure of natural theology and like endeavours (including arguments from religious experience), there is no establishing them on the basis of experience or reasoning. Moreover, unlike those commonsense beliefs that are fundamental, religious beliefs, particularly in our epoch, are not seen as being fundamental and as such universally accepted either intra-culturally or across cultures. But the commonsense beliefs in question (beliefs like Moore's truisms) are so accepted. We can hardly avoid recognizing that people require sleep and that water is wet and that we human beings must have it once in a while, but our very noetic structure would not come crashing down if we ceased believing in God or ceased believing we are immortal. These beliefs, by now in our culture, as they *perhaps* are in all modern cultures, are, culturally speaking, optional. They do not have proper basicality and they may well, for all the parity argument can show, be irrational. Finally religious concepts, as we shall see in the arguments of this book, and as is widely believed by believers and non-believers alike, are problematic.[8] I shall argue the stronger claim in this book that they are not only problematic but that certain key religious beliefs are actually incoherent. But, whether or not that strong claim can be made, they are at least problematic in a way that many commonsense beliefs are not. Moreover, religious concepts are not problematic because of the acceptance of some contentious epistemological or semantical theory or other but are widely sensed to be problematic by many moderns quite independently of their adopting any such theory. (It may be relevant that children in the course of their socialization into our culture are not infrequently very puzzled by such conceptions.) They are, as it were, pre-analytically problematic though certain theories may enhance and conceptually direct our sense of their being problematic.

As a philosopher doing second-order conceptual analysis, I can get equally puzzled about the proper *analysis* of God and the soul on the one hand, and about the past and what it is to have a sudden thought on the other. But that second-order puzzlement about the proper analysis of the past or what it is to have a sudden thought can, and indeed should, go hand in hand with there being a firm agreement about particular claims and ways of uncontroversially establishing their truth, as (for example) establishing the truth of "Abraham Lincoln was the American President during the Civil War" and "Jones suddenly thought that it might rain and went back for his umbrella". But "God spoke to Jones" or "Jones has a soul" are not something whose truth we know how to settle and we are not clear in making such utterances what, if anything, we are talking about when we speak of God and the soul. We are, that is, not only unclear about the correct *analysis* of these terms, we are uncertain as to whether they make sense at all. Our doubts are not only second-order doubts but first-order doubts as well. With the past and with sudden thoughts, by contrast, they are *merely* second-order doubts. We are, that is, in no doubt at all about the reality of what we are talking about in speaking of the past or in the having of sudden thoughts.[9] The engine is idling when we have doubts here. Our doubts are mere Cartesian doubts, not real doubts, as when we have doubts about God and the soul.

V

It has been asked why in various of my writings I give so much attention to atheism. The same question, plainly, could be asked about this volume. Isn't that, the questioning could continue, like taking in religion's dirty linen? Atheism among the philosophers of our time is as common as the common cold. Why, standing where we are now, knowing what we know, make such a big deal about "the death of God"? It is, after all, as evident as evident can be.

I share, as the argument of this book and several others as well makes plain, that fairly widespread intellectual judgment, taking it to be only slightly hyperbolic.[10] Still, that notwithstanding, it reveals in us a depressing human blindness—and most particularly so if we are lucky enough to be members of the intelligentsia—if we do not also find the death of God a cultural problem. It might very well not be a personal problem for some of us at all, but it should be evident that it is now a cultural problem, a problem deeply anguished over by many thoughtful and sensitive people in our society and societies like ours.

To not care about atheism and its denials in such a circumstance reveals a distressing historical and psychological blindness; our very preoccupation with the "post-modern condition" in effect attests to that. It takes a not inconsiderable obtuseness about our lives as human beings not to feel the chill of modernity, not to be capable of feeling the power of Nietzsche's words in *Thus Spoke Zarathustra*:

'Whither is God?', the madman cried, 'I will tell you. *We have killed him*—you and I. All of us are his murderers . . .' What were we doing when we unchained the earth from its sun? Whither are we moving? Away from all suns? Are we not plunging continually? Backward, wideward, forward, in all directions? Is there still any up or down? Are we not straying as through an infinite nothing? Do we not feel the breadth of empty space? Has it not become colder? Is not night continually closing in on us?[11]

I write in the tradition of the Enlightenment and, as does Jürgen Habermas as well, in defence of modernity against both pre-modernity and post-modernity. Put otherwise, in effect, I try to show here, as against post-modern Heideggerian and Derridian challenges, that there is no nihilism that lies at the heart of humanism. Still, and that notwithstanding, it betrays a certain spiritual blindness not to see the loss in metaphysical comfort given (1) the demise of the age of faith with the, to borrow Max Weber's idiom, relentless disenchantment of the world and (2) the replacement of Cartesian certainty in later modernism by a through and through fallibilistic outlook. Indeed with not a few of us this fallibilism has become such a deeply embedded, routinely accepted, background assumption that we are hardly even aware of it as an assumption. And with that mind set, there is no longer even a trace of any nostalgia for the Absolute. But, it is also true, that for many, decentredness remains a problem and, for some, it leads to a raging against reason. It is simply to be blind not to see in our cultural circumstance the depth of our culture shock here.

It could be responded that all of this should have been played out in the eighteenth and nineteenth centuries when the core intellectual issues vis-à-vis religion and secularism were, emotional responses aside, settled. It is now rather late in the day, the response could continue, to be seeking such metaphysical comfort or going on a quest for certainty. The issue of atheism *should* no longer be on the philosophical agenda. Again I too believe that, but to ignore that it is, in fact, still on the cultural agenda for many people and on the philosophical agenda for some of them reveals a cultural blindness and perhaps, where there is an unwillingness to argue the case of belief versus unbelief, it reveals as well intellectual arrogance. Such an attitude is something like the mirror image of Christian fundamentalism. It may be wearisome for some of us now, after so much critical water has gone under the cultural bridge, to argue the case against pre-modernity yet again, but it is at least a cultural necessity.

It is important for us to realize that we are living in the time of a long spiritual interregnum. The old faith with its essentially pre-modern outlook is not yet quite dead and a firmly New World outlook—a *Weltgeist* for a New Age—is still in the long process of forming and is not yet firmed up. In such a cultural condition Heideggerians and Derridians flourish along with talk of post-modernity and nihilism. It is with this backdrop that a probing, non-evasive discussion of belief and unbelief, a discussion of Judaism/Christianity/Islam as over and against forms of atheism is a necessity.[12] These alternative frameworks need to be juxtaposed with clarity and non-evasiveness as, culturally speaking, deeply challenging and disturbing options between whole ways in which we can respond to our ensnarled lives. Against post-modernity, I argue that there really is a *should* to be argued here that is actually worth bothering about and is not something which is just to be dismissed with irony. These frameworks that are our options carry with them alternative moral visions and we should sort ourselves out with respect to them.

However, the main thrust of my argument in this volume is directed to doing my bit to bring to a completion what central earlier figures in the Enlightenment started. I see it, that is, as a mopping up operation. In my optimistic moments (moments which are just some of my moments) I allow myself to hope that in two hundred years or so religion will no longer be on the agenda in our society's attempt to come to grips with itself, but that, notwithstanding that, human beings will still be making sense of their lives and the moral lives of people will remain intact even though belief in God and God-substitutes will have passed from the cultural scene. My hope is that the loss of religious belief will not, as it need not, bring with it a moral wilderness. Indeed my hopes here run deeper. I look to a time—dream of a time—where, with the development of the productive forces, and with that the transformation of society, there will be a greater human flourishing than we have now and that we will finally have, free at long last of sexism, racism and the division of society into classes, what the youthful Marx called a truly human society, and this on a world wide scale. It is easy to sneer at such a belief, to treat it as Marxist naïvety. Even as a hope, to say nothing of a program, it is easy with superior deconstructionist wisdom to be ironical here. Indeed, I think it is altogether too easy to make sport of that "great nineteenth century illusion", the very idea of progress. Be that as it may, my principal task in this volume is not to make thunderous cultural prognostications about the course of history or to articulate a grand theory or some grandiose meta-narrative. My task is a different one. It is to argue, within the bounds of what in an Anglo-American and Scandinavian philosophical culture is a standard philosophical methodology, that, however the *Weltgeist* goes, what cognitively speaking is the case is that central strands of religious belief are so problematic that they are best judged to be incoherent, but that, notwithstanding this, there is no *reason* to despair if there is no God or to think that life or morality would be without point in a Godless world. It is not that nothing would change with the death of God. The habits of the heart as well as the habits of the head, if God-talk were generally acknowledged to be incoherent, would in important ways be transformed, though this can and should (*pace* Sartre) take place without our coming to live in an entirely different "moral universe", let alone our finding life in a Godless world a moral wilderness. To not lose one's nerve and to continue to have a sense of social solidarity and some conception of a humane social order in an utterly secular world is in effect to affirm a form of humanism.[13] This humanism, as it were, cuts against both a religious orientation, which is essentially a pre-modern stance, and a post-modern stance. But the sustained object of my critique in this volume is directed at what in effect is a series of pre-modern religious turns, unless one wants to count either Wittgensteinian fideism or Christian positivism (Braithwaite and Hare) as post-modern forms of taking, in spite of everything, a religious turn. These, however, are turns Derrida and Lyotard might find to be rather quaint forms of post-modernism. In any event, I am concerned here to defend essentially the values and basic conceptual framework of the Enlightenment against repeated and varied turns to religion from, on the one hand, forms of metaphysical religiosity to, on the other, forms of Wittgensteinian fideism and other forms, radical and non-radical, of religious revisionism.

NOTES

1. Richard Swinburne, *The Existence of God* (Oxford: The Clarendon Press, 1979); H.A. Meynell, *The Intelligible Universe* (Totowa, NJ: Barnes and Noble, 1982); Anthony Kenny, *Faith and Reason* (New York: Columbia University Press, 1983); Terence Penelhum, *God and Skepticism* (Boston: D. Reidel, 1983); Penelhum, "Do Religious Beliefs Need Grounds?"*Nederlands Theologisch Tijdschrift* 80.3 (1986): 227-37; Swinburne, "Faith and Reason," *The Journal of Philosophy* LXXXII.1 (1985): 46-53; and Shabbir Akhtar, *Reason and the Radical Crisis of Faith* (New York: Peter Lang, 1987).

2. Penelhum, "Do Religious Beliefs Need Grounds?"

3. Penelhum, *God and Skepticism*. See also William Alston's discussion of it in his review, *The Philosophical Review* XCIV.4 (1985): 599-602.

4. See my references to Wittgensteinian fideists in chapters 6 through 11. See also D.Z. Phillips, *Beliefs, Change and Forms of Life* (Highlands, NJ: Humanities Press, 1986); D.Z. Phillips, *Primitive Reactions and Reactions of Primitives* (Oxford: Exeter College, 1983); and John W. Cook, "Magic, Witchcraft and Science," *Philosophical Investigations* 6.1 (1983).

5. Penelhum, *God and Skepticism* 157.

6. Penelhum, "Do Religious Beliefs Need Grounds?" and his *God and Skepticism*.

7. Richard Rorty, *Philosophy and The Mirror of Nature* (Princeton, NJ: Princeton University Press, 1979) and Richard Rorty, *Consequences of Pragmatism* (Minneapolis: University of Minnesota Press, 1982); Charles Taylor, "Overcoming Epistemology," *After Philosophy*, eds. Kenneth Baynes *et al.* (Cambridge, MA: The MIT Press, 1982) 464-88; and Taylor and Alan Montefiore, "From an Analytical Perspective," *Meta-Critique*, ed. Garbis Kortian (Cambridge, Eng.: Cambridge University Press, 1980) 1-26.

8. For a fine cluster of arguments that bring out how much this is so, see here the exchange between John Skorupski and Robin Horton. John Skorupski, "Science and Traditional Religious Thought I & II," *Philosophy of the Social Sciences* 3 (1973): 7-115 and "Science and Traditional Religious Thought III & IV," *Philosophy of the Social Sciences* 3 (1973): 209-30. Robin Horton, "Paradox and Explanation: A Reply to Mr. Skorupski I," *Philosophy of the Social Sciences* 3 (1973): 231-56 and Robin Horton, "Paradox and Explanation: A Reply to Mr. Skorupski II," *Philosophy of the Social Sciences* 3 (1973): 281-312. Skorupski, "Comment on Professor Horton's 'Paradox and Explanation'," *Philosophy of the Social Sciences* 5.1 (1975): 63-70.

9. G.E. Moore, *Philosophical Papers* (London: George Allen and Unwin Limited, 1959) chapters II, VII, IX and X; A.E. Murphy, "Moore's 'Defense of Common Sense'," *The Philosophy of G.E. Moore*, ed. P.A. Schilpp (New York: Tudor Publishing Company, 1942) 299-318; and Gilbert Ryle, *Collected Papers*, vol. II (London: Hutchinson, 1971) chapters 11, 14, 23, 24 and 27.

10. Kai Nielsen, *Contemporary Critiques of Religion* (London: Macmillan, 1971); Nielsen, *Skepticism* (London: Macmillan, 1973); Nielsen, *An Introduction to the Philosophy of Religion* (London: Macmillan, 1982); Nielsen, *Philosophy and Atheism* (Buffalo, NY: Prometheus Books, 1985); and Nielsen, "Religion and Rationality," *Analytical Phi-*

losophy of Religion in Canada, ed. Mostafa Faghfoury (Ottawa, ON: University of Ottawa Press, 1982) 71-124.

11.   Cited by Mark C. Taylor in his "Descartes, Nietzsche and the Search for the Unsayable," *New York Times Book Review* 1 February 1987: 3.

12.   I speak of atheism as distinct from agnosticism here quite deliberately. For my argument that agnosticism, where it contrasts with atheism, is a non-starter, see my *Philosophy and Atheism* 9-28, 55-75, 77-104.

13.   Sidney Hook, *The Quest for Being* (New York: St. Martin's Press, 1961) 73-102.

CHAPTER 1

On Mucking Around About God: Some Methodological Animadversions*

I

THERE IS CONFUSION AND PERHAPS EVEN INCO-
herence not only in the philosophical and theo-
logical accounts of religion, but in certain central strands of first-order religious discourse itself. Not only the talk about God but first-order God-talk
itself, it is at least plausible to argue, is in certain fundamental respects
incoherent.

While there is a strong temptation in thinking about religion to think
this, could it really be the case that religious talk generally or religion or,
at the very least, Judaism or Christianity, actually is incoherent? If we take
Wittgenstein seriously this could not be possible. For him what is given
are the forms of life, and the forms of language are the forms of life. He
reminds us that ordinary language is all right as it is; it does not need
any philosophical subliming. Our task as philosophers, Wittgenstein would
have it, is to give a perspicuous representation of that language. We must
come, if we would dispel philosophical perplexity, to command a clear
view of the language in question where it is actually at work. Our philosophical accounts of a particular domain of discourse may be confused,
but it makes no sense to say that a whole domain of discourse is itself
confused. In certain moods and when we speculate in certain ways we
slip into perplexities about a whole domain of discourse, though when we
are in such perplexities we usually do not see these perplexities as being
about a domain of discourse. We do not see them as confusions about
the workings of our language, though that is in reality what they are. But
once we see them as such confusions and command a sufficiently clear
view of our language in that domain for our philosophical perplexities to
wither away, the philosopher's task is completed. The only proper task

*First published in the *International Journal for Philosophy of Religion* (1984).

for a philosopher, Wittgenstein argues, is clearly to display the structure of the language area that perplexes us philosophically—or at least to characterize it with sufficient clarity such that our philosophical obsessions are dispelled. But this is all that can be done. There can be no question of criticizing the perplexing area of discourse itself. What we need to recognize is that the forms of language, which are also the forms of life, are the philosopher's *given*. It makes no sense, Wittgensteinians claim, to say that they are incoherent or to claim that they are irrational or somehow mistaken or incorrect or inadequate to capture the complexity of life. We are, rather, limited to displaying their structure.

Such a Wittgensteinian conception of philosophical activity is aptly summarized by Alice Ambrose:

> '. . . What a mathematician is inclined to say about the objectivity . . . of mathematical facts, is not a philosophy of mathematics, but something for philosophical *treatment*. The philosopher's treatment of questions is like the treatment of an illness' (p. 91). This statement, although appearing rather late in Wittgenstein's *Philosophical Investigations*, orients the reader interested in what distinguishes Wittgenstein's conception of philosophical activity from the traditional conception. The traditional philosopher considers himself to be solving problems, whereas, according to Wittgenstein, there are no problems, in any usual sense, to solve. There are only linguistic obsessions to be removed. Obsessions transmute into problems 'misunderstandings concerning the use of words, caused, among other things, by certain analogies between the forms of expression in different regions of language' (p. 43). The result is dissatisfaction with our ordinary language, as if our way of speaking 'does not describe the facts as they really are' (p. 122). But nothing is gained, and no practical advantage is even desired of a philosophical re-description (p. 122). Language as used by the metaphysician 'goes on holiday' (p. 19). Nonetheless, this use is a symptom of a deep disquietude. The therapy for this disquietude (the technique for 'solving' philosophical problems) is according to Wittgenstein to 'command *a clear view* of the use of our words' (p. 49), whereupon the problems should dissolve, '*completely* disappear' (p. 51). Not solution, but dissolution, is the aim; and not to reform language, but to describe it, and in so doing to 'bring words back from their metaphysical to their everyday use' (p. 48).[1]

Philosophical perplexities arise when "language goes on a holiday," when we fail to command a clear view of our language and develop, in reflecting about certain deeply embedded concepts in our language, confused metaphysical conceptions of these concepts—concepts which display themselves in the working of our language. The philosopher, who knows what he is about, destroys such a house of cards by clearly displaying the functions of our actual language at the point where philosophical perplexities arise. When that is done, the perplexity, like a neurotic obsession, will, or at least should, dissolve, for what seemed like a profound problem will now be seen to be a muddle arising from a failure to understand the workings of our language.

II

For approximately a decade after the publication of Wittgenstein's *Philosophical Investigations* (1953), this striking conception of philosophy captivated many (mostly younger) philosophers already influenced by analytical philosophy, and repelled a considerable number of the older generation of philosophers trained in a very different tradition. Indeed the repulsion, like the reaction to Richard Rorty today, was not just, or sometimes at all, intellectually based but came, quite understandably, from an arousal of their anxieties. By now, this Wittgensteinian metaphilosophical message does little more than provoke a yawn from most philosophers, though there are a few philosophers, deeply influenced by Wittgenstein, who in their philosophical practice, though less and less in their programmatic statements, continue to operate with such a conception of what proper philosophical activity comes to. (Richard Rorty, in a rather qualified way, has done something to reverse this trend.)[2]

Both in reacting against it and operating with it, philosophers of religion have been deeply influenced by this Wittgensteinian conception. Philosophers whom I have dubbed, perhaps tendentiously, Wittgensteinian fideists have, at least in practice, accepted it, while other philosophers, often indignantly, have rejected it as evasive and utterly wrongheaded.

It is, I believe, more difficult than most of the parties to this dispute have realized to sort out what is at issue here. Wittgensteinian fideism is very easy to parody. They are those chaps who advert to the fact that there are various language-games, including religious language-games, and that they all are in order just as they are. There can, these chaps believe, be no legitimate question about the coherence of these language-games. It is enough to note that a language-game, including a religious language-game, is played. Some, of course, play religious language-games and some don't; but there can be no legitimate dispute about whether playing or not playing is the more reasonable activity, or whether one is or is not justified in engaging in such activities.

However, while it is easy and indeed even tempting to go ironical about such a position and to ridicule and lampoon it, it is not so evident that there may not be a reading of it which teaches something very deep and important indeed. I continue to feel ambivalent about Wittgensteinian fideism, feeling both (a) that there is plainly something very unsatisfactory about it; and (b) that it touches something deep about religion and, more generally, about forms of life and "groundless believing" that our overly rationalistic philosophical attitudes obscure from us.[3]

I want to see if I can run some of this to the ground. Let me start by returning again to the beginning of this chapter. If this Wittgensteinian conception of philosophical activity is correct, it does not make sense to make the statements I made in the very first two sentences of this chapter. To ask, "Could religious talk or Christianity be incoherent or unintelligible?" would be like asking "What is the tone of pitch?" But, Wittgenstein notwithstanding, it does not seem to me that such a question concerning religion or Christianity is a senseless one or that my first two statements are sense-less. I am, in fact, not unsurprisingly, strongly inclined to believe that they are true. More generally, I am not so confident that such a Wittgensteinian conception of philosophical activity will serve so well in the philosophy of religion, though I am, of course, aware that certain eminent analytical practitioners of the philosophy of religion have conceived of their task at least in part in this way.

I want to try here to show that such putative statements as "The Christian concept of God is incoherent" are themselves intelligible by (a) giving grounds for asserting that they are true; and (b) showing what would count against their truth. If I can establish this, I shall have most certainly shown that such a statement is intelligible. If such a statement is *intelligible* (though perhaps false) the conception of what it is to do the philosophy of religion set forth by such distinguished philosophers of religion as D.Z. Phillips, John Hick, William Alston and Ninian Smart will not do. Such ways of going about things will then be seen to be but a first step. Moreover, if such a general statement concerning the philosophy of religion can be expanded to other domains, the very conception of philosophical activity set forth by Wittgenstein will have been shown to be inadequate. (Even without that generalization, it will to some degree have been shown to be inadequate if such a conception of philosophical activity is not adequate to thinking about God and religion.)

III

Let us start by asking: What evidence can be given for the truth of the claim that the Christian concept of God is incoherent? I think the following will give us some evidence. Christians and Jews say, "God made the heavens and the earth." Compare that sentence with "Fred made bread and soup." And forget here, at least for the nonce, the sense (perhaps the analogical sense) "made" is to have in the first sentence or what, if anything, it could mean to say that something was made out of nothing. Perhaps it is like making a tune out of nothing? What I want to ask is *what* is "God" supposed to stand for in such a sentence and how is the referent of that term to be identified? If "Fred made bread and soup" was used in some determinate linguistic environment, we would know how to identify "Fred" and we would readily enough, if we are practised speakers of English, know what *kind* of reality "Fred" referred to, even if we did not know who Fred was, and we would, in such a circum-stance, understand what it would be like to be extra-linguistically taught, say by ostensive teaching, who and what "Fred" referred to. He could readily, in many circumstances, be pointed out in a crowd: "That chap there with the big ears and dark glasses is Fred." We know what it would be like to point him out and distinguish him from some other chaps. It is a term whose referent is teachable both extra-linguistically by pointing and intra-linguistically by definite descriptions.

Now "God" and "Fred" are very different. For whatever may be the case in certain primitive religions or whatever might have been the case in the early days of Judaism and Christianity, it is plainly the case in developed forms of Judeo-Christianity that there is no pointing to, or any other extra-linguistic teaching of, the referent of "God". In this respect, at least, "God" is not at all like "Fred". Can we teach what "God" refers to intra-linguistically by definite descriptions? Jews and Christians say that God is "the maker of the heavens and earth," "the being transcendent to the world, upon whom all other beings depend and who depends on no one or no thing," "the being of infinite love to whom all things are owed," "the heavenly father of us all," "the infinite sustainer of the universe," and the like.

It is fair enough to say that we understand *something* of these phrases. They are not plain gibberish as is "the colour infinite transcendence," "the procrastination eats expectations," or "the fiddler plays brown." Even such phrases could, of course, be *given* sense, but just as they stand they do not have sense in the corpus of English. They are not like the unproblematic definite descriptions that could be applied to Fred: "The director of the Glenbow," "the chap with the rusting Volvo," "the man who is married to Shirley," "the lad who graduated first in his class at Winston Churchill High in 1962." But, while the alleged definite descriptions associated with God are not gibberish, as is "the fiddler plays brown," they are also not unproblematic like the above definite descriptions associated with Fred. With them we could point out what we were talking about. The Glenbow could be readily enough identified in certain circumstances and "director" could be taught by a variety of ostensive and linguistic techniques. But while there is an activity we could point to for someone who did not understand someone making soup, there is no comparable pointing to—or indeed any pointing to at all—someone making the heavens and the earth. Indeed, someone who thought there just might be would surely show by that he did not understand religious discourse. Still, if someone is puzzled about what "God" refers to, they are going to be equally puzzled about what it is we are talking about when we speak of "the maker of the heavens and the earth." And similar things obtain for the other alleged definite descriptions associated with "God". They are, to put it minimally, not unproblematic in the way the definite descriptions associated with Fred are.

Surely, for Christians, Jews and Moslems, God is an Ultimate Mystery, that ultimate mystery that believers believe answers to their deepest needs. But, that notwithstanding, *what* is it they are referring to or talking about when they use the word "God" or the phrase "the Ultimate Mystery"? If they cannot say at all, why should we, who are not Christians or Jews, believe they are talking about anything at all or saying anything coherent when they say things like "God is my saviour in whom I stand in need"? And why should they think their term "God" stands for or answers to anything at all, when they use it in their religious discourses, if they have no idea of what it is they are talking about when they use the term "God"?

IV

What seems at least radically unsatisfactory about Wittgensteinian fideism is its refusal to face this question. Perhaps, in some way I do not see, this is the wrong question to ask and "the question" should be disposed of as we would dispose of "a question" which purported to ask what kind of non-natural property does "good" signify? But that the above question about God is such a pseudo-question would have to be shown. It looks, at least, as if that God-question is a significant question and indeed an absolutely central question to ask in thinking about religion. To put it in what I think is a minimal way, at least it needs to be shown how that question rests on a mistake, if indeed it does rest on a mistake. The burden of proof cuts against the Wittgensteinian here. It is not enough to say God-talk is in order as it is, and Jewish or Christian belief cannot be at all vulnerable to disbelief because people can play Christian and Jewish language-games. It would appear at least to be the case that, if no account at all can be given of *what* or *who* we are talking about in speaking of God, belief in God is incoherent, and that, if this is our situation after all, the Jewish and Christian religions, as well as other religions invoking such a conception, are incoherent and should not be belief-systems and ways of life to which we should subscribe.

V

Wittgensteinians aside, it could be argued, and in some circles no doubt it would be argued, that my way of arguing has too many affinities with a by now thoroughly discredited logical positivism. Talking in the way I do would not only make nonsense or a mishmash out of religion and theology, it would, as well, in effect, turn a good bit of firmly entrenched natural science into such nonsense or such a mishmash. Molecular biology, for example, is not debarred from explaining biological phenomena in physical-chemical terms because the relevant chemical processes are unobservable apart from the biological processes they explain. But molecular biology is surely not properly described as nonsense or pseudo-science. Logical positivists, even less than post-positivist analytical philosophers, would not even dream of rejecting molecular biology or dream of claiming that such a perfectly in-place science needed de-mythologizing or rational reconstruction in order to count as genuine science. But why then isn't what is good for the goose good for the gander? If molecular biology, when so logically structured, can pass muster, why can't theology, if it is so logically structured? Isn't a refusal to take God-talk as being on a par in this respect with molecular biology-talk pure secular prejudice against religion? Isn't the *ideology* of the atheists or secular humanists showing?

This would be fair enough to say if there were this logical parallel, but there isn't; and *here* an old fashioned logical positivist argument is perfectly in place. The relevant physical-chemical processes are unobservable, but they are only *contingently* unobservable because we cannot now observe them, have no coherent conception of what it would be like to observe them, or no provision is made for observing them even in the theory. But there is no *logical* ban on the very possibility of their being observed as there is in the case of God-talk.[4] Anything that could possibly be observed would not be the God of developed Christian and Jewish religious discourse, but no such *logical* ban is made on the physical processes of molecular biology or on any other domain of natural science. And that makes all the difference in the world. It makes the difference, that is, between terms having an empirical sense or not.

VI

Suppose someone says that, since "God" does not refer to an empirical reality, of course it does not make *empirical* sense. It makes, instead, *metaphysical* sense. But what that means is, to put it minimally, anything but clear. Perhaps "God" is like "2" for people who go Platonistic about numbers and talk portentously of mathematical objects. But that is just bad metaphysics, for people who are troubled by nominalism. Nominalism and Platonism take in each other's dirty linen. We need numbers to do physics and a lot of rather interesting and uninteresting things as well. But that does not mean we need to reify "2" into some kind of queer object. We have these mathematical conceptions we repeatedly use, and indeed some of them may be indispensable to us in all sorts of practical ways, but that is no reason to ramify our ontology so that a physical object ceases to be a pleonasm.

I think such a response is a perfectly plausible way of being tough-minded. But suppose it strikes someone instead as being bloody-minded and dogmatic. So let us allow mathematical objects to read Platonistically for the nonce. There is, let us now assume, some kind of *sui generis* mathematical reality; numbers are eternal. And let us also assume the same thing about logic. So we can, given these assumptions, no longer say that a physical object is a pleonasm, or that there are no eternal objects. But surely this does not take us to a metaphysical reality; such a conception has not yet been given sense. We can and should say, given these assumptions, that we cannot say the concept of God is incoherent because it is incoherent to speak of eternal realities. But God is also said to be an *infinite* individual, an infinite person, transcendent to the world. Acknowledging that there are eternal realities such as numbers gives us no purchase on this. We still do not understand what we are supposed to mean when we speak of an "infinite person" or "an infinite *individual* transcendent to the world."

Suppose it were in turn replied that we do get some sense of that here, for in knowing that numbers are eternal we know, by a few more manipulations, that $2 + 2 = 4$ would be true even if there were no world, and this gives us some sense of what it is for something to be transcendent to the world. (This assumes, of course, that we know what mathematical truth is and that notion, more than common sense realizes, is problematic. But we are assuming here, counterfactually, that it is not.) Even if there were no universe, $2 + 2 = 4$ would still be true. This gives us a sense of something being independent of the world or being non-dependent on the world, and this in turn gives us some sense of what it is to be transcendent of the world.

I think, to get started that way shows how mistaken it is to Platonistically reify numbers, but, as I said, I am, for the nonce, allowing such reifications. So we have a sense of transcendence that is equivalent to eternality. It is not incoherent to say God's existence is necessary (i.e., eternal) in the way numbers are necessary, and that God does not depend on the world, also in the way numbers do not depend on the world, is also evident. If there is a God, he has those features. God could no more be created or constructed than "2" could be created or constructed.

So, after all, "God is transcendent to the world" need not be incoherent. Moreover, since God is a mystery—indeed an ultimate mystery—it is not supposed to be a crystal clear conception but still—and this is what is crucial—it is also not an incoherent one either.

Such a conception of transcendence probably does not give the believer all that he wants in the notion of transcendence. Still, it is not implausible to say that it gives him some inkling here. So let us ride with that. But the transcendence (eternality) of numbers gives us no sense of what it would be like for an *individual* to be transcendent (eternal) except to say, unhelpfully, that individuals are transcendent *just like* numbers are. Tokens are eternal just like types are. But that sounds, at least, like nonsense, for, allowing Platonism, *types* are just what *must* be eternal (transcendent) but no sense has been given as to how a token, an individual, can be eternal. Indeed, by contrast with a type, it is just the sort of thing that cannot be eternal.

We also have no understanding of how an individual can be infinite. We understand that there are an infinite number of natural numbers, but we do not understand what it is to speak of an infinite individual or an infinite person. Moreover, even assuming the reality of Platonic entities, we do not understand what it means to say a person is transcendent to the world, or that a person, or indeed anything else, made the world. Our understanding of the eternality of numbers gives us no foothold here.

Suppose we are told, as theologians have repeatedly told us, that predicates applied to God do not have the same sense as the predicates applied to created beings or other realities. That is fair enough. "Running" in "Charlie is running" and in "Charlie's nose is running" do not have the same sense, and yet both could be expressive of perfectly true propositions for all of that. But with "running" here we have a clear analogy. We cannot, if we are to convey anything coherent, have a complete equivocity as in "He slaughtered the bull" and "The pope issued a papal bull." But no plausible analogy has been made between "individual," as used in "infinite individual," "individual transcendent to the world," and "individual" as used in talk about human beings or, for that matter, German Shepherds.

VII

I have made a lot about how we do not understand what "God" refers to. We do not, where "God" is construed non-anthropomorphically, understand *what* or *who* God refers to. We cannot identify God extra-linguistically. There is nothing like ostensive teaching here and we cannot identify God intra-linguistically either, for the alleged definite descriptions are just as puzzling as is the term "God". Puzzled about what we are talking about in speaking of God, we will be equally puzzled about what we are talking about in speaking of "the infinite other who made the world."

However, some might say that this just reflects a stubborn belief on my part that there can be nothing but physical realities, and that all I have shown by such maneuvers is that God is an *utterly different kind* of reality than a physical reality. It was anticipating this sort of objection that I allowed in—much against my intuitions on these matters—Platonic entities. But I also showed in the previous section these realities are also not good models for what Divine Reality (if such there be) would be like. Someone, particularly someone of Wittgensteinian persuasion, or someone who had read a lot of John Wisdom, might say that this only shows the *kind* of reality that God is is *sui generis*. What it is must be shown on its own terms.

To so argue is an evasion. It has the classical difficulties of the *via negativa*. If we can only say what God or anything else is *not* and if we cannot at all say *positively* what he is, then we in reality do not know what he is, for there are myriads of things and even considerable numbers of *kinds* or *types* of things that anything is not. If I ask you to believe in somorlo—to trust somorlo—but cannot ostensively teach you what "somorlo" refers to, or introduce you to "somorlo" by definite descriptions, but can only say that somorlo is not this or that, you are still in the dark about what somorlo is.

We know clearly enough what *kind* of reality "Fred" refers to and we have some sense of what kind of reality "2" refers to, if we want to talk about "2" in these referential terms at all. We can at least conceptually identify "2" but we can only conceptually identify "God" by using terms which are at least as perplexing as "God" is.

There are terms used in the hard sciences which we cannot ostensively teach either. My talk of there being no logical ban on the possibility
of their being observed is, it might be argued, not to the point anymore
than is the positivist's point about verifiability *in principle*, where counterfactuals have to do all the work. If we say "All sentient life will be destroyed
forever" is verifiable in principle, we must be saying something like this:
though all life has been destroyed forever, yet if there were to be some
life, as in reality there can't be, if this proposition is true, that life could
observe that all sentient life had been destroyed forever. But then some
semi-sentient life would be observing that there was no sentient life at all.
These remarks, to put it minimally, are not unproblematic.

Are the relevant counterfactuals about God similarly problematic?
I say that anything that could be observed could not be the God of advanced
Judeo-Christianity. (Homeric gods are another matter.) That remark, if
you will, is what Wittgenstein would call a grammatical remark. There is
no *similar* ban on observing the fundamental entities of molecular biology.
Similarly, we haven't the remotest idea of how to observe the fundamental
particles of physics. Indeed, we suspect that they cannot be observed and
this also goes with being a non-instrumentalist in the philosophy of science
and thinking that they are part of the furniture of the universe (something
very different from "the maker of the universe"). But this does not rule
out the counterfactual "If we were in a very different position and had
radically different instruments—instruments of a radically different kind
than we have now—then perhaps we would be able to observe them." This
seems at least to be a harmless counterfactual, quite unlike the one about
all sentient life and, contrasting it with the God counterfactual, we can
also see that the God counterfactual is very different and indeed very much
more problematical. We say of God: anything that could possibly be
observed would not be God, but if we were to observe God, though indeed
we do not even know what it would be like to do so, he would look like
thus and so. This is, to put it mildly, a very problematic counterfactual,
while the fundamental particles counterfactual is not at all so problematic.
After all, we understand why there is a logical ban on seeing the Platonic
entity (the type) "2" while we have just seen a token "2". And indeed
there are plenty of them around to be seen. But if a neutrino is part of
the furniture of the universe, just like a grain of sand only very, very, very
much smaller, then there can be no *logical* ban on its being observed.
But God, like the Platonic entity "2", is the kind of entity that in principle
cannot be observed.

This much the *via negativa* can establish. God is not on a
continuum—either one way or the other—with a grain of sand. There is
a coherent logical ban on observing God, and if it makes no sense to speak
of directly observing or experiencing God, it makes no sense to speak of
indirectly observing God either. We must, to say anything intelligible, have
a non-vacuous contrast here.

VIII

I have been concerned, running against the Wittgensteinian stream and a number of other streams as well, to show that certain central strands of first-order Christian-Jewish-Islamic religious discourse are incoherent. Minimally, I have tried to give good reasons, though perhaps not decisive reasons, for believing that the proposition "The Christian concept of God is incoherent" is true. That, if true, is sufficient to refute Wittgensteinian conceptions of religion or at least Wittgensteinian fideism. To show that such a claim not only is intelligible, but that it may very possibly also be true is to change the agenda of the philosophy of religion from its present agenda back to something more like the agenda of the days of positivism and of ordinary language philosophy, where it was not just assumed that religious discourse is coherent. Where this assumption is not made, the central arguments in the philosophy of religion turn not on whether God's existence could in some way be proven but rather the stress is on the question of whether God-talk of the appropriate sort is or is not coherent. J.L. Mackie to the contrary notwithstanding, this is where I think the questions in the philosophy of religion should be returned. This is the point from which it should start.

Notwithstanding what I have said and the cogency of my arguments (if indeed they are cogent), it is certainly possible for someone to wonder if the central strands of a whole domain of discourse could actually be incoherent. Second-order talk about the discourse might be incoherent but not, it is natural to say, the first-order discourse itself. But to deny this does not seem at all counter-intuitive to me. When we read the Icelandic Sagas, *Egal's Saga und Najl's Saga*, for example, and we come across a conception of fate, we may well find it incoherent or, even more extremely, when we read accounts of the cosmology of highland New Guinea—what their culture heroes do and the like—we recognize that such talk is incoherent. (I do not want to say that the line between what is incoherent and what is just outrageously false is always a sharp one. The Sagas talk of certain people being shape-changers. Is this a false belief or an incoherent one?) Similarly (*pace* Winch) we can come to see that Evans-Pritchard was right: it just isn't the case that the witchcraft accounts of the Azande are not in fact true, they *couldn't* be. Given such a recognition about certain central discourses of other tribes, why should rather parallel discourses in our tribe be so exempt? It is counter-intuitive and deeply ethnocentric to think that they should be.

I have also been concerned here to show that Wittgensteinian concerns of what good philosophical methodology or activity should look like have not well served us in the philosophy of religion. And I suspect similar things should be said for political and social philosophy, the philosophy of the social sciences and the "non-foundational" parts of moral philosophy. (Perhaps they are the only parts which should continue to exist?)

IX

All of that notwithstanding, it is still the case that Wittgenstein—particularly the Wittgenstein of *On Certainty*—touched something very deep indeed about the nature and extent of our groundless believing and about the necessity and propriety of it. He, as Richard Rorty has cottoned on to, has given us, without a lot of longwinded pedantry, strikingly good reasons for setting aside the standard questions of metaphysically-based and epistemologically-based philosophy. He has shown us how we can neither find nor do we need to find some kind of philosophical foundationalism (even an "anti-foundationalist foundationalism," if you will) to set aside the standard epistemological and metaphysical questions: questions about solipsism, the external world, anti-realism and the like. He shows us how there can be no genuine question about whether "the sun will come up tomorrow," "whether there are other minds," "whether there is an external world," "whether time is real," "whether there are numbers," "whether any memory beliefs are reliable," and the like. With a thorough understanding of Wittgenstein, we will no longer have the strange urge to ask those "questions". These are not questions to be solved but "questions" which his philosophical therapy, or a philosophical therapy like it, will dissolve. And similar things can be said, I have argued, for extending his method for general scepticism to scepticism about morality.[5] We are as rightly justified in believing that it is wrong to torture little children just for the fun of it as we are in believing that the sun will come up tomorrow or that we have bodily organs. But Wittgenstein generalizes from a one-sided diet; his philosophical therapy will not work so well for "Is there a God?", "Do we have souls?", "Is communism superior to capitalism?", "Is active euthanasia ever justified?", and the like. Achieving a clear command of how a language-game works will not dissolve our perplexities or tell us what we should think about these matters.

NOTES

1.   Alice Ambrose, "Review of Ludwig Wittgenstein's Philosophical Investigations," *Philosophy and Phenomenological Research* SV.1 (1954): 111.

2.   Richard Rorty, *The Consequences of Pragmatism* (Minneapolis: University of Minnesota Press, 1982) 19-36.

3.   Kai Nielsen, "On the Rationality of Groundless Believing," *Idealistic Studies* XI.3 (1981): 217-29. See chapter 9 of this book.

4.   Kai Nielsen, "The Intelligibility of God-talk," *Religious Studies* 6 (1970).

5.   Kai Nielsen, "On Needing a Moral Memory," *Metaphilosophy* 25.3 (1983): 277-306.

CHAPTER 2

God, Necessity and Falsifiability*

────────────────────────────

IT IS DIFFICULT TO KNOW WHERE TO START IN talking about religion. People are puzzled about it and taken up with it in very different ways, but many philosophers' deepest perplexities turn on whether they can make any tolerable sense out of key religious concepts. Where they want to believe, this sometimes leads even to a profound emotional harassment, for in certain moods at any rate the most fundamental concepts of their religion seem quite meaningless to them.

In its own right, this reaction is philosophically puzzling, since for the most part both believers and non-believers, as participants in the same culture with the same forms of life, know how to use religious discourse. In our culture, they both have a participant's grasp of God-talk. At this level there is no significant lack of understanding; they both know how to operate with religious discourse. But knowing how to use this self-involving form of discourse does not imply that there is no bewilderment about its use. Both believers and non-believers alike are baffled by what it is all about.

It is no longer news that a very pervasive kind of disbelief consists in the conviction that key segments of God-talk are not stammering efforts to talk about an ultimate mystery, but meaningless or incoherent stretches of discourse. God-talk, it is held, does not succeed in fulfilling the putative cosmological claims which believers confusedly think they are making when they use such language. Non-Neanderthal believers, on the other hand, though deeply perplexed by the language will continue to claim on pain of ceasing to be believers that, though such talk is perplexing, it is not utterly meaningless or incoherent. In reality such utterances do have a kind of substantive content which enables their users to make intelligible, affirmative, cosmological assertions concerning a mysterious ultimate reality.

────────────────

*First published in _Traces of God in a Secular Culture_, ed. G.F. McLean (Staten Island, NY: Alba House, 1973).

Though they are mystifying utterances, they manage to present themselves as factual claims, that is as true or false utterances about what there is. The believer must take his stand here, but this is precisely where many a religious sceptic is sceptical.[1]

There is a natural response and defensive stratagem on the part of the religious believer that cannot be allowed. I have in mind the kind of fideism which would claim that though the believer's utterances are meaningless, he can believe them anyway. This is nonsense if anything is,[2] for unless we know at least in some minimal sense what it is we are to believe, it is logically impossible for us to either believe or disbelieve. I cannot believe or fail to believe in some putative proposition unless I understand to at least some extent the meaning of "p". Whether we like it or not, we are faced with the very central and fundamental question of whether God-talk does have sufficient intelligibility to give it enough coherence to make faith justifiable. Can we show that God-talk has the kind of intelligibility which would make reasonable, philosophically informed, and perceptive human beings become or remain Jews, Christians, or Moslems?

While religious sceptics do not think that religious discourse has this kind of intelligibility, believers obviously think that it does. How could we rationally decide whether God-talk has sufficient intelligibility to make Christian, Jewish, or Islamic belief acceptable options among the conflicting ways of life?

Theology of Falsification: A. Flew

Part of the issue here emerges from the much discussed "theology and falsification" issue and from what has been dubbed Flew's challenge.[3] Suppose two fast friends, a believer and a sceptic, are standing together aboard ship on a starry night. The believer remarks to his friend, "How can we really deny that God made all this?". The sceptic replies that awe-inspiring and vast as all this is, he cannot see the hand of God in it. "From a human point of view," the sceptic continues, "there are perfections as well as imperfections and order as well as disorder in nature, but there is no reason to say God created or ordained it all." Whatever the believer points to as evidence for God's creative activity, the sceptic interprets naturalistically. On close observation they seem to be using different terminology to describe the same phenomena. Finally, an observer of this discussion begins to wonder if there is anything more than a purely verbal and attitudinal difference between the believer and his sceptical friend. When the believer asserts "God made all this," or "God loves his children," what is he asserting that is different from the assertions of the sceptic with his thoroughly naturalistic orientation?

Surely, if he is doing anything more than talking about natural phenomena in a high-toned manner, he must show the difference between asserting and denying such putative statements as God created the heavens and the earth and God loves his children. If this cannot be done—if it is not possible to show at least what conceivable experiences count for and against the claim that God created the heavens and the earth and that God loves his children—then these putative statements are devoid of factual and cosmological significance. They purport to make factual statements and are actually used by believers with that intent. Nevertheless, they are devoid of factual content if no experiential statements, not even statements recording what it is logically possible to experience, count for or against their truth.

However, as Flew points out, this at least seems to be just the situation we are in vis-à-vis religion. Sophisticated believers so use such key bits of God-talk that nothing counts or even is allowed to count against their truth. If even in principle nothing can count against their truth then neither can anything count for their truth. Thus, in reality such theistic claims are devoid of factual or cosmological significance. Flew's challenge comes to this: the theist seems to use such key theistic utterances as "God created the heavens and the earth," or even "There is a God," in such a way that they are compatible with anything that could conceivably transpire. If this is so, then they are devoid of factual significance. To show that they do have the kind of factual significance and intelligibility the believer requires, the believer must show what conceivable turn of events would count against his putative assertions. He must describe a conceivable turn of events which, if it were to transpire, would be sufficient to warrant the claim that it is not the case that God created the heavens and the earth and it is not the case that God loves mankind.

Of course, as a believer he does not believe that such states will occur. However, if his God-talk is to have factual content, he must not rule out the logical possibility that one could specify an empirically identifiable state of affairs, which, were it to transpire, would warrant the assertions, "There is no God," "God does not love his children," or "God did not create the heavens and the earth."

Much modern scepticism and religious perplexity revolves upon the conviction that theists cannot adequately meet this challenge. Non-anthropomorphites cannot state in straightforward empirical terms under what conceivable conditions they would give up making such key theistic claims. Thus they seem not to be making any real claims at all.

Many have assumed that such a challenge is not really serious because in a somewhat hidden form it presupposes the correctness of the now thoroughly discredited logical empiricist claim that an utterance is at least cognitively meaningless unless it is verifiable (confirmable or infirmable) in principle. But no such general criterion of meaning is presupposed or even involved in Flew's challenge or in my argument. What is involved is the following: an utterance is devoid of *factual* content—and thus can make no factual assertion—if it is not directly or indirectly confirmable or infirmable in principle. This chapter will examine the reasonableness of this assumption.

Many would categorically deny that this is a proper assumption when the subject of our discourse is God. God has the kind of existence, if he exists at all, that makes it impossible to characterize the logic of God-talk in such a manner. God is a necessary being; his non-existence is inconceivable. If he exists, he exists necessarily. Thus, his existence is either logically necessary or impossible. Because there can be no question of an experimental or empirical identification of God, Flew's challenge is not to the point. The only possible identification of God would be a purely conceptual one. If this can be done at all, it will be accomplished through a conceptual analysis which will establish that "There is a God" is *logically* necessary and "There is no God" is a contradiction.

Such a claim leads us to the topic of necessary existence. To evade Flew's challenge, one must establish that the concept of necessary existence or necessary being is a coherent one, that God has necessary existence, and that a purely conceptual identification of God is possible. This will answer the most pressing questions about the intelligibility and coherence of God-talk.

God as a Logically Necessary Being:
C. Hartshorne

I agree that if God exists his existence is necessary. More to the present point, I also agree that if the word "God", as it has come to function in the Jewish-Christian-Islamic tradition, is expressive of a coherent concept, it must be possible to make sense of the notion of necessary existence. But the crucial question remains: can one make sense of necessary existence.

On a certain understanding of Anselm, Malcolm and Hartshorne have tried to explicate and defend a concept of necessary existence. It commits them to regarding God as a logically necessary being and to treating "There is a God" and "God exists" as analytic statements, that is, as statements expressing logical necessities.[4] Though some of the arguments are subtle, because I have discussed the issue at length elsewhere and Malcolm and Hartshorne have been devastatingly criticized by others, I shall be moving here too brusquely and dismissively really to get to the bottom of that issue.[5] Nevertheless, before progressing to my major topic, I wish to indicate the lie of the land and provide some grounds for believing that another conception of necessary existence needs to be appealed to, if this appeal is to serve as an adequate model for explicating the concept of God.

In brief, it is propositions or statements, not beings, that are logically necessary, because it is to propositions or statements rather than to beings or forces that such predicates are applicable. It makes no more sense to speak of a being which is logically necessary than it does to speak of a stone being alienated. Furthermore, there are no existential statements that are logically necessary. J.N. Findlay is perfectly right: if God is treated as a logically necessary being—having logically necessary existence—then the concept of God, like the concept of a round square, becomes self-contradictory. We would thus know for certain that God's existence is impossible, for the very concept of a logically necessary being is self-contradictory.[6]

Wherever x denotes a being or Being, it is never self-contradictory to deny that there is an x. The negation of an existential statement is never a self-contradiction. It is indeed true that "God is eternal" is analytic; it is also analytic to say that God could not cease to exist or come to exist. Thus, "God died" or "God ceased to exist," when taken literally, is a contradiction in terms.[7] By definition God is eternal, and it does not make sense to assert that an eternal being ceased to exist. Nevertheless, it is perfectly intelligible and consistent to assert that there are no eternal beings, and from conceptual analysis alone, it would follow that if there are no eternal beings now, there never were and never will be. This does not establish the truth of the existential statement "There is an eternal being" or the falsity of "There are no eternal beings." Assuming the intelligibility of the phrase "eternal being," conceptual analysis alone cannot establish the existence or non-existence of such beings. Thus, it cannot establish the existence of God.

Though Malcolm has claimed that the denial of a priori existential statements is only a dogma, no convincing example of an a priori existential statement has ever been given. Hume's famous remarks in this regard in his *Dialogues Concerning Natural Religion*[8] would seem to be a truism, namely, that whatever can consistently be said to exist can consistently be said not to exist. When I assert that x exists, I can also consistently deny that statement. As Findlay shows, this is independent of whether there are synthetic a priori statements, for in contrast to existential statements those which are said to be synthetic a priori do not categorically assert the existence of anything.[9] The synthetic a priori statements "Nothing can be red and green all over," and "Every event has a cause" do not make the categorical assertion that anything exists. Knowing the truth of the second assertion does not tell us if there are any events. We know only that if there are any events, they have causes. No existential statement can be logically necessary. The very concept of "a logically necessary being" is self-contradictory.

Metaphysical Statements: M. Charlesworth

Many would meet Flew's challenge by simply denying that, in order to be factual, an assertion must be verifiable or falsifiable in principle or, as I prefer to put it, confirmable or infirmable in principle. They concede that empirical propositions must be in principle confirmable or infirmable, but add as a counterbalancing factor that one must not assume gratuitously that only empirical propositions have factual or descriptive meaning.[10] Why can there not be unverifiable statements of fact; why can there not be metaphysical factual statements that are neither confirmable nor infirmable in principle; does not the word "empirical" qualify facts?

It will be argued that I, Flew, and a host of others are still caught up in a dogmatic and unjustified positivistic spirit. There are certain factual statements, which many have called "metaphysical statements," that are in perfectly good logical order but are not even in principle confirmable or infirmable.

It is surely incumbent upon me to examine some arguments for that claim. One is made by M.J. Charlesworth in his "Linguistic Analysis and Language About God."[11] Charlesworth points out that it is one thing to say that an assertion is a meaningful statement of fact only if we know what would count against its truth; it is "quite another thing altogether to say that an assertion is meaningful only if we know what would count against its truth in the way in which we know what would count against the truth of an empirical assertion."[12] Believers who are at all orthodox take "God will protect me and judge me" to be a factual statement. It is indeed true, Charlesworth agrees, that to be a genuine factual statement (to make a meaningful factual assertion) something must count against its being true. It is also true that to understand such utterances we must know what would count against their being true.[13]

So far there is agreement between Charlesworth, Flew and myself. But, Charlesworth adds, not all "counting against their truth" need be linked to empirical verification. In the case of metaphysical statements, including key theistic assertions, we know what would count against their being true in the sense that "their validity is shown by showing the self-contradictoriness of their contradictories."[14] If, for example, we can show that the assertion "Everything happens by pure chance" is absurd, then "the metaphysical statement that the world exhibits 'order' or 'design'" is meaningful.[15] Metaphysical statements do have meaningful opposites; they do make a non-vacuous contrast: "What is denied by metaphysical statements is some kind of absurdity or self-contradictory 'state of affairs' and this, so to speak, is not nothing."[16]

This argument has several flaws. To show that "stones are females" is absurd does not show that "stones are males" or "stones are not females" is meaningful. "It is false that procrastination drinks melancholy" or "It is not the case that colourless green ideas divorce" are no more meaningful than "Procrastination drinks melancholy" or "Colourless green ideas divorce." All we have done is to put the negative sign, which itself is quite intelligible, before a meaningless collocation of words. Where what we are denying is a contradiction, we should remark that a contradiction cannot be in every sense meaningless. We must understand at least that, given the meanings of the individual words in question, we cannot string words together in this way and assert anything. But being meaningful in this way cannot carry the implication of being assertive. If a given utterance contains a genuine self-contradiction, it cannot be used for stating anything that can be true or false. To try to do so would be to attempt the impossible, namely, to assert at one and the same time and in the same respect the truth of mutually incompatible propositional elements. In effect, a self-contradictory utterance functions to negate itself and thus it cannot assert; it is self-cancelling and ends by affirming nothing at all. Such a sentence unsays what it says and so ends by failing to assert anything. A self-contradictory utterance does not discuss or classify anything; thus it could not possibly assert anything.

When Charlesworth says that the denial of a metaphysical statement asserts a "self-contradictory 'state of affairs,'" he puts "state of affairs" in quotation marks. He does this because he must realize, however dimly, that a state of affairs, a fact, can no more be contradictory than a colourless idea can be green. A self-contradictory statement in principle lacks the power to refer; that is, it is senseless to speak of its referent. Thus its denial cannot refer either, because it does not actually deny that a certain state of affairs obtains. Contradiction and self-contradiction are features of languages not of facts.

In this connection, a defense of Charlesworth might assert that "if necessarily false statements assert what can in principle never be the case, the denial of such a statement must assert what in principle must always be the case."[17] In reality, however, Charlesworth cannot be defended in that way, because "can in principle never be the case" means "logically impossible to be the case." In turn, this implies "it makes no sense to speak of something being the case here." When I deny a self-contradictory statement, I do not assert that another state of affairs must be the case. I simply give one to understand that words cannot intelligibly be so used.

At the very most, it might be claimed that I disguisedly asserted something about the meanings of words. If I deny that there are any married bachelors or colourless green ideas, I am proclaiming that it is senseless to speak of married bachelors or colourless green ideas. I am not asserting that there must be bachelors or green things, and, since "unmarried bachelors" and "coloured greens" are pleonastic, I am not asserting that there must be married bachelors or coloured greens either. "Unmarried" and "coloured" do not really qualify their noun here; they are, in such a linguistic environment, ersatz adjectives which do no linguistic or conceptual work.

If Charlesworth drops the part about "self-contradictory 'state of affairs'" and restricts his claim to "metaphysical statements deny some kind of absurdity," he has said something too vague to be of any philosophical value. If I deny that the moon is made of green cheese or that Nelson Rockefeller could swim across the Atlantic, I deny an absurdity, but it certainly does not follow that I have made a metaphysical statement. I have instead simply uttered an empirical truism. What special kind of absurdities do metaphysical statements deny? From Charlesworth's example, it would seem that they deny statements whose meaning is, to put it mildly, very unclear. An example is his "Everything in the world happens by pure chance." Assuming that "Everything happens by pure chance" is not self-contradictory or empirically false, what kind of absurdity does it have? It has a similar kind of absurdity as "Procrastination drinks melancholy," namely that, while it seems to assert—it has a declarative form—we do not have a use for it any more than we have a use for "Procrastination drinks."

My above remarks need the following qualification. The two phrases differ in that in certain quite non-metaphysical contexts there is a humdrum use for "pure chance" which Nagel has shown to be perfectly compatible with determinism. It is the use of chance in a sentence like "It was by pure chance that we met at the Klausen Pass."[18] If we construe "Everything happens by pure chance" in that way, it indeed becomes a genuine statement; but it also becomes an absurdly false empirical statement. Thus, its denial is not a metaphysical statement either. There is no other use for "pure chance", or at least no other use has been given. Where it is not an empirical absurdity or a contradictory notion, it has no determinate meaning. Like "Procrastination drinks melancholy," or "Disenchanted stone couples suffer alienation," it is without a determinate meaning or use in any *Sprachspiel*; and hence its denial is also without such a use. Since this is so, it cannot be used to assert what is the case or what must be the case.

At one point Charlesworth says that we show the truth of metaphysical statements "by showing the self-contradictoriness of their contradictories." In this case we have, in addition to the above difficulties, others as well. We have shown metaphysical statements to be analytic and, by definition, analytic statements are devoid of factual or substantive content.[19] Charlesworth is correct in pointing out that not all analytic statements are tautologies. However, he is mistaken in thinking that only tautologies, e.g., "A is A," assert nothing at all or are not assertions. Tautologies "do not deny anything, either a possible state of affairs or an impossible 'state of affairs,'" but "Bachelors are unmarried" does not, as I have shown, deny anything either. "A logically impossible state of affairs," like "a round square," is a senseless collocation of words.[20] Anyone who understands the meaning of the constituent terms understands that nothing could answer to that putative description. (It, of course, should not be confused with more mundane uses of language which are perfectly in order, e.g., "The situation in Vietnam is an impossible state of affairs.") "Bachelors are unmarried" signals (indirectly indicates) that certain linguistic conventions are being observed and that for any words with equivalent uses in the same or a different language, it would not make sense to deny such a statement.

Charlesworth maintains that accounts like mine are accounts in which "an arbitrary metaphysical assumption" has been unwittingly or surreptitiously introduced. In view of my above argument, Charlesworth surely needs to give us in precise detail exactly what metaphysical assumption or assumptions have been made.[21] I do not see that I have done anything of the sort here. It seems to me that in arguing against Charlesworth, I have only appealed to the logic or style of functioning of the English language. I would not want to say that my arguments are in any way simply relative to the English language, for certainly what I have said here could be translated into German or French without loss of cognitive content. In fine, I did not make metaphysical assumptions in anything I have said here; I simply appealed to the uses of language.

T. Corbishley vs Nowell-Smith on
Empirical Limitations

In the original university discussion of Flew's chal-
lenge, Thomas Corbishley tried to meet the challenge directly by showing
that there are factual statements which are neither confirmable nor infirmable even in principle. I feel that Nowell-Smith's reply to Corbishley utterly
devastated his central contentions. However, since others disagree and
the issue is a fundamental one, I shall briefly review the arguments.

Corbishley argues that Flew's "notion of what constitutes a fact is
in need of enlargement," and that Flew is right in claiming that God is
not observable.[22] "There is a God" is not equivalent to or entailed by
any statements concerning observable phenomena. Corbishley remarks
that he would "gladly concede to Mr. Flew that when I assert that God
is a fact, I do not mean by that statement that God is observable in the
sense in which gardeners are observable."[23] Even in principle God is not
directly observable. Corbishley should have added that since he is not
in principle directly observable, he cannot be indirectly observable either.
But Corbishley maintains that God is a fact in a "deeper sense" than any
contingent thing is a fact. He believes that it is a fact, and practically speaking
an indubitable fact, that God exists, because if God were not, "nothing
would ever happen at all."[24]

Since this is so, Corbishley meets Flew's challenge in the following
way: ". . . in reply to the question 'What would have to occur or to have
occurred to constitute for you a disproof of the love of, or of the existence
of, God' the only thing to be said is, quite literally, 'Nothing'."[25]
Corbishley takes the question of God's existence to be the key metaphysical
question; he maintains that only "the non-existence of anything at all would
constitute for me a disproof of the existence of God."[26] Given the fact that
"that condition is just not possible," is it not evident that "There is a God"
has factual intelligibility and is manifestly true? Flew's very way of posing
the question begs the whole issue. There can be no situations which are
incompatible with God's existence, for if there are any situations at all (and
there are), then God exists. Given the range of application of the word
"God", we cannot apply the principle of non-vacuous contrast which is
applicable to ordinary descriptive statements. Given what God is, it is
logically impossible that there could be a state of affairs incompatible with
his existence. "God exists" and "I exist" are not the sort of assertions
for which it is "possible to find out anything that could be regarded as
'counting against' or being incompatible with their truth."[27]

Corbishley contends that Flew only makes this challenge as he does
because he uncritically presupposes the common empirical dogma that
"unless facts are visible, audible, tangible or somehow observable by sense-
experimentation, they are not only ungettable; they just are not facts."[28]
Indeed if x is properly called "a gardener" or "a policeman", then x must
surely be something that can be seen. But, Corbishley asks, what is the
justification for claiming "that all facts must be of the same class as

gardeners or policemen"? To reply "that only the empirically observable
is of value for philosophizing" is to make another dogmatic metaphysical
statement that, like "I exist" or "There is a God," is not open to falsification. We must firmly recognize that there are many factual statements not
open to empirical confirmation or disconfirmation. Corbishley maintains
that there are plain factual statements which are compatible with any and
every conceivable empirical state of affairs. "God exists" or "There is
a God" are such statements. Thus Flew's challenge is simply irrelevant
to them.

There are a host of difficulties in Corbishley's attempt to meet Flew's
challenge. P.H. Nowell-Smith only points out a few; but, as Nowell-Smith
avers, there are many more. Those which come out in attempts to meet
Nowell-Smith's reply and arguments of that type will be examined in the
next section. In the remainder of this section I shall reproduce the crucial
(and to my mind quite adequate) substance of Nowell-Smith's rejoinder,
leaving further and more complicated points to the subsequent discussion.

Nowell-Smith remarks that "Corbishley does not answer Flew's main
contentions; he evades them and he feels justified in so doing because
he attributes to Flew a crude sensationalism which he thinks is self-
refuting."[29] As we have seen, Corbishley thinks that Flew holds that "an
unobservable fact is not a fact."[30] This would make it impossible for Flew
to believe that there are magnetic fields; but Flew, like anyone else in the
modern world who has his wits about him, believes that there are such
realities. Moreover, it would be absurd for him not to believe in their reality,
and for this reason we are strongly inclined to agree with Corbishley that
there must be something wrong with Flew's empiricist philosophical
principles.

However, Nowell-Smith counters that such a criticism is wide of
the mark, for Flew need not say that things like magnetic fields, opinions,
or other minds must be observable in order to be facts. "All he requires
is that it should be possible to produce evidence for or against their
existence; and this can easily be done. A pattern of iron filings is evidence
for a magnetic field and Flew's paper is evidence for the existence . . .
of his opinions."[31] Although some empiricists have tried, we cannot identify the meaning of abstract entities, e.g., Flew's opinions, magnetic fields,
orthodoxy or the British Constitution "with their actual and hypothetical
manifestations." Nowell-Smith points out that Flew does not commit this
error. "He makes no attempt to develop a theory on this point."[32] He
only argues, and rightly so, that if such statements as "a magnetic field
can be set up by induction," or "the British Constitution is unsatisfactory"
makes sense, we must "be able to say, at least roughly, what would count
as evidence for or against them."[33] Contrary to Corbishley, this does not
commit one to the claim that only what can be observed can exist.

It is Corbishley's preoccupation with this issue that blinds him to
the point of Flew's parable. The point of the parable is just this:

> God is invoked as an explanation. But if an explanation, of whatever sort, be it
> empirical or metaphysical, is to explain it must explain why things are like this

and not like that. Newton's laws explain the movement of the earth; they would not be an explanation if they were true no matter how the earth moved . . . . And for the same reason, the hypothesis that God exists can only explain what happens on earth provided that it explains why this happens and not that.[34]

Indeed tautologies and other analytic statements and propositions that become true by being uttered, e.g., "I am now speaking," are not falsifiable in principle. Here Flew's challenge is irrelevant. But "There is a God" is not analytic, and "surely Corbishley does not want to maintain that 'There is a God' is necessarily true because it becomes true by being uttered."[35]

Nowell-Smith makes a further important point about "There is a God" that is very frequently overlooked. Contrary to what Corbishley maintains, "the proposition that God exists must follow and not precede propositions about what God is and does."[36] Before we can sensibly ask whether God exists, we must have some idea of "what it is that is said to exist."[37] Because an existential statement asserts "that there is (or is not) a subject of a certain kind," we must know or at least have some idea of what kind. If our God-talk is to be intelligible, we must give or it must be possible to give the criteria that govern the use of "God". How are we to do that? What are we talking about when we use the word "God"?

Corbishley does not treat "God" as something that can be taught by ostension, for he does not want to say that God can be directly apprehended. In some sense we are to infer the existence of God from experience. We say God must exist because of *y*, and *y* could not exist without God's existing. (It is like "There are people on the island because there are footprints there, and there could be no footprints if there were no people.") But we have to know what it is we are to infer in order to be able to assert that there is a God. For such an inference to be possible, there must be an intelligible set of conditions associated with "God", and it is here that we face classic difficulties.

One condition that is associated with "God" is "love". God is said to love all mankind. We then discover that "God loves all mankind" is taken by the faithful, or at least by the theologically sophisticated faithful, to be compatible with any and every empirically specifiable state of affairs. No matter what happens, no matter how horrible the situation we envision, it is still held to be compatible with "God loves all mankind." At this juncture, Nowell-Smith asks, what does the word "love" mean in "God loves all mankind" if "God is said to love no matter what happens."[38] The point that Corbishley misses is this: since we cannot ostensively teach "God" in order to be able to assert intelligibly that there is a God, we must come to know what "God" means through descriptions. We must teach and learn the meaning of "God" intralinguistically. Perhaps "God" is but an umbrella term for certain definite descriptions, but at any rate we learn the meaning of "God" intralinguistically by ascertaining that certain conditions are associated with "God". "Love" is one of them. To be able to understand the Jewish-Christian use of "God" we must be able to understand what it means to say "God loves his children." But in order to understand such a statement, we must understand what counts for and against its truth. As Nowell-Smith well says:

We do *not* ask that God's love should be identical with human love; but to be
called "love" at all, it must be distinguishable from hate. Even if we believe that
God never does, has or will hate his children we must know what sort of situation
would lead us to say that he does, even though this situation never arises. Unless
"God loves" is contrasted with something it is meaningless.[39]

Behind this claim of Nowell-Smith is a general conceptual point about
descriptive discourse. If a word in a sentence is descriptive (functions
descriptively), it "not only means what it does but also excludes what it
does not mean."[40] In making factual statements we must utilize what
Nowell-Smith calls descriptive sentences; but a descriptive sentence is quite
comparable to a descriptive word. To be intelligible, they both must exclude
something and have a positive meaning. In fact, this inclusion and exclusion
are two sides of the same coin. "A descriptive sentence not only describes
a state of affairs but excludes contradictory states of affairs."[41] When it
is said that a factual statement must be falsifiable in principle, we are given
to understand that it is a statement made by the employment of such a
sentence, viz., "a descriptive sentence." Only such sentences could be
used to make falsifiable statements. To understand "God" we must be
able to understand sentences like "God loves his children," "God is angry
with men for their sins," "God is merciful to those who are truly peni-
tent," "God is a jealous God," and the like. If "God" is used in an intelligible manner, these sentences must be descriptive sentences. Since this
is so, we must be able to meet Flew's challenge and say what would have
to occur to constitute evidence against the love of God. Corbishley has
not shown how the believer can either meet or justifiably evade Flew's
challenge. He has not shown how we can prove that our crucial God-talk
has a proper sense if one cannot meet this challenge.

C.B. Daly, W. Norris Clarke, and
Arguments of Universal Intelligibility

C.B. Daly finds Nowell-Smith's arguments uncon-
vincing and responds in a way that is reasonably typical of a number of
metaphysicians.[42] Nowell-Smith argued that for something to be a genuine
explanation of any sort "it must explain why things are like this and not
like that." To this Daly replies:

But if the theist's reason for asserting the existence of God is the finitude or contingency of any and all finite being, then quite obviously the assertion is not open
to empirical verification or falsification in the sense intended and the proposed
tests display an enormous *ignoratio elenchi*. Flew's falsificatory occurrences occur
in an already existing world whose *existence* is taken for granted; the theist invokes
God as the *Cause of the existence of the world*. Nowell-Smith supposes that the
"God-hypothesis" will imply one kind of world: the "no-God-hypothesis" a different
kind of world. But the theist's proposition is that on the "no-God-hypothesis" there
is no kind of a world. Father Corbishley, S. J., was perfectly right in retorting
to Flew: "In reply to the question 'What would have to occur or to have occurred

to constitute for you a disproof of the love of, and of the existence of God?' the
only thing to be said is, quite literally, 'Nothing.' The Theist declares, if there
is any kind of world, God exists. His alternative is, either God or nothing. He
invokes God, not to explain why the world is 'like this, and not like that,' but
to explain how there can be a world at all."[43]

In a similar vein W. Norris Clarke has argued that the principle
embedded in Flew's challenge is not "applicable to arguments of universal
intelligible exigency."[44] If we look at the actual logic of God-talk, he
claims, we will see why. When believers reason about their belief, as when
they try to establish the existence of God, it is quite natural for them to
reason as follows: "All finite beings demand an infinite or self-sufficient
being as their necessary ground of intelligibility. Given finite beings, it
necessarily follows that there is an infinite being." If they do reason this
way—and many religious people do—the very logic of their argument
requires that they assert that every finite or contingent being requires an
infinite ultimate cause or ground. Since this is so, it is hardly appropriate
to ask the believer who has made that argument to name a finite state of
affairs which would count against this claim.

The finite state of affairs would have to be intelligible to be so specified, and it is the believer's precise point here that no finite state of affairs
is intelligible without the infinite as its ground. The argument proceeds
from this general character of finitude or contingency; hence no particular
grouping of finite or contingent being affects the issue so long as they are
still finite. Thus, Daly and Clarke both conclude that the only way to falsify
the argument is by attacking the validity of the argument. This can be done
only by showing that there is nothing intrinsic to finitude such that finite
beings, to be understood at all adequately, must be understood as requiring
the infinite as their sufficient reason. God is thus asserted as the necessary
conclusion of an argument, not as a contingent fact of experience.

There are a myriad of difficulties and perplexities about these claims.
First a general point: both Fathers Daly and Clarke seem to be pulling
themselves up by their own bootstraps. In speaking of arguments, demonstrations, proofs and the like, they are assuming the intelligibility of the
premises and conclusion while it is just this which is at issue. What is the
meaning of Father Clarke's first premise, viz., "All finite beings demand
an infinite or self-sufficient being as their necessary ground of intelligibility"?
It is precisely such utterances that raise a problem about the intelligibility
of God-talk. People are puzzled about the phrase "infinite or self-sufficient
being". They are finite beings; they know what it is to demand a raise,
or a divorce, or an end to hostilities in Vietnam; they even know vaguely
what it is to demand the moon. But what, if anything, does it mean to
demand an infinite or self-sufficient being?

What are people talking about when they talk about "an infinite
being" or "a self-sufficient being"? Fred says "There is a glacier on
Neptune," Maria denies that there are any glaciers there. We understand
their utterances; we know what is at issue; and we know what would decide
the issue, although at present we may not know how to decide that issue.
But if Father Clarke says "There really is an infinite being" and Corliss

Lamont says "No, there isn't," the problem of what really is at issue between them arises. What is Father Clarke affirming and Lamont denying?

What, if anything, does "infinite being" refer to? "Infinite being" purportedly refers, but what it supposedly refers to cannot be observed even in principle. Perhaps it no more succeeds in referring than do "round-square" or "contradictory state of affairs" or "roglid". How could it actually refer, if even in principle we cannot distinguish observing, encountering, and apprehending such a being from failing to observe, encounter, or apprehend such a being? Both Clarke and Lamont recognize that there are finite beings, though Lamont may not like talking about them in this way. They might even both agree that these finite beings demand an infinite being as their necessary ground of intelligibility, though Lamont could say that nevertheless there is no such infinite being. "Men and other finite beings exist and they seek a necessary ground of intelligibility, but there is no necessary ground of intelligibility and there is no infinite being." He might add "Even if there were a necessary ground of intelligibility, men need not seek it in an infinite being." These last two utterances do not seem to be incoherent or unintelligible; they most certainly do not appear to be contradictory. If they are contradictory, their denials would be analytic and surely Clarke would not want that.

Would Father Clarke seriously try to maintain that either (1) "If there are finite beings then there is an infinite being" or (2) "If there are finite beings and if there is a necessary ground of intelligibility, then there is an infinite being" has the same tight logical force as "If there are red pencils then there are coloured pencils" or "If there are valleys then there is some ground above the valley"? If he does, he is maintaining that they are analytic, and is therefore faced with the fact that his crucial premises are actually truths of language. From truths of language, no truths of non-linguistic fact can follow.

If, like Father Copleston, he denies that they have that tight logical force then, given that we logically cannot observe an infinite being and that no empirically identifiable state of affairs will indirectly verify it, how can Clarke claim that he has ground for asserting that his premise is true and Lamont's false? If their truth conditions are the same, how can he even distinguish them? That they are verbally different no one denies, but so too are "Marie sweats" and "Marie glows." Isn't the only difference between what Clarke and Lamont say is that Father Clarke likes to use "infinite being" with all its emotive overtones, while Lamont does not? If the above argument is right, can there be any more difference between them on substantive grounds than between Hans and Erik when Hans asserts "He took the elevator" and Erik asserts "He took the lift"?

The believer, of course, wants to claim that he is asserting something more than the non-believer, but if the above is correct, he is unable to say or explain what more he is asserting. His key phrase certainly at least appears to be devoid of cognitive meaning. It purports to refer to something that is not naturalistically specifiable, but it fails to indicate what it would be like for either a believer or a non-believer to know or to have reason to believe that such a reference has been successfully made.

In order to initiate his theistic argument so that we can inspect its validity, its premises must be intelligible in the requisite sense. This is precisely the logically prior question that Clarke tries to bypass. However, as my above argument shows, it cannot be so readily bypassed or in fact bypassed at all, for there are very serious questions concerning the intelligibility of his premises.

Intelligibility and Theistic Reasoning

This point is of sufficient importance to approach it from a different direction. Corbishley, Daly and Clarke argue that since every finite being and presumably every conceivable finite being as well requires an infinite and ultimate cause or ground, then no disconfirming or falsifying evidence could occur for the statement "There is an infinite ground of all finite things." Any mentionable piece of evidence would refer to a finite being and every finite being, if it is to be intelligible and thus recognizable, requires an infinite cause or ground. The existence of anything at all counts as evidence and, presumably, conclusive evidence for the existence of God (an infinite and self-sufficient being). The existence of nothing at all or the non-existence of the world would establish the falsity of "There is a God." Thus, given the scope of "There is a God" or "There is an infinite being," it is concluded that Flew's test is not a fair one.

For the sake of continuing the discussion, I will put aside my earlier arguments which do indeed have force here. It still can be pointed out that it is precisely the factual intelligibility of utterances with such an unrestricted generality that Flew's and Nowell-Smith's arguments challenge. "There is a God" or "There is an infinite ground of the world" are said to connote (a) "Every and any finite being requires an infinite and ultimate ground." But (a) could not be a factual assertion or statement, for it does not assert that things are like this and not like that. It does not characterize or assert a distinctive state of affairs at all. As Flew and Nowell-Smith show, these features are exactly the hallmark (defining characteristics) of factual statements. Yet (a) and "There is a God" and "God acts in the world" are presumably all factual statements. Since they do not have the logic of factual statements, they cannot actually be factual statements. The believer's beliefs about the logical status of his religious utterances are mistaken.

It will not suffice for Clarke or Daly to reply that (a) and "There is a God" are both very unusual factual statements, i.e., statements of supernatural, transempirical, or transcendent fact for the very intelligibility of these phrases is one of the crucial points in question. Simply to assume their intelligibility would be another instance of lifting oneself up by one's own bootstraps. We understand something of the logical behaviour of factual statements; these theistic statements are not used in that manner. To be told they are special "metaphysical", "non-spatiotemporal", "supernatural" factual statements does not help us, for if we are vague about the meaning of "God" we will be equally puzzled by the meaning of these phrases.[45]

Daly cannot adequately defend such philosophical theology by claiming that the theist "invokes God, not to explain why the world is 'like this and not like that' but to explain how there can *be* a world at all," for theists claim that, mysterious as it is, it is a fact that God exists. Presumably this is used to explain another fact, namely that the world exists or that there is a world.[46] As we have seen, "There is a God" is not a factual statement. If this is so, neither is "There is a world" a factual statement; it does not characterize or assert the existence of a state of affairs. Its denial, "There is nothing" or "It is not the case that the world exists" fails to describe even a conceivable state of affairs. Thus, "There is a world" cannot be a factual statement. As we have seen, a factual statement must have an intelligible opposite which also asserts a state of affairs. "There is a world" does not have such an intelligible opposite, i.e., its denial is not a descriptive statement. Appearances to the contrary, neither "There is a God" nor "There is a world" are actually used to make factual statements.[47]

Even if all my previous arguments are rejected as inadequate, there are still grave defects in Clarke's and Daly's contentions. Apart from the difficulty of speaking intelligibly of an "infinite being" or a "totally self-sufficient being," it appears to be quite possible that finite beings could demand or require "an infinite or self-sufficient being as their necessary ground of intelligibility" without their demands or requirements being met. A man might demand loyalty from his employees as a necessary ground for his peace of mind; if he was at peace with himself, we could conclude that it is likely that employees are loyal. Similarly, if "finite beings" is intelligible and an infinite being is a necessary ground for its intelligibility, then we can conclude that an infinite being exists. But why say that an infinite being is a necessary ground for the intelligibility of finite beings? My watch is a finite being and I am a finite being. That I have a watch and that there are such artifacts is made perfectly intelligible in terms of human purposes (why people have such artifacts), the activities of watchmakers, the behaviour of springs and wheels, etc. My existence is made perfectly intelligible in terms of the activities of my parents, environment, biological and psychological capacities, and the like. Similar things hold for other finite beings: everyday observation, and understanding of the different aims of people, and an understanding of scientific explanations make their existence perfectly intelligible. Surely many ordinary-sense finite beings and finite states of affairs can be and are made intelligible without any recourse to God or theology at all.

At this point Daly's argument becomes pertinent. He contends that it is not what or how finite beings or states of affairs are, but that they are, which requires a self-sufficient, infinite being. We need an explanation of why there are contingent or finite realities at all. According to Daly, we must invoke God to explain why there is a world at all. In that sense only God can make finite, contingent existence intelligible.

By now the verbal legerdemain in such a contention has also been exposed. We know there are finite beings. We also know that they are intelligible, that is to say, we know that there is no conceptual ban on understanding why any of them are the way they are and behave the way they do. In fact, our knowledge of them is considerable. But if finite beings demand or require an infinite being for their very intelligibility, then we seem forced to admit that there is an infinite self-sufficient being. However, reflection on the actual ways in which we understand finite beings, individual things and processes, and the corpus of our scientific laws and generalizations makes it evident that we do not require an infinite being to make sense out of them or to make them intelligible.

It is said that we do not go deeply enough in this quest, but simply explain one fact by another. We invoke laws, together with statements of initial conditions, to explain particular occurrences. We explain some laws in terms of other laws, but finally our laws are not backed by further laws. Their support ultimately rests on descriptions of the way things are. Those who use existentialist terms could speak here of "brute facticity". Similarly and typically, we explain human actions by exhibiting their rationale.[48] But finally, in search of ever deeper explanations, we would simply have to appeal to descriptions of the norms of human behaviour, how they arose, and the human wants to which they minister. Again we are reduced to "brute facticity," to a description of the way things are.

Such explanations, no matter how good, will not satisfy Daly or Clarke, for to terminate the request for explanations in this way does not, they believe, press deeply enough. It does not, they maintain, make finite beings really intelligible, since we are finally left with the brute fact that there are finite beings. As Daly puts it, we have not explained ". . . the most radical and fundamental fact about any fact, the fact that it is."[49] Accepting this remark at face value is to let language play a trick on us. Even if we do not and cannot explain finite beings in this so-called "deeper sense", it does not follow that we have not made them intelligible in any of the standard senses of "explain".

It is an evident fact of experience that in these senses they are intelligible, but it is not at all evident that finite beings are intelligible in that further metaphysical sense. That there is anything at all might be just the very "mystery of existence" which will never be explained.[50] It may perhaps be true that *if* it is to have an explanation, it must be explained in terms of an infinite and self-sufficient being. But why assume that there is such an explanation or that reality is intelligible in that way? To say that there must be a reason for everything is to invoke a principle that, to say the least, is not self-evident and may not hold in all domains.[51] It is reasonable to expect that any individual occurrence has a cause or that all human actions have some sort of rationale or at least some motivating conditions. That is, we explain how, what, and why things are by means of other things of a perfectly contingent sort.[52] But why extend the principle of reason to a radically new and thoroughly mysterious context, that is, to explain that there is anything at all? Why assume, as do so many theists, that there must be a reason, ground, or cause for the fact that there is anything at all? Why even assume that there actually are such *ultimate* explications? Perhaps an appeal to God, "the Cause of the existence of the world," is simply an appeal to an empty formula that appears to explain without really doing so. This possibility has not been ruled out or rendered at all implausible by Corbishley, Clarke or Daly.

Language and Theistic Reasoning

That this last possibility may be an actuality is reinforced by the fact that Corbishley, Clarke, and Daly have difficulty in getting their argument stated in an intelligible fashion. Daly speaks of "God as the Cause of the existence of the world."[53] Here "cause" is used in an idiosyncratic and perhaps even in an unintelligible way. To say that "The sun caused the snow to melt," "Overwork caused his collapse," or "Economic instability helped cause the rise of Hitler" is to assert that a relationship holds between two independently identifiable states of affairs. As they rightly insist, God is not independently identifiable and the world is not a state of affairs, for "the world" is an umbrella term for all the finite things that there are. Thus necessary conditions for an intelligible employment of "cause" are absent in the phrase "the Cause of the world." Yet they take this phrase as essential in elucidating "God". Even if the world were "a kind of thing" that could be identified, what causes the world still cannot be independently identified.

Language has gone on a holiday in an even more obvious manner in a further remark of Daly's. He begins in a controversial but tolerably straightforward way by remarking that when the believer asserts there is a God and the atheist denies it, they are not simply differing in their picture preferences or in attitude. "The difference is, in the fullest sense, one as to what is so, and therefore as to the facts."[54] However, in the next remark he slides into nonsense disguised in the same way as the nonsense of "This sentence is false." The offending sentence is this: "The difference is as to what precisely is the most radical and fundamental fact about any fact, the fact that it is."[55] In other words, Daly is trying to say "It is a fact that facts are." But isn't that fact, if it is a fact, simply a further fact, i.e., one of the facts in the class of facts? If so, then that facts are is not a further fact about facts. If, on the one hand, it is simply a fact that facts are, then it is a member of the class of facts and as such it is denoted by "facts are." If so, then how can it be a further fact about the whole class of facts that facts are? If, on the other hand, it is not a fact that facts are, then the statement "It is a fact that there are facts" is false. Moreover, if it logically cannot be a fact that facts are, then "The fact that any fact is" or "A fact that facts are" is not only an odd bit of English, but a collocation of words without an intelligible use.

This can be seen in still another way. Compare
(1) There are facts.
and
(2) There are no facts.

Assuming that (1) can be asserted or denied, to assert (2) (if (2) can be asserted at all) is to deny (1). But (1) for Daly is supposedly a metaphysical statement of fact. Thus, (2), as a proper denial of it, must be on the same logical level and thus must be a "metaphysical statement of fact." This cannot be, for (2) is nonsense. Suppose we say "There are no facts" is true, i.e., it asserts a fact. Then it is false, for there is a fact. Suppose we try to assert instead that "There are no facts" is false; then again there are facts. We unsay what we say, for we tried to assert that there are no facts. But "true" and "false" are complementary terms. It makes sense to say that a factual statement is false only if it also makes sense to say that it is true. As we have seen, it makes no sense to assert that (2) is true; thus it cannot make sense to assert that (2) is false. Far from being, as Daly must believe, an obviously false factual statement, (2), like "This sentence is false," is a bit of disguised nonsense. In this case, (2) is also nonsense, for (1) is the denial of (2) and hence is on the same logical level. Or, if it is felt that somehow it is too strong to claim that (1) is nonsense, it is at least plain that (1) cannot be a factual statement, metaphysical or otherwise, for it must be on the same level as (2), which has been shown not to be a factual assertion of any kind.

It does not help Daly if (2) is said to be nonsense by way of being self-contradictory or to be meaningful in the way self-contradictions are. In such an assertion, appearances to the contrary, (1) must be analytic, as the denial of a self-contradiction. In that case (1) is indeed meaningful, not as a substantive statement of fact, metaphysical or otherwise, but as a truth of language or as a conceptual remark depending for its sense on the use of language.

The above arguments are designed to show that certain key putative statements made by Daly cannot even be meaningful substantive assertions; thus he cannot really have a case. If for some reason my arguments are mistaken, it still has been shown that, even if Daly's statements are somehow meaningful after all, we still have no good reason for believing that finite beings can only be explained by reference to an infinite, self-sufficient cause or ground of all finite existence or that there is or even can be any explanation of why there is anything at all.

Relevance of Falsifiability Theory to Theistic Issues

We should also note some further defects in Clarke's argument. Clarke speaks of falsifying an argument, but an argument cannot be true or false. It can be valid or invalid, sound or unsound, conclusive or inconclusive. This is the manner used for logical appraisal of arguments. By contrast, statements can be falsified or verified, though they cannot be valid or invalid. To attack or defend the validity of the argument is to beg what exactly is in question, namely that there is an argument, i.e., a formal ordering of meaningful statements, that can be either valid or invalid. Flew and I have questioned whether in such talk there are cognitively meaningful or, as the believer intends factually significant statements which could serve as premises in an argument. Clarke's very setting up of his claim begs the question; it assumes that he does have an argument which is either valid or invalid, and thus must have meaningful statements as premises. This last difficulty may simply be a slip on Clarke's part that could be avoided by a more careful statement of his case. Nevertheless, this needs to be done.

Finally, let me return for one last time to Daly. Daly remarks:

> The Flew and Nowell-Smith tests belong to science, not to metaphysics. They leave the metaphysical question unasked, and they therefore beg all the questions. For in asking "Why is the world like this, when it might have been like that?" they refuse to see that that question could not arise unless we first had answered the question, "Why is there anything at all, when there might have been nothing?"[56]

This is wrong on two quite obvious counts. When my wife asserts "We have no coffee" she is not making a scientific statement. Yet "the Flew and Nowell-Smith tests" are applicable to her remark: we can say what it would be like for it to be false and it asserts "that things stand thus and thus and not otherwise." More importantly, it is plainly not the case that we must have answered the question, "Why is there anything at all when there might have been nothing?" before we can answer the question "Why is the world like this when it might have been like that?" I haven't the faintest idea concerning the answer to the question: "Why is there anything at all?" I am not even certain that it is an intelligible question. It can indeed be emotionally significant, but that is another matter. But it may not be a literal question; in fact, I am inclined to agree with Tillich that it is not a literal or genuine question at all.[57] I can and do raise certain questions concerning why the world is one way rather than another. Sometimes I even answer them, e.g., "Why is there no coffee in the pantry?" "Because I forgot to bring some home from the store yesterday"; or "Why do you constantly break your lead when you write?" "Because you bear down so hard." These are trivial, but they are questions of the requisite type nonetheless. More general questions about why the world is like it is, e.g., "Why do frustrated people respond with aggression?" and "Why is there no lasting peace in the Near East?" can be asked and sometimes answered by people who have no understanding at all of Daly's metaphysical question.

There is no reason for saying, as Daly does, that Flew's challenge displays an "enormous *ignoratio elenchi*."[58] It is not only that "There is a transcendent cause of the world" is not open in a straightforward sense to empirical verification and confirmation; Daly has not been able to show what it would be like for it to have any kind of test at all. He claims that while "the theist's language is adequate to the facts of experience, the atheist's is not." But he has not been able to show how or even that this is so; he does not illustrate how it fits consistently with his further claim that it is a mistake to assume that "the God-hypothesis" will imply one kind of world and "non-God-hypothesis" another.[59] If they both imply the same kind of world, what does it mean to say that one is more "adequate to the facts of experience" than the other? If they both imply the same kind of world, neither need ignore any of the facts of experience or select arbitrarily from the facts of experience.

More basically, Daly claims, as do Corbishley and Clarke, that (1) "On the 'no-God-hypothesis' there is no kind of world" and (2) "If there is any kind of world God exists" are both fundamental truths. But they have not shown that it is self-contradictory or nonsensical to assert (3) "We live in a Godless world" or (4) "Though there is no God, we do live in a world with reflective but often cruel human beings." If they cannot do this, and ruling out empirical verification as they do, how can they know or have any grounds for believing that (1) and (2) are true or even have any truth-values? Moreover, if they did establish that (3) or (4) are self-contradictory then (1) and (2) would be analytic. In that case, (1) and (2) would be devoid of the factual/metaphysical significance so essential for their case.

My examinations of this issue, so central to any account of God-talk and the quest for God, may have seemed wearisome. As Charlesworth, Corbishley, Daly, and Clarke are trying to do what is plainly impossible anyway, why waste time with the details of their views? My answer is three-fold: they, and many others, clearly do not think they are trying to do what is impossible. As representatives of an ancient, socially effective institution, their arguments against a claim to end all such metaphysical arguments need to be given careful consideration. If what I said here has not advanced philosophy, it should have advanced understanding between philosophers. Secondly, some of their responses to the "Theology and Falsification issue" are indeed natural and influential responses that deserve an effective reply.[60] Whether I have succeeded in doing that here, the reader must decide for himself.

Thirdly, it is felt in certain circles that a view like mine is still a partial holdover from a largely discredited positivism. Some feel that attention to a more metaphysically oriented approach would show the superficiality of my view. In discussion, Professor John Macquarrie has even remarked that my view is "old fashioned". Fashions change and I am little concerned with whether it is or is not "old fashioned". I am concerned with whether what I say is so and with whether it is indeed superficial. I have tried to show here that it is not superficial and that the criticism directed against such an analytic approach by the Catholic philosophers I have discussed will not withstand critical scrutiny. Perhaps there are better criticisms directed against this approach by philosophers working from a Catholic background, but they remain unknown to me. I issue here an open invitation to improve on these arguments and meet this analytic challenge. If my arguments have been near their mark, the verification/falsification argument remains an unmet challenge to theists. For theistic religion to meet the expectations of their adherents, "There is a cause of the universe" and "There is an unfathomable Divine Love which governs the order of history" must be shown to have a factual status. But theistic utterances of this sort are devoid of factual significance.

NOTES

1.   Some of the key considerations here have been brought out by Paul Edwards and Ronald Hepburn. See Edwards' article "Atheism" and Hepburn's "Agnosticism," *The Encyclopedia of Philosophy*, ed. Paul Edwards, vol. 1 (New York: Macmillan, 1966) 74-89 and 56-59.

2.   See my "Wittgensteinian Fideism," *Philosophy* XLII (1967): 191-210.

3.   I have characterized Flew's challenge rather fully in my "On Fixing the Reference Range of 'God'," *Religious Studies* II (1966): 13-30. For the original statement of it see Antony Flew, "Theology and Falsification," *New Essays in Philosophical Theology*, eds. A. Flew and A. MacIntyre (London: SCM Press, 1955) 96-99.

4.   Norman Malcolm, "Anselm's Ontological Arguments," *Philosophical Review* LXIX (1960): 41-62, and Charles Hartshorne, *The Logic of Perfection* (LaSalle, IL: Open Court, 1963).

5.   See the following two chapters of this book. See also here the criticisms of Malcolm's position in the *Philosophical Review* LXX (1961): 56-109; Robert Coburn in "Professor Malcolm on God," *Australasian Journal of Philosophy* XLI (1963); and John O. Nelsen, "Modal Logic and the Ontological Proof for God's Existence," *The Review of Metaphysics* XVII (1963): 235-42.

6.   J.N. Findlay, "Can God's Existence Be Disproved?" in *New Essays in Philosophical Theology*, eds. A. Flew and A. MacIntyre (New York: Macmillan, 1964) 47-56.

7.   Nietzsche, of course, never intended it literally. In his *The Joyful Wisdom* (New York: Ungar, 1960), he remarks that to say "God is dead" is to say "that the belief in the Christian God has become unworthy of belief."

8.   David Hume, *Dialogues Concerning Natural Religion* (New York: Hafner, 1948).

9.   J.N. Findlay, "Can God's Existence Be Disproved?" 71-75.

10.   See F.C. Copleston's remarks on this in his debate with A.J. Ayer. A.J. Ayer and F.C. Copleston, "Logical Positivism: A Debate," *A Modern Introduction to Philosophy*, eds. Paul Edwards and Arthur Pap (New York: Free Press, 1965) 726-50.

11.   M.J. Charlesworth, "Linguistic Analysis and Language About God," *International Philosophical Quarterly* I (1961): 139-67.

12.   *Ibid.* 165.

13.   *Ibid.* 140.

14.   *Ibid.* 165.

15.   *Ibid.*

16.   *Ibid.* 163.

17.   F.R. Harrison, "Mr. Geach's Interpretation of the 'Five Ways'," *Sophia* II (1964): 35.

18.   Ernest Nagel, "Determinism in History," *Philosophy and Phenomenological Research* XX (1959-1960): 291-317.

19.   M.J. Charlesworth, "Linguistic Analysis and Language About God" 165.

20.   *Ibid.*

21.   *Ibid.* 140.

22.   Thomas Corbishley, S.J., "Theology and Falsification," *The University* 1 (1950-1951): 9.

23.   *Ibid.*

24.   *Ibid.* 10.

25.   *Ibid.*

26.   *Ibid.*

27.   *Ibid.*

28.   *Ibid.* 11.

29. P.H. Nowell-Smith, "Theology and Falsification," *The University* 1 (1950-1951): 12.

30. *Ibid.*

31. *Ibid.* 13.

32. *Ibid.*

33. *Ibid.*

34. *Ibid.* 13-14.

35. *Ibid.* 14.

36. *Ibid.*

37. *Ibid.*

38. *Ibid.*

39. *Ibid.* 16.

40. *Ibid.*

41. *Ibid.*

42. C.B. Daly, "The Knowableness of God," *Philosophical Studies* IX (1959): 90-137.

43. *Ibid.* 103-104.

44. In a private communication to me. But see also W. Norris Clarke, "Analytic Philosophy and Language About God," *Traces of God in a Secular Culture*, ed. G.F. McLean (Staten Island, NY: Alba House, 1973).

45. The best that could be done here is to appeal to what is sometimes called the *sui generis* character of the language or what is less piously called the idiosyncrasy platitude, viz., that "every mode of discourse has its own logic." Making such an assumption, one might argue that the sense of "fact" and "factual statement" in God-talk is different than in other areas. One is either aware of what these facts are or one is not. Ultimately one can only understand them in their own terms. I have tried to give grounds for rejecting such a view in my "Wittgensteinian Fideism."

46. C.B. Daly, "The Knowableness of God" 104.

47. I am, of course, speaking of non-anthropomorphic concepts of God. Where God, like Zeus, is conceived anthropomorphically, it is simply false that there is such a God.

48. See here William Dray, *Laws and Explanation in History* (London: Oxford University Press, 1957) chapters III and V; and William Dray, "The Historical Explanation of Actions Reconsidered" and Kai Nielsen, "Rational Explanations in History," *Philosophy and History*, ed. Sidney Hook (New York: New York University Press, 1963) 105-35 and 296-324.

49. C.B. Daly, "The Knowableness of God" 105.

50. See here Milton K. Munitz, *The Mystery of Existence* (New York: Meredith, 1965).

51. See Arthur Danto, "Faith, Language, and Religious Experience: A dialogue," *Religious Experience and Truth*, ed. Sidney Hook (New York: New York University Press, 1961) 137-49.

52. Kurt Baier, *The Meaning of Life* (Canberra: University College, 1957).

53. C.B. Daly, "The Knowableness of God" 103.

54. *Ibid.* 105.

55. *Ibid.*

56. *Ibid.*

57. In *Philosophical Interrogations* I asked Tillich if this "question" could conceivably be answered and whether, if it were logically impossible to answer it, it could literally be a question. Tillich replied, "There is no doubt that the question, 'Why is there something, why not nothing?', is not a question in the proper logical sense of the word. There is no answer to it, as I myself have concluded by referring to Kant's mythical God who asks this question with respect to himself and cannot answer it." Paul Tillich, "Inter-

rogations," *Philosophical Interrogations*, eds. Sydney and Beatrice Rome (New York: Holt, Rinehart & Winston, 1964) 403.

58.   C.B. Daly, "The Knowableness of God" 103.

59.   *Ibid.* 105.

60.   I have tried to come to grips with more direct efforts to answer Flew's challenge rather than to challenge its presuppositions in my "Religion and Commitment," *Religious Language and Knowledge*, eds. W.T. Blackstone and R.H. Ayers (Athens: The University of Georgia Press, 1972) 18-43; Kai Nielsen, "Eschatological Verification," *Canadian Journal of Theology* IX (1963): 271-81; "God and Verification Again," *Canadian Journal of Theology* XI (1965): 135-42; and "On Fixing the Reference Range of 'God'," *Religious Studies* II (1966): 13-36. I am indebted to Kenneth Stern and John Miller for their helpful comments on an earlier version of this chapter.

CHAPTER 3

Necessity and God*

I

WHILE ORTHODOX BELIEVERS *INTEND* TO BE asserting a fact when they say "There is a God," "God exists," "God does in reality exist," or "Something and one thing only is omniscient, omnipotent and infinitely good," they seem not to be able to say what would or could, even in principle, count toward establishing either the truth or the falsity of such statements. Though "God" and "There is a God" are part of the corpus of English in a way "The central meaning process is difficult to measure" or "The ground of all-in-all cannot transmute itself into Being-for-itself" are not, yet for all that, such God-talk is in a certain important respect problematic.

It should, however, surely be asked: who is the philosopher to set up such entrance requirements—entrance requirements far more stringent than those a linguist would use—for determining when a given mark is a genuine word or a string of words is an intelligible sentence? Yet, believers claim that it is a fact that God exists, though it seems to be logically impossible to find out *what* this fact is. In this way "God" is like "Being itself", "The Absolute" and "The Ground of all-in-all".

Given these conflicting considerations and given the failure of Wittgensteinian fideism, it may be worthwhile to leave the sturdy ground of the plain man and see if some theological concepts of ancient vintage will help beef up the claim that God-talk is intelligible. Here I want to study some claims that God is a Necessary Being. I want to examine the persistent and tantalizing claim that somehow God is a *logically* necessary being (a being whose non-existence is logically inconceivable) and that "God exists" and "There is a God" is a logically necessary truth or at least a proposition whose truth can be known a priori.

On the one hand, Hartshorne and Malcolm, following Anselm, claim that the fool contradicts himself when he says that there is no God and,

*First published in the *International Journal for Philosophy of Religion* X.1 (1979).

on the other, J.J.C. Smart and J.N. Findlay, following Hume, contend that the concept of a logically necessary being, or of a "logically necessary fact", or of a factual statement which is logically true, is a contradiction in terms.[1] Here questions concerning the intelligibility of God-talk and questions concerning whether God exists come together, for if Anselm is right, to show that "God exists" is *intelligible* is to show that God does exist, and if Smart and Findlay are right "There is a God" is, for a religiously adequate concept of God, a contradiction.

Who is right here? Perhaps (as I believe) both sides are wrong. The best way to look into this matter is to consider the following two questions:

1.   Should God be conceived of as a *logically* necessary being? Is the concept of a logically necessary being intelligible or free from absurdity?
2.   Are there existential statements that are logically necessary or a priori or necessarily true?

Malcolm, Hughes and Hartshorne think that the Hume-Kant answer to 2) is a mere dogma. Is it? I do not think so. But Malcolm is surely right in saying we should argue out this Humean thesis against cases. Furthermore are we, as Findlay, Malcolm and Hartshorne think we are, pushed, when we honestly and carefully think of God, to take his existence to be either logically necessary or impossible?

II

Findlay's argument here is crucial. It starts, as Hughes and others aver, with a sensitive elucidation of what constitutes the proper object of a religious reverence. Findlay goes on to claim that *given* this attitude of reverence and *given* a propensity to reason, a reflective religious man is inescapably driven to conceive of God as a logically necessary being.

Let us follow out Findlay's subtle analysis. Findlay remarks:

> Religious people have, in fact, come to acquiesce in the total absence of any cogent proofs of the Being they believe in: they even find it positively satisfying that something so far surpassing clear conception should also surpass the possibility of demonstration. And non-religious people willingly mitigate their rejection with a tinge of agnosticism: they don't so much deny the existence of a God, as the existence of good reasons for believing in him. We shall, however, maintain in this essay that there isn't room, in the case we are examining, for all these attitudes of tentative surmise and doubt. For we shall try to show that the Divine Existence can only be conceived, in a religiously satisfactory manner, if we also conceive it as something inescapable and necessary, whether for thought or reality. From which it follows that our modern denial of necessity or rational evidence for such an existence amounts to a demonstration that there cannot be a God.[2]

Findlay thus attempts to show that if we conceive of God in a religiously adequate way, we will come to see that such a concept of God is self-contradictory. This is not, Findlay hastens to add, to say that the various gods of idolatry and mythology are self-contradictory conceptions or that other anthropomorphic conceptions of God are self-contradictory conceptions, but that they are not *adequate* objects of religious attitudes. Moreover, there are many uses of the word "God" which are so aseptic that they are clearly compatible with atheism. We must pin down a fully developed theistic conception of God by trying to discover what would count as an "adequate object of a religious attitude".

There are, Findlay argues, a number of descriptive phrases which taken together draw a rough boundary around the attitudes in question. It is important to note that these attitudes are not indifferently evoked in any setting. There is a range of situations in which they normally and most readily occur. This is true of any attitude-expressing word. The words "angry", "anxious", "fearful", and the like have incorporated into their very *use* or *meaning* "a reference to the sorts of thing or situation to which these attitudes are the normal or appropriate response."[3] Fear (for example) is an attitude which is readily evoked only in certain situations. That is, it is appropriately evoked in situations in which there is menace or potential injury. If I said "I'm afraid but I know there is nothing dangerous about the situation", I would not be saying something that was absurd; but if I uttered that sentence and said "and my attitude is perfectly appropriate, perfectly justified," I would be saying something absurd. Similar things can and should be said for anger. We cannot without a confusing linguistic deviation say that *any* object of any attitude is an *appropriate* object of that attitude. A simple examination of English usage or some other natural language will make it apparent that our attitudes have certain standard objects. It is by reference to them that we determine whether our attitudes are or are not appropriate or normal.

In trying in a given case to determine which attitude is appropriate, we can ask whether ordinary, reasonably knowledgeable and sane native speakers would in such and such circumstances say that such and such attitudes are justified or appropriate. All that "philosophy achieves in this regard is merely to push further, and develop into more considered and consistent forms the implications of such ordinary ways of speaking."[4] What can and should be inquired into is "whether an attitude would still seem justified, and its object appropriate, after we had reflected long and carefully on a certain matter, and looked at it from every wonted and unwonted angle."[5]

This is just what Findlay does for "a religious attitude". What would count as a fully adequate object of a religious attitude? What would it be like? By approaching it in this way we can see what a God adequate for religious purposes would come to.

Findlay, rather like Rudolf Otto, says that a religious attitude is one in which we will in appropriate circumstances tend to abase ourselves before some object, "to defer to it wholly, to devote ourselves to it with unquestioning enthusiasm, to bend the knee before it, whether literally or metaphorically."[6] The God of a believer is something toward which the believer has an attitude of total commitment, abasement, deference and utter devotion. God, by definition, is *worthy* of worship. That is to say, the appellation "God" would not be used unless it referred to what was taken to be *worthy* of worship and utter devotion. It is analytic to say "A religious attitude is a worshipful and devout attitude" when one is talking about a Jewish-Christian-Moslem religious attitude. (There is no worship in Therevada Buddhism.)

What are the objects of such attitudes? Religious attitudes, Findlay points out, presume *superiority* in their objects. We feel as if we are nothing before the object of such an attitude. But "such an attitude can only be fitting where the object worshipped and reverenced exceeds us very, very vastly: in power, wisdom or other valued qualities."[7] (Recall Job and Job's reaction when God speaks to him out of the whirlwind.)

Consider some actual objects of religious attitudes. People have worshipped many things. They have worshipped stones, phalli and bulls, but— and this is central—not *as* stones, phalli or bulls. When it is realized that these things do not have an indwelling, mysterious power, religious attitudes toward stones, phalli or bulls no longer seem appropriate. We worship what we believe to have "surpassing greatness in some object." But if we continue to reflect we will say—as many religious people have—that an adequate object to such an attitude could not be limited in any manner. It would be "wholly anomalous to worship anything limited in any thinkable manner." All limited superiorities have the taint of relativity. Being dwarfed by mightier superiorities "they lose their claim upon our worshipful attitudes."[8] That to which we turn in awe, reverence, devotion and utter debasement must be thought to have "an unsurpassable supremacy along all avenues." It must somehow be all-comprehensive and totally unlimited. Everything else that exists must be dependent on such an object of reverence.

Reflecting on what would be an adequate object of an attitude of worship and reverence, we are irresistibly led to the paradoxical claim that it cannot be anything which merely happens to exist. As Findlay puts it himself:

> The true object of religious reverence must not be one, merely, to which no *actual* independent realities stand opposed: it must be one to which such opposition is totally *inconceivable*. God mustn't merely cover the territory of the actual, but also, with equal comprehensiveness, the territory of the possible. And not only must the existence of *other* things be unthinkable without him, but his own non-existence must be wholly unthinkable in any circumstances. There must, in short, be no conceivable alternative to an existence properly termed 'divine': God must be wholly inescapable, as we remarked previously, whether for thought or reality. And so we are led on insensibly to the barely intelligible notion of a Being in whom Essence and Existence lose their separateness. And all that the great medieval thinkers really did was to carry such a development to its logical limit.[9]

In turning to God, we turn to that to which we, if we are religious, will utterly abandon ourselves. The conditions we associate with the word "God", if our religious attitude is appropriate, are conditions such as: being *all* wise, *all* good, *all* powerful, etc., etc. God by definition must possess all these perfections to a *superlative* degree. Of anything of which we could appropriately say "My Lord and My God", we would withdraw that appellation upon the discovery of any imperfection at all.

We should also note that God must *not* simply possess these features, as a mere matter of fact, for then they wouldn't be *inalienably* His own. We would find it idolatrous to worship a being who just happened to have these qualities while something else might have had them. We are led, Findlay argues, "irresistibly, by the demands inherent in religious reverence, to hold that an adequate object of our worship must possess its various qualities *in some necessary manner*."[10]

A god that can satisfy religious needs and claims must be in every way inescapable. Such a god is a God "whose existence and whose possession of certain excellence we cannot possibly conceive away."[11]

To conceive of God thus, Findlay argues, is to conceive of an adequate *object* of a religious attitude. With this much ground cleared, Findlay springs his trap and comes up with his *ontological disproof* of the existence of God. He says that it is plain that these very requirements for an adequate object of a religious attitude entail "for all who share a contemporary outlook . . . not only that there isn't a God, but that Divine Existence is either senseless or impossible."[12]

Findlay makes it perfectly clear in his reply to criticisms by Hughes and Rainer that in speaking of a "contemporary outlook" he is not limiting this to those who would deny that there are synthetic a priori statements and claim that all necessary propositions are analytic. Even if we take a Kantian position and admit *synthetic* a priori statements, Findlay's claim still has force. His claim is that Divine existence is an existence whose "non-existence is inconceivable." No other God could be religiously adequate. Divine existence is either impossible or logically necessary. If God exists his existence is *logically* necessary. But such a conception is self-contradictory for those people who agree with Kant that "it couldn't be *necessary* that there should ever be anything of any description whatever." On such grounds it is obviously self-contradictory to claim that there is an *x* whose non-existence is inconceivable. The very logical requirement for the proper use of "God", namely that of a Being whose very "*existence* and whose possession of certain excellences we cannot possibly conceive away," is self-contradictory. Anselm's argument in reality entails not that God must exist but that "There is a God" is self-contradictory. Even if we allow existence to be a property, we still—on Kantian premises— could only say "hypothetically that if something of a certain sort existed, then it would exist necessarily, but not, categorically, that it actually existed."[13]

Findlay says that if one is 1) willing to accept his account of an *adequate* object of a religious attitude, an account which involves the contention that God must either exist necessarily or not at all, and 2) if one accepts Kant's view that (in the same sense of "necessary") there are not any logically necessary facts of existence, then one is logically committed to the assertion that there can be no God. Relative to such premises we have proven—demonstrated—the non-existence of God.

Findlay makes a familiar point—a point Ryle, Waismann and

Lazerowitz have stressed—that this argument, as any argument, can at a certain cost be evaded. He points out:

> . . . there can be nothing really 'clinching' in philosophy: 'proofs' and 'disproofs' hold only for those who adopt certain premises, who are willing to follow certain rules of argument, and who use their terms in certain definite ways. And every proof or disproof can be readily evaded, if one questions the truth of its premises, or the validity of its type of inference, or if one finds new senses in which its terms may be used. And it is quite proper, and one's logical duty, to evade an argument in this manner, if it leads to preposterous consequences. And Hughes and Rainer are within their rights in thinking my conclusions preposterous: only I don't agree with them.[14]

Findlay goes on to apply this general contention to his present argument:

> I admit to the full that my argument *doesn't* hold for those who have desire to say that God exists in some necessary and unescapable manner . . . . Nor will it hold for those who are willing to say, with Rainer, that one might *come* to perceive the necessity of God's existence in some higher mystical state, nor for those who say, with Hughes and St. Thomas, that God himself can perceive the 'necessity' of his own 'existence', though both this 'existence' and this 'necessity' are something totally different from anything that we understand by these terms . . . . But my argument holds for all those thinkers . . . who accept Kant's view that there aren't any necessary facts of existence and who also can be persuaded to hold that a God who is 'worth his salt' must either exist necessarily (in the same sense of 'necessary') or not at all. The force of my argument doesn't depend, moreover, on my recent analysis of necessity in terms of tautology: it holds on *any* account of the necessary that can be squared with the above conditions.[15]

Findlay's remarks here seem to me not at all to entail or give logical support to any relativistic, historicist or fideist doctrines. He has merely dramatized the fact that logic is not everything and that a rationalism which thinks that it is, is both irrational and illogical. But there are surely certain premises which are more reasonable to hold, or premises which have greater utility, or premises for which there is more empirical evidence, or premises which square better with the ways we do, and conceivably can talk and think, than do their rivals. Findlay's point, I take it, is that it is more reasonable or plausible to hold both of the premises he holds than their opposites and that jointly they entail the non-existence of God. But given this type of inconclusiveness in philosophical arguments—any philosophical argument no matter how well conceived—it is certainly rational, as J.J.C. Smart powerfully argues, to turn to considerations of *plausibility* in assessing rival philosophical claims. The most we can hope to achieve in any important philosophical argument is to show that a given account is more plausible than any of its rivals. But often to achieve this much is to achieve something of a very considerable importance, e.g., suppose that we could establish that mind/body identity theory was more plausible than any of its rivals. This would clearly be of very considerable importance. Findlay, I think, would claim that his argument for the non-existence of God fares very well looked at in this light.

However, we must not forget that reasonable men have denied both premises in trying to refute the claim that it is self-contradictory nonsense to assert the existence of a religiously adequate God. Malcolm and Hughes have denied that logically necessary existence is self-contradictory or in some way impossible; Penelhum and Hick have agreed that it is indeed nonsense to speak of *logically* necessary existence but have argued that it is not true that a concept of a religiously adequate object of worship commits one to a belief in a logically necessary being, though it does commit one to a belief in a necessary being. I think the Penelhum-Hick "out" is a much more plausible alternative than the Malcolm-Hughes "out", but I want here to examine the Malcolm-Hughes argument, for I think it raises central issues both for philosophical theology and for metaphysics generally. There is a persistent tendency to try to make logical considerations do more work than they can possibly do and a deep and understandable urge to try to establish certain crucial existential claims a priori. I want to show, once again, in the light of plausible contemporary counter-moves, that such a conception of existence is incoherent.

Perhaps there are non-tautological *logically* necessary existential statements. Perhaps certain existential statements are after all true a priori. It may indeed be true, as Malcolm claims, that it is a dogma, an unproved assumption of modern analytic philosophy, that no sentences of the form "There is a so and so" or "Such and such exists" function to assert logically necessary truths. It is Malcolm's contention that there is no reason *not* to claim that *sometimes* "x exists" or "there is an x" are necessary propositions whose truth can be determined independently of any empirical investigation or any simpler type of looking and seeing.

Hughes makes similar claims. It is true enough that no tautology can be existential, but, Hughes argues, we should question the claim that *all* necessary or a priori propositions or statements are tautologies. Hughes agrees with Findlay that "God exists" is a necessary proposition but he stresses that it is non-tautological. In saying "God exists" the theist must admit that, *in this special case*, his proposition is *necessary without being tautological*. The Findlay-type atheist must show, Hughes argues, that it is logically impossible for there to be a non-tautological, non-analytic necessary *existential* proposition. We have seen that while Findlay will countenance *synthetic* a priori propositions, he will not countenance *existential* a priori propositions. Thus we have here a head-on conflict.

Against Hughes' claim isn't it plain, as Hume classically argued, that for any proposition of the form "x exists" or "There is an x" we can always meaningfully or intelligibly deny that x exists or that there is such an x? We can always say "It is not the case that x exists" or "It is false that there is an x" without contradicting ourselves. In no case is "x exists" an a priori truth.

In reply to this classical Humean claim it has been argued that such a Humean position is committed to at least one of the following two unjustified and unjustifiable assumptions: 1) to say that a statement is a priori is to say that it is analytic, or 2) only analytic statements are a priori. I agree that one should not accept the first statement, for it is obviously false. But the second statement seems to me to be true. However, as we have seen, Findlay does not accept it and does not need to accept it to make his argument. He needs to maintain only the Kantian claim that there are no a priori existential statements. I agree with Findlay that such a claim is enough to rule out the possibility of there being a *logically* necessary being. But to make this claim doubly clinching, I want to go on to argue that only analytic statements are a priori. But even if my following arguments on that topic seem in one way or another unconvincing, bear in mind that the kind of statements which might be synthetic and a priori are all *hypothetical* statements; they do not *categorically* assert the existence of anything. So even if my argument fails, we still have no good grounds for believing that there can be a *logically* necessary being. Only if we can come up with a convincing example of an existential a priori statement will Findlay be undermined in this direction.

I now return to the problem of whether only analytic statements are a priori. Kenny has argued against my position in the following way; on the one hand, an analytic statement is a statement the denial of which is self-contradictory, or it is a definition or a statement logically following from a definition; a priori statements, on the other hand, are statements expressing a priori truths and, as Kenny puts it, "a priori truths are truths which are known on logical grounds alone."[16] It is his contention that not all a priori statements—statements expressing a priori truths—are analytic. He claims that the following statements are a priori without being analytic:[17]

    1.   Nothing can be both red and green all over at the same time.

    2.   Temporal precedence is transitive but irreflexive.

Kenny gives no argument at all to establish that they are not analytic. Yet it seems to me that it is only because of its ambiguity that 1) might be thought *not* to be analytic. Such a sentence-type, like the sentence-type "Tadpoles are young frogs," is sometimes used analytically and sometimes empirically. Someone might carefully look to see if down under the red, one might detect a layer of green—the red having a certain transparency; or if down under the green, one might detect a red as one sometimes sees a brown bottom through greenish water. If someone used the sentence-type 1) in that way one could tell that he was making an empirical statement. If instead he employed the sentence-type to make a claim to which evidence is *in principle* irrelevant and if it were also a remark which no one who understood the conventions of the language would regard as a remark which could be intelligibly denied, then he would be employing that sentence-type analytically. Sentence-tokens of that sentence-type, depending on the context, can be used in either way; sometimes they are used to make empirical statements and sometimes analytic statements and, as Waismann in effect points out, sometimes it may not be clear just which way the user proposes to use them. The same thing can be said for 2). (The user, even when he understands the distinction just made, may not be clear how on a given occasion he is using such a sentence.) It is this ambiguity or, if you will, indeterminateness of 1), that tricks us into thinking that it (evading the differences between sentences and statements) is an a priori yet non-analytic statement. But we have no good grounds for thinking we have any a priori but non-analytic truths and the Humean argument, given above, for claiming that statements of the form "x exists" are never a priori truths seems, at least, to be a sound one.

If a theist replies that in the special case where "God" becomes the value of the variable x the proposition becomes a necessary one, the *onus probandi* is surely on him to show that there is something very special about the concept of God that makes "God exists" or "There is a God" necessary propositions.

The dialectic could go on, for a theist can reply "Well, what is special about God is that God *by definition* is a self-existent being or a being whose non-existence is inconceivable." But nothing is accomplished by such a move on his part. We do not know what can count as "a self-existent being" or a "being whose non-existence is inconceivable," for these terms have no established use in our language. Moreover, the reason we do not understand them, and the reason why they do not have an established use is that we do not understand how "self-existent" or "logically impossible not to exist" could qualify or characterize being. Where an existential statement has an established employment in a natural language, we understand what it would be like to negate or deny it; we understand what it would be like for it not to be true. Since it is always logically possible to conceive of the non-existence of any being whatsoever, we find the notion of a self-existent being—a being whose non-existence is inconceivable—to be an inconsistent claim. This is what gives us an ontological disproof of the existence of God if we try to conceive of God as a *logically* necessary being. It is that which gives Findlay's argument force.

This sounds question-begging and *in a way* I suspect it is. But note this: "self-existent being" or "being whose non-existence is inconceivable" have no established use in the corpus of English. Particularly when we try to conceive of the latter as a being or as being, we do not understand what could possibly count as an exemplification of such an alleged being. "Self-existent being" is like "talkative stone". It is senseless, self-inconsistent use of language. As far as I can see, all I can finally do toward establishing this is to get you to carefully reflect on our usage (or, if you will, simply reflect on your own live usage) and see that this is so, as you see that it makes no sense to call a puppy an old dog. It is this final appeal to usage and to the fluent speaker's *linguistic* intuitions that gives one the *impression* that the question is being begged. But it seems to me we have hit rock bottom here.

It should be noted also that there is something very fishy about making "God" a *special case*. This seems most particularly evident when we keep in mind that the very coherence of the concept of God and first-order God-talk is itself in question. We cannot just assume we have an intelligible religious language-game or form of life.

However, it could be argued, and has been argued, that there are other quite intelligible cases of logically necessary or a priori existential propositions. Not all existential propositions can be denied without self-contradiction. This is Malcolm's belief and we must now look into his evidence for it. Consider the following six cases:

1) There is an infinite number of natural numbers.
2) There is a prime number greater than seven.
3) There are minds.
4) There are material objects.
5) There were material objects.
6) There is a universe.

First we should note that 1) through 6) are all odd; perhaps they are all even logically odd. But to say this certainly shouldn't by itself constitute a condemnation or even a criticism of them. To point to the logical oddity of an utterance is for me merely a device to put one on guard. It warns us that all *may* not be well with these utterances—language may have gone on a holiday. But, odd or not, we still have here prima facie cases of necessary existential statements, i.e., statements whose truth is determined on logical grounds alone, that is, existential statements that are somehow true a priori.

Let us consider the mathematical cases first. Malcolm takes, as his major non-religious case, the so-called existence theorems of mathematics, e.g., 2) "There is a prime number greater than seven." Here Malcolm's claim has, I believe, been successfully attacked by Allen and Abelson.[18] We should first note that "necessary existence" has no established usage in mathematics, though Malcolm implies that it has. Yet there is a distinctive sense of "exists" in mathematics. Mathematical existence is established in a different way than empirical existence. Instead of some complicated looking and seeing, the mathematician proves or demonstrates the existence of a "mathematical entity" by a formal deductive procedure. But proof, deductive demonstration, in mathematics, as anywhere else, is always relative to a set of postulates. The existence theorems of mathematics, as Allen points out, are not guaranteed by intuition; they are conclusions derived by rule from Peano's postulates. It is indeed true that the existence theorems do not hold in virtue of their meaning alone; that is to say, Malcolm is correct in claiming they are not analytic; but they follow from postulates, at least one of which must be an existential (factual), logically contingent postulate, if the system is not to be various. Their truth cannot be determined on logical grounds alone. Existence in mathematics is never a matter of definition and it is never a purely a priori matter.

Furthermore, if we make a close analogy between "There is a God" and "There is an infinite number of natural numbers" or "There is a prime number greater than a million," we will get something which Malcolm and no defender of the ontological argument would want: namely that, as our existence theorem only follows if we make certain *postulations*, so we must postulate the existence of God to prove His existence. But this is not what we wanted to do, for by postulating His existence the very question of His existence has now been begged at the outset.

Let us take some of the other purported examples of necessary (a priori) existential statements. We should note initially that 3) through 6) have a decidedly metaphysical flavour. They are hardly a part of ordinary discourse. Malcolm or any Wittgensteinian might very well reject them as sham statements—statements which have no home in any form of life—

statements which play no role in any living form of language, have no role in any language-game. I would indeed assert this myself; and that we must go this far afield for necessary existential statements is itself significant. But less cautious defenders of necessary existence (such as Hartshorne) trot them out, so let us see, at least for the sake of the argument, what can be made of them.[19]

Consider first 3) "There are minds." Some might think that indubitable, and in a plain Moorean sense of "indubitable" it most surely is indubitable, but the question at hand is whether it is a logically necessary proposition or an a priori truth. It would, I think, be reasonable to argue that "there are minds" follows logically from the statement that normal human beings have minds and one might argue that "Normal human beings have minds" is a necessary (a priori) truth. But this last statement seems to me a necessary truth because it is analytic. However, we cannot derive a non-analytic proposition from an analytic one and thus we can only conclude that there are minds if we can add the existential proposition "There are normal human beings." But "There are normal human beings" and even "There are human beings" are contingent propositions. The conditions under which they would be false can be stated. They are most certainly not a priori truths. Thus we have no grounds for asserting "There are minds" is an a priori truth.

Consider now 4) "There are material objects." Someone might say this is entirely indubitable and again in a plain Moorean sense it is. But the question is whether it is an a priori proposition or a necessary proposition that no conceivable experience can refute. It seems to me—as it does not seem to Baier—that it is not an a priori proposition.[20] "Material object", as Austin has taught us, is a philosopher's term of art. We do not learn it by ostensive definition. But, as Baier points out, we learn it by reference to words so learnt. At first we learn words like "bottle", "rock", "cat", "sock", "toothbrush", by being shown and being allowed to or made to handle the things bearing these names.

> Later, we learn the word "thing" which can be used as a generic expression for any of these and others like them whose names we have not yet learnt. Later still, we learn to distinguish between those which are called "things" . . . and those which are called "animals", "plants", and "visual (or optical) phenomena" such as rainbows, clouds, and shadows.[21]

Now someone might ask, as Baier did, "how could a man who had come to understand 'material object' in this way, be unaware that there were some?" He could have learned some of his words like "bottle" or "rock" from a dictionary, but he could not "learn all of his words that way, for how would a person acquire the ability to understand the words in the dictionary?"[22] He would have to learn some of these words through ostensive teaching.

It is tempting to object:

> But can one be sure that the tables and chairs, the houses and stones, the shoes and ties, by reference to which he has learnt the expression 'material object' really are material objects, and not just bundles of ideas or sensations or phenomena?

> This question, however, is not legitimate, for tables and chairs and the like are the sorts of things we mean by 'material objects'. The question makes no more sense than the question whether apples and oranges, grapes and plums really are fruit. There is of course another question which is perfectly legitimate, namely, whether material objects really are bundles of ideas or collections of electrons and so on, but whatever the true answer to this question it cannot reverse the truth that tables and chairs are material objects.[23]

Thus we are *tempted* to say 4) "There are material objects" is a necessary truth. But we should resist this temptation, for it in reality is not a necessary proposition or an a priori truth. It remains a contingent proposition as Baier's own fantasy case shows. We can conceive of a situation in which no one was aware of physical objects and in which there might be no physical objects. Suppose as a result of a cataclysmic nuclear war there are only a few survivors left on earth. Picture them being blown about in the air by heavy winds too far from each other to see each other; totally paralyzed, their tactile, but not their visual senses destroyed. Suppose further they are looking up into the sky seeing only what is above them. Thick smoke and heavy clouds hide all material objects they might otherwise see from the corner of their eyes, as well as the moon, the sun and the stars. Yet, as Baier points out, they might be perceiving something, i.e., they "might see flashes of lightning, rainbows, or auroras, hear claps of thunder and howling storms" and the like.[24] Nevertheless, the objects of their perception would not be material objects, but various visual, auditory and olfactory phenomena. Now perhaps perception entails that the percipient have a body, and thus we would still have at least one material object on our hands. But it is *conceivable*—that is to say it is logically possible—that only the phenomena seen by the percipient remain, i.e., lightning, clouds, wind, thick smoke, etc., without there being a percipient actually to perceive it. That is to say, we can describe a state of affairs in which only this exists. Thus we can conceive of what it would be like for there to be no material objects and thus 4) "There are material objects" is not an a priori truth.

This indeed does knock out the necessary status of 4) "There are material objects"; but, it might be replied that Baier's argument about how we learn "material object", "rock", "turtle", "thing" and the like establishes the necessary status of 5) "There *were* material objects." *Given* the use of these terms, i.e., "sock", "bottle", "thing", it is "indubitable that at least at the time when the child began to learn his language, there were material objects." But this only shows that 5) has basically the same kind of status that "There are an infinite number of natural numbers" has. Given the truth of certain *empirical states* of affairs, viz., that there are or were some things we call rocks, trees, flies, dirt and the like, and given that some people come to learn that there are such objects and come to use "rocks", "trees", "flies", "dirt" and the like as labels for these things, for which "material object" is an umbrella term, then it follows that "There were material objects" is true. But its truth depends on these empirical conditions and thus it is not an a priori truth. For the truth of 5), as in the case of "mathematical entities", rests on the truth of certain non-linguistic empirical facts, i.e., that there at one time were rocks, trees, dirt, flies and the like. That there were and still are such entities is an empirical truism but this hardly relieves statements like "There were rocks" of their empirical status.

The case, however, with "God" is very different. It is not learned intralinguistically; it is not an umbrella term for objects we come to learn ostensively. Malcolm and Hartshorne, like Anselm, want to say that given the use of "God"—a term whose meaning we do not learn by having God pointed out to us—we, if we will reflect on its meaning, can come to understand that "There is a God" is an a priori truth (a logical necessity). It is not, as in the other cases, that we can derive "There is a God" from certain empirical statements of non-linguistic fact plus certain linguistic conventions.

6) "There is a universe." This appears to be an existential proposition, but what could conceivably falsify it or what would count as evidence against its truth? It is tempting to say that nothing could conceivably falsify it. This temptation should be resisted. To see what is involved here we should first come to recognize that 6) needs interpretation. But on its two most plausible readings it is either nonsense or analytic. If "universe" is a very generic term for "All the things there are" then 6) becomes:

6') "There is all the things there are"
or more charitably and grammatically:

6") "There are all the things there are."
But here, depending on how we take "There are", we either have a tautology or nonsense. We have a tautology when "There are" means "exists", for then we are saying "All the things there are exist" or "All the things that exist exist." We have nonsense if "There are" functions as it does when we exclaim "There are all the Beatles together."

If we do not treat "universe" as a generic term for "All the things there are" or (if this is not a pleonasm) "All the finite things there are" then "the universe" is a phrase without meaning. So again with 6) we do not have an existential factual statement that is a necessary proposition or an a priori truth.

III

There is another line of argument against Findlay and Smart that has recently been taken by Bowman Clarke.[25] Clarke attacks their claim "that logically true propositions assert nothing but merely reflect our use of words, the arbitrary conventions of our language."[26] He attempts to show that such a claim is mistaken if it is taken in a way that would undermine a construal of "There is a God" as being 1) logically necessary and 2) non-vacuous and assertive. Clarke, unlike a classical rationalist, is perfectly prepared to concede that "There is a clear and intelligible distinction which can be made between logically true propositions and factually true propositions."[27] But, he argues, it is not a fact that the one "asserts nothing" and the other does, nor is it a "fact that one 'reflects our use of words' and the other does not."[28] It is not true, Clarke is at pains to claim, that if "There is a God" is a logically necessary truth, that it then merely reflects our use of words and asserts nothing whatsoever.[29] Rather it asserts a necessary state-of-affairs and its denial asserts an impossible state-of-affairs.[30]

Surely Clarke is correct in asserting that analytic statements or logically true propositions "in a language which describes the world," e.g., any natural language "asserts nothing whatsoever about terms, words, rules or conventions. They are indeed not statements about language."[31] " 'Puppies' is an English word that has the same meaning in English as the phrase 'young dogs' " is indeed a statement about language, but "Puppies are young dogs" is not a meta-linguistic statement but is in the object-language. According to Clarke, it asserts a necessary state-of-affairs.

Indeed, Clarke continues, it does not assert a contingent fact but it does not follow from this that it asserts nothing or that it is uninterpreted. It most certainly is interpreted as are many analytical statements or necessary propositions. They have subject and predicate terms and the subject terms at least are referential; "Puppies are young dogs," Clarke in effect argues, is not a vacuous formula. Similarly, "A is red and A is not red" asserts something, namely "a state-of-affairs in which the state-of-affairs asserted by the first contingent proposition and the state-of-affairs asserted by the second contingent proposition are incompatible."[32] That is, it asserts a *necessary* state-of-affairs or a necessary fact. The proposition asserting it is most surely not uninterpreted and thus it is a mistake to say it asserts nothing when all that we can sensibly mean by that is that it does not assert an empirical state-of-affairs. Rather it asserts "a necessary state-of-affairs— one that could not be otherwise."[33]

As we have seen, such statements are *not* about language. In that sense it is incorrect to say they "reflect our use of words" and if, alternatively, we mean that they " 'disclose' to us something of the language," this is indeed true, but contingent propositions also disclose to us something about our language and yet we are still willing to say both that they tell us something non-linguistic and that they are assertive. But if this is so, then, it would seem, we have no grounds for denying logically necessary statements are also assertive. It is indeed true, Clarke stresses, that "a logically true proposition can be determined to be true solely on the basis of the syntactical and semantical rules alone, whereas a factually true proposition cannot," but this does not make logically true propositions empty or vacuous; it simply reflects the fact that "a logically true proposition asserts a necessary state-of-affairs, one that could not be otherwise no matter what the contingent state-of-affairs might be . . . ."[34] Since this is so, one can, Clarke argues, correctly assert, as he maintains Findlay correctly asserts, that "There is a God" is logically necessary and still avoid Findlay's reductio that "There is a God" becomes completely vacuous, for "There is a God" asserts a necessary state-of-affairs or a necessary fact.

Even on Clarke's own grounds there are radical defects in his argument. He has not adequately met the standard Humean objections concerning necessary existence. One can indeed agree that logically necessary statements are not characteristically, if ever, about language while *not* agreeing that they assert some "necessary fact" or "necessary state-of-affairs". Indeed we may have some fairly intelligible paradigms of a "necessary state-of-affairs"—a state-of-affairs that could not be otherwise. With all their corpulence and age, it could not be that either Erhard or Strauss could run the mile in less than four minutes. And it could not be the case that there are toadstools at the centre of the earth. That the sun will rise tomorrow is another necessity. But these necessary states-of-affairs are *factual* necessities, not the necessities Clarke needs. The propositions asserting them are *contingent* propositions, not *logically* necessary propositions asserting logically necessary states-of-affairs. But the very force of Smart's and Findlay's thrust is, of course, to point out that no sense has been given to "*logically* necessary fact" or "*logically* necessary states-of-affairs" or "*logically* impossible states-of-affairs". Clarke makes it sound as if his phrases make sense by neglecting the qualifier "logically". He tells us "a logically false proposition asserts an impossible state-of-affairs . . . ." This appears to make sense for "an impossible state-of-affairs" has a use, viz., "The state-of-affairs in Bonn is impossible" or "The situation in Viet Nam is impossible." But no use has been given for "a *logically* impossible state-of-affairs", unless it is to be stipulated as an ersatz referent for a self-contradictory statement—even assuming we can intelligibly speak of the referent of a statement. But still how in such a circumstance a "fact", "situation", "state-of-affairs" is being referred to remains utterly opaque.

When people have said self-contradictory and logically necessary statements are vacuous, they most certainly did not mean they were uninterpreted. As part of a natural language their individual terms, or at least the non-syncategormatic ones, have an application. What they were asserting is that the sentence as a whole is not used to assert anything, for such sentences do not make statements which amplify our knowledge, that is to say, they do not inform us, except by indirectly teaching us something about our language. "Puppies are young" or "Puppies are young dogs" do not tell us anything that we do not already know, if we know the meaning of "puppy". They assert no fact or non-linguistic state-of-affairs of which we might otherwise be unaware. No use at all has been given to a "logically necessary state-of-affairs". If x is a state-of-affairs or fact, it is something one might not be acquainted with, but it is still something with which one might come to be acquainted. But a logically necessary proposition does not tell us, directly or indirectly, of any non-linguistic state-of-affairs. It cannot reveal to us any non-linguistic fact of which we might have been unaware. When people have incautiously said such propositions were about language or reflected our use of language, they have meant to say or at least should have meant to say that these utterances do not inform us— facts concerning the function of language apart—about the world. To the extent that they inform us at all, they inform us about the uses of our language.[35] They do not do that by being statements about the language but they reveal the unscheduled implications of the language (and similar languages) in a way that no factual statement can. "My pencil is red" does not so reveal the workings of my language but "A red pencil is a coloured pencil" does. It does not assert some elusive logically necessary state-of-affairs but it reveals a rule of language, or more broadly a rule about the nature of certain concepts: "You can't call x 'red' unless you also allow that x is coloured." It is a fact that there is such a rule, but it is a rule about our language or about the nature of our concepts. If we construe "There is a God" to mean "There is a logically necessary being," so that "There is a God" becomes logically necessary, then "There is a God" can no longer assert a fact or "a necessary state-of-affairs" or any state-of-affairs at all. It will reveal, as "Red things are coloured" reveals, something of the workings of our language or the structure of our concepts. Thus Clarke's labour to avoid Findlay's reductio comes to nought. We have no idea of what a "logically necessary state-of-affairs" or a "logically necessary fact" is like, and thus we have no understanding of "logically necessary existence". If God's necessity is this kind of necessity then we have no understanding of "God".

To establish the fact that there is logically necessary existence or that there are logically necessary beings, we must establish that there are a priori existential propositions, i.e., propositions which categorically assert the existence of something whose truth does not depend on any non-linguistic empirical facts. While we should not simply take it as a dogma that there are and can be no logically necessary existential propositions, it remains the case 1) that no plausible example of such a proposition has been adduced and 2) that there are good theoretical reasons for believing that there are no such propositions. We can, of course, certainly say of many propositions, e.g., "There are coloured things if there are red things," that they are a priori truths. What we have not been able to establish is that there are any categorical existential statements without hypothetical riders, e.g., "There are coloured things", which are a priori truths.

I did not simply assume that there are no a priori existential statements. I examined alleged counter-examples to what seems to be evidently true, namely that there are no existential a priori truths, and I have shown that none of them counts as a genuine disconfirmation of the claim that there are no a priori existential statements. In line with this I have examined "There is a God" on its own merits as one such counter-example. If my arguments have been correct I have shown that the alleged counter-examples are only alleged counter-examples and not genuine counter-examples. In spite of the renewed interest in establishing by philosophical argument that there is a logically necessary being, we still are in such matters essentially with Hume. There is good reason to think that "a logically necessary being" like "round square" is a contradiction in terms. Thus if God is conceived of as a logically necessary being, we have very good reason to believe that this concept of God is self-contradictory and thus that it is a self-contradiction to assert that there is a God.[36]

NOTES

1. Charles Hartshorne, *The Logic of Perfection* (LaSalle, IL: Open Court Publishing Co., 1962); Norman Malcolm, "Anselm's Ontological Arguments," *The Philosophical Review* LXIX (1960); J.N. Findlay, "Can God's Existence be Disproved?" and J.J.C. Smart, "The Existence of God," *New Essays in Philosophical Theology*, eds. Antony Flew and Alasdair MacIntyre (London: Macmillan, 1955). See also the comments on Findlay's essay by Hughes and Rainer in the same volume.

2. J.N. Findlay, *op. cit.* 47-48.

3. *Ibid.* 49.

4. *Ibid.* 50.

5. *Ibid.*

6. *Ibid.*

7. *Ibid.*

8. *Ibid.* 51.

9. *Ibid.* 52.

10. *Ibid.* 55.

11. *Ibid.*

12. *Ibid.* 54.

13. *Ibid.* 56.

14. *Ibid.* 71-72.

15. *Ibid.* 75.

16. Anthony Kenny, "God and Necessity," *British Analytical Philosophy*, eds. A. Montefiore and B. Williams (London: Routledge & Kegan Paul, 1965) 143. Adel Daher has effectively criticized this essay, as well as some related arguments by Plantinga in his "God and Factual Necessity," *Religious Studies* 6.1 (1970).

17. *Ibid.* 143, 146.

18. See H.L. Allen and Raziel Abelson, *The Philosophical Review* LXX (1961).

19. Hartshorne used no. 6 against me in argument.

20. Kurt Baier, "Existence," *Aristotelian Society Proceedings* LXI (1960-61): 26.

21. *Ibid.*

22. *Ibid.* 27.

23. *Ibid.*

24. *Ibid.* 28.

25. Bowman Clarke, "Linguistic Analysis and Philosophy of Religion," *The Monist* 47.3 (1963): 365-86. But see, in criticism, Adel Daher, "God and Logical Necessity," *Philosophical Studies* (National University of Ireland) XVIII (1969).

26. *Ibid.* 380.

27. *Ibid.* 383.

28. *Ibid.*

29. *Ibid.* 397.

30. *Ibid.* 382.

31. *Ibid.*

32. *Ibid.*

33. *Ibid.*

34. *Ibid.* 384.

35. If this is said to be a way of informing us about the world, it is a way of informing us about our *concepts*, about the *uses* or *functions* of language. That is to say, it is not about English or German or French. We learn, for example, something about the *use* of 'dog', 'hund', or 'chien'. But that is not a lesson in English, German or French, but about the common employment of these terms.

36.   These arguments, of course, do not touch scholastic arguments which construe God's necessary existence in quite different terms. I have considered some of these arguments in my "God, Necessity and Falsifiability," *Traces of God in a Secular Culture*, ed. George F. McLean (New York: Alba House, 1973) 271-304. See also the exchange between D.R. Duff-Forbes and John H. Hick in the *Canadian Journal of Philosophy* 1.4 (1972): 473-88 and Terence Penelhum, *Religion and Rationality* (New York: Random House, 1971) 31-48, 365-80.

CHAPTER 4

Truth-Conditions and
Necessary Existence*

I

MY OBJECTIVES ARE TWOFOLD. I WANT FIRST TO show (mainly following John Hick) that there is a conception of necessary existence or *aseity*, distinct from a conception of "logically necessary being", which is at least prima facie plausible; and second to show, with respect to this specific conception, that there are relevant questions about stating truth-conditions which are unsatisfied and perhaps even in principle unsatisfiable, and that these are questions which must be met before such a prima facie plausible conception can be taken to give us the basis of a satisfactory theological elucidation of what it is to speak of God. I shall argue that it is doubtful whether these questions about truth-conditions can be met.

I should add that my arguments in the second half of this chapter have a certain "empiricist ring" and that arguments of this general sort are, of course, challengeable and indeed have been challenged. I have tried to provide a general account and defense of such an approach in my *Contemporary Critiques of Religion* (London: Macmillan Ltd., 1971), my *Skepticism* (London: Macmillan Ltd., 1973) and in my *Reason and Practice* (New York: Harper and Row, 1971), chapters 21 and 31-36 and I will not repeat those arguments here. What I shall do, however, without relying on arguments contained in those books, is (1) to raise specific considerations to show why there is a problem about truth-conditions and identification which such a conception of necessary existence does not resolve in the way a conception of logically necessary existence perhaps would, were it coherent, and (2) show that it must do so to be a viable account of God. With (2) I shall be going against the stream, for it is often (perhaps usually) thought now, though Hick to his credit does not think so, that with such an account of necessary existence we legitimately can bypass such allegedly empiricist considerations.

---

*First published in the *Scottish Journal of Theology* 27.3 (1974).

One further preliminary. I referred initially to this account of *aseity* or necessary existence simply as "a prima facie plausible account," not only because I think that the considerations I shall raise in Section III of this chapter show it in fact to be an unsatisfactory account but also because of the more direct, quite different and unfortunately overlooked arguments made by Stuart R. Brown, *Do Religious Claims Make Sense?* (New York: The Macmillan Co., 1969), pp. 153-6 and by Colin Lyas, "On the Coherence of Christian Atheism", *Philosophy*, vol. XLV (January 1970), pp. 13-17, which raise penetrating and perhaps even reasonably decisive arguments against the utilization of such a conception of necessary existence, if it is (as it is) to give us some understanding of a God who is a "being than which a greater cannot be conceived." Perhaps, after all, such a being could intelligibly be said to be a being who could annihilate himself, if he chose to do so, and perhaps it is even religiously appropriate for him to do so. Such remarks are usually thought to be absurd, exhibiting an evident failure to understand the grammar of "God". But Brown and Lyas both have deployed careful arguments to show that they are not absurd at all. Be that as it may, my own target and method of attack in this chapter will be a different one and my account (which in no way depends on the viability of their account) is not one with which Brown at least would have much sympathy.

II

Powerful arguments have been deployed against Malcolm's, Hartshorne's, and Plantinga's attempts to show that there are or can be existential statements—statements asserting the existence of something—which are logically true or true a priori. If these arguments are correct, it is nonsense to claim that there could be something such that if its existence is logically possible, then it exists. If this is so, it appears to be a field day for Findlay and his ontological disproof of the existence of God; that is, it looks as if Findlay's argument is correct: a religiously adequate conception of God is that of a logically necessary being, and the conception of a logically necessary being is a self-contradictory conception. However, this short way with God or God-talk will not work. What we must do is challenge Findlay's premise that the only adequate object of a religious attitude or of a theistic religious attitude would be a logically necessary being. That is to say, we should challenge the claim that God is properly conceived as a *logically* necessary being.

Hick proceeds to do this with vigour and I would like initially to follow out his argument here.[1] He first argues that it is a mistake to think that what is allegedly signified by a self-contradictory concept—a logically necessary being—could possibly be an appropriate object of a religious attitude. Findlay should carefully note exactly what he is saying: surely it is perplexing—to put it conservatively—to claim that what is purportedly signified by a self-contradictory conception is an *adequate* object of a religious attitude. What is referred to by a self-contradictory conception (even if we can intelligibly speak this way) could not be an adequate object of a religious attitude. If we recognize that a logically necessary being is a contradiction in terms we should also recognize that it could not possibly be an adequate object of religious attitude. It would on the "contrary be an unqualifiedly inadequate object of worship."[2]

It seems to me that Hick is right here. We must reject Findlay's claim that a God adequate for religious purposes must be conceived in such a way that "God exists" is a logically necessary or a priori truth.

Yet we appear at least to get in trouble if we do this. We *seem* to be rejecting the God of the Bible. The biblical writers and orthodox Jews, Christians and Moslems conceive of God as the Lord of all. He is taken to be incomparable, eternal, unlimited—wholly necessary in every conceivable way. Even Neo-Thomist philosophers such as Father Copleston conceive of God as a being whose non-existence is inconceivable.

We must, however, beware of the construal that most philosophers are prone to put on "conceivable". We must avoid simply importing into a *religious* context the use of "conceivable" that is typical in logic, where "*x* is conceivable" comes to mean "*x* is not self-contradictory" or more liberally "*x* is not self-contradictory or *x* is semantically deviant, e.g., not like 'is or red' or 'Jones is a natural number' ". The same thing must be said of "necessary". To say that there is no sense of "necessary" or none that has been coherently explained apart from the logical necessity of statements is simply false. As Peter Geach has remarked, even a superficial acquaintance with modal logic will show how mistaken it is to treat "necessary" in such a univocal way. And modal logic apart: to say that "necessary" can only refer to "logical necessity is equivalent to saying that whatever cannot be so, *logically* cannot be so—e.g., that since I cannot speak Russian my speaking Russian is logically impossible".[3]

There is a further point to be made here. Hick points out that for the biblical writers it is indeed true that the existence of God was not regarded as something open to question. They conceived of God as sheer given reality—a reality of which these biblical writers were as vividly aware, or thought they were as vividly aware, as they were of their own physical environment.[4] God as a Holy Will, as the *mysterium tremendum et fascinans*, is the maker and ruler of the Universe. He is the sole rightful sovereign of men and angels. He is the ultimate reality and determining power of everything other than himself. His creatures—as Job came to see— have no standing except as the objects of his grace.

Yet if this is said, does this not imply that they, after all, conceived of God as a logically necessary being—as a being whose non-existence is logically inconceivable? Hick's reply here is significant.

> But, it might be said, was it not to the biblical writers inconceivable that God should *not* exist, or that he should cease to exist, or should lose his divine powers and virtues? Would it not be inconceivable to them that God might one day go out of existence, or cease to be good and become evil? And does not this attitude involve an implicit belief that God exists necessarily and possesses his divine characteristics in some necessary manner? The answer, I think, is that it was to the biblical writers psychologically inconceivable—as we say colloquially, unthinkable—

that God might not exist, or that his nature might undergo radical change. They were so vividly conscious of God that they were unable to doubt his reality, and they were so firmly reliant upon his integrity and faithfulness that they could not contemplate his becoming other than they knew him to be. They would have allowed as a verbal concession only that there might possibly be no God; for they were convinced that they were at many times directly aware of his presence and of his dealings with them. But the question whether the non-existence of God is *logically* inconceivable, or *logically* impossible, is a purely philosophical puzzle which could not be answered by the prophets and apostles out of their own first-hand religious experience. This does not, of course, represent any special limitation of the biblical figures. The logical concept of necessary being cannot be given in religious experience. It is an object of philosophical thought and not of religious experience. It is a product—as Findlay argues, a malformed product—of reflection. A religious person's reply to the question, Is God's existence logically necessary? will be determined by his view of the nature of logical necessity; and this view is not part of his religion but part of his system of logic, if he has one. The biblical writers, in point of fact, display no view of the nature of logical necessity, and would probably have regarded the topic as purely academic and of no religious significance. It cannot reasonably be claimed, then, that logically necessary existence was part of their conception of the adequate object of human worship.[5]

In fine, they thought it was unthinkable, impossible, inconceivable that there be no God: his reality is manifest; he is inescapable; his existence is quite necessary. But there is no reason to believe that he was conceived of as being a *logically* necessary being; there is no reason to believe that his non-existence was taken by these writers to be *logically* inconceivable. Moreover, if some few did so reason they would have been in error, as Malcolm's critics have made apparent. But here their error would be an error in logic: an error in philosophical theology which blurs their *characterization* of their religious response. But they need not fall into this error for they could, still without committing such a philosophical blunder, take God's existence to be necessary, for they could take the necessity of Divine Existence to be a brute factual necessity.

Hick also claims, again with considerable plausibility, that both Anselm and Aquinas thought of God as having factual necessity rather than as having a logically necessary existence.[6] I shall not pursue this historical point here. Yet it should be apparent by now that *if* their conceptions of necessary being are to be viable, they cannot have had in mind the malformed conception of a logically necessary being.

Findlay and Malcolm would be abusing language and obscuring the issue if they were to persist in their claim that such a *factual* necessity is not enough because a being with only factual necessity would *merely happen* to exist and a fully adequate object of a religious attitude could not *just happen* to exist. The following considerations establish this. Findlay and Malcolm present us with a dilemma: "Either God's existence is logically necessary or he merely happens to exist". But in pointing out that one half of the dichotomy is self-contradictory Findlay has in effect removed the dichotomy. If all objects are said to be either round squares or non-round squares and it is found out that there, logically speaking, can be no round squares, then it is pointless to go around characterizing all objects as non-round squares, for "non-round squares" can have no intelligible opposite. Having concluded, as Findlay has, that "the notion of necessary existence has no meaning, to continue to speak of things merely happening to exist, as though this stood in contrast with some other mode of existing, no longer has any validity".[7]

To this, it can well be countered, that there is a non-vacuous contrast between things that just happen to exist and things which exist necessarily. So, "contingent existence" is not, after all, pleonastic. This is true but since "*logically* necessary existence" is self-contradictory, the contrast between "existing necessarily" and "just happening to exist" will have to be drawn *within the class of realities* that, as a matter of *logical* possibility, might not exist now or might never have existed. (Malcolm is right in claiming that if God does not exist now, he never existed and he never will come to exist. That is, God by definition is eternal, but that does not make God's existence logically necessary.[8])

Hick tries to spell out more fully what is meant by a "factually necessary being". It is not enough to contrast transient existence with eternal existence and to identify divine necessity with the latter. Something might exist eternally simply because it in fact was never destroyed, though at all times it could be destroyed. An eternal being need not be indestructible or the source of all power. (Of course, if it were in fact destroyed it would not be eternal.) But God—as the ultimate Lord of all—is not capable of being destroyed or of being created. It is further, Hick argues, true that God is ". . . incorruptible, in the sense of being incapable of either ceasing to exist or of ceasing to possess divine characteristics".[9]

God—Hick's factually necessary being—is "an incorruptible and indestructible being without beginning or end."[10] These are but aspects of a "more fundamental characteristic which the Scholastics termed *aseity* ('self-existence')." The core notion of *aseity* is that of completely independent being. Each item in the universe depends upon some factor or factors beyond itself; not even all incorruptible and indestructible beings have this *aseity*. Aquinas thought human souls, angels and the heavenly bodies were incorruptible and indestructible, except by an act of God. They are eternal and necessary beings, but they lack *aseity*. "Only God exists in total non-dependence; he alone exists absolutely as sheer unconditioned self-existent being."[11] God has unlimited superiority over all other beings; he is, by definition, the greatest possible being—a being in whom absolute trust may be placed. All other realities depend on him and he in turn depends on no other reality; nothing can threaten his cause, everything else depends on him; there are no sufficient conditions for existence.

In short, "What may properly be meant . . . by the statement that God is, or has necessary existence as distinguished from contingent existence is that God is without beginning or end and without origin, cause or ground of any kind whatsoever. He is as 'the ultimate reality', 'unconditioned, absolute, unlimited being.' "[12] Yet "that God is, is *not* a logically necessary truth; for no matter of fact can be logically necessary. *The reality of God is sheer datum,*" though unlike *other* necessary beings, God is the sole self-existent being: that is the sole totally unlimited, totally independent being. God, Hick avers, "is an utterly unique datum."[13]

The existence of God cannot be causally explained since a self-existent being must be uncaused and therefore "not susceptible to the causal type of explanation." Bertrand Russell's question—who created God?—can only be a joke or a failure to understand what is meant by "God". We can best define "God" as follows:

> God is an eternal, incorruptible, indestructible reality who creates all beings other than himself and is not and cannot be dependent on or created by anything else.[14]

Such a reality has both necessary being and *aseity*; that is, it always will be, always was and, as a sheer matter of fact, cannot nor could not nor will not be able not to be.

Such a concept of God as self-existent necessary being is—Hick argues—perfectly intelligible; it is indeed a mysterious, awe-inspiring notion, but a God who is not mysterious and awe-inspiring would not be the God of the Judaic-Christian-Islamic tradition. But the important thing to see here, Hick argues, is that such a concept is perfectly intelligible. Given, Hick continues, that God as necessary being is an intelligible concept, the crucial question remains: "Is there a being or a reality to which this concept applies?" To ask this question is, in effect, to concede that "God exists" is intelligible and to ask how can we know or have grounds for believing that God exists. Can we by religious experience or through revelation come in some way to confirm or render credible the claim that God exists; or can we in some way and in some sense prove, after the fashion of the cosmological argument or the argument from design, that God exists? Or is it the case, as Hick himself thinks, that we must accept divine existence solely on *faith*? Knowing what it *means* to say "There is a God," I can have *faith* in God and accept it on *faith* that God exists.

III

I, however, obstinately remain stuck several steps back, for I am not convinced that Hick or anyone else has been able to show how the concept of a factually necessary, self-existent being is intelligible where that concept is interpreted as Hick interprets it or where it is interpreted so that we can continue to conceive of God as transcendent to the cosmos; that is where "God" refers to something in some way "over and above the universe." But surely the onus is now on me to show that this is so.

First—and this will surely support Hick—we can and should make the Ziffian point that we have *some* understanding of the conditions that Hick associates with the word "God". These conditions may indeed be problematic, but it still remains true that we have some understanding of them. If God is the sole independent, unlimited eternal being there cannot be two Gods—a God of good and a God of evil—and God could not cease

to be or come to be or be created and the like. But similar linguistic manoeu-
vres can be made with "The Absolute is unfaithful" or "Ziff heard a
picture". If Ziff heard a picture, then Ziff heard something and Ziff could
at that time hear and the like. If the Absolute is unfaithful it is not to be
trusted, not to be confided in and perhaps it should be divorced from the
contingent. But "The Absolute is unfaithful" or "Ziff heard a picture"
are surely, except as metaphors, nonsense. That we can make *such* moves
with "God" does not show that such wordstrings as "God is the sole
independent, totally unlimited, eternal being" are not nonsensical or
incoherent uses of language.

What more do we need to establish the intelligibility of such uses
of language? Giving up anything like the ontological argument and with
it giving up any attempt to make a purely *conceptual identification* of God,
we need some *empirical anchorage* of our term. We need, as Hick himself
on other occasions has stressed, some way of showing what would *in principle* satisfy the conditions he associates with the term "God". Now, as
Kierkegaard quipped, we cannot expect God to be a Great Green Bird.
Paul Edwards to the contrary notwithstanding, we do not conceive of God
as a Being with some kind of huge body.[15] A God that could be observed,
that could be seen or apprehended in any literal way, would not be the
God of the Judeo-Christian-Islamic tradition. Yet in our very first-order
religious discourse, we sometimes talk of *seeing* God, of apprehending God,
of an awareness of God, of the experience of God, of living in the presence
of God and the like. Our God-talk even allows us to speak or rather sing
of seeing the face of the invisible God. Yet we must be careful not to rule
out metaphor in an arbitrary and insensitive manner. But we must also
not forget that genuine metaphors can—to use a metaphor myself—be
cashed in; that is, to use another, they can in principle be redeemed in
the sound currency of straightforward assertion.

Searching for this empirical anchorage for "God", we need to ask
what sort of a thing or being or reality or force we are talking about when
we speak of something as the sole, independent, totally unlimited, eternal
being? Hick speaks of it as *sheer datum* and as a *unique datum*. But what
would it be like to experience or fail to experience or in any way encounter
this Being—this sheer datum? A unique datum or even any old datum at
all is in virtue of the very meaning of "datum" something that could be
encountered, that could be identified. Yet what criteria do I use in order
to decide whether I or others did or did not correctly identify that putative
datum? What would even in principle count as experiencing or failing to
encounter, an eternal, utterly unbounded, indestructible, immaterial reality,
who creates all other realities but is itself uncreated and is in no way dependent on anything else? What would have to be the case, what would we
have to experience now or in the future, in this life or in the next, in order
for us to have any grounds at all for asserting rather than denying or denying
rather than asserting that there is such a reality?

Hick himself avers that we should, for the sake of clarity, set out
"God exists" in a Russellian way, i.e., "There is one (and only one) x
such that x is omniscient, omnipotent, etc." Now, to put it in a Peircean

way, what *conceivable experiential* states of affairs, events, actions, occurrences and the like would lend even the *slightest* probability to the claim that there is one (and only one) *x* such that *x* is eternal, uncreated, incorruptible, indestructible, immaterial, unlimited and a totally independent creator of all other realities? If (as Hick himself believes) the above phrases are so put together that they can be used to make what is purportedly a factual statement and if it and its denial are both equally compatible with *all conceivable experienceable* states of affairs, then the putative statement and its denial are both without factual content, without factual significance.

However, as Hick is most rightly concerned to uphold, "God exists" is *thought* by the believer to be a factual statement—to have factual significance. All reasonably orthodox believers believe that it is a fact that God exists. But if "There is a God" is compatible with anything and everything that we might conceivably experience now or hereafter, "There is a God" is without factual meaning—it is devoid of factual content or significance. Yet for Hick and for believers generally "There is a God" must have factual content.

The above point is indeed an old point, but, old or not, it seems to me to be well taken.[16] And here Hick, though not Ziff, agrees with me, for he argues for a kind of "eschatological verification" which will, he believes, give the necessary empirical anchorage to God-talk such that it will enable us to establish that "There is a God" and the like have factual significance.[17]

Once we construe "God" as a factually necessary being after the manner of Hick, or for that matter after the manner of Aquinas, we are led, if we are clear-headed, quite inexorably to what has been called Flew's challenge or rather misleadingly "the theology and falsification issue". If with Malcolm and Findlay we stay with a *logically* necessary being, we can avoid Flew's challenge, but only at the cost of making "There is a God" self-contradictory. To make out a case for "God exists" being an intelligible factual statement and for Divine Existence being necessary, though factually necessary, we are led to a consideration of the theology and falsification issue and to the noetic claims of religious experience. But there again, as is well known, we face a host of standard difficulties, difficulties that cannot be avoided by utilizing the concept of *aseity*.[18]

NOTES

1. John Hick, "God and Necessary Being," *Journal of Philosophy* LVIII (1961): 725-34; and "Necessary Being," *Scottish Journal of Theology* XIV (1961): 353-69.

2. John Hick, "God and Necessary Being," *Journal of Philosophy* LVIII (1961): 728.

3. In his essay on Aquinas in G.E.M. Anscombe and P.T. Geach, *Three Philosophers* (Oxford: 1961) 83.

4. John Hick, "God and Necessary Being," *Journal of Philosophy* LVIII (1961): 728. See also in criticism here Adel Daher, "God and Factual Necessity," *Religious Studies* 6 (1970).

5. *Ibid.* 729.

6. *Ibid.* 729-31.

7. John Hick, "God and Necessary Being," *Journal of Philosophy* LVIII (1961): 731.

8. This has been convincingly argued by P.T. Brown, "Professor Malcolm on Anselm's Ontological Arguments," *Analysis* (1961).

9. John Hick, "God and Necessary Being," *Journal of Philosophy* LVIII (1961): 731.

10. *Ibid.* 732.

11. *Ibid.* 733.

12. *Ibid.*

13. *Ibid.*

14. John Hick, "God and Necessary Being," *Journal of Philosophy* LVIII (1961): 733.

15. Paul Edwards, "Some Notes on Anthropomorphic Theology," *Religious Experience and Truth*, ed. Sidney Hook (New York: 1961) 242.

16. I have argued this and have generally elucidated and criticized Ziff's account in my "The Intelligibility of God-talk," *Religious Studies* 6.1 (1970). See as well Robert Hoffman, "On Being Mindful of 'God': Reply to Kai Nielsen," *Religious Studies* 6.3 (1970).

17. Hick develops this in his "Theology and Verification" reprinted in *The Existence of God*, ed. John Hick (New York: 1964) 253-74. I have criticized Hick's account in my "Eschatological Verification," *The Canadian Journal of Theology* XVII (October 1963). Hick has replied to this in the second edition of his *Faith and Knowledge* (Ithaca, NY: 1966) 196-99 and I have in turn responded in my *Contemporary Critiques of Religion* 71-79.

18. I have argued against specifically Neo-Thomistic conceptions and utilizations of *aseity* in my "God, Necessity and Falsifiability," *Traces of God in a Secular Culture*, ed. George F. McLean (New York: Alba House, 1973) 271-304.

CHAPTER 5

Rationality, Intelligibility, and Alasdair MacIntyre's Talk of God*

I

PHILOSOPHERS AND THEOLOGIANS—AND NOT without reason—have raised challenges concerning the rationality of religious beliefs and the intelligibility of religious conceptions. But it is also true that the range of response to these challenges is by now well mapped and the argumentative ground well-trodden. However, Alasdair MacIntyre has re-examined these issues in a highly original, perceptive and interesting manner. While avoiding what F.C. Copleston has characterized as a "positivist orientation" (a set of assumptions and commitments which is much broader than the distinctive views we associate with logical empiricism), MacIntyre persists in arguing that belief in God is *for us* irrational and indeed not even compatible with our understanding God-talk.[1] This—particularly when freed from any kind of positivist orientation—is a paradoxical claim as well as a challenging one of both theoretical and ideological importance.

I shall argue that MacIntyre fails to sustain his claims, significant and perceptive as they are. In so arguing I shall proceed by laying out his central contentions in some detail and then critically scrutinizing them. I do this because of their importance, their unfamiliarity and because they have occurred in scattered places rather than in a central chunk of argument. I shall bring them together into a coherent whole, display their rationale and try to show how notwithstanding their perceptiveness they will not withstand critical examination.

II

MacIntyre in arguing for the incoherence of God-talk is very explicit about rejecting verificationism. Indeed MacIntyre

---

*First published in *The Philosophical Forum* V.3 (1974).

believes that verificationist arguments of the type which Ayer and Flew have developed are in reality unjustified and unjustifiable empiricist dogmas and that any recognizable form of verificationism will *not* set or characterize correctly the logical limits of what can be intelligibly said or coherently believed but in fact will turn out to be the very kind of worldview which verificationism would rule out.[2]

MacIntyre, like Pascal, for whom he has a deep sympathy, is sceptical about claims, including sceptical claims, to have indubitable first principles. He stresses that there is an important historical dimension in our thought which is almost totally neglected by Anglo-American philosophers. In analyzing religion or morality, we should not think that we are analyzing and trying to give a perspicuous representation to an unchanging structure of concepts.[3] What we should recognize instead is that most of our concepts undergo considerable change in different historical periods and different cultural settings. To take a notorious example: a crucial mistake of moral philosophy in the Anglo-Saxon countries, MacIntyre observes, is that it is notably unhistorical.

> Books are too often written about 'the' moral vocabulary apparently on the assumption that there is an unchanging structure of concepts. It is too often assumed, when moral philosophers apparently disagree about 'good' and 'ought' that they are holding rival and competing views of the same concepts, rather than elucidating very different concepts from very different historical periods.[4]

In examining philosophical and ideological debate, we need more often to try to view the matter as if we were anthropologists from another culture. This is exactly what MacIntyre, atheist that he is, does in discussing the debate between atheists and theists.[5] It is MacIntyre's belief that intellectualist accounts of the loss of belief or of religious scepticism are mistaken. "It is not the case," he tells us, "that men first stopped believing in God and in the authority of the Church, and then subsequently started behaving differently. It seems clear that men first of all lost any over-all social agreement as to the right ways to live together, and so ceased to be able to make sense of any claims to moral authority."[6] The fragility of religions in our culture is not due to philosophical or theological argument or to the sceptical onslaughts of a speculative atheism, which finds its profound exemplars in David Hume and Bertrand Russell, but is due "to its role in our social life."[7]

Furthermore (and this is a very considerable departure from standard modes of philosophizing) in understanding religion and in coming to grips with questions concerning the coherence of religious concepts, we should pay particular attention to social structure. If we try to understand religion or any of the other modes of social discourse apart from it we will surely flounder. What is involved here comes to the fore if we consider some relations between religion and social structure during the height of the Industrial Revolution. Religion is, as MacIntyre puts it, "always at least an expression of a society's moral unity, and it lends to that unity a cosmic and universal significance and justification."[8] But the sense of moral unity was destroyed with the sharp class divisions developing during the Industrial Revolution, with the rise of capitalism and with the destruction of relatively stable and closely integrated village communities as the peasants moved in mass into the cities and became an urban proletariat. The older forms of community were undermined and with that rapid alteration of social structure it became the case that there no longer existed "shared and established norms common to all ranks in the community, in the light of which everyone stands either vindicated or convicted by their own conduct."[9] Such a moral orientation did not exist for the working class in the teeming industrial cities, torn as they were "from a form of community in which it could be intelligibly and credibly claimed that the norms which govern social life had universal and cosmic significance and were God-given."[10] The social structure of their society was such that the officially endorsed norms, though universal in *form*, actually served the partial and partisan interests of the capitalist ruling class. These moral norms worked to enhance the interests of the rich by disciplining the poor; in such a cultural environment it could no longer be credibly claimed that these moral norms were God-given and not man-made.

In such a society with such class divisions and such class conflict, religious concepts came to lose their point and so their intelligibility (rationality), for they cannot in that environment do what they exist (at least in part) to do, namely to provide a framework for the activity we call "religion" which in turn gives symbolic and ritualistic expression to a culture's moral unity. Religion can no longer give expression to our society's moral unity or to the moral unity of the society of the Industrial Revolution for the very simple reason that such societies have no moral unity. As the Industrial Revolution developed, people found themselves in situations where social change was very rapid and where moral practices were anything but unalterable. This very condition of their lives "made ordinary men far more conscious of the actual and potential variety of competing and conflicting moralities and ways of life and the need to choose between them, and thus it was undermining the notion of one true morality."[11]

But Judaism and Christianity require such a conception of a single True Morality. If this notion is incoherent or unbelievable, then Judaism and Christianity are themselves incoherent. It is MacIntyre's claim that religion becomes unintelligible where there is no moral unity.

To this it is not unnatural to object that, while it shows, if the argument is sound, that *in a sense* religious discourse is unintelligible, this is not the strong and (or so many philosophers have thought) interesting sense of "unintelligible" in which philosophers should be interested. MacIntyre's argument does nothing to show that "God created the heavens and the earth" is unintelligible in the way "Nixon sleeps faster than Dean" is unintelligible. We, as far as anything MacIntyre has shown is concerned, understand what it asserts. We are not lost, as we are with the Nixon remark, about what it could *mean* and it is not, as in the Nixon remark, a deviation from a linguistic regularity; in fact because we understand so well what it means we recognize that in our present cultural context it is pointless, though we also recognize that the same remark would not lack point in another cultural context. But these considerations show, as clearly as can be, that, in the sense which has been of interest to philosophers, MacIntyre's very remarks are evidence that such God-talk is intelligible. They only show (if sound) that such talk is unintelligible in the sense of being pointless (and in that way irrational) in a cultural milieu such as ours.

However, when all of the above considerations are taken to heart, there is left open the following retort. A man of strong religious convictions could argue against MacIntyre, and generally against such accounts, that if God-talk is only unintelligible in the sense of being pointless in a class-divided Industrial or post-Industrial milieu, we should, as moral agents, direct all our energies to recapturing the sense and indeed even the reality of an integrated community—something desirable on other grounds as well—such that the eschatological hopes at the core of Christianity could again be felt with force. They, he could argue, give a significance to life in a way no purely secular or humanist ideals can. If such religious ideals are lost or become pointless in a certain environment, then we should seek to regain an environment in which they will not be pointless and in that way unintelligible.

To reply in turn that this is turning Christians into a tribe of Don Quixotes is not an adequate rebuttal—though it is important not to lose sight of—for a Kierkegaard would surely in turn respond that this is precisely what we should expect in the alienated, forgetful world in which we live. In such a world a Christian should and indeed humanly speaking must be a Don Quixote—a knight of faith seeking to make a reality of that which is militated against by the whole thrust of our culture.

Generally what should be observed at this juncture is that, unless there are some other ways in which religious conceptions can be seen to be unintelligible, such remarks about social structure will do little to establish that belief in God is irrational for contemporary Western or westernized persons. Secularization has cut deep in our culture; that is to say, there has been a massive transition from beliefs, activities, and institutions presupposing beliefs of a traditional Christian kind to beliefs, activities and institutions of a non-religious kind. But this does not show that there should not be knights of faith who would struggle against such a social order.

III

It is significant to note that MacIntyre himself raises a related objection to his own account, though it seems to me that he has done little to answer it. He turns to what many philosophers would believe to be the heart of the matter when he remarks:

> Is what I have said so far merely sociological comment of a kind that could have no bearing on the truth of any Christian theological claims? It seems to me that this is not the case for the following reason. One could not make this comment on the argument unless one was prepared to deny that the claims of the Christian religion included a claim about its necessary relevance to the forms of social life and its ability to give a meaning to secular social life in every kind of circumstance. Historically, indeed a central claim of the Christian religion has been that

it is able to incarnate itself within different forms of social life and to lend to them a meaning and a justification which they would otherwise lack, but the tendency of my argument has been to show that Christianity confronted with the secular life of the post-Industrial-Revolution society has in fact found it impossible to lend meaning to that life or to enable people to understand and find justifications for living out its characteristic forms. It is rather that Christianity has been shaped and reshaped by the forces of modern secular life. Thus in so far as the claims of Christianity are themselves social, so far the claims of Christianity are impugned by the actual history of modern society. It is always possible for the theologian at this point to modify his claims. It is always possible for him to assert that the Christian gospel is a body of eternal and unchanging truths, and that it is related to the changing forms of secular social life. Such a version of orthodoxy will be immune to any suggestion of refutation by or modification as a result of sociology or social history.[12]

In response to the claim that Christianity is a body of eternal and unchanging truths not dependent on the changing forms of secular social life, MacIntyre remarks that in actuality theologians have not generally responded that way. That is to say, they have not treated Christian doctrine as if it were so independent of society. Contemporary theologians (he mentions Tillich, Bonhoeffer and Robinson) who have tried to interpret Christianity to make it relevant to contemporary culture have in effect expunged it of any theological content and indeed often of any logical consistency.[13] We have with such theologians what MacIntyre has elsewhere described as a religious vocabulary linked with an atheistic substance. If we take the popular Tillich—the Tillich without his grandiose and quite unintelligible metaphysical conceptualization—we have a perfect example of this reinterpretation for modern man turning into what is in effect an atheism with all religious and theological content eviscerated, leaving us only some, by now empty, religious vocabulary. "God" is not a referring expression of any kind standing for a, or the, supernatural being governing the world; to think that this is how "God" functions is, Tillich tells us, to misconstrue "God". Rather "God" is a word we use for whatever it is that we care most deeply about. We gain a deeper understanding of the nature of God, the more fully we come to understand man's most ultimate concerns. Indeed to talk about God is to talk about man's most ultimate concerns. This, MacIntyre is quick to point out, is just the familiar Feuerbachian form of atheism baptized with a new name.[14]

This is hardly fair, as I have pointed out elsewhere, to Tillich or even to his understudy Robinson, for they also utilize metaphysical constructions which, while rejecting supernaturalism, do not admit of such an atheistic or naturalistic explication, but MacIntyre could reasonably respond that it is (a) the above secularist side of Tillich and Robinson that has been so influential—that has caught up so many people—and (b) it is this side which is clearly intelligible in terms of the most ubiquitous categories of understanding of contemporary culture. And if we take the side, deleting a concern for Tillich's at least seemingly incoherent ontology, religion is gelded.

However, a recognition that there is this tendency to eviscerate religion, to make it intelligible to modern man, is not enough to answer MacIntyre's objection to his own claim that his sociological comment has no bearing on the truth and thus in an important sense on the intelligibility of the truth-claims of Christianity. He admits that besides the Tillichs, Bonhoeffers and Robinsons, there is Kierkegaard, Barth and revivals of Catholic orthodoxy. Their claims and readings of Christianity, with its doctrine of God, do not depend, for their coherence, MacIntyre avers, on their accounts' squaring with secular culture. MacIntyre even points out that "Barth's message is that any attempt to justify belief in God or any attempt to comprehend God's ways by translating revelation into terms other than its own is bound to fail."[15] Those fortunate enough to have God's revelation have some measure of understanding; those without it are utterly in the dark. And while this leaves us with the important cultural fact that many people—perhaps most people—in our culture are untouched by religion, find the whole enterprise bafflingly pointless, this does not show that such concepts do not make sense. Indeed there is play space here for the Barthian or Neo-Orthodox theologian to explain why it is to be expected that so many people in our culture are on such (from their point of view) barren ground.

So such sociological comment, unsupplemented by philosophical argument about the incoherence (logical impropriety) of the concept of God or revelation, will not show that religious concepts, for modern man or anyone else, are unintelligible or do not make sense. It shows that for many they are baffling and largely uncomprehended, but it does not show that there are not in our culture the conceptual resources and the human resources as well to gain sufficient understanding of them to be able to take them to heart. There is certainly ample room for that species of self-deception which Kierkegaard called "double-mindedness", but that does not show that religious conceptions are not understood by anyone or that what some believers understand (believe they understand) could not be communicated.

MacIntyre remarks that with the theological orientation we have learned from Kierkegaard and Barth, we come to have "a closed circle, in which believer speaks only to believer, in which all content is concealed."[16] Indeed there is a point about the content, but it is less evident, given the wide appeal of Kierkegaard, whether we have here the closed circle of an in-group theology. Perhaps when we get to the allegedly distinctive theological content this does happen, but the obscurity and at least seeming closedness may, instead, be due to the elusiveness of these theologians with respect to the traditional issues of philosophical theology—an elusiveness we do not feel when reading Aquinas or Scotus. If the latter is the case, this would seem to indicate that it is something in their "philosophical style" and not in the nature of the theological concepts themselves which occasions the breakdown in understanding.

IV

        If what I have argued hitherto is near to the mark, MacIntyre's almost anthropological approach will not settle the problems with which we are concerned. It will not in any appreciable degree help us resolve the question of whether belief in God is an intelligible and coherent option for educated Westerners in the Twentieth Century and it will not enable us to ascertain whether belief in God is for us irrational or for that matter rational.

        MacIntyre, however, gives some more purely conceptual arguments for his claim that for us religious claims are unintelligible. In his "Is Understanding Religion Compatible with Believing?", he begins by setting a conceptual puzzle that should exercise both Christians and sceptics (atheists or agnostics).[17]

> In any discussion between sceptics and believers it is presupposed that, even for us to disagree, it is necessary to understand each other. Yet here at the outset the central problem arises. For usually (and the impulse to write 'always' is strong) two people could not be said to share a concept or to possess the same concept unless they agreed in at least some central applications of it. Two men may share a concept and yet disagree in some of the judgments they make in which they assert that objects fall under it. But two men who disagree in every judgment which employed the concept—of them what could one say that they shared? For to possess a concept is to be able to use it correctly—although it does not preclude mishandling it sometimes. It follows that unless I can be said to share your judgments at least to some degree I cannot be said to share your concepts.[18]

The difficulty, for contemporary belief (and this is not unrelated to what we have been saying about social structure), MacIntyre argues, is that it at least appears to be the case that sceptics and believers disagree in toto in their judgments on some crucial religious matters.[19] The crucial condition, stressed by Wittgenstein, for mutual comprehension and intelligibility, is lacking, namely *agreement in judgments*. If a sceptic and believer are not prepared to assert any of the same things about God or sin or salvation, their concepts cannot be the same and indeed about these matters there can be no mutual understanding and communication, for there is no sharing of concepts. But this, MacIntyre claims, is exactly the position we are in vis-à-vis the disputes between believers and sceptics. In our cultural context they simply do not and cannot understand each other. (Here it is clear that MacIntyre is not referring to the eviscerated conception of Christianity of Tillich, Robinson, Van Buren, Braithwaite or the death-of-God theologians, but to the central strands of Christian belief which perhaps receive their fullest theological expression for our time in the theology of Karl Barth.) Neither side will accept this characterization, MacIntyre contends, but nonetheless this is the position to which they are committed.

        Before we proceed further there is an obvious question which should be considered—a question which MacIntyre slides over. Why should the above considerations—assuming for the moment they are well taken—show that for twentieth-century-educated Westerners key religious concepts are unintelligible? Would it not at best show that for some they are and for some they are not and further—since the drift is toward scepticism (to what elsewhere MacIntyre characterizes as a *passive atheism*)—that the numbers of people who find the central religious beliefs of Judaism and Christianity unintelligible are numerous and increasing?

Yet, even if this is so, this would remain clearly a purely sociological or socio-psychological matter. It is an empirical belief about society of the kind that would ultimately have to be backed up with statistics. It allows for the fact that there still are educated Westerners who find (or believe they find) such religious beliefs intelligible. That they are a small cultural enclave does not show that they are *mistaken*; that the passively atheistic educated majority could not come to understand their beliefs does not establish that what such religious people believe to be intelligible is really not intelligible.

MacIntyre does not, as I have remarked, confront this directly, but there is one paragraph, early on in his "Is Understanding Religion Compatible With Believing?" which indirectly could be taken as showing—given the sociological situation we here described, given the fact that believers and sceptics do not share certain concepts and given certain other beliefs to which they are committed—that contemporary sceptics and believers alike are committed to a set of unintelligible beliefs. Christians—think particularly of the Protestant Neo-Orthodoxy of Barth, Brunner and the Niebuhrs—want to claim that atheism is primarily rooted in the will. Sinful humans pridefully reject what they in part do not understand; but if this is so then it cannot be the case, as Christians also argue, that religious concepts are not understood by sceptics for sceptics could only so reject them if they understood them. The Neo-Orthodox account gives to understand that the sceptic both understands them and fails to understand them. Thus the Christian account is internally inconsistent exhibiting that this conceptualization of God is unintelligible. Moreover, again according to MacIntyre, the sceptic who says that religious beliefs are flatly unintelligible gets into comparable difficulties, for he also "has to explain the meaning of religious utterances in order to reject them (that is, he never says—as he would have to if they were flatly senseless—"I can't understand a word of it")."[20] Sceptics claim to be able to explain the meaning of religious beliefs so as to show that they really are unintelligible. But this very much looks, at least, as if they were saying that these beliefs are both intelligible and unintelligible. It looks at least, MacIntyre claims, as if believer and sceptic alike were inconsistently claiming that a common understanding of religious belief is both necessary and impossible and this shows that their concepts are incoherent and their key religious beliefs, including of course belief in God, unintelligible.

It seems to me that this argument is not at all adequate to establish that religious beliefs are unintelligible. It does perhaps show that a certain key theological argument of Neo-Orthodox Protestants and a certain sceptical theological or meta-theological argument are inconsistent. But this only shows that these particular attempts perspicuously to display key religious

concepts come a cropper; it does not show that the religious concepts themselves are unintelligible. Moreover, the Neo-Orthodox Protestant theologian
could easily modify his account by claiming that sinful man has some
understanding—though still a terribly corrupted understanding—of the key
concepts of God, sin and salvation, though it still remains the case that
this understanding is so minimal that without grace his understanding will
be so corrupted—suffering from hubris as he is—that he will reject God
and not take the steps which will make it possible for him to receive God's
revelation. This is indeed a slight shift in theological posture but not such
a radical one that it—or something like it—should not be available to a
Christian to avoid the unintelligibility that goes with inconsistency.

The sceptic has even a smaller modification to make, if any modification at all. (I say "if any modification at all" because (a) not even Ayer,
Hägerström, Hedenius or Flew ever said or implied that religious utterances
are flatly senseless and (b) there is good reason to believe that their actual
accounts are in accord with what I will forthwith characterize as "a modification" of the sceptical position.) Sceptics could and have said that religious
utterances are *syntactically* in order (make syntactic sense) but are *semantically* incoherent because in non-anthropomorphic employments of "God"
we have no conception of what could count as a referent for "God" and
sentences made by the use of such terms, while purporting standardly to
have an assertive role, do not actually function in that way, for we (believer
and non-believer alike) have no conception of what would count toward
establishing their truth or their falsity. They purport to have truth-values
or truth-conditions but we have no understanding of what their truth-values
or truth-conditions are so that we are able to understand what counts toward
establishing their truth or their falsity. In those crucial ways we find them
unintelligible, though we do understand them in the sense that we understand how to use God-talk so as to make non-deviant utterances and we
can readily enough recognize deviant utterances. Sceptics, as well as
believers, understand the syntax of God-talk—and in that way can explain
its meaning—but sceptics find its alleged semantic claims utterly baffling.
Indeed they find them so baffling that they can make no sense of their
alleged truth-claims. They have no understanding of *what* those "claims"
claim. They purportedly assert some mysterious states-of-affairs but it is
utterly unclear what states-of-affairs, facts, or cluster of facts are being
asserted.

The syntax and indeed the pragmatics of religious discourse are
such as to show that in certain key respects it is idiosyncratic from other
forms of discourse and that conditions for successful reference which obtain
for those other forms of discourse do not obtain for key bits of religious
discourse—principally talk of God. Our very understanding of the context
of religious talk and its syntax leads us to this, but then no coherent account
follows of what reference and truth could come to in non-anthropomorphic
religious discourse so that in that crucial respect we have no understanding
of the discourse and find it utterly unintelligible or at least so problematic
that we cannot make sense of it. In this way the sceptic can at least plausibly
state his claim without inconsistency.

The short of it is that neither the Neo-Orthodox Protestant theologian nor the sceptic need put his account so that he is asserting, as MacIntyre would have it, that a common understanding of religious concepts (minimally an understanding of syntax) is both necessary and impossible.

V

Even if in some way MacIntyre could extricate himself here, two further very natural objections arise concerning MacIntyre's analysis. The first would be to deny what MacIntyre claims, namely that sceptics and believers disagree in toto in their judgments concerning religious matters. Is not Martin Hollis far closer to the mark than MacIntyre when he claims that sceptics and believers "agree in most particulars. Otherwise the believer will be entitled to claim that the unbeliever does not understand what he is disagreeing about. Mystery is divine truth to the believer and human nonsense to the unbeliever. But both can agree where it sets in"?[21] This, as the saying goes, is "right on" and does it not show, *pace* MacIntyre, that there is some agreement in judgment between believer and sceptic?

I shall turn in short order to MacIntyre's attempt to rebut that argument, but for a moment let me turn to a second argument against MacIntyre's account. This objection is quite different from the first and it is the objection that MacIntyre spends most of his time trying to meet. Anthropologists claim to understand concepts which they do not share; indeed they must be able to do this (or so it would seem) to have any anthropological understanding at all. They identify such concepts as *mana* or *tabu* without using them. In short common understanding does not require, as MacIntyre (following Wittgenstein) has claimed, a sharing of concepts and any agreement in judgments at all.

MacIntyre, as I have remarked, spends most of the essay now under consideration in rebutting this objection. I shall return to it after I have considered his first and brief response to the first and—to me at least—more natural objection to his account.

VI

In responding to the first objection MacIntyre remarks that appearances are deceiving and sceptics and believers do really disagree in *toto* in their judgments over religious matters and do not in reality share key concepts of Christian discourse. Concepts such as God, sin and salvation have no counterparts, MacIntyre contends, in non-religious discourse where believers and sceptics do agree in judgment. And when

secular predicates such as 'powerful' 'wise' and 'good' are transferred to a religious application they undergo change such that a new element signifying a new
concept enters. The transition from 'powerful' to 'omnipotent' is not merely quan-
titative. For the notion of 'supreme in this or that class' cannot easily be transferred
to a being who does not belong to a class (as God does not). And thus a new
concept has been manufactured.[22]

Where there is a shared vocabulary, suggesting (but only suggesting) shared
concepts, but no actual agreement in judgments, we still do not have shared
concepts and without actual shared concepts we have no mutual understanding. This, MacIntyre maintains, is just the state believers and sceptics
are in vis-à-vis religious concepts, though it is true that outside religion
sceptics and believers tend to agree in the non-religious judgments they
make while using concepts which are often superficially like the quite
different concepts used in religious contexts.

    Even if we are justified in claiming that the difference is sufficiently
great such that we can speak of a new concept when "wise", "good",
"powerful", or "loving" is used of God, it still is not clear that MacIntyre
has successfully rebutted the first objection. (That we are so justified is
far from clear for it is not evident that we have any very clear criteria for
when we do and when we do not have a new concept. Yet I let that pass,
for, intuitively or pre-analytically, we have some sense of what we are saying
here and hopefully and presumably analysis could in time, if philosophers
were to go to work at it, set out the criteria with which we actually work.)
Why assume, even with such distinctive conceptions as "God", "sin",
and "salvation", that there is no agreement in judgment concerning the
application of these terms and thus no sharing of the concepts expressed
by them? The sceptic, living in Christendom or in that present-day secular
culture which is an outgrowth of Christendom, understands, as well as the
Christian, that it cannot be correct to say that "Hitler is God-incarnate,"
though there is no similar conceptual impropriety, given the language-game
which Christians play, and which most sceptics can play too, in saying
"Jesus is God-incarnate." Similarly it cannot be correct (given that language-
game) to say that "Rabbits sin" or "Salvation is hydraulic" while it is correct
to say "Christians sin" and "Salvation comes through God's grace." This
is as clear evidence as there can be that there is some agreement in judgment
about the particulars of belief and about where belief sets in, e.g., God
is mysterious and there are mysteries which can only be taken on faith,
but that $2 + 2 = 4$ and that grass is green are not and cannot be objects
of religious faith. MacIntyre is just plainly wrong in denying that in our
time there is no agreement in judgment between believers and sceptics
over religious matters.

    There is a further and very different objection to MacIntyre's
account, pressed by both Richard Brandt and William Alston, which appears
at least to undermine it (though I shall argue that the matter is actually
much less decisive, particularly if MacIntyre would give verificationism
its due, than appears at first blush).[23]

    MacIntyre argues that we share concepts if we do *not* disagree in
toto in judgments. We need, that is, this minimal agreement to share

concepts and only if we share concepts can we understand each other. Alston first disambiguates this claim in an important way. He shows that taken in one way it is a truism and taken in another way it is "certainly false."[24] But he also shows later that these are not the only readings which can be given to MacIntyre's thesis. If we include analytic statements and conceptual remarks in what it is to agree in judgment, then, Alston points out, MacIntyre's remark is most certainly true. If we do not agree, say concerning the concept of omnipotence, that being omnipotent is to be able to do anything whatsoever, then we are clearly not using "omnipotent" to express the same concept. To have the same concept we must agree at least about the analyticity or (in Wittgenstein's sense) the grammaticality of some of the utterances made by the use of terms which are at least thought to express the same concept. We need to have some agreement on which remarks are grammatical remarks to share the same concept. But, as Alston points out, this does not seem to be the reading MacIntyre gives to his claim. Rather, MacIntyre seems to be only talking about substantive judgments or the sort of judgment which makes claims about the correct *applications* of a term, e.g., is so-and-so a pencil, so-and-so a smile or is some particular an act of gratitude. But if this is the correct reading of MacIntyre's thesis, then it is false, for we "can think of many cases in which two people do not agree in any applications of a term, but nevertheless obviously share the same concept (use the term in the same sense)."[25]

To illustrate his meaning Alston uses the example of the concept of a sea serpent. Two sailors, one from a rather backward culture and the other from a rather less backward culture, may utterly disagree about what particular things are or are not sea serpents while still sharing the same concept. *A* from the backward culture may assert on some determinate occasion that so-and-so are sea serpents and *B*, looking at the same objects, may deny that these things are sea serpents and indeed deny that there are in fact any sea serpents at all. But they, for all that, still could have the same concept of a sea serpent, that is to say, they could have the same concept and yet disagree not only on that occasion but in fact on all occasions about whether a given animal was or was not a sea serpent. They would indeed have a different concept if one took a sea serpent to be a kind of eel or muraina characteristically found in the Mediterranean and the other took a sea serpent to be a sea monster of serpentine form. But let us suppose they both take a sea serpent to be a sea monster and both agree in general about the characteristics of a sea monster, but, when travelling through the Indian Ocean, *A* asserts the large venomous snakes they both see are sea serpents and *B* denies that they are, and indeed denies that in fact there are any such monsters. Like sea-nymphs and unlike Sea ravens (cormorants), they, he claims, are mythical creatures, but he agrees that there could have been such creatures; they are in no way a *conceptual* impossibility. Here we have two people totally disagreeing about the application of "sea serpents" and so in one plain sense not agreeing in judgment concerning them while still sharing the same concept.

MacIntyre could respond that *A* and *B* do not really disagree in

toto about the application of the term "sea serpent" because, while indeed
B does not agree that any of the venomous sea snakes that A points out
are sea serpents, i.e., sea monsters, B still does agree with A that if they
were to see a serpentine marine animal of terrifying proportions that that
would indeed be a sea serpent. B does not apply the concept of a sea
serpent to anything but he in part agrees with A about what would count
as one. They can and do agree on paradigms and so they share the same
concept. They do not disagree in toto about the application of "sea serpent."

Building on his above response MacIntyre could go on to remark
that for the contemporary sceptic the concepts of God, sin and salvation
unlike the concept of a sea serpent are such that the sceptic—when the
concept of God is not anthropomorphic, i.e., Zeus-like—is unable to form
any idea of what the terms "God", "sin", or "salvation" are being applied
to, could be applied to or what could count as such a God, or as sin or
as salvation. He may find the notion of an "infinite-non-spatio-temporal
individual" something he can make nothing of; he may well be as lost
with that as he is with the notion that a plant is an ox. He does not understand what could even count as an application of such a notion and it is
this crucial sense in which the sceptic and believer do not at all agree about
the application of the term and thus do not share the same concept and
thus do not understand each other.

However, as Alston points out, if MacIntyre takes this turn in specifying what he means for a concept to have the same application or to fail
to have the same application, he is plunging into what Alston calls "the
bottomless abyss of difficulties with the verifiability criterion of meaningfulness."[26] Indeed MacIntyre himself, I think mistakenly throwing the
empiricist baby out with the positivist bathwater, rejects anything that smacks
of such a positivist or verificationist orientation. But unless he takes such
a verificationist turn here he seems to have backed himself into an unhelpful
truism or into an account which is, as Alston puts it, "certainly false."

Generally it might be thought that apart from the above arguments
MacIntyre's thesis is plainly faulted by anthropological practice, for anthropologists do indeed come to understand the beliefs and conceptions of
people in alien cultures without sharing their concepts. But in the essay
under consideration and in two later ones, MacIntyre powerfully argues,
following to this extent Evans-Pritchard and Winch, that a necessary condition for gaining an understanding of an alien culture is to gain an understanding like that of a participant or at least something approximating that
of a participant. We must come to understand the norms governing the
rule governed behaviour of the culture in question and we must come to
see something of the point of those norms. Without that we will have no
understanding of what they do and we will have no understanding of their
concepts. But this participant's understanding involves some sharing of
concepts and thus it is not the case that anthropological understanding
provides a massive counter-case to MacIntyre's thesis. Moreover, in understanding his thesis here we come to see that it should be taken much more
in the positivist or verificationist spirit than Alston allows. But then there
seems at least to be a conflict between the way MacIntyre sometimes argues
and his rejection of verificationism.

VII

In his "Rationality and the Explanation of Action," MacIntyre rightly points out that "in discriminating between what is rational and what is irrational we must not mistake the standards of normal belief and behaviour in our own age for the standards of rational belief and behaviour as such."[27] Agreeing on this point with Trevor-Roper, he rightly criticizes liberal historians and anthropologists such as Frazer and Tylor for their ethnocentric characterizations of rationality and irrationality. Indeed their ethnocentricity led to misdescriptions of other cultures and their way of viewing rationality led to too great a confidence in the adequacy of the categories of our own age and provided them with an untenable way of drawing a distinction between "reason" and "superstition".[28]

What is interesting to note in the present context is that Father Norris Clarke, in a perceptive criticism of MacIntyre, has in effect argued that in his argument to exhibit the irrationality and unintelligibility of Christian belief, MacIntyre makes, in a sophisticated way, the very errors he warns us against above.

Clarke points out that MacIntyre's most fundamental reason for claiming that for us—situated as we are—belief in the God of Christianity is unreasonable and indeed that the very understanding of Christian belief is incompatible with believing in it, is that "understanding it leads to the discovery that its specifically religious content is relevant only to certain cultural contexts now past."[29] To this Clarke responds, rather obviously and along the lines I argued earlier, that from the fact that particular cultural conditions make a belief either harder or easier to believe nothing follows one way or another about the warrantedness or lack of warrant of the belief. Surely there is no doubt at all about the sociological generalization that it is harder for an educated European now to believe in Christianity than it was in the Middle Ages. This may even be true in part because of the pervasiveness and efficacy of science and technology. In making such socio-logical claims MacIntyre is on safe but truistic grounds, but the truth of these sociological beliefs does not establish the truth or even probability of the contention that Christian beliefs are false or that Christianity is "merely the product of those social contexts more favourable to belief in it. . . ."[30]

What MacIntyre must show is that Christianity is so culture-bound and culture-caused that it is in reality best viewed, as Clarke puts it, as "a purely human construction resulting from social needs or pressures peculiar only to certain cultural contexts, and therefore not at all what it claims to be—namely, a response to an objective divine revelation historically communicated to man in the person of Jesus Christ."[31]

Against this claim of being so utterly culture-caused and bounded, it can be pointed out that Christianity has existed for some considerable length of time and in some very varied cultures and that there has been what Cardinal Newman called a "Development of Christian Doctrine." That our scientific culture somehow shows the ethnocentricity and irrational-ity (pointlessness) of Christianity is also not evident and flies in the face of the fact that in scientifically advanced cultures there are "hundreds of thousands of converts to Christianity every year including many scholars and scientists. . . ."[32]

Perhaps they "are really the most misguided, self-deceived, intellectually blind, and least excusable of all the long parade of believers in Christianity down to the present day," but surely that could not be reasonably asserted without very considerable argument and evidence.[33] But MacIntyre has nowhere done this. What most centrally he must do, and has not done, is to "present some sample analyses of basic Christian doctrines which are dependent for their intelligibility and relevance upon a social context that has now passed away."[34] This would be a crucial start in any effort to establish that Christianity is so culture-caused and culture-bound that it is little more than the tribal folklore of a few cultures which, in virtue of their material power, have dominated the world and with that domination have spread their proselytizing religion along with other elements of their culture throughout the world.

NOTES

1.   Alasdair MacIntyre, "Is Understanding Religion Compatible with Believing?" *Faith and the Philosophers*, ed. John Hick (London: Macmillan, 1964). Father Copleston has set out his claims about a "positivist orientation" in his *Positivism and Metaphysics* (Lisbon: 1965) 9. I have made some critical remarks about Copleston's way of viewing things in my *Reason and Practice* (New York: Harper and Row, 1971) chapter 36.

2.   Alasdair MacIntyre, "Positivism in Perspective," *New Statesman* 59 (April 1960): 490-91; Alasdair MacIntyre, "A Kind of Atheism," *The Manchester Guardian* (July 1966); and Alasdair MacIntyre, *Marxism and Christianity* (London: Gerald Duckworth Ltd., 1969) ix.

3.   Alasdair MacIntyre, *Against the Self-Images of the Age* (London: Gerald Duckworth Ltd., 1971) 80, 86, 95.

4.   *Ibid.* 86.

5.   Alasdair MacIntyre, "The Debate About God: Victorian Relevance and Contemporary Irrelevance," *The Religious Significance of Atheism*, eds. Alasdair MacIntyre and Paul Ricoeur (New York: Columbia University Press, 1969) 53.

6.   Alasdair MacIntyre, *Secularization and Moral Change* (London: Oxford University Press, 1967) 54.

7.   Alasdair MacIntyre, *Against the Self-Images of the Age* 25.

8.   Alasdair MacIntyre, *Secularization and Moral Change* 12.

9.   *Ibid.* The extent to which this claim is an overstatement is shown in Richard Norman's *Reasons for Action* (Oxford: Basil Blackwell, 1971) 160-72.

10.   *Ibid.* 15.

11.   Alasdair MacIntyre, "The Debate About God: Victorian Relevance and Contemporary Irrelevance" 43. See also MacIntyre, *A Short History of Ethics* (New York: The Macmillan Company, 1966) 110-28, 215-26, 265-66.

12.   Alasdair MacIntyre, *Secularization and Moral Change* 66-67. There is a crucial and unfortunate ambiguity in this passage. MacIntyre remarks: "Thus in so far as the claims of Christianity are themselves social, so far the claims of Christianity are impugned by the actual history of modern society." If "social" is taken in a fairly straightforward way this argument does not go through at all. Religion, like morality, could be a social category in the straightforward sense that it is something a culture shares. If that

were the case, the claims of Christianity would not necessarily be undermined by a shift in the *Zeitgeist*. Its claims could still be true even though people ceased to acknowledge them. MacIntyre's argument would only go through if the claims of Christianity were social in the sense that the concepts used in those claims were social in the more restricted sense that they were *constitutive concepts*, like the concept of chess, such that their very existence and the reality they signify were created, sustained and determined by constitutive rules similar in logical form to the constitutive rules of chess. This *may* be so for the concepts of religion; D.Z. Phillips writes as if this were so. But that this is so has not been established and MacIntyre makes no attempt to show that it is so.

13.   *Ibid.* 68.

14.   MacIntyre, *Secularization and Moral Change* 68-69 and "The Debate About God: Victorian Relevance and Contemporary Irrelevance" 27-28.

15.   MacIntyre, *Against the Self-Images of the Age* 15.

16.   *Ibid.* 19.

17.   Alasdair MacIntyre, "Is Understanding Religion Compatible with Believing?" *Faith and the Philosophers*, ed. John Hick (London: Macmillan, 1964).

18.   *Ibid.* 115.

19.   *Ibid.*

20.   *Ibid.* 116.

21.   Hollis, "Reason and Ritual," *Rationality*, ed. Bryan R. Wilson (Oxford: Basil Blackwell Ltd., 1970) 236.

22.   MacIntyre, "Is Understanding Religion Compatible with Believing?" 116.

23.   Richard Brandt and William Alston, "Comments," *Faith and the Philosophers*, ed. John Hick (London: Macmillan, 1964).

24.   William Alston, *op. cit.* 154.

25.   *Ibid.*

26.   MacIntyre, *Against the Self-Images of the Age* 257.

27.   *Ibid.* 244.

28.   Norris Clarke, "Comment," *Faith and the Philosophers*, ed. John Hick (London: Macmillan, 1964) 147.

29.   *Ibid.*

30.   *Ibid.*

31.   *Ibid.* 148.

32.   *Ibid.*

33.   *Ibid.*

34.   *Ibid.*

CHAPTER 6

The Coherence of
Wittgensteinian Fideism*

I

STUART C. BROWN ARGUES THAT WITTGENSTEIN-
ian fideism is internally incoherent.[1] It is, he
claims, a philosophical view about religion which is committed to two propositions both of which cannot with consistency be jointly held. On the one
hand, as fideists, the Wittgensteinians are committed to the view that there
is no common standard of reference by which the issues between belief
and unbelief could be rationally adjudicated: the respective beliefs, in fine,
are incommensurable. (Brown calls this the *incommensurability-thesis*.)
Yet, on the other hand, fideists also believe that there are criteria of truth
and falsity in religion. (I shall call this the *truth-thesis*.) Brown's claim is
that the *truth-thesis* and the *incommensurability-thesis* are both integral
to Wittgensteinian fideism, but that they are incompatible and thus
Wittgensteinian fideism is internally incoherent.

Brown and I are one in believing that Wittgensteinian fideism rests
on a mistake, and we both agree that D.Z. Phillips is a paradigm case
of a Wittgensteinian fideist, but I am far from confident that Brown has
been able to establish that such a fideism collapses because of purely
internal difficulties.

(D) and (E) below are the statements of the *truth-thesis* and the
incommensurability-thesis respectively. Brown's argument—to state it more
fully—is that they both cannot be consistently held when taken in conjunction with (A), (B) and (C) below, and that (A), (B) and (C) are undeniable.

My trouble begins with not being able to see why (B) is undeniable,
and thus I do not see that it is true that the Wittgensteinian fideist must
reject either (D) or (E) because (1), (A), (B) and (C) are undeniable, and
(2) because of the way (A), (B) and (C) are related to (D) and (E). Brown's
list is as follows:

(A) Any belief fundamental to any religious tradition conflicts with one or more

---

*First published in *Sophia* XI.3 (1973).

'infidel' beliefs, i.e., with beliefs which qualify a man as an unbeliever in relation to that tradition.

(B) If there are criteria which determine certain beliefs as true, then those beliefs, together with any to which someone who holds them is thereby committed, are commensurable with any conflicting beliefs.

(C) There can only be criteria of truth and falsity to be found within a religious tradition if some fundamental beliefs of that tradition are true.

(D) There are criteria of truth and falsity to be found within any given religious tradition.

(E) No religious belief is commensurable with any infidel belief.[2]

II

Brown claims that (B) is undeniable. This seems to me thoroughly questionable when one keeps in mind how Phillips (Brown's paradigm Wittgensteinian fideist) construes "religious belief" and "truth" and "falsity" in religion.

(B), we may recall, is the proposition that "if there are criteria which determine certain beliefs as true, then those beliefs, together with any to which someone who holds them is thereby committed, are commensurable with any conflicting beliefs". That is to say, if I believe that it has been below zero for ten days in a row, then I am also committed to believing that the water is frozen in the pail that has been sitting on my front lawn those ten days past, and I treat as commensurable with that last belief the false belief that there are two live goldfish swimming around in a pail of water sitting on my front lawn. If there are criteria which determine the truth of p, then we have grounds for believing q to be true, if being committed to p also commits us to q, and we also have grounds for believing that any belief in r which conflicts with q is false. But to so conflict with q, r must be measurable (assessable) by the same standard as q and so be commensurable with q.

"To deny this one would need to maintain that the reasons which show q to be true have no bearing on the truth or falsity of r."[3] But then, if we made such a denial, we would be reduced to the absurd view of being committed to maintaining that q and r, while remaining conflicting beliefs, could both be true.

After setting out this argument, Brown then rightly points out that Phillips does not defend such an eccentric view of "true", where "true" becomes an ellipsis for "true only for some particular group," and thus, like "large" and "small", a relative term. For Phillips, as for most of the rest of us, "if something is true it is true *sans phrase*".

From these considerations, Brown concludes that given that "true" is employed in its normal way, (B) appears at least to be analytic, and if (B) is analytic or even in some other way undeniably true, and if (A) and (C) are also undeniable (as Brown argues they are), then we cannot consistently and simultaneously hold the two indispensable claims of Wittgensteinian fideism, namely (D) and (E).

When one turns back to a consideration of what Phillips is actually arguing, Brown's argument appears less decisive than it may have seemed at first sight. For while Phillips does *not* give a relativistic reading of "true", he does give a distinctive reading for religious beliefs of "true" and "belief" (in the latter he follows Wittgenstein). Given these readings, I shall argue, (B) will be neither analytic nor undeniable. What Phillips does (and here he also follows Wittgenstein) is to deny, given the employment of "true" in them, that the normal relations holding between matter-of-fact propositions hold for those distinctive situations where we cross types between religious propositions and purely matter-of-fact propositions.

An illustration used by Phillips will translate this into the concrete and bring out what he intends. Suppose p is the religious proposition expressing the religious belief "God is in heaven." Someone who did not understand religious beliefs, i.e., didn't know how to play that language-game, or at least didn't understand that particular religious belief, would quite understandably conclude that this committed such a religious believer to the absurd proposition q, "Some astronauts might catch a glimpse of him." (This is parallel to "It has been below zero for ten days" and "The water in the pail in my front yard must be frozen.") And if the believer were really so committed, this in turn would allow it to be the case that q' ("Some astronauts saw God") or r ("They did not see God") are both candidates for true or false religious propositions. On such a view, they are all (p, q, q' and r) taken to be commensurable.

Contrary to this, it is Phillips' contention—and it seems to me an entirely reasonable contention—that it shows an utter misunderstanding of what Christianity is all about to think that q, q' or r could be possible utterances in that mode of discourse.[4] In that mode of discourse no question of their truth or falsity could even arise except perhaps in a claim that q and q' are *necessarily* false. But plainly they are not at all commensurable with p. Yet p—"God is in heaven"—is a proper religious utterance in such a mode of discourse, and q, q' and r are indeed infidel beliefs which show that someone who seriously employs them, where the engine is not idling, is not a Christian believer or even any kind of religious believer with even a tolerably close family resemblance to a Christian believer. That is to say, they illustrate the sort of considerations that would lead one, as the Wittgensteinian fideists do, to assert (E).

An examination of that case also brings to the fore the need to disambiguate (B). There are many people with little or no understanding of religion who would try to construe p literally and who take q, q' and r to be commensurable with p. They take q to be something which a believer who accepted p is committed to if certain factual conditions obtain. But it is just such propositions as q and q' which Phillips would maintain, and I believe rightly, are such that no Christian believer, who had any tolerably adequate religious understanding, would entertain even as possible religious claims.

Anyone who held such an infidel belief would show himself to be an unbeliever, but not in the way a man would who asserted "There is no God; there is no heaven, the world is full of pointless, purposeless evil." These beliefs also qualify as infidel beliefs, but they are infidel beliefs which do not necessarily show a lack of understanding of religious beliefs, though they do categorically reject core Christian beliefs. By contrast, q, q' and r show a lack of understanding of religious belief. They are conflicting beliefs but they are clearly not commensurable beliefs. They are beliefs, Phillips argues, which belong to a different language-game. The truth of "God is in heaven" and the truth of any claim about what astronauts might see or fail to see is not settled in the same way. This is basic for Wittgensteinian fideists and indeed for Wittgenstein himself, though it is not clear that Wittgenstein would speak of either the truth or falsity of religious beliefs. However, it is clear that both Wittgenstein and Phillips do not think that q, q' and r are confirmable or disconfirmable by reference to such empirical propositions or even commensurable with them. Yet q, q' and r would ordinarily be thought to be infidel beliefs which conflict with Christian beliefs, though here it is the whole class of beliefs which are conflicting. That is to say, a man who asserts (attempts to assert) either "The astronauts found heaven and saw God," or "The astronauts failed to find heaven or God," shows in his very assertion (attempted assertion) that he is an unbeliever, though an unbeliever not because he rejects a religious belief he understands, but an unbeliever by way of not even understanding the religious belief in question. But these beliefs are conflicting with religious beliefs in the quite plain sense that one could not hold them and be a believer. But this shows clearly that (B), far from being analytic, is in fact false, for here we have incommensurable infidel beliefs which conflict with religious beliefs which hold in virtue of the very criteria for "true Christian belief". (I am assuming for the sake of this discussion what Brown also assumes, namely that there are criteria for true religious beliefs.)

Brown might try to defend the analyticity or at least the undeniable truth of (B) by claiming that q, q' and r in my above example do not, after all, really conflict with religious beliefs. They do not conflict, he might argue, because they are not even in the same mode of discourse and show no understanding of the relevant religious beliefs or of what it is to believe in God. Since this is so, they cannot really conflict with religious beliefs and thus I have not produced a genuine counter-instance to (B).

This betrays the ambiguity of "conflicts" in (B) and it is this that prompted my remark that (B) needs disambiguating. If, on the one hand, in (B) "conflicting belief" is just an infidel belief which a believer could not hold and remain a religious believer, then I have produced a counter-instance to (B) and Brown's claim is false. If, on the other hand, "conflicting belief" in (B) means an infidel belief on the same *logical level* as a religious belief, then (B) is trivially (that is truistically) true. But I see no good grounds for so pre-empting "conflicting beliefs", given the fact that much unbelief rests on claims about the incoherence and not on the falsity of fundamental non-anthropomorphic Christian beliefs.

However, even such denials, e.g., "There is neither God nor heaven," *need* not in all linguistic environments be construed as conflicting commensurable beliefs, for someone who made such a statement might not be asserting it because he believed that it was false that there is a heaven or that God exists, but because he thought that either or both of those notions were incoherent. His "There is neither God nor heaven" has the import of saying that he rejects such notions because he believes them to be incoherent. Thus "There is neither God nor heaven," on such a quite natural reading, is also both non-commensurable and conflicting with very key religious beliefs. If Brown replies that on such a construction "There is neither God nor heaven" is no longer a conflicting belief, then this shows that he is salvaging his position by stipulative re-definition.

III

Brown goes wrong because he fails to keep in mind just how Phillips construes "religious belief" and "true". Consider such Christian utterances as "God is our saviour," "We shall meet after death," "God is the Creator of the heavens and the earth," or "God is in heaven." They should not be construed, Phillips avers, again following Wittgenstein, as either statements of fact or expressions of attitude.[5] Rather we should construe them as verbal pictures which govern the lives of Christian believers. As Phillips puts it (attributing this conception to Wittgenstein), "these pictures are unshakeable beliefs in the sense that they form the framework within which those who live by them assess themselves and the events that befall them."[6] In believing that we shall meet after death, the believer need not at all believe in some incoherent conception of some putative future state of affairs in which people, as disembodied agents, will survive the death of their bodies. Rather to be immortal is to be in one's own life in God and to be free of the snares and temptations of mortal life.[7] And to have such a belief is to be governed by a certain picture; it is not to accept as probably true or even to try to make sense of some would-be factual claim that a certain very problematical future event will occur. A believer, in living in accordance with a Christian picture of eternal life, could come to agree with Flew and Penelhum that it makes no sense to speak of surviving bodily death. He need not be trying to think of his own funeral and at the same time trying to think of himself as witnessing his own funeral. Rather in thinking of his own death and in thinking of meeting those he cares for after death, he can be thinking of his life as a whole and attaching a certain very strong value to friendship and personal relationships.

It is tempting to say that this in effect shows that such pictures are not expressive of anything that is or even could be literally true. But however tempting this is, it is still, Phillips argues, mistaken, for "We shall meet after death" on such a construction could only be figuratively true, if we could at least in principle indicate something of what it would be like for it to be literally true. Yet this we cannot do, for we have "no original context of literal truth which the religious pictures can distort or deviate from."[8] But then we can hardly talk about its being figuratively true either.

Rather what we must come to see is that "We shall meet after death" is an "embodiment of a reflection on, or vision of, the meaning of life and death".[9] It very well could be "an expression of belief that people should act towards each other, not according to the status and prestige that people have acquired or failed to acquire, during the course of their lives, but as children of God, in the equality which death will reveal."[10]

Religious beliefs, including a belief in eternal life, are not opinions or conjectures about what is the case, or predictions about what will happen, or retrodictions about what has happened. Rather, these fundamental religious beliefs are visions in terms of which much of the believer's life is lived. They are not assessed or even assessable, Phillips claims, by an appeal to evidence; rather these beliefs provide pictures one lives in accordance with, draws sustenance from, and judges and assesses one's life and one's environment by.

It is in the light of this conception of religious belief that we should understand Phillips' conception of religious truth—a conception in which "religious truth" and "truly religious" come close at least to being equisignificant.[11] After talking about belief and religious pictures, Phillips goes on to remark:

> It is of the utmost philosophical importance to recognize that for the believers these pictures constitute truths, truths which form the essence of life's meaning for them. To ask someone whether he thinks these beliefs are true is to ask him whether he can live by them. . .[12]

But here "true belief" surely undergoes a sea change. Asking about them is very different from asking whether it is true that the continued existence of the Atlantic salmon is threatened. But since "belief" is very distinctive in "religious belief" and since religious propositions are not statements of fact, "truth" in this domain must also be construed differently. When we see how differently, we will look on the conflict between sceptics and believers in a new way. Phillips stresses that while it makes sense to ask what is truly religious, it makes no sense to ask whether religion is true or false or whether religious utterances make true or false statements, if in doing that one invokes some conception of confirmation or disconfirmation or some conception of an external test.

If we look to the natural environment of "God is truth" or "To love God is to know the truth," we will come to see, Phillips contends, that they "are not a class of second-best statements, hypotheses awaiting confirmation. . ."; rather they are "a body of truths", i.e., principles to live by, which have played an important part in man's efforts to regulate and make sense of his tangled life.

In asking whether in the domain of religion as such we have truth or whether in the domain of Christianity we have such truth, we are not asking, Phillips argues, something of the type we would be asking if we asked whether the ship leaving Halifax is bound for London or whether the Atlantic rift is pushing the continents apart. Rather, we are using "truth" in a way much closer to the way we would be using it if we were to assert that there is a lot of truth in the claim that it is better to give than to receive.

To dispute about the truth here is very unlike arguing about whether a prediction will come true or arguing over whether what a factual statement alleges to obtain really does obtain, e.g., "There are storks in Iceland." Rather it is to argue over an ethical matter, to wit, over the worth of generosity. A man who says that he has come to see the truth in the maxim that it is better to give than to receive is giving us to understand that he will strive after generosity, and try to orient and regulate his life in accordance with that maxim. A similar thing obtains for anyone who assents to "Christ is the truth, the life and the way" or "God is truth." He is not taking a world-historical stance but is announcing and affirming how he will strive to live. "Truth", as "belief", has a very different use here than it has in scientific and factual domains.

Such an account of "truth" and "belief" is of crucial importance for Wittgensteinian fideists and the core of it, if not Phillips' particular detail, has both attracted and repelled many people who think seriously about religion.[13] There is something here which is important and has, I am convinced, "a ring of truth about it"; yet, I am also convinced, it should be looked on with a very jaundiced eye. This fideistic account indeed has been and should be attacked frontally.[14] But to try to undermine it by exhibiting internal inconsistencies in a skeletal formulation of it which ignores how it gives flesh to the *commensurability thesis* through its elucidation of the nature of truth and belief in religion is almost certain to fail, primarily by only deftly refuting a straw man.

NOTES

1.   Stuart C. Brown, "Fideism, Truth and Commensurability," presented at the Forty-Sixth Annual Meeting of the American Philosophical Association, Pacific Division, San Francisco, 23 March 1972.

2.   *Ibid.* 3.

3.   *Ibid.* 4.

4.   D.Z. Phillips, *Death and Immortality* (London: Macmillan, 1970).

5.   D.Z. Phillips, *Faith and Philosophical Enquiry* (London: Routledge and Kegan Paul, 1970) 204-22.

6.   D.Z. Phillips, *Death and Immortality* 68.

7.   *Ibid.* 60.

8.   *Ibid.* 66.

9.   *Ibid.* 67.

10.   *Ibid.* 66.

11.   D.Z. Phillips, *Faith and Philosophical Enquiry* 150-53.

12.   D.Z. Phillips, *Death and Immortality* 71.

13.   See here the interesting review discussion of *Faith and Philosophical Enquiry* by S.C. Thakur in the *Australasian Journal of Philosophy* 49.3 (1971): 324-29; the essays by Tziporah Kasachkoff, "Talk About God's Existence," *Philosophical Studies* (The National University of Ireland) XIX (1970): 181-92; and Paul Edwards, "A Critical Examination of 'Subjective Christianity'," *Question* 4: 93-110.

14. I have tried to do this in various ways in my "Wittgensteinian Fideism," *Philosophy* XLII.161 (1967); "Language and the Concept of God," *Question* 2 (1969); "God and the Forms of Life," *Indian Review of Philosophy* I.1 (1972); *Contemporary Critiques of Religion* (London: Macmillan, 1971) chapter 5; and in my *Skepticism* (London: Macmillan, 1972) chapter 2.

CHAPTER 7

Reasonable Belief Without Justification*

IS IT NOT A MISTAKE TO TRY TO JUSTIFY A BELIEF where there could be no substance to a doubt whether it is true? Are not people who express a doubt *in such circumstances* expressing a doubt—more accurately *trying* to express a doubt—where there is no longer any *ground* for doubt? And is this not irrational?[1]

If we start with our various social practices, our various language-games, the embedded and habitual ways in which we do things with words to fulfill various of our purposes, do we not readily push back or get pushed back in reflecting on them, and in a quest for justification, to some very fundamental beliefs—beliefs which are either constitutive or regulative of those practices—which we can perhaps best call framework-beliefs and which are beliefs we cannot justify? Indeed are they not beliefs it makes no sense to either try to justify or to doubt? Doubt here appears, at least, to be empty. No further *real possibility* exists which doubt might exclude.

The following are examples of framework-beliefs of a plainly non-religious and non-metaphysical kind. "Things do not just vanish without cause", "In situations of the same type a substance A (say snow) will react to substance B (say heat) in the same way", "There is a continuity of nature", "My image of some x (say the Empire State Building) is an image of that x (say the Empire State Building)", "I cannot fail to know my own intentions".[2]

I want first to ask whether there are similar religious beliefs—beliefs which have a similar status and in a similar way are as unproblematical. But in asking that I wish first to make some preliminary points about how religious framework-beliefs function, though something very much like it applies to all framework-beliefs. We should, in trying to examine framework-beliefs, avoid isolating certain of them and in effect treating them like axioms.

*First published in *Body, Mind and Method: Essays in Honor of Virgil C. Aldrich*, eds. D.F. Gustafson and B.L. Tapscott (1978).

When we do this with "There is a god" we treat that proposition as the lynch-pin belief of the whole system of religious beliefs with the consequence of making it appear that if this belief cannot be shown to be justifiable, then none of the other beliefs of that system which presuppose it can be known to be justifiable either. This isolation is a time-honoured way of going about things shared by many believers and non-believers alike. But all the same it ought to be questioned. So to treat "There is a god" is, according to D.Z. Phillips and Stuart Brown, in effect to think of God as if he were an object, though indeed a very special and exalted "supernatural object" among the objects of the universe.[3]

Questions about the reality of God must not be so construed and belief in God must be viewed, to make sense of it, as part of a whole system. Moreover, we should view these questions as questions about what *kind* of reality divine reality really is. What is at issue, Phillips and Brown claim, is comparable to the question of what *kind* of reality physical objects have. There is no *finding out*, they maintain, whether God is real or not, as there is a finding out of whether unicorns are real. If we are realistic, we will come to realize that there is no more any genuine *finding out* whether God is real than there is a way of finding out whether physical objects are real. In this respect both God and physical objects are very different from Santa Claus and unicorns, where such an investigation can be made. Moreover, where there is no possibility of finding out that so-and-so is real, there is no possibility of *failing* to find out either, and thus there is no possibility of *genuine doubt*. The real question in both cases is the question about the *kind* of reality physical objects and God have. Phillips and Brown take these questions to be importantly similar. The first is about whether it is possible to speak of truth and falsity in the physical world and the second "is a question of sense and non-sense, truth and falsity, in religion".[4]

To this it is natural to respond that if we start by asking what *kind* of reality God has, we commit the fallacy of the complex question. We assume, that is, that God *has* a reality and that God could be real when it is these very things that we want to query. Surely it is important to understand, if we can, what *kind* of reality we are talking about, if indeed there is such a reality, and it is, no doubt, a mistake to construe God as a "super-object" among objects, but we also very much want to know whether there is such a reality, whether there is anything of that sort, whether that kind of reality has an exemplification or whether it is *simply* a conception in a conceptual scheme of a determinate language-game. (I take it that these are all facets of the same basic question.)

I suspect Phillips and Brown and Wittgensteinian fideists generally would in turn respond that this is still in effect treating God as if he were a physical object or something like a physical object.[5] But I do not see that this need be so and to show that it is so, if it is so, would require argument. Why can we not sensibly ask if what is *claimed* to be divine reality is *indeed* a reality at all? What is wrong with asking if that claimed reality is indeed something which actually exists? ("Something", we should not forget, has many different uses in many different linguistic environments.) Perhaps belief in God is not a belief in any *kind* of reality at all, but a belief in a kind of unreality arising from conceptual confusion and/or

human need? (*Perhaps* there is trouble here with "actually exists"?) Neither
Phillips nor Brown have been able to block that question or show it to
be a pseudo-question that no one would ask who had a good understanding
of religious language-games.

    We should also recognize that in talking about what Phillips—perhaps
pleonastically—calls "the physical world" we have a reasonable understanding of what speaking of truth or falsity comes to. In speaking of physical
objects, e.g., the tomatoes are ripe, the swallows are late in returning this
year, we perfectly well understand under what conditions these statements
would be true and under what conditions they would be false. But it is
not so clear that we know how to distinguish between truth and falsity in
religion, e.g., "God created Adam", "All men are tainted by original sin".
In a certain way there is sense and nonsense in religion. There are deviant
and non-deviant religious utterances. But what truth or falsity would come
to in religion is not clear. Before we can confidently say that "God created
Adam" is false, we must have some idea of what it would mean to say
it is true or probably true. But it is such questions that are bothersome.
Moreover, *pace* Phillips, if we do not construe God's existence as a matter
of fact, what are we to construe it as: a matter of convention, a notional
demand of a certain conceptual system, a conception arising out of pressing
behavioural needs or hopes, a matter of fiction or what? To say that it
is a fact that God exists, as I believe most believers would say, is not to
give to understand, as Phillips believes, that God is being construed as
something within the conceptual framework of the physical world. God
is thought to be a transcendent reality and to assert that God exists is to
assert that there is such a transcendent reality—that it is a fact that there
is such a transcendent reality.[6] This does not, at least on the surface,
appear incoherent or logically odd, and it is the sort of thing that most
Jewish and Christian believers would say, and indeed on reflection would
still want to continue saying, for, as Hägerström puts it, to abandon such
a conception is to abandon what is pervasively and understandably felt
to be the life-blood of Christianity or Judaism.[7]

    Thus it does not seem to me to be true that either Phillips or Brown
have given us good grounds for claiming that scepticism about the existence
of God, conceived of as a being who happens to have created and continues
to take an interest in the universe, is based upon or rests upon a misconception or a mistake. It does not seem to me that they have at all shown
that one cannot, while properly using religious discourse, while playing
religious language-games, raise within that language the possibility of God's
non-existence.[8] The sceptic's critique and questions are not to be taken
as something which is *just directed against the language of religion*.

    Pace Brown, scepticism about the reality of God need not just, or
perhaps not even at all, be scepticism about whether it is possible to think
and talk about matters in the way in which religious persons do.[9] A
sceptic could agree that many people do think and talk in that way but
still could consistently deny one or another of the following: that they intelligibly, coherently, reasonably, justifiably or truly can, where the latter
is a denial that they can succeed in so talking in making remarks—where
fundamental religious claims are at issue—which (a) are either true or false

or (b) are either true or at least probably true. The sceptic need not be reduced, as Brown and Phillips believe, to remarking that "Religion doesn't mean anything to me" or "I don't see the point of it". He might, like some of Dostoevsky's sceptical characters, very much see the point in such talk and yet remain quite incapable of belief.

However, it could be responded that the sceptic owes us some account of his uses of such terms as "intelligibly", "coherently", "reasonably", "justifiably", or "truly". If these terms, in part at least, take on the distinct meaning they have, or come to have, because of the distinctive language-games or practices they enter into, and there is little in the way of cross-form of discourse criteria for their proper employment, then, Brown and Phillips could respond, the sceptic's challenge about coherence, reasonability, justifiability and the like is an empty one, for the criteria for what is reasonably, coherently and justifiably done or believed in and about the substance of religion are determined by the constitutive rules of the religious discourse itself. In this important way religious discourse is *sui generis*. However, it is by no means evident that the criteria of such concepts are so totally context-dependent and form-of-life relative.[10]

However, let us for the occasion assume that they are so form-of-life relative and with this assume with Brown, as it is at least somewhat plausible to assume, that the sceptic's challenge reduces to the complaint that religion doesn't mean anything to him, that it seems to him to have no point at all. If that is the case, it may well be, as Brown argues, that there is not a sufficient community of judgment—that is agreement in judgments—for the believer and the sceptic to argue out their case against the bar of reason and come, even in principle, and with infinite patience and attendance to the facts and their implications, to a reasoned and justified conclusion as to who is right or even to such an agreement concerning who is more likely to be right or wrong. No determination of truth or justifiable belief on either side may be possible here. The conflict, Brown would have us believe, may be like his construal of the conflict between an art lover and a boor.[11]

Brown describes that conflict as follows: when the matter to be argued is about what is the most reasonable way to construe a situation or interpret the facts, there can be no rational resolution between the disputants unless there is a considerable community of judgment. That is, there must be a considerable agreement, albeit often implicit and unarticulated but still operative, between the disputants in their reactions, attitudes, framework-beliefs and whole ways of looking, talking and behaving. Within a given culture or cluster of cultures—say in the West today—there is such a community of judgment between art critics even when they very fundamentally disagree. They all belong within a more or less common tradition of art. But—or so Brown contends—"there seems nothing for the boor and the lover of art to discuss about art". If the boor says that the only pictures he likes are those with fishing scenes in them that remind him of his fishing expeditions or those with plump women in them, there is no room for dialogue and argument between him and the lover of art. They just have incommensurably different ways of looking, talking and behaving, with no way of showing or justifying that one way of doing these things is the more adequate or the more reasonable. The believer and unbeliever, he claims, are in the same or at least in a very similar situation to that of the art lover and the boor.

Brown in his *Religious Belief* puts his central claim powerfully as follows:

> Corresponding to the fundamental religious belief in the existence of a god there is, in art, the belief that there are objects worthy of aesthetic appreciation. In each case the belief is so embedded in a way of looking, talking and behaving that to doubt it is to question the point of that way of looking, talking and behaving. For the possibility of God's non-existence no more occurs within religion than the possibility of there being no works of art (in the normative sense of 'objects worthy of aesthetic appreciation') occurs within art. Furthermore the point of worship can no more be specified in non-religious terms than the point of attending to works of art can be specified in terms acceptable to the boor. One can only explain in religious terms why the behaviour described as 'worship' is appropriate, i.e., why thanksgiving, repentance and so on are appropriate. There is, then, a point beyond which the demand for justification becomes too radical even to make sense. And the questions 'Is there really a god?' and 'Are there really works of art?' do not have sense in the way in which 'Are there really any angels?' and 'Is Anti-art really art?' have. For these latter questions can be raised within the appropriate way of thinking and discussed in its terms. But the former questions are detached from the ways of thinking to which they purport to relate. We understand them not so much as demands for justification or as doubts to which there could be any substance but as expressions of an attitude, of a failure to see any point in what goes on in art or religion.[12]

It is tempting to say what Brown says, but it also seems to me to be the case that this Wittgensteinian move deserves querying. Is there really no common ground between the boor and the art lover? The art lover can ask the boor why he only likes paintings with fishing scenes and plump women. When the boor explains why it is he likes only these he can in turn be asked why he should go on only liking these. If he responds that these are the only interesting or good pictures, then there is, of course, room for argument and reasoning and judgment. If, alternatively, he says, "For no reason", then he in effect concedes his liking is arbitrary. And again there could be argument, discussion and dialogue. Why, after all, should he continue to be so arbitrary? What we need to recognize is that all along the line there is room for dialogue and argument. There is no a priori reason why in such contexts there even could not be what Habermas calls undistorted communication.

As Phillips has himself come to concede, the various language-games, within a given family of languages at least, are not insulated from each other.[13] There are all sorts of overlapping of criteria and rationales and relevant shiftings of perspectives. Justification does come to an end in any given dispute, but justificatory questions from a shifted perspective can start up again and it seems doubtful that it has been established that there are any fixed points at which all justificatory questions for *whatever purposes* must simply come to an end and that all we can say is this is what we do. No doubt in certain circumstances for certain determinate reasons we can reasonably say just this and break off discussion and be justified in terminating a request for justification. Life is short and all sorts of practical and human considerations intervene. But that is a different matter from the one that we have been discussing. What is less evident is that there are points at which justification *must* come to an end because (a) it makes no sense to ask at this point for any purpose or reason, for any kind of justification at all and (b) no intelligible questions are possible in such a context about what it is we are doing and thinking. Why, after all, should the boor so limit himself by being so arbitrary? Isn't it very possible that he is missing something worthwhile in life that might enhance his human flourishing? For understandable *causes*, we, in our bourgeois and pluralistic cultures, are inclined to be wary about comparative judgments about such choices or preferences. But it is surely far from evident that there is nothing to be said here and that decision is king. This claim itself should come up against the bar of reason.

Granted, at least for the sake of this discussion, that religion, art, morality and science are forms-of-life and that their fundamental beliefs are distinctive and interlocked ways of looking, talking and behaving such that to challenge any of these beliefs is to challenge this whole way in looking, talking, and behaving. Yet, why is it not possible to do just that? Can one not quite rationally, from a prudential or class point of view, challenge taking the moral point of view?[14] It certainly seems at least that one can. Even more evidently, one can challenge the point or the rationality of taking a Christian or Jewish point of view. And indeed one can do it even for taking any religious point of view at all. It is, to put the matter cautiously, not evident that argument cannot develop about such matters. And it is not evident where or even that there is a distinct point where argument must stop and we can only take sides in accordance with certain attitudes.

Brown claims that questioning concerning the possibility of God's non-existence *cannot* legitimately occur *within* religion.[15] But this cannot be correct, given the doubt and wrestling of many of the most profound men of faith. Some of them were torn by doubt. Sometimes they even affirmed their faith when they felt that the probability of God's non-existence was very considerable indeed. Their acceptance was rooted in trust and commitment, not in a knowledge that God exists. A Jew or a Christian cannot renounce his faith in God, but his faith can be tried. He can surely come to wonder and to be filled with doubts concerning whether, after all, there is a God, while still fervently praying to that God of whose existence he is so unsure. This can and does happen within religion.

Such a doubt is so central that it can put into question *the point* of a whole way of looking, talking and behaving, though, as Dostoevsky's *Shatov* dramatically shows, it is quite possible, while not believing in God, all the same to *want* to believe in God and to see very clearly the point of that religious way of viewing the world while still recognizing, or at least believing, that such a belief is belief in a myth and, because of this, also coming to believe that, after all and regrettably, there is no point in so looking at the world, since God does not exist. One can quite consistently believe this and be fully convinced that if only God did exist, there would very much be a point in so looking, talking and behaving. And plainly, if God were a reality, such activity would have a very considerable point.

In sum, it does not seem to me that a good case has been made for the claim that with the question "Is there really a god?" we have reached a point where the demand for justification is too radical even to make sense. The key framework-proposition, the most fundamental belief of the Judeo-Christian tradition, has been broached. It is indeed deeply embedded in distinctive religious language-games, but we can—or so it seems at least—perfectly intelligibly ask whether there really exists such a reality or whether there is anything of that sort at all. That does not, even within religion, appear to be an unintelligible or even an idling question. "Is there really a god?" need not be just an expression of an attitude but can, as well, be a genuine doubt concerning whether there is in reality a reality of a certain determinate kind or whether there in reality even could be. The sceptic, or at least certain sceptics, e.g., Santayana or Hepburn, *pace* Brown and Phillips, could very well see the point of religion, if only there were a god. In that way a sceptic can be very unlike the boor.

Let us now take a somewhat different tack. Certainly the study of Wittgenstein encourages us to believe that there are fundamental beliefs, including fundamental religious beliefs, which are deeply embedded in our language. As children we, in acquiring a language, are simply trained to think and respond in a certain way. We learn, as we learn to speak, certain beliefs and they are learned in such a way that alternatives are not even envisioned. We do come subsequently to revise and even reject *some* beliefs we so learn, but the suggestion is that other beliefs and indeed whole systems of belief are so deeply embedded that, learning our language as we have and having the language we have no means for a justification or a criticism of such whole systems of belief. As Brown well puts it:

> Someone who does not share such beliefs simply stands outside the tradition of those who do. It is, for instance, part of our tradition to believe that we ought not to do what is harmful to others. What could we say to someone who asked us to justify this belief? It would be no good telling him that it is in a man's long term interests to avoid doing harm to others. For even if that were true it would not be to the point if what is to be justified is the belief that it does in itself matter whether harm results to others from what we do. From the point of view of those who share this way of looking at things someone who demands justification of such a belief is beyond the pale. The appropriate response to him would seem to be, first to explain why there could be no answer to his question and then, perhaps, to try to change his way of looking at things.[16]

There are many human practices, such as the above moral practices, or the viewing and prizing of art, which are not, except perhaps incidentally, a means to some further human end and which could not, as some other practices can, be justified by reference to the end they serve.

These last claims seem to be at least plausible—though in some other context I would like to see them argued out—but what I am now concerned with is their application to religion.[17] Brown tells us that belief in God, indeed even the belief that there is a god (understood as the belief that there is an object worthy of worship), like belief in the value of art or the belief that we ought not to harm others, is a belief "which neither admits of nor requires justification".[18]

It does not seem to me that the analogy is a good one. People with a deep need to believe, people who see (or think they see) the point in religion and the point, more specifically, of believing in God, are sometimes just unable to believe. Such people think that the belief in the alleged transcendent reality denoted by the term "God" is such a scandal to the intellect, requires such credulity and intellectual evasion, that they cannot believe and indeed would not wish to be able so to dupe themselves so that they could in time come to believe. There are in our culture believers and non-believers and there are many people struggling in between. Many of them very much want an account of that admitted mystery denoted by the term "God", which is at least sufficiently plausible not to require a crucifixion of one's intellect or, alternatively, a justification on moral grounds for accepting such an account, even though it does require such a crucifixion of one's intellect. Moreover, and independently, they—or at least some of them—are perplexed on moral grounds whether any object (any being) could be *worthy of worship*. The perplexity comes from reflecting on morality and religion itself. In such contexts the engine is not idling. And it is not analogous to the case of someone who is just indifferent to moral or aesthetic considerations and can see no point in either activity. Some doubters and some critics of religion can see the point of it very well and are not indifferent to the considerations underlying religion, but they also recognize that, in contrast to morals and aesthetics, in religion certain cosmological claims are quite evidently and unequivocally a part of that religion and that these claims at least appear to be so problematic as to make their acceptance of questionable rationality by people with such an understanding. Such a sceptic wants to ascertain, if it can be ascertained, whether it is indeed irrational for him to continue to accept these fundamental religious beliefs. Brown and Phillips, and those other philosophers whom I have (perhaps tendentiously) called Wittgensteinian fideists, have not, as far as I can see, blocked these questions. Because of their at least apparent reasonability, it seems at least to be the case that the belief that there is a god—or indeed belief in God—is a belief which does require justification for its reasonable acceptance. To put it minimally, it does *not* appear, at least, to be a belief that we can reasonably accept as groundless but still perfectly in order.

NOTES

1. Here I am deeply influenced by the powerful anti-Cartesian line about doubt and certainty and the need for a contextually dependent context for doubt taken by Peirce and by Wittgenstein in his neglected *On Certainty*.

2. I am indebted to Norman Malcolm here both for some of the examples of framework-beliefs and for his discussion of framework-beliefs. See Norman Malcolm, "The Groundlessness of Belief," *Reason and Religion*, ed. Stuart Brown (London: The Macmillan Press Ltd., 1977). See as well in the same volume Colin Lyas, "The Groundlessness of Religious Belief"; and G.H. von Wright, "Wittgenstein On Certainty," *Problems in the Theory of Knowledge*, ed. G.H. von Wright (The Hague: Martinus Nijhoff, 1972) 47-60.

3.   D.Z. Phillips, *Faith and Philosophical Enquiry* (London: Routledge and Kegan Paul, 1970) and Stuart Brown, *Religious Belief* (London: The Open University Press, 1973). Paul Tillich in his cumbersome and often obscure way says similar things.

4.   D.Z. Phillips, *op. cit.* 3 and Stuart Brown, *op. cit.* 37-39.

5.   D.Z. Phillips would no doubt respond that the above remarks reflect how, given the dominant scientistic paradigm of intelligibility, philosophical reflection itself easily falls prey to scientistic pressures. To think, for example, that God is something that could be located or identified is to betray a misconception of the kind of reality God has. It shows, Phillips would have it, a misunderstanding of, on the one hand, the anthropomorphic and mythic conceptions of God and, on the other, of modern religious conceptions alive in genuine first-order Jewish and Christian discourse. Still, once we recognize that God is not the sort of reality that could be located, the problem remains how are we to understand—or even do we understand—what this putative ultimate reality is that we are talking about and do we understand at all what would justify our saying that the truth of "There is a god" is even a trifle more probable than its denial? If the answer to this last question is in the negative and we do not understand what it is we are talking about in speaking of God, then it seems to me that it is not just a scientistic or positivist prejudice to question the coherence of such talk. See D.Z. Phillips, "Philosophers, Religion and Conceptual Change," *The Challenge of Religion Today*, ed. John King-Farlow (New York: Science History Publications, 1976) 196-97.

6.   There would still be dispute about how to construe "transcendence" here, but at the very least, many believers would find it essential to try to articulate some non-symbolic reading of "transcendent to the world." See Ninian Smart, "Mystical Experience," *Sophia* I.1 (1962): 24-26. Yet, it is doubtful if such a conception of "metaphysical transcendence" can be given a coherent reading. To substitute what Ilham Dilman calls "religious transcendence" is: (a) in another way to fall prey to the pressures of philosophical reflection under the dominant scientistic paradigm, and (b) to substitute a conception which will not meet the *religious* expectations of very many Christians and Jews. See Ilham Dilman, "Wisdom's Philosophy of Religion Part II, Metaphysical and Religious Transcendence," *Canadian Journal of Philosophy* V.4 (1975): 497-521.

7.   Axel Hägerström, *Philosophy and Religion*, trans. R.T. Sandin (London: George Allen and Unwin Ltd., 1964) 224-59.

8.   Stuart Brown, *op. cit.* 38.

9.   *Ibid.* 39.

10. Steven Lukes and Martin Hollis have shown that such an extreme contextualism cannot be correct. See their essays in *Rationality*, ed. Bryan R. Wilson (Oxford: Basil Blackwell Ltd., 1970) 194-239. But, as I have tried to show, problems remain. See my "Rationality and Relativism," *Philosophy of the Social Sciences* 4.4 (1974) and my "Rationality and Universalism," *The Monist* 59.3 (1976): 441-55.

11.   Stuart Brown, *op. cit.* 36-41.

12.   *Ibid.* 39.

13.   D.Z. Phillips, *op. cit.* 77-79.

14.   See my "Rawls and Classist Amoralism," *Mind* (January 1977).

15.   Stuart Brown, *op. cit.* 39.

16.   *Ibid.* 40.

17.   I do argue them out in the article cited in note 14 and in my "Rawls' Defense of Morality," *The Personalist* 59.1 (1977): 93-100, and my "Rationality and the Moral Sentiments," *Philosophica* 22.2 (1978): 167-92.

18.   Stuart Brown, *op. cit.* 40.

CHAPTER 8

Religion and Groundless Believing*

I

IT IS A FUNDAMENTAL RELIGIOUS BELIEF OF JEWS and Christians that a human being's chief end is to glorify God and to enjoy him forever. Human beings are not simply creatures who will rot and die, but they will survive the death of their present bodies. They will, after the Last Judgment, if they are saved, come into a blissful union with God, free finally of all sin, and they will be united in heaven in human brotherhood and love. But for now, that is, in our "earthly" condition of life, we stand in division both inwardly as self-divided creatures and against each other as well; a kingdom of heaven on earth is far from being realized. We humans—or so Jews and Christians believe—are sinful creatures standing before the God of mercy and of love whose forgiveness we need and to whom everything is owed.

The thing to see here is that being a Jew or a Christian is not just the having of one framework-belief, namely a belief that there is God. And it is not just, as some philosophers seem to assume, the having of that belief and the having of another, namely that we will survive the death of our bodies. Rather, as Wittgenstein and Malcolm stress, what we have with a religion is a system, or as I would prefer to call it, a cluster of inter-locking beliefs, qualifying and giving each other sense and mutual support.[1] We have here a world-picture which not only tells us, or purports to tell us, what is the case but orients and guides our lives and can touch profoundly—if we can accept such a world-picture—our hopes and expectations as well. To be a Jew or a Christian is to be a person whose sense of self and sense of the meaningfulness of life is tied up with that world-picture.

It has seemed to many philosophers, believers and nonbelievers alike, that key concepts in this world-picture—God, heaven, hell, sin, the

*First published in *The Autonomy of Religious Belief: A Critical Inquiry*, ed. F.J. Crosson (Notre Dame, IN: University of Notre Dame Press, 1981).

Last Judgment, a human being's chief end, being resurrected and coming
to be a new man with a new body—are all in one degree or another problematic concepts whose very intelligibility or rational acceptability are not
beyond reasonable doubt. Yet it is just this sceptical thrust—or so at least
it would appear—that Wittgenstein and certain Wittgensteinians oppose
as itself a product of *philosophical* confusion.[2] In the systemic home of
various ongoing and deeply entrenched language-games, these concepts
have a place, and in that context they are, and must be, perfectly in order
as they are. Within those language-games no genuine questions of their
intelligibility or rational acceptability can arise and criticisms from the
outside—from the vantage point of some other language-game—are always
irrelevant, for the criteria of intelligibility or rational acceptability are always
in part dependent on a particular language-game.[3] It might be thought
that the phrase "genuine question" in the above is a tip-off marking what
in effect is a *persuasive* definition and showing, as clearly as can be, that
such questions can and do arise over such general criteria within the
parameters of such language-games. But the response would be that no
one who commanded a clear view of what she or he was saying and doing
would try to make such a challenge or search for such general criteria
of intelligibility or rationality, for she would be perfectly aware that she
had no place to stand in trying to gain such a critical vantage point. There
just are no criteria of intelligibility or rationality *Überhaupt*.[4] Such a
person has and can have no Archimedean point in accordance with which
she could carry out such a critique.

Genuine criticism, such Wittgensteinians argue, will have to proceed
piecemeal and within the parameters of these different but often interlocking
language-games. Critique, if it is to cut deep and be to the point, must
be concrete (specific) and involve an extended examination of the forms
of life from *within*. For such a criticism to be a genuine possibility the
critics must have a sensitive participant's or participant-like understanding
of these forms of life as they are exhibited in the language-games with
which they are matched. (Perhaps it is more adequate to say the language-
games are embedded in forms of life!)

In such a context criticism is in order and is an indispensable tool
in the *development* of a tradition, but there is—so the claim goes—no
genuinely relevant criticism possible of language-games as a whole or of
forms of life. There is no coherent sense, such Wittgensteinians argue,
in which we can speak of a confused language-game or an irrational form
of life or of a full-fledged, conceptually distinct practice which is irrational
or incoherent.[5] Our language-games are rooted in these practices and are
not in need of justification or of a foundation. In fact the whole idea of
foundations or grounds or justification here is without sense. Foundationalism is a philosophical mythology. There is no logic which can give us the
a priori order of the world. Rather our logical distinctions are found in
or become a codification of distinctions found in our various language-
games. But the sense—the intelligibility—of our language-games cannot
be coherently questioned. There is, they claim, no coherent sense to the
phrase "a confused language-game" or "a confused but conceptually
distinct practice" or "an irrational form of life." We indeed have a deep

philosophical penchant to go on to question, to ask for foundations for, to try to justify such practices, language-games, or forms of life. But it is just here that we fall into transcendental illusion. We do not recognize the import of Wittgenstein's full stop and we dream of justification where none exists or even could exist.

Both understanding and genuine criticism must, initially at least, proceed by seeing how the various concepts interlock and how in the form of a whole system—a cluster of concepts—they make sense. There is no understanding them in isolation. We come to understand their use by coming to see their place—their various roles—in the system. There is no understanding "the chief end of man" outside of something like a religious context and there is no understanding the distinctive end of man envisioned by Christianity without understanding its concept of God. And there is no, so the claim goes, even tolerable understanding of Christianity's concept of God without understanding the Christian concept of the end of man and man's highest good. And in turn to understand that, it is necessary to make sense of a man's surviving the death of his present body and coming to have a resurrection body in a resurrection world. There is no more breaking away the Christian conception of the end of man or man's highest good from such cosmological conceptions than there is a way of breaking away the conception of the Last Judgment from them. And in turn the concepts of heaven, blissful union with God, human brotherhood, love, and sin do not stand on their own feet but gain their distinctively Christian sense from their interlocking with these other concepts of Christian life. These concepts and many others like them cluster together, and we cannot understand them in isolation. Moreover, they stand and fall together.

II

Yet, these crucial Wittgensteinian points notwithstanding, there is a certain probing of those concepts which is quite natural and which can—or so it at least appears—be carried out in relative isolation from the examination of the other concepts of the cluster, provided we have something like a participant's grasp of the whole cluster. We, in wondering about the resurrection body in the resurrection world, naturally wonder how identity is preserved in the switch or in the resurrection or in reconstitution of the body. Who is it that is me in the interim between the decay of the "old body" and the emergence of the "new" one, and in what space and in what world in relation to our present familiar world of everyday life and physics is this resurrection world? Is it even logically or conceptually possible for a rocket to be shot up to it? Somehow this all seems fatuous—a plain getting of it wrong—but what then is a getting of it right, what is it that we are talking about, and does it make sense? Does it help our understanding at all to say that we must just understand it in its own terms? Does it help particularly the perplexities we feel at this juncture to relate such conceptions to the other conceptions in our

religious language-game? It is not at all clear to me that, about these particular worries, it does help much, if at all, to relate these philosophically
perplexing conceptions to other religious conceptions. Even more important
is the role of the concept of God here. While gaining its meaning in a certain
determinate context in a cluster of concepts, the concept of God can still
have, in relative isolation, certain questions addressed to it. We glorify
God and find our chief joy in him, but *who* or *what* is the God we enjoy
and how appropriate is the use of personal pronouns in such talk? We
have the word "God" but is it a proper name, an abbreviated definite
description, a special kind of descriptive predicable or what? It surely
appears to be some kind of referring expression, but what does it refer
to? How could we be acquainted with, or would we be acquainted with
or otherwise come to know, what it stands for or characterizes? How do
we—or do we—identify God, how do we individuate God, what are we
talking about when we talk of God, do we succeed in making any successful
reference when we speak of God? What or who is this God we pray to,
love, find our security in, make sense of our lives in terms of, and the
like? Our cluster of religious concepts will help us somewhat here. We
know he is the God of love who transcends in his might and mystery our
paltry understanding. *Some* Jews and Christians believe he is that being
whom we will somehow meet face to face when we are resurrected and
our sins are washed away, and we know that he is a being of infinite mercy
and love with whom we may somehow, someday, be in blissful union in
a world without division, strife, or alienation, where love and brotherhood
(sisterhood) prevail. This helps to some extent to locate God in *conceptual*
space but only to some extent, for still the nagging question persists: what
is it or *who* is it that is this being of infinite love, mercy, power, and understanding of whom we stand in need? What literally are we talking about
when we speak of this being or what kind of reality or putative reality do
we speak of when we speak of or even talk to God? (If we have no conception
of what it is to speak literally here, then we can have no understanding
of the possibility of speaking metaphorically or analogically either, for the
possibility of the latter is parasitic on the possibility of the former.) Suppose
someone says there is no reality here and "God" answers to nothing at
all—stands for, makes reference to, nothing at all. How are we to answer
him and show he is mistaken? And how are we to answer the other chap
who looks on the scene and says he does not know how to decide such
an issue? He does not understand what it would be like to succeed in making
reference with "God", but not knowing that, he also does not know—
indeed cannot know—that "God" does *not* stand for anything either. If
we don't understand what could count as success, how could we understand
what could count as failure? All these people can play Jewish or Christian
language-games with such a cluster of concepts, but they remain thoroughly
perplexed about what, if anything, they are talking about in speaking of
God. If that is so, how can we possibly be justified in saying that the concepts
in question are unproblematic and are in order as they are? We know
what it is religious people do with such words; we can do similar things
with words as well, and we understand full well the uses of language
involved. We could do it all quite competently in a play if necessary. But

though we can speak and act and at least seem to share a common under-standing, we cannot decide whether "God" does, or even could (given its meaning), secure reference—stand for something, refer to something actually real—and we do not agree about or understand how to go about settling or resolving or even dissolving that issue. But how then can these key concepts or conceptions be unproblematic?

III

Some, whom I have called—perhaps tendentiously—Wittgensteinian fideists, would respond that the core mistake in what I have been arguing is that I continue to construe God as an object or a thing or entity of some sort. That this is a governing assumption for me, as it is for Flew as well, is revealed in my and his repeated request for a specification of the referent (denotation) of "God", in our asking repeatedly *who* or *what* is God.[6] We both are, it could be argued, looking for the substance answering to the substantive and sometimes at least that is a mistake of such an order as to show a fundamental confusion about the logic of God. It confuses the surface grammar of the concept with its depth grammar.

There is no more question, they claim, of finding out whether God exists than there is of finding out whether physical objects exist. The putative question "Is God real?" makes no more sense than does the question-form "Do material objects exist?" It is true that a man who rejects religious belief and does not believe in God is not cut off from reason—is not thereby shown to be irrational—as is the man who does not believe there are any physical objects. Indeed we would not know what to make of a child's doubting the reality of physical objects, but we would understand very well a child's not believing in God or an adult's coming not to believe in God. The kind of unquestionable propositions that Moore and Wittgenstein take to be bedrock unquestionable propositions may, in their normal employments in normal contexts, very well be propositions it really makes no sense to question. They are framework-beliefs. Whatever other differ-ences they may exhibit, they are propositions which are not, or at least so these Wittgensteinians claim, *testable empirically* and thus are, in that way, not grounded in experience.[7] There is no finding out whether they are true or false. The fact that the basic teachings of religion cannot properly be called knowledge should cease to be paradoxical, shocking, or perplexing when we reflect on this and on the fact that these various framework-beliefs—certain of them as we are—are still not bits of knowledge. Moreover, that is not distinctive of religion and ideology but is a feature, as Wittgenstein shows, of many quite unproblematic domains as well.[8] All language-games have their framework propositions and, as they are something we cannot be mistaken about or in any way test or establish, they are not bits of knowledge. Doubting, establishing, believing, finding out, and knowing are activities which only make sense within the confines of language-games, and they require each other for any such single activity to be possible. But such contrastive conceptions cannot be applied to the framework propositions themselves. And while it is perfectly true that cultural changes can and do bring about changes in what we do and do not regard as reasonable, what realism requires, Wittgenstein argues, is a recognition that we do not have and cannot come to have a historical vantage point which will tell us what, such historical contexts apart, is "really reasonable."[9] (Indeed such talk may very well have no coherent sense.) What we have in various areas are different and often incommensurable beliefs which are, for many at least, unshakeable beliefs which regulate their lives. But there is no finding out which, if any of them, are really true. There is, such Wittgensteinians argue, no establishing "philosophical foundations" which show that some or all of them have a rational underpinning. Such rationalist hopes are utterly misguided.[10]

To understand what we mean by "God", to grasp its role in the stream of life, is to come to understand its role in such religious activities as worship, prayer, and the praise of God. That is where we come to understand what it is that we believe in when we believe in God. That is where the experience of God will have some reality, and it is in those surroundings that "Thou art God" has clear sense. There God becomes a reality in our lives, and it is there where it becomes clear to us that the existence of God is neither a theoretical nor a quasi-theoretical nor even a metaphysical question. We respond, if we are religious, to religious talk, and on certain appropriate occasions some of us even sing out "God is our God above all other Gods." Some Wittgensteinians have even claimed that "God exists" in its actual logical form (its depth grammar) is not something which actually is, as it appears to be, in the indicative mood. Most definitely, such Wittgensteinians claim, it is not a statement of fact or even a putative statement of fact. "God", they also claim, is not a term concerning which it makes any sense at all to look for its referent. In Christian and Jewish language-games "God is real" is a grammatical truth.

IV

These claims deserve a critical reception. "God is unreal. God is but a figment of our imaginations born of our deepest needs" are not deviant English sentences. There are a number of language-games in which such talk is quite at home. But as believers don't speak that way, it will be claimed that the above sceptical utterances are not at home in religious language-games. (But again, believers could act in a play and speak that way or write novels, as Dostoevsky did, in which characters say such things.) At least some believers understand such talk and there are many ex-believers and doubting Thomases and people struggling in various ways with religious belief. In their struggles and in their expectable and understandable wrestlings with faith, such talk has a home. Questions about whether God is really a figment of our imagination quite naturally arise. Moreover, their typical contexts are not the bizarre and metaphysical contexts in which we can ask whether physical objects are real or whether memory beliefs are ever reliable. In our lives, that is, they are, for believer and nonbeliever alike, not idling questions like "Is time real?"

It might be responded that it is necessary to recognize that for a medieval man asking "Is God real?" would be such an idling metaphysical question. Perhaps that is so—though that would have to be shown; after all, Machiavelli was a late medieval man—but, whatever we should say for the medievals, what is true in cultures such as ours is that such questions repeatedly arise in nonphilosophical contexts where the engine is not idling. Why are they not in order in those contexts? What grounds have we for saying they are not real doubts or that they would never be asked by anyone who understood what he was asking? That some people—even that many people—do not question these propositions does not show they are "unquestionable propositions." That they are plainly not *just* theoretical questions does not show that they are not theoretical at all. Perhaps changes over time and, in our culture, about what is taken to be reasonable and what is not, have changed our responses to these questions and our attitudes toward worship, praise, and prayer. But then we need to recognize just that and consider what that involves and what philosophical significance it has.

It is indeed true that we need an understanding of God-talk to understand the sense of sentences such as "I take my illness as a punishment," "Your sins are forgiven," "God is merciful to sinners," and "He has experienced God's mercy," but we also need, to understand them properly, to see how they fit into a system. (We can speak of a "system of salvation" and we need not think of it as a theoretical system.) But none of this precludes or makes unnecessary asking about the referent (alleged referent) of "God". Granted "God" does not stand for an object among objects, but still what does "God" stand for? None of the above has shown that to be a pseudo-question.

V

Wittgensteinians—as is most evident in the work of Winch, Dilman, and Phillips—try very hard to avoid facing that issue. Indeed they struggle to show that in reality there is no such issue at all.[11] I have tried to expose the nerve of some of the issues here and to maintain against them that there appears at least to be a real issue here.

Wittgensteinians will contend that language-games and forms of life are neither well-founded nor ill-founded. They are just there like our lives. Our understanding of them and assurance concerning them is shown by the way we go on—by how we employ them—whether we claim, in our philosophical moments, to understand them or not. There is no showing

that the evaluative conceptions and norms, including the norms of reasonability embedded in them, require a justification, a foundation, or even
an explanation. Indeed, if they are right, the first two are impossible and
even the third (i.e., that they require explanation) may be impossible as
well, but, impossible or not, such things are unnecessary. The urge to
attempt such justifications and explanations is very deep—as deep as
the very subject that has traditionally been called "philosophy". But
Wittgenstein schools us to resist this urge. If he is near to the mark, reason—
the use by human beings of the various canons of rationality—requires
that we resist it. Such general inquiries about religion and reality are
senseless. There neither is nor can be a *philosophical* underpinning of
religion or anything else. But such philosophical foundationalism is not
needed. It is not something the loss of which undermines our capacity
to make sense of our lives. Bad philosophy gives us the illusion that religion
requires such a foundation and sometimes succeeds in so infiltrating
religious conceptions that they do come to have incoherent elements which
should not be accepted. Good philosophy will help us spot and excise those
nonsensical, metaphysical elements. But when purified of such extraneous
metaphysical elements, religious belief is both foundationless and not in
the slightest need of foundations or of some philosophical justification.

I do not intend here to rise to the fundamental metaphilosophy issues
raised by this Wittgensteinian rejection of the search for "philosophical
foundations." Such a way of viewing things is plainly less popular now
than when Wittgenstein and some of his followers first pressed it home.
Yet it seems to me that philosophers have not so much answered it, or
shown it to be a pointless lament, as simply to have ignored it. I think
that this is a mistake and that a philosophical practice that survives taking
this challenge seriously will look very different indeed from the practices
that went before it.

However, I don't want to speak of that grand issue here but only
to face some of its implications for religion, if one takes to heart
Wittgenstein's critique of the pretensions of philosophy. I agree, of course,
that religion can have no such philosophical or metaphysical foundations.
I do not even have a tolerably clear sense of what it means to say that
there is some *distinctive philosophical* knowledge that would give us "the
true grounds" of religious belief. I am no more concerned than are the
Wittgensteinians to defend such a metaphysical religiosity and I am not
concerned to replace it with some distinctive atheological "*philosophical
knowledge.*"

However, our perplexities and difficulties about God and religion
are not just in a second-order context where the engine is idling. Most
of them are not like perplexities about how we can know whether there
is an external world or whether induction is justified or whether our memory
beliefs are ever reliable. It is not just the talk about God-talk that perplexes
us but certain central bits of the first-order talk itself. People with a common
culture and a common set of language-games are very much at odds over
whether we can know or justifiably believe that there is a God and this
can be, and often is, linked for some with an intense desire to believe

in God or, for that matter (though much less frequently), not to believe in God. It is common between myself and Wittgensteinian fideists that we do not think that there is any metaphysical Santa Claus that is going to provide us with answers here, to wit with some distinctively "metaphysical knowledge" which will assure us that there is or is not, must or cannot be, that putative reality for which "God" is the English term.

Using their own procedures, procedures I take within a certain scope to be perfectly proper, I started by looking at religious language-games we all can play and concerning which we at least have a knowledge by *wont*. When we look at certain religious language-games and—indeed from inside them—put questions which are perfectly natural, questions that plain people ask, and ask without suffering from metaphysical hunger, we will see that perplexities *arise* about to whom or to what we could be praying, supplicating, or even denying when we talk in this manner. Where "God" is construed non-anthropomorphically, as we must construe "God" if our conception is not to betray our belief as a superstition, it appears at least to be the case that we do not understand who or what it is we believe when we speak of believing in God. It is not just that we do not understand these matters very well—that is certainly to be expected and is quite tolerable—but that we are utterly at sea here.

Such considerations make scepticism about the reality of such a conception very real indeed. And that very scepticism—as Dostoevsky teaches us—can even come from someone who has a genuine need or at least a desire to believe. That scepticism is common enough and, if I am near to my mark, could be well-founded, even in complete innocence of or in utter irony about philosophical foundations for or against religious belief.

NOTES

1.   Ludwig Wittgenstein, *On Certainty*, trans. Denis Paul and G.E.M. Anscombe (Oxford: Basil Blackwell, 1969); and Norman Malcolm, "The Groundlessness of Belief," *Reason and Religion*, ed. Stuart C. Brown (Ithaca, NY: Cornell University Press, 1977) 143-57.

2.   Wittgenstein in *On Certainty* and again in a somewhat different way in his *Philosophical Investigations*. See Rush Rhees, *Without Answers* (London: Routledge and Kegan Paul, 1969); the article cited in the previous note from Malcolm; D.Z. Phillips, *The Concept of Prayer* (London: Routledge and Kegan Paul, 1965), *Death and Immortality* (New York: St. Martin's Press, 1970), *Faith and Philosophical Enquiry* (London: Routledge and Kegan Paul, 1970) and *Religion Without Explanation* (Oxford: Basil Blackwell, 1976); Ilham Dilman, "Wisdom's Philosophy of Religion," *Canadian Journal of Philosophy* V.4 (1975) and "Wittgenstein on the Soul," *Understanding Wittgenstein*, ed. G. Vesey (London: Macmillan, 1974).

3.   In addition to the above references, note as well Peter Winch, "Understanding a Primitive Society," *Rationality*, ed. Bryan R. Wilson (Oxford: Basil Blackwell, 1970) and "Meaning and Religious Language," *Reason and Religion*, ed. Stuart Brown.

4.   See the above references to Phillips and Winch and, most centrally, Wittgenstein, *On Certainty*. I discuss further facets of this in my "Reasonable Belief Without

Justification," *Body, Mind and Method: Essays in Honor of Virgil C. Aldrich*, eds. Donald Gustafson and Bangs L. Tapscott (Dordrecht, The Netherlands: D. Reidel, 1979).

5. Most of the above references are pertinent here but note, as well, D.Z. Phillips, "Philosophers, Religion and Conceptual Change," *The Challenge of Religion Today*, ed. John King-Farlow (New York: Neale Watson Academic Publications, 1976) 190-200.

6. See my *Contemporary Critiques of Religion* (New York: Herder and Herder, 1971) and my *Skepticism* (New York: St. Martin's, 1973); and see A.G.N. Flew's *God and Philosophy* (London: Hutchinson, 1966); and A.G.N. Flew's *The Presumption of Atheism* (New York: Barnes and Noble, 1976).

7. Norman Malcolm, "The Groundlessness of Belief."

8. Ludwig Wittgenstein, *On Certainty* and G.H. von Wright, "Wittgenstein On Certainty," *Problems in the Theory of Knowledge*, ed. G.H. von Wright (The Hague: Martinus Nijhoff, 1972) 47-60.

9. Wittgenstein, *On Certainty* 43, 80.

10. Again, *On Certainty* seems to me a crucial reference here. See also Stanley Cavell, *Must We Mean What We Say?* (New York: Charles Scribner's Sons, 1969).

11. Such accounts have been powerfully criticized by Robert C. Coburn, "Animadversions on a Wittgensteinian Apologetic," *Perkins Journal* (Spring 1971): 25-36 and by Michael Durrant, "Is the Justification of Religious Belief a Possible Enterprise?" *Religious Studies* 9 (1971): 440-54 and in his "Some Comments on 'Meaning and Religious Language'," *Reason and Religion*, ed. Stuart Brown, 22-32.

CHAPTER 9

On the Rationality of Groundless Believing*

*The difficulty is to realize the groundlessness of our believing.
At the foundation of well-founded belief lies belief that is not
founded.*

Ludwig Wittgenstein

I

THERE ARE THREE REMARKS OF NORMAN Malcolm's with which I should like to begin. The first is his remark that

> In our Western academic philosophy, religious belief is commonly regarded as unreasonable and is viewed with condescension or even contempt. It is said that religion is a refuge for those who, because of weakness of intellect or character, are unable to confront the stern realities of the world. The objective, mature, *strong* attitude is to hold beliefs solely on the basis of *evidence*. (204)[1]

Surely the response of intellectuals to religion is more complex and varied than that, but there is enough truth in this exaggeration and in Malcolm's further remark "that by and large religion is to university people an alien form of life" to make it an important sociological datum to keep before our minds when we consider religion. A religious human being, a person who prays and goes to church and all that, is something of an anomaly among present day Western intellectuals and particularly among philosophers. That form of life does seem very alien to many of us.

The second remark of Malcolm's I should like to quote is both characteristic and important.

> Religion is a form of life; it is language embedded in action—what Wittgenstein calls a 'language game.' Science is another. Neither stands in need of justification, the one no more than the other. (212)

Indeed, as he remarks a few pages earlier, "one of the primary pathologies of philosophy is the feeling that we must justify our language games" (208). Malcolm, following Wittgenstein, argues that there is nothing here to be

*First published in *Idealistic Studies* (1981).

grounded—nothing that could be either well-grounded or ill-grounded; a "language game is not based on grounds. It is there—like our life."[2]

Malcolm is, however, very aware that there is a deep and tenacious resistance to this on the part of philosophers. A sociological remark of his, which will serve as my third and last quotation, accurately and importantly notes a certain pervasive state of affairs which obtains among philosophers in North America.

> The desire to provide a rational foundation for a form of life is especially prominent in the philosophy of religion, where there is an intense preoccupation with purported proofs of the existence of God. In American universities there must be hundreds of courses in which these proofs are the main topic. We can be sure that nearly always the critical verdict is that the proofs are invalid and consequently that, up to the present time at least, religious belief has received no rational justification.
>
> Well, of course not! The obsessive concern with the proofs reveals the assumption that in order for religious belief to be intellectually respectable it *ought* to have a rational justification. *That* is the misunderstanding. It is like the idea that we are not justified in relying on memory until memory has been proved reliable. (210-11)

The point is, is it? Is this a good analogy and, the analogy apart, is this general counterenlightenment posture of Malcolm's, which I believe is Wittgenstein's as well, the realistic, perceptive and indeed—if such appraisal terms are applicable here—the correct posture to take?

Both Malcolm and Wittgenstein believe that people—and most particularly people with a philosophical bent—have an irrational fear of groundless beliefs. But this, they believe, is a philosophical pathology which requires philosophical therapy, a therapy which Malcolm seeks to provide in his "The Groundlessness of Belief."

Malcolm wants to say—and he takes this to be Wittgenstein's conviction as well—that pervasively in our lives there are central beliefs, beliefs he calls framework-beliefs, which are accepted, as religious people accept certain of their key religious beliefs, steadfastly and not as conjecture, but for which there are no reasons. As difficult as it is for us to grasp and accept, what needs to be recognized, Malcolm contends, is that much of our believing—believing which forms our lives—is groundless believing on the basis of no evidence, and, he claims, it is believing for which there could be no evidence. Indeed, where we are talking about genuine framework-beliefs, this is how it must be. There could be no grounds for them.

Throughout our lives there is and must remain any number of beliefs which have a firm but groundless acceptance. But—so the claim runs— the confused Cartesian penchant to try to transcend this is in reality the irrational heart of rationalism. Beliefs—beliefs which are central to our lives—can, and indeed many must, have this groundless acceptance and not be any the worse, or even in the slightest degree unreasonable, for all of that. We sometimes do, of course, have groundless beliefs which are silly or plainly falsifiable such as the belief that flowers have feelings or that tomatoes are poisonous. But the groundless beliefs in which we are interested are not of that sort, but are more fundamental beliefs some of which play an important part in our lives. Some of the examples given by Malcolm are the following:

1. Things do not just vanish without cause.
2. In situations of the same type a substance A (say snow) will react to a substance B (say heat) in the same way.
3. There is a continuity of nature.
4. My image of some x (say the Empire State Building) is an image of that x (say the Empire State Building).
5. I cannot fail to know my own intentions.

Consider the first example as a plain and mundane enough instance of a groundless belief. If I cannot find my keys, I would not, even after an extended search, seriously consider the "hypothesis" that they had inexplicably ceased to exist: that they just "vanished into thin air." Here my mind is firmly closed and this is true of most people concerning such matters. Yet, as Malcolm remarks, "it is possible to imagine a society in which it was accepted that sometimes material things do go out of existence without having been crushed, melted, eroded, broken into pieces, burned up, eaten or destroyed in some other way" (200). There would, for such a society, be behavioural differences between them and us. If they lost their keys, they would give up the search sooner than we would, be less inclined to the hypothesis that they had been stolen, and more inclined to use "they just vanished" nonmetaphorically. Even their "attitude toward experiment, and inference from experimental results, would be more tentative" (200).

However, Malcolm does not believe that we could rightly dismiss the beliefs of such a tribe as being radically incoherent and thus irrational. In certain fundamental ways their beliefs and behaviour differ from ours but in other very central ways their beliefs are like ours and they reason in the way we do. "Although," as Malcolm remarks, "those people consider it to be possible that a wallet might have inexplicably ceased to exist, it is also true that they regard that as unlikely. For things that are lost do turn up later; or if not, their fate can often be accounted for. Those people use pretty much the same criteria of identity that we do; their reasoning would resemble ours quite a lot. Their thinking would not be incoherent. But it would be different, since they would leave room for some *possibilities* that we exclude" (201, italics mine). Moreover, it is not the case, Malcolm claims, that it is evident that one tribe's position here is better supported by the evidence than the other's. Indeed "each position is compatible with ordinary experience" (201). Sometimes, though not very often, familiar objects do disappear without adequate explanation. But this fact is fully accepted by both sides though they draw radically different conclusions from it and place the fact in very different interpretative frameworks. But we cannot justly score, as we might at first be tempted to think we can, either view as irrational and incoherent because it flies in the face of the evidence. We do not have available to us here one of our standard ways of showing a belief or network of beliefs to be unjustified and, where persisted in with such an awareness, irrational. So while—or so Malcolm claims—neither view can be shown to be unreasonable, our own minds are firmly shut against the other tribe's view. We would not "be willing to consider it as even *improbable* that a missing lawn-chair had just ceased to exist" (201). We would not seriously entertain such a suggestion and it is "no exaggeration to say that this attitude is part of the foundations of our thinking" (201). It is, as Malcolm remarks, something we do not even try to support with grounds and yet *such* unsupported beliefs, contrary to the usual view of the matter, are not at all unreasonable; but they are all the same groundless and there are rational alternatives to them. They are part of our framework of thinking and so can properly be called framework-beliefs. Yet we have no sound basis for regarding them as superior or more rational than the alternative framework-beliefs as my above remarks about a straightforward case show. Such a belief, as the one I have just examined, is part of our world picture (*Weltbild*); it is an unreflective and unsupported "part of the framework within which physical investigations are made and physical explanations arrived at," but it is not, Malcolm would have us understand, in the slightest unreasonable or rightly suspect for all of that. Such beliefs, as Wittgenstein puts it in *On Certainty*, are the "matter-of-course (*selbstverständliche*) foundation for our investigations."[3] They are part of a system or network of beliefs and, as the matter-of-course foundation of our thought and action, they typically go unmentioned. (The other beliefs I listed at the beginning of this section are similar framework-beliefs and have a similar status.)

It is also important to stress, as Malcolm does, following Wittgenstein, that "all testing, all confirmation of a hypothesis, takes place already within a system" (202). This system provides the boundaries within which we ask questions, carry out investigations, and make judgments. The framework-principles are necessary in carrying out a search for evidence, in confirmation and disconfirmation, and in justification. But justification must come to an end, and at some point we must believe and act without justification. That point comes when in pushing for justification we arrive at the framework-propositions of the system. They are the propositions which are assumed, usually unconsciously, in testing and in justification but are not themselves put to the test or justified. Indeed, Malcolm stresses, they not only are not, they cannot be so tested. We have no realistic understanding of what it could even mean to justify a framework-belief to say nothing of a whole system of such beliefs.

That there must be such an end to testing and justification is not the result of human fallibility or weakness but is, on Malcolm's understanding, the conceptual requirement "that our inquiries and proofs stay within boundaries" (203). Malcolm and Wittgenstein use the example of calculation to illustrate this claim. We will, depending on our mathematical proficiency, have to check different calculations, but certain of them, e.g., $5 \times 5 = 25$, will be regarded as certain by all adults who know how to calculate with any proficiency at all. Moreover, if we try to ask for a justification of the certainty of all our calculations, we will, if we think this through, have to recognize that at some point we will have to be finished with justification and all we can do is point out that this is just how we do calculate. At some point a justification of calculation, or for that matter anything else, must just come to an end. Wittgenstein remarks that we would in the end, faced with the persistent philosophical critic who supposed that *all* the calculations we make are uncertain and who would rely on none of them, be reduced to replying that this is not how we play the language game of mathematics and to appealing to the fact that this language game is played. This sceptic says that mistakes are always possible and that consequently he will not rely on *any* calculation. We can respond that such a man is crazy but we can hardly show that he is in error. We seem at least to be reduced to talking about different reactions and different attitudes. "We," as Wittgenstein puts it, "rely on calculations, he doesn't; we are sure, he isn't."[4] We can, of course, use words like "crazy" or "irrational" here but—or so Wittgenstein and Malcolm believe—we seem to have no grounds to justify one reaction rather than another and we seem to have no way of showing one such way of reacting and believing to be more reasonable than another. Justification, the establishing what is the more reasonable or believable, has come to an end. We are caught in a cultural and conceptual web where we, if we are not to fall into illusion, must come to realize that there is no "transcendental frame" we can get back to which will show us what is the right way to view things, which framework-beliefs or principles are true or probably true. It is indeed not even clear that the concepts true or false have a genuine application here. To be realistic we must simply come to recognize that "we grow into a framework" which we do not question but, trusting it, we reason and act in accordance with it. Whatever real doubts are raised, whatever claims are made, and whatever conclusions are drawn, they are drawn within its confines. We have—and can have—no Archimedean point in accordance with which we could justify such framework-propositions or assess them or establish their reasonableness. But it is likewise true that there is no such vantage point in accordance with which acceptance of these framework-propositions, where they are placed in their proper setting, can be shown to be unreasonable. This system of framework-propositions forms the way we think and act and what we take to be justified or unjustified, reasonable or unreasonable. It is our given and no sense can be given to "getting back of it" and somehow showing it is worthy or not worthy of acceptance. These framework-propositions are central segments of our common ways of thinking and speaking in the human situation in which we find ourselves. And in our socialization, these common ways of thinking and acting are pressed upon us in such a way that *we* have no alternative to them. Moreover, even if we could come to learn to play different language games and become socialized in very different but, in some other context, culturally common ways of speaking and acting, we would still have just learned these different and often incommensurable ways of reacting. We would not have acquired a more reasonable or even a less reasonable way of acting and viewing our lives. We would have moved from one groundless system of beliefs to another groundless system of beliefs. But there is nothing wrong with—

nothing unreasonable about—these systems of belief for all of that. The very notion of one being grounded in reason and another not, or one being more reasonable or better justified than another, is utterly without application.

II

Colin Lyas, in a response to Malcolm's "The Groundlessness of Religious Belief," challenges both Malcolm's characterization of groundlessness and what he says concerning the groundlessness of *religious* belief.[5]

Malcolm, Lyas points out, does not clearly distinguish between those beliefs (including religious beliefs) for which grounds are *not sought* and those beliefs for which grounds *could not be intelligibly sought*.[6] Considering the latter putative class, are there really any beliefs which could be *reasonably* held, or at least not unreasonably held, which are not held for a reason and for which it is unreasonable, perhaps even senseless, to look for grounds? Is that class empty and, indeed, perhaps necessarily empty? Are there in this sense groundless beliefs that a reasonable person still might have? Malcolm believes, faithfully following his master, that there are and that these very beliefs are essential for our lives as human beings.

We can best proceed here indirectly and back step a bit. Lyas points out that it is incontrovertible that there are many beliefs that people have for which they do not *in fact seek* grounds. If we ask, "Is it *ever* reasonable for them to have such beliefs and act on such beliefs?" the answer clearly should be, "Yes, it is," for there are circumstances where the need to act with dispatch or the comparative unimportance of the matter and the effort involved to sort it out make it reasonable to accept *de facto* groundless beliefs for which in other circumstances grounds could reasonably be sought. In such circumstances we can reasonably accept *de facto* groundless beliefs.

It does not, however, follow that any of these beliefs, which can be reasonably believed though they are not believed for a reason, are also groundless beliefs in the further sense that they are beliefs for which it would not make sense to seek grounds, or that they are beliefs for which grounds could not be reasonably sought. For the type of beliefs discussed in the previous paragraph where we do not in fact seek grounds for them, we are being reasonable under the circumstances in not seeking grounds for them, but it is also true, at least for some of them, that these are beliefs for which grounds could be reasonably sought. That is to say, there is for some of them at least no conceptual ban on seeking grounds or overwhelming empirical difficulties involved in such an enterprise, and it is further *not* true that we have no idea at all of what a justification would look like here. But are there any beliefs, which we might reasonably hold, where there is a conceptual ban on justifying them: where the very idea of justifying them makes no sense or is ruled out a priori?

Given this disambiguation of "groundless belief," we should realize that our central question should be whether there are any groundless *reasonable* beliefs in this latter sense or senses. (Remember everything we reasonably believe we do not believe for a reason.) Most crucially, are there any beliefs which we should hold or which are reasonable to hold for which grounds could not be sought, i.e., it would be a mistake (some kind of conceptual blunder) to seek grounds for them?

In the initial statement of his argument (the statement Lyas was responding to), Malcolm was indeed not sufficiently clear about the kind of groundlessness he was talking about, but a sympathetic reading of his text, with a background reading of *On Certainty*, should, I believe, lead us to believe that it is this latter type of groundlessness that he principally had in mind. Indeed, in his subsequent reformulations Malcolm makes that quite clear. But, even in his initial general formulation of his case, Malcolm remarks, "grounds come to an end. Answers to How-do-we-know? questions come to an end. We *must* speak, act, live without evidence" (208).[7] Malcolm, as we have seen, like Wittgenstein and Winch, speaks of justification as properly taking place only *within* a domain of discourse, *within* a form of life, a framework or system.[8] But, they claim no justification can possibly be given of a form of life, language game, framework-belief, framework or system itself. One cannot properly apply talk of justifying or failing to justify such concepts when employed in framework-propositions and in such contexts. Yet Malcolm also stresses that the groundlessness of forms of life and language games is not the same as the groundlessness of an arbitrary opinion. It is the groundlessness of something to which the very concept of a ground is inapplicable. Talk of justification or the giving or failing to give grounds, he argues, makes no sense here.

Malcolm, Winch, and Wittgenstein would say, I suspect, of such framework-propositions, of the beliefs they express, and of forms of life as well, that they *cannot conceivably have grounds*. To look for a ground for them is to show that one does not understand them. But then should we not say that it is as misleading to say they are groundless as to say they are grounded? If they could not *conceivably* have a ground, any more than heat can have a colour, then what is the point or even the sense of calling them groundless?

The point, it can in turn be replied, is to call our attention to the fact that they are still centrally embedded beliefs which guide and constrain our thought and action and which are themselves *without grounds, without justification*, and indeed without even the *possibility* of a justification or a grounding. But so what, if it really is the case that the search for grounds here makes no more sense than does the search for the colour of heat? In that sense they are very unlike the plainly groundless and arbitrary belief that fluoridated water will poison you.

III

Whatever we say here, our central problem still remains whether there are any beliefs that it is reasonable to hold are of a type of which it can be correctly said that the search for grounds for them is senseless? Are there actually beliefs of such a type or could there even be beliefs of such a type, such that if someone were to look for grounds for them, we would be in a position correctly to say that that person had not understood what was involved in having that sort of belief?

If I have understood Malcolm correctly, he is claiming that it is a mistake—a conceptual mistake—to look for justification of or a ground for framework-principles of the type I listed in the first section. At least this is the most sympathetic reading of Malcolm's account, and, assuming it is correct, I want to query this claim of Malcolm's.

I think that we could usefully start this inquiry by emphasizing a distinction utilized by Lyas in his criticism of Malcolm's account. Malcolm, Lyas claims, fails to distinguish, where it would be important for him to make such a distinction, between two kinds of framework-principles: *constitutive* framework-principles and *regulative* framework-principles. Only the former, Lyas maintains, are necessarily groundless in the way Malcolm and Wittgenstein maintain framework-principles are groundless. And it is only these which can be reasonably accepted as principles concerning which the very idea of seeking a ground for them rests on a mistake. Lyas illustrates his distinction from science, but (or so it seems to me, but not to Malcolm) he could readily have done so from religion, morality, or any domain of discourse. Constitutive framework-principles are principles which are constitutive of a certain procedure essential for a given activity. The examples from science given by Lyas are: "It is wrong to ignore the result of a properly conducted experiment" and "If there is a contradiction in a scientific theory it is worthless." Lyas remarks that there must be such a body of constitutive principles if there is to be such a thing as science.[9] If we take together the various constitutive principles that there are, they jointly spell out for us what it is to engage in science. They are constitutive for they together constitute scientific procedures without which there would be no such thing as science. Lyas would have us believe that while they are groundless or unjustifiable, they are not for all of that beliefs which are not typically reasonably held. They are, in contrast to *regulative* framework-principles, principles of a formal sort which tell us how the world is to be approached, if it is to be approached scientifically. They are, Lyas contends, constitutive principles of science because without them there is nothing resembling what we now know as science.[10] They are principles which mesh well with Wittgenstein's and Malcolm's conception of justification and with foundationless but still reasonably held beliefs. They in effect limit what could count as justification in a given domain, and without them there could be no justification. They are our yardstick without which there would be no measuring—no justification—in this domain, but as the standard in that domain they themselves cannot be justified.

Regulative framework-principles by contrast are principles which are accepted in the various domains of discourse because they regulate in an overall way the distinctive activities of that discourse. Examples of principles so regulating scientific discourse are "Nature is continuous" and "Things do not just vanish without cause." But, Lyas argues, these regulative principles, unlike constitutive principles of science, are not constitutive of science or anything else but are instead nonformal principles over which questions concerning their justifiability do, or at least can, arise and in the fire of such questioning such principles sometimes do get abandoned. Consider the framework-beliefs which at least some scientists have held but which in the course of scientific change have come to be challenged: "The speed of light cannot be exceeded" or "Events cannot move backwards in time." I am not claiming these challenges have been successful, but they have on some occasions been coherently and carefully made. But if this can be so for such general claims which regulate certain areas of science, how can we be so confident that it is impossible to question the claim that nature is continuous or that things do not just vanish without cause? Some scientists—we should not forget—do talk of the continuous creation of matter.

Malcolm and Wittgenstein to the contrary notwithstanding, such basic regulative framework-beliefs do seem to be beliefs that can be responsibly questioned and challenged. (In his reply to Lyas, Malcolm does not even take up these at least seemingly persuasive objections.) Against Malcolm, Lyas argues that the beliefs which Malcolm claims to be groundless, yet still reasonably held beliefs concerning which it makes no sense to look for a justification, are in reality not such beliefs, for they are not constitutive framework-beliefs but are regulative framework-beliefs whose justifiability can be challenged. Changes in such framework-beliefs do not need to occur groundlessly. Rather they are, at least sometimes, made for a reason. Scientists, using the constitutive procedures of rational empirical inquiry, can sometimes justify the adoption of certain regulative principles. For constitutive principles no question of their justification or lack thereof can even arise but still we can and do use these principles in justifying regulative principles.

It might in turn be responded that something like this rests on the myth of the framework. In not taking a critical attitude toward both constitutive and regulative principles, we are blocking inquiry. We should beware of what is, in effect, by conceptual fiat a breaking off of question-asking in problematical realms because it is often or perhaps even typically the case that in such contexts the word "why?" or its cognates gets used once too often and leads us to ask "questions" that cannot even in principle be answered. A considerable intolerance of "nonsense" may lead to a breaking off of questioning just where it might be deeply enlightening to question. Yet, as in traditional metaphysical contexts, there are alleged questions which are plainly not—*when taken at face value*—genuine questions. Consider "Is time real?", "Are physical objects real?", "Are memory beliefs ever reliable?", or "Are calculations ever certain?" Either, sensibly enough, such alleged questions are asking for an elucidation of a concept or they are quite senseless. Any proof that time is unreal would be less certain than I am certain that I drank my coffee after I poured it in the cup and I further am more certain that $2 + 2 = 4$ than I am of the soundness of any argument that no calculations are ever quite certain. But it is far from clear that to query all constitutive principles, let alone all regulative framework-principles, is so obviously to ask senseless questions. Indeed, something must stand still and be used as our measure while doing the questioning, but from that it does not follow that there are any propositions or set of propositions that we cannot query. What follows is that we cannot—logically cannot—question them *all at once*. But this does nothing to show that there are any self-certifying ones we cannot coherently query, or that there are any principles which are immune to any sort of justificatory question.

Perhaps the reliance on groundless framework-principles—particularly of the regulative sort—as principles capturing beliefs which are beyond question or reasonable doubt, and yet are principles which are reasonably held, reflects a new kind of fideism, a new attempt to avoid facing the consequences of a thoroughgoing fallibilistic view of the world. It is not enough to say, as Malcolm does at one point, that we "grow into a framework; we don't question it" (203). We plainly could grow into a framework and still subsequently come to question it. Indeed, it may very well be the case that for any framework we grow into we should come to question it. That is what it is to come to have a critical attitude, and a failure to do so might very well signify a diminishment of our rationality. In fact, doing things like that, i.e., taking such a critical stance, is precisely what critical, rational people do.

There is plainly something that is right in this Pragmatist-Popperian response. This is what rational people do at least in civilizations such as our own and a failure to do so is a diminishment of our rationality. But, without taking any of this back, we should also realize that there is something remarkably superficial in that response as well. Is it not plainly the case, as Malcolm and Wittgenstein stress, that we can respond in such a critical way to framework-beliefs only in specific and special situations? Is it not crazy to think we could do this generally? Without at a given time some beliefs holding fast, there can be no systematic questioning of whole systems of framework-beliefs. Such a Cartesianism is simply an impossibility. With many such beliefs holding fast, we could perhaps critically assess some specific framework-beliefs—particularly if they are regulative-beliefs— when there is some specific reason to query them. But this could be done only if there were a myriad of matter-of-course framework-beliefs which we do not question but simply use—matter-of-factly assume—in such questioning. Without some such beliefs standing pat there could be neither doubt nor questioning. Moreover, framework-beliefs, constitutive and regulative, define a system, and, as Malcolm puts it, "a 'system' provides the boundaries within which we ask questions, carry out investigations and make judgments" (202). Only in operating within such a system do we understand what it is to justify something, to query it, to make an investigation, to make judgments, to carry out investigations. We need this (in large measure) culturally defined and culturally and historically variable Archimedean point to carry out any such inquiries. Without it operating, without its utilization, we simply do not understand what we are to do to put the varied claims made in the system to a test or to back them up with evidence or in any way to assess them.

To do this, it could in turn be responded, not only involves the myth of the framework, it involves the myth of the whole and the myth of the seamless web as well. Surely we cannot reject or critically assess all these framework-propositions at once, but we can, at least in principle, reject any one of them and there are none that cannot *seriatim* be subject to critical inspection.

We cannot, à la Descartes or Husserl, free ourselves from all perspectives or all frameworks in assessing beliefs. We need somewhere to stand; and, if we are to do any assessing, we must have some criteria of assessment, but, to make a variation on a previous argument, it does not follow from this that there is some privileged framework that cannot be assessed in terms of some other framework. It does not follow from the fact that some framework must be in place for there to be any reasoning or assessment at all, that, while within the framework of each system there is criticism, explanation, and justification, we cannot reasonably expect that there could be some sort of justification, at least in the form of pragmatic vindication, of the framework-propositions of the system. And it plainly does not follow, from any of the considerations set out by Malcolm or Wittgenstein, that there is any framework-proposition that is immune, at least in principle, to such critical assessments. Wittgensteinians such as Malcolm are making a dogmatic, groundless claim—a claim that is hardly a framework-belief in any established language game—when they assert, as Malcolm actually does, that "within a language game there is justification and lack of justification, evidence and proof, mistakes and groundless opinion" but that "one cannot properly apply these terms to the language game itself" (208).

IV

There is a twisted skein of argument here where positions on all sides are problematical. I think we can safely say that it is an open question whether regulative framework-principles and beliefs are justifiable. We are on somewhat more contestable ground only if we say that there are no good a priori reasons for denying that they cannot be justified. Yet, on the Wittgensteinian side, it is also correct to observe that it is very easy, while doing philosophy, to ask the question "Why?" once too often. Moreover, it is reasonable to maintain that there are framework-beliefs which underlie all our thinking even though we do not have any clear criteria for determining exactly when we have and when we do not have a framework-belief. Finally, Wittgensteinians can point out that it is difficult to see what the justification of at least certain very fundamental framework-beliefs or principles could come to. We have no idea what it would be like to do it or what would count as success.

Still, the claim that we have shown that there can be no justification here looks very much like a Wittgensteinian dogma. Yet, to utter Waismann's lament, cannot philosophers learn from experience? Is it not a fact that there just are these diverse, historically and culturally contingent incommensurable frameworks? We grow up in one or another of these frameworks and we may indeed use the beliefs and principles of one framework to criticize another framework or particular beliefs within frameworks other than our own, though the exact relevance or even the legitimacy of such an activity remains in doubt. However, we should not forget that the fact that we have been socialized into a particular cultural pattern (social structure) does not establish, or even indirectly reveal, any superior rationality on our part. We just learn a particular framework *ambulando*. We, that is, grow into and learn it as we do our mother tongue and then we, for the most part at least, act in accordance with it and can scarcely imagine anything else. Even the direction of revolt—if we revolt—is determined or at least strongly conditioned by this system. Moreover, there is no reasonable or fully coherent alternative to living in accordance with such culturally determinate forms of life. Can we possibly, except perhaps at a very few checkpoints, step out of our language, culture, history, and our determinate historical situation? It looks very much as if Hegel was right in denying that we can.

Perhaps this Wittgensteinian sort of thing, so pushed by Malcolm, Winch, Dilman, and Phillips, is in reality a subtle form of romanticism reacting—overreacting—against the ethnocentric elements of the Enlightenment. An underlying message of such a conception is tolerantly to give to understand that all forms of life—including, of course, all framework-principles of such forms of life—are, as far as we can possibly ascertain, both equally reasonable and equally unreasonable. Indeed such notions hardly apply to them. There just are these incommensurable framework-beliefs in incommensurable belief systems. Between them no relevant comparison or assessment can be made. But is this not—or is it—in turn to erect, as Robin Horton believes, a counter-myth to counter certain mythical beliefs of the Enlightenment?[11]

NOTES

1.   Norman Malcolm's first version of "The Groundlessness of Belief" was in *Reason and Religion*, ed. Stuart C. Brown (Ithaca, NY: Cornell University Press, 1977), where it was also criticized by Colin Lyas and Basil Mitchell, followed by a brief response from Malcolm. In his *Thought and Knowledge* (Ithaca, NY: Cornell University Press, 1977), Malcolm has given us a somewhat expanded and clarified account. I shall cite that text and all page references to that text will be given in my text.

2.   Ludwig Wittgenstein, *On Certainty* (Oxford: Basil Blackwell, 1969) paragraph 559.

3.   *Ibid*. paragraph 167. Quoted by Malcolm, *Thought and Knowledge* 202.

4.   *Ibid*. paragraph 217.

5.   Colin Lyas, "The Groundlessness of Religious Belief," *Reason and Religion*, ed. Stuart C. Brown (Ithaca, NY: Cornell University Press, 1977) 158-80.

6.   This point is to a degree clarified in Malcolm's reworking of his essay in *Thought and Knowledge*. I have incorporated those clarifications into my discussion in the text.

7.   This, of course, is also a characteristic point of Wittgenstein's.

8.   Peter Winch, "Understanding Primitive Society," *Rationality*, ed. B.R. Wilson (Oxford: 1970).

9.   Colin Lyas, *op. cit*.

10.   Reflection on the work of Paul Feyerabend may engender the worry that this may be a disguised bit of essentialist mythology.

11.   Robin Horton, "Science and Traditional African Thought," *Rationality*, ed. B.R. Wilson (Oxford: 1970).

CHAPTER 10

Wisdom and Dilman on the Reality of God*

I

REACTING AGAINST PHILOSOPHERS SUCH AS Braithwaite, Hare and Van Buren, caught in what not a few would believe to be an essentially positivist rut, John Wisdom and Ilham Dilman forcefully argue that there is more to religion than commitment to a way of life and yet they both are, like Braithwaite and Hare, adamant in maintaining that believers and non-believers need not differ, and indeed will not differ, when they are informed, reflective and philosophically sophisticated, "in what they expect by way of a life after death" and, more importantly still, they will not differ in what "they infer about what lies beyond the reach of the senses" (194).[1] Moreover, they agree that not only can we not make any valid inferences about what lies beyond any possible reach of the senses, we cannot directly know—encounter, become acquainted with—such a reality either.

Wisdom holds, as unequivocally as he ever holds anything, that religious beliefs speak of and indeed can only speak about the world we know by means of the senses. This leads Wisdom to argue that believers should no longer construe God as a transcendent reality. Dilman, by contrast, thinks that Wisdom has been led into error here and that he is in effect confusing *metaphysical* and *religious* transcendence, importing an incoherent metaphysical conception of transcendence into the language of faith.[2]

Dilman makes a rather perplexing claim that we should examine. If we play, he tells us, Christian or Jewish language-games, if we are reasoning and acting in accordance with those modes of discourse with their distinctive framework-beliefs, we must simply take as *given*, as not to be challenged by philosophy, the "Christian idea of God as a *transcendent* being, beyond time and our senses" with a "Kingdom outside the world" (499). But we need to be careful here for we should not take this as committing us to

*First published in *Religious Studies* 16 (1980).

an epistemological and presumably a metaphysical theory of any kind at all (499). In accepting such notions—as all Christian and Jewish believers must—we are not accepting a *philosophical* account of any sort, including any account of a theory "about what is meant by 'God' in the scriptures . . ." (499). But how then are we to take such remarks about transcendence? Dilman says, surprisingly, and to me at least remarkably, that it is "a direct statement about the kind of God Christians worship" (499). And then, making perfectly apparent his Wittgensteinian, neutralist and second-order conception of philosophical activity, he remarks that the philosophic task, given such a direct statement about the kind of God Christians worship, cannot be to criticize this concept, but one to "elucidate its logic".[3] This means giving a perspicuous representation of the "Christian idea of God as a transcendent being, beyond time and our senses", "with a Kingdom outside the world". But—and this is the striking thing which makes Dilman's account very different from the usual thing—this does not mean we must construe God's transcendence on some model of an invisible Gardener (499).[4] It does not mean that we have to invoke any distinctive metaphysical doctrines at all.

I am not about to accept such meta-philosophical, meta-theological restrictions on what can constitute proper philosophical activity and on what our squarification base in philosophy should be. But I do not wish to challenge this here, at least not immediately and directly. Instead I will continue for the sake of the discussion to make the sort of assumptions that are being made by Dilman about the nature of philosophy and, recognizing that they are both not uncontroversial and not unusual, go on to see, particularly given his way of doing philosophy, what kind of elucidation of God's transcendence Dilman can give us and to ask of it whether it matches our pre-analytic understanding of that mysterious God Christians, Jews and Muslims worship and whether it squares with our well-considered convictions as informed and reflective human beings.

II

One of the first things we need to do, Dilman argues, is to break the spell of a philosopher's way of regarding such phrases "beyond our senses", "transcendent", "timeless", "outside this world" and the like. We are accustomed to seeing them against the backdrop of metaphysical philosophies and what Axel Hägerström called metaphysical religiosity.[5] These notions, Dilman claims, have been thoroughly and trenchantly exposed and are indeed incoherent conceptions not tied into any genuine language-games. But this should not at all intimidate the philosopher of religion trying to make sense out of Christian and Jewish religious discourses. For there are *religious*, specifically Christian and Jewish, construals of these notions, which are quite distinct from such metaphysical construals. Moreover, they do not suffer from the defects of these metaphysical conceptions. That sometimes philosophers, including Christian and Jewish philosophers, mix them up only attests to the fact that philosophical mistakes are made, including often deep meta-philosophical mistakes about how best to proceed.

Dilman tells us that when the Christian God is described as being "beyond our senses" it is "the world of the senses" that is in question. In religious discourse "the world of the senses" is not used to contrast with "the world of intelligible objects"; rather what is being talked about is a way of living and conceiving of one's life "in which we seek the satisfaction of sensual pleasures, bodily appetites and their derivatives—the desire for riches, power and fame" (501). A person taken up in such a mode of life is a person whose concern for these pleasures and satisfactions overshadows all his other concerns (501). In saying God is "beyond our senses" one is saying that God will not be found in such a world, that a person with such a conception of life, living in such a world, can never find God. The thing to see is that if a genuine knight of faith were to say "that God is not visible to the senses, he would not be making the epistemological point that you cannot see God through a telescope, but a different conceptual point, namely that God does not reveal himself to one who is immersed in a life of the senses" (501). If one is claimed by the flesh, one necessarily turns away from God and cannot respond to the events in one's life from the perspective of the love of God. Here we can see that we have a conceptualization of the transcendence of God that in no way commits one to the metaphysical conception of transcendence that Wisdom rightly criticizes (506).

There is no explaining what in genuinely religious terms it means to believe in a transcendent God without bringing in such distinctive *religious* conceptions. It is a central aspect of Wisdom's work—an aspect which Dilman accepts as the correct way to view the matter—that God is so conceived that he is not conceived of as "an object among or beyond the objects we know . . ." (519). That point is a conceptual point, but to deny that God is either an object or a "super-object"—a "supernatural something"—is not, Dilman contends, to suggest "that God is a myth or that he does not exist" (514). But it does imply a rather more subtle point than is in the minds of many people about what it does mean and does not mean to believe in God or to affirm his existence (519). To come to understand what it means to believe in God, it is central to come to understand what it means to worship, thank, fear or love God (519).

III

Let us start by asking what it is on Dilman's account to love God and to be thankful to God for one's existence. A believer who gradually becomes "immersed in the world of the senses," i.e., taken up in "the satisfaction of sensual pleasures, bodily appetites and their derivatives—the desire for riches, power and fame," is a person who has been "claimed by the flesh" and cannot love God or have a sense of what Dilman calls religious transcendence (506).[6] Nor is it the case that God could reveal himself to a person as long as that person remained in such a state (501). If "these concerns for these pleasures and satisfactions overshadow all other concerns," if these claims have such a settled hold on him, then "he can no longer look at things and respond to them from the perspective of the love of God" (501). Dilman goes on to remark that this "antithesis is bound up with what it *means* to believe in a transcendent God; you cannot explain what kind of God Christians believe in without bringing in such matters" (501). It is in this sense that the remark that God is not visible to the senses makes a conceptual point (501). We need to recognize that "God is transcendent in the sense that turning toward him means 'renouncing the amenities of the world' " (502). Such a person, if he also comes to love the afflicted for themselves alone, thereby loves God. That is what it is to love God and to have an understanding of God's transcendence. Yet such a person might very well, and with perfect consistency, reject, as either nonsense or false, any metaphysical claim that tries to make "God" refer to a being, to being or to an entity that exists independently of the universe and which is an entity or a being or being of a radically different kind than any of the entities or beings in the universe. Yet such a believer, Dilman contends, continues to believe in God's transcendence, in the *religious* sense just specified, while rejecting any belief in the reality of a *metaphysically* transcendent being. Indeed he would typically regard such a conception as incoherent.

We come to understand what God is and what his transcendence is by coming to understand what love is. We understand the latter by coming to understand selflessness. The sort of selflessness that Dilman has in mind is the way in which the Good Samaritan was selfless in attending to the dying stranger by the roadside. In an important way, this is to deny oneself without any silliness such as regarding the body as evil or renouncing simple pleasures. "A selfless person", Dilman remarks, "is not one who is incapable of passion, one who finds no joy in life. He is one whose pleasures are not self-centered, not of the kind in which the 'ego thrives' " (514). If one is selfless, one cares for others and for ideals such as justice and human freedom and equality in a way that is not measured by their utility to the person doing the caring or of any projections about how things will turn out. "Whether or not one serves justice does not depend on the outcome of one's actions; it depends on one's attitude of will" (505). His very love of justice is its own reward. What gives him heart to struggle for the achievement of justice is not, in any important way, what may lie in his own future but simply that justice may be achieved and a human flourishing obtain. To be so unequivocally committed is to "die to the world", "to transcend the world", "to transcend the sense", "to not be held captive by worldliness" and this is what it is for "the kingdom of God to be within one". This is what it is to love God and to believe in a transcendent God, a God transcendent to the world. To have such an attitude to life is to transcend the world. To find God "is to accept and love everything that happens, recognizing that there is no reason why it

should be so and not otherwise" (503). To be thankful to God for one's
existence is to accept and indeed to joyfully accept one's life as a life in
which one gives one's self to justice without reservation and in which one
does not put considerations regarding one's future before one's concern
for justice (505). In that perfectly metaphysically unproblematic way one
dies to the world.

IV

        Dilman has contended, not implausibly, that what
it means to believe in God is shown in what it means to love God and
to be thankful to God. We have, in attempting to follow out Dilman's reasoning here, shown something of what, on Dilman's account, it is to love God
and be thankful to him and in that way we have come to have some understanding of what it is, on his account, for a believer to believe in God and
to believe in his transcendence. It is important to recognize that this account
is *Metaphysik-frei* and that to believe in a transcendent God in Dilman's
distinctive sense in no way commits the believer to an epistemological or
metaphysical theory. It is a characteristic philosophical mistake, a mistake
that philosophical therapy should seek to cure, to try to account for God's
transcendence by invoking a metaphysical and epistemological theory in
which "the antithesis between what belongs to this world and what is supernatural" is turned into "a contrast between what is here and what lies
elsewhere, beneath, behind or beyond space, or into a contrast between
what is now and what is to come later" (503). With such a philosophical
move, Dilman contends, as Wittgensteinian fideists generally do, "one will
either deny God's transcendence or transform it into something logically
incoherent" (503).[7] God is transcendent but, as we have seen, God is not
to be construed as a being beyond the objects with which we are familiarly
acquainted (519). To have a genuine sense of transcendence (this religious
transcendence) is to come to understand and to take to heart the incontrovertible fact that this universe—our world—"is absolutely devoid of finality,"
while at the same time feeling thankful for this world and feeling a sense
of gratitude for one's life and for the world, no matter what one's condition
or what happens. One feels, if one has this religious sense of transcendence,
gratitude for the world as one feels gratitude for beauty. Moreover, the
gratitude the believer feels and the beauty the believer sees in the world
is inseparable from his sense of the contingency of life (578). The love
and gratitude that emerges at such an appreciation must therefore be
"unconditional or invulnerable to what is so", since it is inseparable from
an awareness of the contingency of life and the utter lack of finality in
the universe.

V

Accounts such as Dilman's have provoked very different reactions. (It should be remembered that Dilman's account is perhaps in a certain way the most developed statement of a view that is also held by Rush Rhees, Peter Winch and D.Z. Phillips and has, as well, a certain resemblance to Paul Holmer's and Norman Malcolm's account of religion.)[8] Such accounts seem to not a few people to be deep and probing, reflecting a genuine understanding of what religion is; to others, however, they seem outrageous accounts which refuse to face fundamental problems about belief in God and which replace genuine philosophical analysis with obscurantist literary schmaltz. I have at different times ambivalently had both reactions. My considered convictions now are that such accounts—and Dilman's in particular—have some deep things to say that philosophers and theologians tend to ignore. In trying to understand what it is to believe in God and what it is to be religious, it is important to have these conceptions clearly before us. But I also believe that in important ways Dilman, like Phillips and Winch, is evasive and in effect obscurantist about how we are to understand the concept of God and about *what* it is we are talking about in speaking of God. He never squarely faces the problem of reference but simply drops hints here and there about what he wouldn't say and makes some elusive remarks about what he would say. I shall try to show what it is of importance that he leaves out of consideration.

Dilman is prepared to accept Wisdom's critique—in reality here very much like a positivist critique—of metaphysical conceptions of transcendence: a critique which seems to exhibit their incoherence in a way not dissimilar to the way in which Wisdom would maintain that Locke's idea of a substratum was incoherent. Dilman accepts this account but is concerned to show that he can accept it without "denying the intelligibility of God's transcendence" (498-9). I shall in turn be concerned to argue that he has not been able to give a reading to God's transcendence which squares with a reflective sense of the core commitments of Christianity and Judaism. It leaves out certain things which are essential to those faiths and does not enable us to sort out what is crucially different between believers and non-believers even when our reference class includes philosophically and scientifically sophisticated people.

Dilman stresses that crucial differences between the believer and non-believer come not only in how they live their lives and face death but also in how they see life as a whole (482). These crucial differences, he believes, are not what on a naïve view they might be taken to be, for these crucial differences remain even when "there is no difference between them in what they expect by way of a life after death and no difference in what they infer about what lies beyond the reach of the senses" (494). But what then are the crucial differences and what, in particular, are the crucial differences not alluded to above? It sounds like Dilman is claiming that the religious believer has beliefs which are "concept forming" while the non-believer does not. Believers, Dilman seems at least to be saying, have beliefs which provide them "with a perspective on life, a fixed framework for their judgments and decisions," while non-believers neither do nor can have such conceptions (494). But surely that, while being questionable in its own right, only gives us what are plausibly necessary conditions for religious belief; it does not provide us with both *necessary* and *sufficient* conditions which would enable us to sort out what marks the crucial differences between believers and non-believers. Certainly various varieties of secular humanists, including Marxist humanists, could have distinctive concept forming beliefs. Like the believer they use them in forming a perspective on life as a whole and in developing a fixed framework for their judgments and decisions. *Perhaps* this makes it true that they have a systematic ideology; but that does not add up to their having a religion; it certainly does not entail that they believe in God. A thorough-going atheist or agnostic could, and typically would, have a perspective on life as a whole with distinctive concept forming beliefs and a fixed (relatively fixed) framework for his judgments and decisions. But this does not convert him into a believer in God.

So what then are the crucial differences between the believer and the non-believer and, most particularly, between the Jew or Christian, on the one hand, and the atheist or agnostic, on the other? It is, Dilman to the contrary notwithstanding, not only religious beliefs which provide or are a measure, means of assessment or criterion, but also the fundamental beliefs of any systematic view of the world such as Marxism, Freudianism or secular humanism (where that differs from Marxism) (485-94). They too can involve a "commitment of the will" and thereby what Dilman calls a "dimension of the personal".

The answer that seems most naturally to insinuate itself at this point as constituting the crucial difference between, say, a Christian and an atheist is that the Christian believes in God and the atheist rejects such a belief. The difference here could (*but need not*) encompass all the differences in affective disposition and moral orientation that Dilman draws to our attention while still essentially involving a difference in intellectual orientation about what kinds of being or entities there are or can be. It is such a difference in intellectual orientation that is crucial, for believers and non-believers very well could have the same moral orientation and affective dispositions coupled with very different intellectual orientations.

Dilman wants to resist this but has he any other way of setting out how we should distinguish between believers and non-believers? I think he believes he has in the way he sets out in detail the moral orientation of a believer who has overcome the "domination of the world" and a non-believer who is caught up in things worldly. But this distinction does not, as important as it is for characterizing an essential difference between people with importantly different moral orientations, capture what crucially distinguishes believers from non-believers, unless we want, by stipulative re-definition, to convert certain atheists and sceptics (Einstein, Russell, Freud, Horkheimer and Adorno for example) into believers. To do this surely would constitute a tinkering with our language-games in a way that a Wittgensteinian could hardly approve. There are through and through atheists who have just that life-orientation that Dilman describes as the heart of what it is to believe in God and to commit your life to God.

Traditionally it has been responded that, Dilman's considerations aside, there still remains an essential difference, for, in addition to having that moral orientation to the world and to life, the believer actually believes that there is a God, that God actually exists. Dilman is in effect obscurantist here. Often he sounds like an atheist or like a "Godless Christian", such as Braithwaite, Hare or Van Buren.[9] It seems to be the case that he is treating God as essentially a moral category, rejecting all distinctive Christian cosmological conceptions as myths, generated by bad philosophical conceptions. Yet he also regards these "Godless Christians" as reductionists and uses, without much in the way of elucidation or demythologizing analysis, God-talk in such a way that it certainly looks as if he is utilizing the full-blown Jewish and Christian conceptions with their embarrassing and indeed very problematic cosmology. That, at least, is the way such talk would naturally be taken. Yet Dilman talks as if he wants to excise these conceptions as bits of bad philosophy that have intruded into religious discourse, but he also repeatedly uses terms which appear at least to carry that traditional sense in contexts which seem at least to call for that troublesome reading. But he does not offer an alternative analysis of the concept of God that at all faces, even to attempt to neatly dispose of them, referential problems. He sometimes reasons as if he had de-mythologized God-talk in a way not radically different from Braithwaite and at other times he uses such talk in a way that seems at least to require the traditional reading of the terms—a reading that he officially rejects. Unfortunately, he does little to show us a way out of the dark woods, for he offers little in the way of an alternative analysis of the concept of God.

VI

I should give the above general criticism flesh. Consider the following religious utterances, all of which either are or are very like utterances liberally used by Dilman in his articles. My problem with them is that while we—as much as we ever have—have some idea what to do with them when construed according to the traditional Judeo-Christian cosmological picture, we are quite at sea about knowing how to take them when to believe in God comes to having and taking to heart a perspective on life as a whole and not at all a conceiving of the object of our belief as an entity or being "among or beyond the objects we know" (509). God remains characterized by Dilman as a "He" and that he is taken to exist but, where belief in God comes just to having an orientation toward and a perspective on life, it is not clear what such talk can mean where such personal pronouns are also used. We have the following utterances all at least apparently tied to such a problematic.

1. God exacts from those who love him to consent to be nothing.

2. A person's life may be touched by God in such a way that it shatters her and she is born to a new life.

3. God is to be worshipped.

4. One can find God only in a life of inwardness.

5. To keep one's inwardness one must subject one's life to God.

6. We give thanks to God no matter what.

7. Some people in their personal lives are turned towards God and some are turned away from God.

He also accepts, as standard remarks of theology which philosophy (on his view) cannot criticize but can only elucidate, the following:

8. God is a person.

9. God is a transcendent being.

10. God is timeless.

11. God is not visible to the senses.

All of these readily warm to the traditional cosmological readings, but it is not clear how they are to be taken on Dilman's account, if they are to be distinct from something which is as available both to the atheist and the Christian as something they all could, and perhaps would, accept as true. He must preserve some distinction here if his account is to be non-reductionistic.

To see how this is so let us concentrate first on the first batch of sentences (1-7). 1 would presumably be paraphrased roughly in something like the following way:

1^1. To take a religious perspective one must attain a detachment from self-interested and self-directed concerns and one must become selfless.

Dilman would, I believe, paraphrase 2 as

2^1. A person, thoroughly taken up with worldly pursuits, taking religion more or less as a convention or with no religious beliefs at all, may come, perhaps through some traumatic experience, such as the death of her son, to have a new set or at least an altered scheduling of moral categories which gives her a sense of selflessness and a detachment from worldly concerns.

Sentence 3 would take the following paraphrase into

3^1. One is to love selflessly and to commit one's life to such a selfless love of humanity. (We can plainly see here how far this is from how such a sentence would normally be understood.)

Similarly 4, 5, 6 and 7 would, I believe, be paraphrased by Dilman in something like the following way.

4^1. One can find genuine liberation only in a life of inwardness.

5^1. To keep one's inwardness one must firmly orient one's life to a life of selfless love and to an acceptance of the finality of finitude in the ordering of one's life and in the attitudes one has toward the world.

6^1. We gratefully and indeed joyfully accept our lives no matter what happens.

7^1. Some people in their personal lives are worldly in their orientation and some people are selfless and detached from the world.

Sentences 8 to 11 are more characteristically theological and such utterances are less frequently employed by Dilman, but he does take them as among the sentences philosophers must just accept from theologians and try to provide a perspicuous representation of them which keeps their original sense. His paraphrases of 8 to 11 would be something like the following:

8[1]. The world as a whole should not be viewed as utterly impersonal but as a place where persons and personal values count.

9[1]. To take a religious perspective on the world as a whole is to attain selflessness and detachment and to overcome worldliness and bondage to the senses.

10[1]. To attain a religious perspective on life is to attain a perspective in which life, including such ideals as justice and the flourishing of human love, is valued independently of how things turn out. Love and goodness are valued in themselves and not just for whatever instrumental value they may happen to have. To attain such a perspective is to attain a life devoted to inwardness.

11[1]. For those immersed in a life of the senses there will be no understanding of the religious perspective.

These paraphrases are rough and no doubt Dilman or someone else with such an approach could improve on them. But I believe I have captured the sort of understanding these Wittgensteinians have of such conceptions. (If they mean something more *of a quite different sort*, they should explain what this "more" is.) These readings—excising the old myth-eaten cosmological conceptions—are all of the sort that are perfectly available to the atheist or sceptic. There are, of course, things here that might be *normatively* disputed but there is nothing here that is not available not just as an object of contemplation but as something to commit oneself to. Perhaps Dilman could provide paraphrases of the above sentences which were less crude, but it does not appear to be the case that these paraphrases would provide us with anything that was not perfectly available to the atheist. It does not appear to be the case, that is, that they would be fundamentally different from the paraphrases I have put in his mouth.

Dilman, as I remarked initially, is anxious to maintain against Braithwaite and Hare that religion is more than a commitment to a way of life. Believers, he claims, see the world as a whole differently from non-believers "even when there is no difference between them in what they expect by way of a life after death and no difference in what they infer about what lies beyond the reach of the senses" (494). I have questioned whether Dilman has been able, without appealing to such metaphysical beliefs, to sort out believers from non-believers, though he has sorted out people with different schemes of values. But the differences captured here are not even co-extensive with those differences which distinguish believers from non-believers. One can have the scheme of values Dilman designates as "religious" and actually be either religious or non-religious.

Dilman, like the other Swansea Wittgensteinians, insists his account is not reductionistic. It does not, he would have it, turn religion into moral parables linked with certain distinctive stories which need only be entertained. But it remains unclear in what way for him religion is anything other than a distinctive moral perspective on life as a whole. (Similar things could be said of Winch and Phillips.) The distinctive cosmological claims seem at least to have been excised and this makes his account appear at least to be very reductionistic indeed.

What saves it—and again similar things could be said here about Phillips and Winch—from being decisively so tagged is its vagueness and its use of religious discourse, having the old ring, in an unexplicated way. There seems to be plenty of room for the old philosophical manoeuvre of first saying it and then taking it all back. Dilman remarks for example:

> You cannot say: 'Believing in God is one thing, trusting in him another'. For responding to God, in the different ways that this finds expression in a man's life, is part of what we *mean* by 'believing in God'. (487)

Normally, in such a linguistic environment, we would take "responding to God" in the old way with all its problematic cosmological freight. Dilman there uses it in such a way so as to encourage that understanding. But he also tells us to reject the old cosmological conceptions as incoherent. But it is difficult to understand how we are to take such a passage—indeed even to understand such a passage—if we construe "God" in the manner dictated by Dilman's conceptions about how such concepts are to be understood. I suppose "responding to God" there is to be paraphrased as "selflessly orienting your life". But it is not clear that this is what Dilman means here and the linguistic environment encourages a richer reading. Lack of explicitness and a surfeit of vagueness ward off more decisive critiques.

Dilman might respond by invoking what has been called the *sui generis* platitude. He might say that sentences 1 to 11 say what they say and no paraphrase will exactly reduplicate their meaning. This no doubt is often, perhaps even always, true but, that notwithstanding, sentences 1 to 11 are very problematic and surely encourage the traditional metaphysical readings that Dilman rejects as incoherent. Many people, including some religious believers, are baffled by them and there are people, even with dispositions to respond as believers (reflect on Dostoevsky's characters), who are also disposed to believe they are incoherent or at least thoroughly problematic. The trouble is to understand them and we must seek what devices we can find to guide us in our understanding. In such a context a paraphrase and a reading may be in order, even if no claim is made to having captured the exact meaning of the paraphrased sentence. Indeed, since the paraphrased sentence was itself unclear, no notion of capturing its "exact sense" makes any definite sense. If we knew what that sense was we would not need the paraphrase. But a paraphrase, which gives a specification of meaning, can be of value in just those circumstances. It can perhaps give us some understanding where before we had little or none.

Dilman generally recognizes this and seeks to provide it for Godtalk, but, if my criticisms are near their mark, he has not been able to articulate a sense of that talk that would distinguish the claims of the believer from those of the religious sceptic. If he now backs away, under such philosophical pressure, from all paraphrase, and invokes the *sui generis* platitude, he will leave us with just the baffling unexplicated talk, with its characteristic perplexities, from which he sought to deliver us. His conceptual therapy will not have worked, for we will remain baffled by talk of God.

NOTES

1.   Ilham Dilman, "Wisdom's Philosophy of Religion," *Canadian Journal of Philosophy* V.4 (1975): 473-524. Subsequent references to this article, which is the principal target of this essay, will be given in the text.

2.   John Wisdom, *Philosophy and Psychoanalysis* (Oxford: Basil Blackwell, 1965) 149-68; and *Paradox and Discovery* (Oxford: Basil Blackwell, 1965) 1-22, 34-56. Besides the essay by Dilman cited in the previous note, see his "Wittgenstein On the Soul," *Understanding Wittgenstein*, ed. Godfrey Vesey (London: Macmillan Press, 1974) 162-92 and his "Paradoxes and Discoveries," *Wisdom: Twelve Essays*, ed. Redford Bambrough (Oxford: Basil Blackwell, 1974) 78-106.

3.   Michael Durrant's alternative characterizations should be contrasted with Dilman's and indeed Malcolm's, Phillips' and Winch's readings here. See Michael Durrant, *The Logical Status of 'God'* (New York: Macmillan, 1973) and his *Theology and Intelligibility* (London: Routledge and Kegan Paul, 1973).

4.   Antony Flew's discussion of the invisible Gardener is, of course, the paradigmatic contrast with Dilman and Wisdom. See A.G.N. Flew, "Theology and Falsification," *New Essays in Philosophical Theology*, eds. A.G.N. Flew and A. MacIntyre (New York: The Macmillan Company, 1955) 96-99.

5.   Axel Hägerström, *Philosophy and Religion*, trans. R.T. Sandin (London: George Allen and Unwin Ltd., 1964) 175-223.

6.   Ninian Smart sets out succinctly the sense of and the import of the traditional conception of transcendence in his "Mystical Experience," *Sophia* 1.1 (1962): 19-26.

7.   Ludwig Wittgenstein, *Note Books 1914-16* 81.

8.   Rush Rhees, *Without Answers* (London: Routledge and Kegan Paul, 1969) 110-32; Peter Winch, *Ethics and Action* (London: Routledge and Kegan Paul, 1972) 8-49; Peter Winch, "Meaning and Religious Language," *Reason and Religion*, ed. Stuart C. Brown (Ithaca, NY: Cornell University Press, 1977) 193-221; D.Z. Phillips, *Faith and Philosophical Enquiry* (London: Routledge and Kegan Paul, 1970); D.Z. Phillips, *Religion Without Explanation* (Oxford: Basil Blackwell, 1976); Paul Holmer, "Wittgenstein and Theology," *New Essays on Religious Language*, ed. Dallas M. High (London: Oxford University Press, 1969); Paul Holmer, "Atheism and Theism," *Lutheran World* XII (1963); Paul Holmer, "Metaphysics and Theology: The Foundations of Theology," *The Lutheran Quarterly* (1967); and Norman Malcolm, "The Groundlessness of Belief," *Reason and Religion*, ed. Stuart C. Brown (Ithaca, NY: Cornell University Press, 1977) 143-57, 186-90.

9.   What I mean by "Godless Christianity" can be seen from reading Braithwaite, Hare and Van Buren. See Richard B. Braithwaite, "An Empiricist's View of the Nature of Religious Belief," *The Logic of God: Theology and Verification*, eds. Malcolm L. Diamond and Thomas V. Litzenburg (Indianapolis: The Bobbs-Merrill Company, 1975) 127-48; R.M. Hare, "The Simple Believer," *Religion and Morality*, eds. Gene Outka and John P. Reeder, Jr. (Garden City, NY: Anchor Books, 1973) 393-427; and Paul M. Van Buren, *The Secular Meaning of the Gospel* (New York: The Macmillan Company, 1963).

CHAPTER 11

Wisdom and Dilman on the Scope of Reason in Religion*

I

JOHN WISDOM ARGUES THAT RELIGIOUS BELIEFS are amenable to reasons which ultimately rest on how things stand here and now.[1] This shows itself in differences between believers and sceptics, differences which Wisdom takes to be real differences and not merely verbal differences plus differences in their attitudes to life. They differ not only in how they live their lives and face death; they differ in *how they see life*. They differ in their perspectives on reality. In reflecting on this and in asking whether what they say about life is true, questions about the rationality of religion and questions about "religious truth" arise.

Ilham Dilman, commenting on Wisdom, takes the following three points to be both crucial and obvious.[2] He even goes so far as to claim that "no philosophy that denies them can . . . be sound" (p. 473).

1. Believers and non-believers differ in how they see life and this difference is crucial to religious belief (p. 473).
2. Religious beliefs are true or false. (Believers talk of them as being true or false and their talk "makes perfectly good sense.") (p. 473).
3. In certain circumstances, "reasoning or reflection which starts from certain features of the world, as experienced by a man in the grip of religious doubt, may clear his doubt and lead him to belief" (p. 473).

I do not think these points are as unproblematical as Dilman believes, and I do not believe that philosophy should take them as unquestionable starting points which any philosophy must square with in order to be sound. 1 and 3 are in the first instance ambiguous. There is a way of taking them which makes them obvious but on reflection, given their ambiguity, they are all the same problematical. How is it that such believers—believers

---

*First published in *Philosophical Investigations* 3.4 (1980).

with no different empirical expectations than such sceptics—see life differently? Is that difference, after all, not merely one in attitude and in picture-preference? Or perhaps the difference is simply one of moral orientation associated with differing picture-preferences? (What, in such a context, is it "to see life differently"? Perhaps that talk just masks a confusion?) And while reasoning and reflection may indeed lead a person to belief, is this not a mere "causal leading"? Moreover, is it enough to justify the belief to show that it is a mistake to believe that? Wisdom's account is ambiguous here. Dilman contends that once this ambiguity is noted and the various possibilities canvassed it becomes evident that we should abandon such attempts at justification. Is it? Finally, it is unclear that any coherent sense at all has been given to talk of a religious truth which is also adequate to meet the religious person's expectations concerning the truth-claims of religion. (We will return to this issue.)

II

Ilham Dilman's "Wisdom's Philosophy of Religion" can reasonably be construed as a response to remarks like those made above. It attempts to show that there is such a thing as religious truth or spiritual truth, that even fundamental religious beliefs are somehow amenable to reason without being beliefs which either require justification or can come to have a justification and that there is, as well, a crucial difference between how believers and sceptics see life and indeed see the world as a whole. He also tried to show what each of these things comes to.

Wisdom (according to Dilman) contends that "if there is a God it must be possible to know there is and to know this without an inference" (p. 474). What this knowledge comes to is not quite what most people would expect. Believing in God, which is necessary but not sufficient for knowing God, is, as far as I can ascertain, a coming to look on life from a distinctive perspective and in the light of that perspective reorienting one's life. People who believe in God not only have different attitudes to life from people who do not, they also interpret many of the events in their lives in a quite different way from non-religious people, and they put them in a different perspective and attach a different significance to many of these events. In that way they see things differently. In this sense, as Wisdom remarks, "some belief as to what the world is like is of the essence of religion" (p. 477). Dilman adds, as a gloss on that remark, that this "means some perspective on life."

Dilman fills out the above conception in the following way: in religious terms to have some belief as to what the world is like is to have a perspective on life; to believe that God exists is to be convinced of and to be committed to a certain perspective on the whole of life and on the world as a whole (p. 477). It is of the essence of religion to have such a view of the world as a whole. Indeed to have a religion is to have a certain perspective on life (p. 478). To believe in the God of the Jewish-Christian tradition is to have a certain perspective on the world as a whole, that is to say, it is to have a *Weltbild*. It is not a question of believing that a very distinctive kind of being or entity exists and of placing one's trust in that being or entity (p. 519).

It is against the background of what a religious understanding comes to, and of what a knowledge of God comes to, that we should understand Dilman's remark about the difference between a believer and sceptic as being like the difference between someone who says the *world* is a garden and someone who says it is a wilderness (p. 477). Dilman brings out what he has in mind here and the important analogies and disanalogies in the following set of remarks:

> The disagreement between those who say there is a God and those who deny this, he argues, is like the disagreement between someone who says that the world is a garden and one who thinks it is a wilderness. It is not like the one between someone who says that it is all taken care of by an invisible gardener and someone who thinks that no such gardener exists. That there is a gardener, unseen, behind the scenes, if there is one, is an additional fact to the appearance of the garden; whereas that the world is a garden or the garden not a wilderness is not something over and above the world's or the garden's appearance. Still those who are familiar with that appearance may find it difficult to know what to make of it, to appreciate what it all adds up to, and while some may see nothing there but a wilderness, others may discern an order and arrangement reminiscent of one to be found in a well cared for garden. So the dispute between them is like disputes about whether someone has been kind or cruel, generous or mean, *after* one knows exactly what he has done, what led up to it, and the circumstances surrounding his actions. It is like disputes about whether or not there is beauty in the picture before us. It is like disputes about whether or not the defendant has been negligent *after* the witnesses have been heard and the beer examined. In all these cases one of the disputants fails to see or appreciate something even though it is in front of his nose and 'visible' in the appropriate sense, and argument guides his apprehension and changes his vision of what is so. (pp. 474-75)

Such remarks will surely provoke the retort that such an account is *reductionistic*. The difference between the believer and the sceptic, it will be claimed, is not just about the character of the world, even the character of the world *as a whole*, but about whether there is a creative sustainer of the world, *transcendent to the world*, where "over and above the world" is construed as in some sense "beyond" or as "supernatural to" the universe.[3]

To take the line that Wisdom and Dilman take, is, C.B. Martin contends, to in effect adopt a pseudo-pantheism that reduces Christian and Jewish belief to something quite different from what it has been and which distorts, in its attempts to rationalize and demythologize that belief, the core cosmological claims of these religions.[4] Religious utterances, on such a reading, would come to have a quite different meaning than they now actually have. Martin is claiming that Wisdom is not analyzing or setting out the use religious utterances actually have, but he is giving them what is in fact a patently new use. (Dilman would resist this particular claim, though he says rather similar things for other elements of Wisdom's account. Yet Dilman's account would no doubt also seem reductionistic to Martin, though Dilman, I am sure, would return the compliment. Is reductionism only a malaise of the other fellow? Does the notion have any unproblematic application in the philosophy of religion?)[5] Martin illustrates what he means in the following passage:

> For instance, the statement 'God is Creator and Judge, merciful and righteous' would be a means of cosmic simplification. Many features that we had not related together would be related in a kind of pattern. Innumerable instances of goodness unexpectedly being rewarded and evil being punished would be related. So many things in nature would be seen to have the look of things kindly devised that we might feel less fear. All this and much more could be accomplished by the pseudopantheistic use of the statement. Of course, what would be accomplished would not be a reference to a particular Being above other beings. It is because of this lack that I cannot take it seriously as a use of religious utterances.[6]

If one thinks of Judaism and Christianity—and theism generally— "as mainly a certain organization of the facts about the world and not as a reference to some kind of ultimate Being outside of the world and beyond comprehension," then, Martin concludes, "atheists and theists may be led gently to agreement."[7] But this agreement, Martin claims, will come at a cost, for such a believer will, as a pseudo-pantheist, wittingly or unwittingly, have transformed himself into a kind of an atheist. Martin would have it that such a pseudo-pantheist does not believe in God, for to believe in God is to believe (among other things) in "a mysterious at least partially incomprehensible reality outside of, transcendent to, the world."[8] Dilman, on the contrary, will argue that that is not what it is to believe in God, but rather that such a traditionalist conception with such a *metaphysical* conception of transcendence is bad philosophy and bad theology, muddling our religious understanding, including our distinctively religious understanding, of God's transcendence.[9]

However, that this is so needs to be established and Martin's argument (if correct) would cut not only against Wisdom, but also against Dilman, Rhees, Winch, and Phillips. It is not Wisdom who seems at least to be a pseudo-pantheist but the Swansea Wittgensteinians as well. Dilman does make a determined attempt to meet such arguments. Putting what is centrally at issue briefly, and in my own way, it could be responded that Martin himself is fully aware of the desperate straits philosophers are in, in trying to give a more coherent and convincing account of the "what more?" than that given in such allegedly pseudo-pantheist accounts. Indeed Martin, like Michael Durrant, thinks that no acceptable account can be given of that "more".[10] However, given that belief, if we are going to make sense of religion at all, we need to recognize the need to cut our costs and retrench incoherent cosmological beliefs and stick to a core, plainly relevant to religious people, that makes sense to reflective, conceptually sophisticated, and informed people living in a world which has experienced the development of science. Moreover, these rejected cosmological beliefs can be viewed as the intrusion of bad metaphysics into religion. Dilman claims that an account of transcendence, God and the differences between believers and sceptics can be given which does not involve that metaphysics, which does not conflict with Scripture and a distinctively religious understanding and which, without mythology and a crucifixion of the intellect, does exhibit real differences between believers and sceptics.

Martin, I suspect, would respond that this is only achieved by setting aside, as muddled and confused, and as inessential to religious belief, what is in reality actually of the *essence* of Judaism and Christianity, namely a belief in a mysterious creator of the world, distinct from (outside of, independent of, transcendent to) the world. To this, in turn, it would be responded, that that is not what is essential to religion and indeed, if that is taken to be essential, it will only succeed in making religion—or at least Jewish and Christian religion—unbelievable to most educated and reflective people with a tolerably good philosophical and scientific training. Just as one can come to see love or geometry in a partially new way, so one can come to see God in a partially new way without, Dilman would argue, losing what is the essence of religion. We should not forget that within the Jewish and Christian traditions the way God has been conceptualized has been repeatedly changed, sometimes under scientific pressures. Why should we think that this either cannot or should not continue? A religious *Weltbild* does not exist in isolation; that is to say, a contemporary Christian's *Weltbild* is not just a religious one and, as Wittgenstein argues, the framework-principles of such a *Weltbild* hang together in a system. There will, given these diverse elements, be pressures on contemporary Christians to modify distinctively religious aspects of their *Weltbild* to have a more consistent system. But there is nothing problematic or untoward about that, for such a criticism is not of the system as a whole or of the fundamental principles of the *Weltbild* but is a form of criticism from *within* the system.

Dilman stresses that having not just a view of life or a perspective on life, but having a view of the world *as a whole*—having a worldview—is of the essence of religion. (But can there not be non-religious worldviews? Must we, or should we, say that, after all, we should alter our ordinary way of speaking and conceptualizing and call them religious?) These religious worldviews (though this on his account seems to be pleonastic) and their central claims have, Dilman contends, a peculiar invulnerability. They are not open to falsification. (Does this, together with their motivational aspects, make them *ideological*?)[11] But *how* then, if they are not open to falsification, can we ascertain whether they or any of their fundamental propositions are true or false? Wisdom and Dilman still speak in such circumstances of seeing how things really stand. But what does this mean here? What would it be like, where such conditions obtain, to do this? How can we establish whose—if anyone's—perspective is the correct one or the more nearly adequate one where there is no even approximate falsification? Recall Wittgenstein's scepticism here. Is it just that we will have different and often incommensurable *Weltbilden*? But then there can be no knowing one perspective rather than another to be the correct one. Perhaps we can, after all, assess whole perspectives by showing, through making connections and disconnections, that one account gives a more perspicuous representation than the other? Perhaps in the past in the more positivistic accounts too much weight has been given to confirmation and disconfirmation: too much weight has been given to testing?

Dilman stresses more than does Wisdom the limitations of reason in religion and the *invulnerability* of such worldviews. As Dilman puts it,

"I do not think that a perspective on life as a whole is in this way vulnerable to any facts, since it determines its possessor's assessment of the facts" (p. 480). This is not to say that it must or even tends to distort one's assessment of facts, for there is, and indeed can be, no getting at the facts perspective-free. There is no alternative to seeing things from a perspective, so, if we even say that the very having of a perspective must distort our assessment of the facts, we deprive "distorting of the facts" of a non-vacuous contrast. *Sometimes* the holding of a distinctive perspective will hobble us and distort our appreciation of the facts in a given case, but to say this must always be so because there is no "perspective-free" viewing of the facts is at least unwarranted and probably incoherent. However, and this is an added element, Dilman maintains that religious perspectives have an invulnerability. "The invulnerability of the perspective," Dilman contends, "is the result of one's determination to stick to certain concepts, to adhere to a particular measure of life. In this respect it has a fixity akin to the fixity of a system of geometrical axioms. Like a fixed star the believer takes his bearing from it in his judgements and decisions" (p. 480). (But can there be no argument and sometimes perhaps even decisive argument about the rationality and justifiability of sticking to certain concepts?)

III

What is crucial to see in this connection, Dilman contends, is that in systems of salvation such as Judaism and Christianity, there are clusters of interrelated beliefs which are *concept forming* and which, for those who subscribe to them, fix a framework and in that way determine a perspective which give those "who subscribe to them a fixed framework for their judgement and decisions" (p. 482).[12]

Those concept-forming beliefs, which *guide* the believer's apprehension in many situations, are those beliefs which are called *true* by many of those who adhere to them (p. 482). Wisdom believes, in a way Dilman does not, that these judgments—the claims believers call true—can be supported and indeed justified, shown to be well-founded or ill-founded, by something which in a way is closely analogous to the way in which judgments about a person's negligence, fairness, or sensitivity can be supported. That is to say, there is a process of reasoning and reflection which, if we can go through with it, will show these beliefs to be either well- or ill-founded (p. 482). It is Wisdom's further belief that if that did *not* obtain, it would make no sense to call these beliefs true.

Dilman regards this view as mistaken. He argues that it involves a mistaken conception of truth.

> Can one intelligibly characterize a belief to which one adheres as "true" if it cannot be supported by reasons or considerations of one kind or another? If one is inclined to think not then he should be reminded of contexts where "true" carries no such implication. We all speak of logical truths and we do not hesitate to acknowledge

an arithmetical proposition such as "2 + 2 = 4" as true although we have no idea how we should go about proving or supporting it. Such propositions *need* no proof. If someone insists that still they *can* be proved, I would reply that the conviction we express when we call them true cannot be increased by such a proof were someone clever enough to devise one. As far as our conviction goes such a proof is an idle wheel, a false support. Worse than this, it obscures the real source of our conviction which lies elsewhere, in the service which what we are convinced is true gives us in so much of our life and thinking, in the way it is interlocked with so much of what we accept and judge by. Its truth then lies in the kind of understanding it makes possible for us in connection with so much that is of interest to us. (p. 483)

Dilman's point is that there are contexts in which the notion of truth is *not* tied up with conceptions of proof, verification, the supporting of what is said and believed to be true with reasons or considerations of one kind or another (p. 483).

This view needs careful and sceptical examination. Let us state and inspect Dilman's argument for it (pp. 483-86). To give an example of the kind of "religious truth" or spiritual truth he has in mind, he takes a remark linked with a story from Plato's *Gorgias*. It is a story Socrates tells there about Judgment Day and the story he tells, he tells *as the truth*. A central "truth" in that story is Socrates' belief that his life will be infallibly judged when it is over. He believes the story to be true and he aims to present his soul in the soundest possible condition. Dilman remarks that "Socrates' faith in its truth does not rest on the kind of evidence with which one would support an ordinary prophecy." His desire to live a good life is not conditional on what will happen to him in the hands of his judges. In believing the story to be the truth, he does not mean that he believes it to be a story "containing reliable predictions or empirically well-founded beliefs." Moreover, he takes it that evidence for his belief that he will be judged in the future is not relevant, because his desire to live a good life is not conditional on what will happen to him in the future. No spiritual concern to live a certain life can enter through a belief which is supported or undermined by evidence. *Evidence is irrelevant to religious belief and, in particular, it is plainly evident that it is irrelevant to such a religious belief.* If we required evidence to support the truth of our belief in a future life in which we will be judged, it would undermine the whole *point* in having such a belief. The story of the Last Judgment in the story told by Socrates embodies or gives expression to certain values. It involves a commitment to accept suffering and even death rather than inflict wrong on others. The story presents a certain *measure for life* for those who accept it as true. Indeed the very word "true" here has a different use than it has in "It is true that the pen is on the table." To say the story is true, Dilman tells us, is to "characterize a measure," a "means of assessment rather than any assessment" that has been made (p. 485). In claiming the story to be true, Socrates states his measure; that is to say, he is not talking about what is or is not so in claiming the story to be true; rather he is setting a *standard* about how to react in such a situation. Dilman adds that Socrates "is saying that no other form of assessment makes sense for him" in such a domain (p. 485). Truth here, he claims, will take such a personal form. (Doesn't this confuse commitment and truth and does not this make "religious truth" thoroughly subjective? Suppose someone were to say that that kind of "truth" is no truth at all. But perhaps, in turn, it should be queried whether to so respond is simply dogmatically to insist on a conception of truth which could have no possible application in a religious domain?)[13]

Religious truths, Dilman claims, are both like and unlike the truth of mathematical axioms. The truth of mathematical axioms is "interlocked with so much of what we accept and judge by, so much on what we agreed on" (p. 485). Dilman claims that the same is true of those religious beliefs that religious believers take to be true. They are bound up in this way with the religious language-games they play. But in the religious case something distinct is involved as well.

> . . . when a religious man calls his beliefs true he means something more than this, since those who deny what he affirms can still carry on with the activities which make up the life they share with him even if they cannot do so in the same spirit. The religious person who affirms the truth of his beliefs is speaking for himself in a way that he would not be doing when he affirms those mathematical truths which he takes for granted when he adds up his accounts or works out his holiday expenses. For accepting the truth of religious beliefs means more than participating intelligently in religious practices. It means finding their sense in his own life. A religious man who affirms the truth of his beliefs is saying something like: "I find them indispensable for most of what I do; there is no part of my life that would make sense without them—I cannot go along with anything else". Thus, what Socrates thinks "personally" is not irrelevant to his claim that what he tells Callicles he tells him as the truth. (p. 485)

Truth in most contexts is impersonal but in this context, Dilman claims, there is no getting at the truth—what is really so—impersonally, for in religious domains how a person thinks, feels, how he commits himself is inseparable from what the truth is. Here "truth" is being used in a rather striking way—a way that should provoke at least initial suspicion—and indeed this distinctive use may capture some of what Kierkegaard meant by "subjective truth." Yet again this conception is surely obscure enough to arouse suspicion.

However, as Dilman remarks, this is not to say that whatever the believer *says* is true. Whether a person really "believes the religious beliefs he subscribes to, whether he believes them to be true, is a matter of what they mean to him, what he makes of them in his own life" (p. 486). (Does this conflate, reduce, or confuse "sincerely believing" or "being truly committed" with "true belief" or "believing what is true" or "believing the truth"?)[14] Dilman seems at least to be saying that, where religious beliefs are at issue, his belief is true if (a) he has a good understanding of the religious discourse in question, (b) he sincerely holds that belief, (c) it goes deep within, and (d) he has made it his own.[15] It is difficult, of course, to ascertain when these conditions obtain; moreover, they can plainly more or less obtain, seemingly making some religious beliefs more or less true, but where these conditions are satisfied it would appear to be the case that a true religious belief is a sincerely held religious belief. This seems at least to make "religious truth" very subjective and it also makes it the case that a "sincerely held but nonetheless false and indeed superstitious religious belief" would no longer even be a conceptual possibility. Perhaps Dilman and Phillips, who holds a similar view, would *not* take this to be a *reductio* or counterintuitive. But it would be nice to know why it isn't, if it isn't.

Dilman somewhat weakens the thrust of this criticism by remarking that "obviously there are limits to what can count as a religious truth, to be found in the religious traditions" (p. 486). They are given in the forms of life and the linked language-games; no *individual* can be the arbiter of them. They determine the limits of possibility in religion. But then he adds—keeping with us (as far as I can see) the problem—that, where

> there is question of whether such limits have been transgressed, the question "Is what he believes true?" *means*: Can I accept it and make it my own? Can I find new life in it? I cannot say "It is true" unless and until I can. (p. 486)

But while this may be a *necessary* condition for religious truth, can it be *sufficient* condition for such truth, if such there be? It would seem at least to rule out the possibility of heretical but false religious beliefs. More interestingly and more importantly, it would rule out, by conceptual fiat, the very possibility of there being people who wholeheartedly make these religious beliefs the measure of their lives and still think, without a lapse into incoherence, that they are myths: deep, humanly compelling moral myths but myths all the same. Such a position, though perhaps rare, does not seem to be incoherent. Surely the burden of proof is on Dilman to show that someone who so conceptualizes the situation must lapse into incoherence.

There would, of course, be argument about what it is to accept such "myths" and believe them and about whether they are indeed properly called myths. No doubt Dilman would say that certain key questions are being begged here, for, he might contend, I am making the contrast between myth and truth on the basis of a conception of truth at home only in factual contexts. But that that is so is not evident, and however "truth" is construed, a distinction between truth and myth would seem to be a genuine one, particularly in the context of religion. As surely the study of history and anthropology makes evident, at least some religious conceptions are mythical. Yet it appears at least to be the case that Dilman's account collapses the distinction between religion and myth. There seems on Dilman's account to be no conceptual space for a Santayana-like figure who accepts, and indeed makes his own, the life-orientation and perspective on life as a whole that Dilman so skillfully displays and yet still asserts that belief in God is belief in a myth—a deep, humanly compelling moral myth but a myth all the same. Dilman must say that such a comment is incoherent but it surely doesn't appear to be and the burden of proof shifts to him.

IV

Dilman argued in talking of belief in religion that we are "not speaking of what becomes knowledge when justified and held with conviction" (p. 486). We should not, he claims, contrast belief in God with knowledge of God. In talking of religious belief it is very important to realize we are talking about something we make our own. "Believing in God is commitment to a certain way of looking at the world and hence of assessing and responding to the contingencies of life" (p. 487). It is not the case that believing in God is one thing and trusting him another. Part of what we mean by "believing in God" is the response to God we find in the believer's life. Where a person has come to have a genuine belief in God, he or she will have come to "care for certain values, show concern for certain things in life . . ." (p. 487).[16]

In the religious stream of life we also draw a distinction between genuinely believing in God and coming to know him. Only a few will claim to have come to know God. Reflective believers recognize the distance that separates them from God and the difficulties in bridging it.[17] So they speak of believing in God rather than knowing God; the latter suggests the having of a direct experience of God, an experience which most believers do not claim to have, though they believe that some believers have this direct knowledge as a result of God's self-disclosure. But to be in a position to receive that, they must "die to the world," i.e., die to one's worldly and ego-centered expectations and self-love. In that state it is possible, but by no means certain, that they can come to *know* God in God's response to them. God can reveal himself *in the hearts* of "those few only who have ceased to expect anything for themselves" (p. 488). (Why "in the hearts"? That surely says something about the nature of "religious knowledge".) "It is," Dilman claims, "in an awareness of *nothingness* that the believer finds God's love, His mercy and forgiveness" (p. 488). In such a condition God comes to reveal himself to him, to make his presence felt and it is in such a condition that the believer comes to know God.

When these things happen, God (if he chooses) reveals himself to or within the believer or the sceptic. With the latter, i.e., the sceptic, people speak of a religious conversion. With respect to this conversion Dilman remarks:

> Here people sometimes speak of having "encountered" God and they may say that they know there is God from personal experience. What such a person encounters is something which he finds he can only identify as God's response— His anger which rips him apart and crushes everything that gave him a sense of being somebody, or His love which makes him put everything he has considered important aside and transforms his whole life. It is he who identifies what he meets in this way, though the criteria which enable him to do so come from the religion with which he has been in contact through the culture it permeates—the culture in which he has his roots. When a man's life has been touched by God in this way the transformation is one that shatters him so that he is born to a new life. (p. 489)

But quite soberly and indeed somewhat sceptically, why should this be viewed, in spite of the depth and intensity of the feelings involved, as an experience *of* God, particularly when any kind of literal understanding of encountering God, being touched by God, standing in the presence of God is clearly out on Dilman's account? Why not take this experience quite naturalistically for what it has every appearance of being, namely, a profound psychological experience of great moral importance to the believer—an experience which reorients the life of the person having the experience? But why give it any remarkable noetic status? There seems, on sober reflection, no reason for characterizing it, as Dilman characterizes it, as a form of direct knowledge of God. (But again is this not to construe "God" in the conventional way—a way which Dilman rejects? The arguments here, as is characteristic in philosophy, are rather tightly linked. Still isn't there something like the bottom line argument that either we, in speaking in this way, are conceptualizing God as having some not unproblematic ontological status or we are, all the window dressing aside, only talking about a moral and psychological reality?)

V

Religious beliefs (more accurately central religious beliefs) are beliefs "which constitute the framework of a particular perspective on life" (p. 490). We can, however, make sense of these beliefs without accepting them. Yet believing in God is never merely—or even principally— an intellectual process, a matter solely of cognition or careful reasoning or reflection. One's will and heart must be engaged as well. The reasoning, to bring belief, must be more than a purely intellectual exercise; it must, as well, be "carried out in terms of moral categories" which engage the will and affect one's concern. In the struggle between belief and unbelief, the conflict of loyalties will not be confined to the intellect but will engage the heart and will. Reasoning "which helps him to sift out his reactions to life will resolve the conflict one way or the other" (p. 491). Reasoning, reflection about religion or, if you will, religious reasoning, cannot bring the person who engages in it to believe in God unless it moves the heart as well as the mind. An unmoved spectator and calculator of the actual could not possibly believe in God or know that God exists (p. 491). It is Dilman's claim that "the kind of allegiance that is involved in religious belief is one that finds expression in those many situations in life which call for deep affective response" (p. 493). It is crucial to understand that the kind of reasoning which may guide a person towards a belief in God is one which in part helps him to sift out his reactions to life (p. 493).

Dilman agrees with Wisdom that ratiocination is involved in religion, but he does not believe we can *justify* belief in God or show a religious commitment to be more or indeed less reasonable than a purely secular one. It is possible for "a person to arrive at a religious belief or a deeper spirituality through reflection on the world or reasoning about his life," but he cannot show his belief to be justified and the sceptic to be mistaken. "We misapprehend the nature of religious reasoning if we think that the reasoning which has guided one man to belief in God ought to lead anyone else to that belief if he gives his heart and mind to it" (p. 493). We should, Dilman claims, disconnect, in thinking about religion and its rationality, the notions of reason and justification. We can show that certain religious beliefs are reasonable framework-beliefs to guide a person's apprehension and orient her/his reaction to life and the world as a whole. But we cannot justify this religious commitment by showing it to be well-grounded and a purely secular orientation by contrast ill-grounded. Both natural theology and natural anti-theology are mistaken in thinking anything like that can be done. There is no justification of fundamental religious beliefs, but they are not irrational for all of that.

This, however, seems to me to involve another emasculation of what religious claims—and most particularly Christian claims—purport to be. Christ, for the Christian, purports to be *The Truth* and *The Way*. To claim this, as Christians do, is not just weakly to give to understand that it is not unreasonable to be a Christian, or that Christianity is one reasonable way of viewing the world as a whole and organizing one's life around that world-picture, but it is to claim that the Christian picture is *The* Truth and *The* Way. In a way some other *Weltbilden* do not so claim, it purports to reveal *the* correct view of the world, the view in accordance with which a person is to live his life. Christianity for Christians of a tolerably orthodox sort is not viewed as just one worldview among others. The Self-Image of Christianity is that it sees itself as making an unequivocal demand on the Christian; it has a categorical quality, a claim to something more Absolute, than anything that is captured in Dilman's or Wisdom's attempted perspicuous representation. Christian believers take their claims to be true. Indeed they take their system of salvation as a whole to be *The Truth*. Dilman's reconstruction does not capture that sense of "true" and "The Truth".

It is not unreasonable to believe, as I do, that there is no conception of truth or *The Truth* in Christianity that coherently meets the religious believer's expectations. We either get a reductionistic account that does not meet his religious expectations or we get a flight into incoherence. But coherent or not, the belief that Christianity is *The Truth* is a key part of the Christian's expectations. Dilman can claim that with his conceptualization of religious truth he saves something of what the believer believes, but what he saves is a very reduced version of the proud claims and the most persistently held and fondest hopes and expectations of Christianity. (Very similar things could be said of Judaism.) Dilman can respond that in the end it comes down to a choice between something like his reconstruction of "religious truth" or false consciousness. But, in turn, it can be responded that with religions and the conception of religious truth so reduced, there is little point left in being religious. The secular humanist too can recognize and acknowledge such import as Dilman and Wittgensteinians generally allow religion.

Still there remains the impression that in the arguments pro and con central questions have perhaps been begged. There seems to be a neutral and still useful starting point from which the argument can be launched that will not initially prejudice the case in one direction rather than another. Dilman could respond that I, like Martin, persist in regarding an account of Christianity or Judaism as reductionistic and as an inadequate characterization of Christianity or Judaism *if* it does not construe God as a metaphysically transcendent reality, distinct from the world and upon whom the world (the whole universe) depends. But it is precisely this metaphysical conception which Dilman and Wittgensteinians generally will not accept.

Such a conception, they rightly recognize, is of dubious intelligibility. We can hardly reasonably claim that an adequate understanding of God-talk should require us to assume such a conception of such dubious intelligibility. (Indeed that it is of such dubious intelligibility is common ground between us.) An adequate account of religion could hardly, it will be claimed, utilize, as an integral element of its account, such a questionable philosophical construction. However, it does not follow from this that we should reject all conceptions of God. Secular critics, Dilman could respond, simply refuse to accept any conception of God that is coherent and non-superstitious, given a contemporary understanding of the world.

So be it. Without such metaphysical constructions belief in God would not be linked to the hopes that have been traditionally and pervasively a part of Christianity, the doubts of agnostics, or the denials of atheists. If, in turn, that is said to be precisely one of the key virtues of such a Wittgensteinian characterization of God-talk, then it should in turn be responded that if we live by this virtue, we will have abandoned the core premises of the Christian faith and rendered it a limited and one-sided moral alternative to secular humanism. Indeed it will be an alternative which in reality has accepted its opponent's ground rules. It has actually, though hardly, as have Braithwaite and Hare, self-consciously accepted its cosmology. So reduced, this neo-Christian *Weltbild* can be easily assimilated into or accommodated by a Marxist humanism without possessing the richness, moral complexity, and systematic coherence of such a view of the world.

NOTES

1.   John Wisdom, *Philosophy and Psychoanalysis* (Oxford: Basil Blackwell Ltd., 1964). The principal essay concerning religion in that collection is his "Gods," *Paradox and Discovery*, ed. John Wisdom (Oxford: Basil Blackwell Ltd., 1965). The principal relevant essays are "The Logic of God" and "Religious Belief."

2.   Ilham Dilman, "Wisdom's Philosophy of Religion," *Canadian Journal of Philosophy* V.4 (1975): 473-522. All page references to this article are given in the text.

3.   Ninian Smart captures the core of this traditional conception well in his "Mystical Experience," *Sophia* 1.1 (1962): 19-26.

4.   C.B. Martin, *Religious Belief* (Ithaca, NY: Cornell University Press, 1959).

5. For an acute discussion of this, see the exchange between Thornton and Mascall, J.C. Thornton, "Religious Belief and 'Reductionism'," *Sophia* 5.3 (1966): 3-16, and in the next issue of *Sophia*, Mascall's response and Thornton's rejoinder. See, as well, my "Some Meta-theological Remarks About Reductionism," *Journal of the American Academy of Religion* (1974).

6. Martin, *Religious Belief* 11-12. However, to reveal something of the complexity of the matter, we should not forget Tillich's remarks about super-naturalism and "The God above God." This is double edged. We should not forget its challenge, but we should not forget its obscurity either.

7. Martin, *Religious Belief* 15.

8. *Ibid*.

9. The second part of his article on Wisdom's philosophy of religion is of particular importance here.

10. Michael Durrant, "Is the Justification of Religious Belief a Possible Enterprise?" *Religious Studies* 9 (1970): 449-55.

11. For a discussion of this see my "On Speaking of God," *Theoria* 28.2 (1962) and my "Reductionism and Religious Truth Claims," *Dialogos* (1974).

12. Compare this to Norman Malcolm's conception of framework-beliefs. Norman Malcolm, "The Groundlessness of Belief," *Reason and Religion*, ed. Stuart Brown (Ithaca, NY: Cornell University Press, 1977) 143-57.

13. For this kind of probing, see A.E. Murphy and Brand Blanshard, *Reason and the Common Good*, ed. A.E. Murphy (Englewood Cliffs, NJ: Prentice-Hall, 1963) 173-82, and Brand Blanshard, *Reason and Belief* (New Haven: Yale University Press, 1973) chapter 6.

14. For an argument that it does, see Paul Edwards, "Kierkegaard and the 'Truth' of Christianity," in his *A Modern Introduction to Philosophy*, 3rd ed. (New York: The Free Press, 1973) 505-22. But see also D.Z. Phillips, *Faith and Philosophical Enquiry* (New York: Schocken Books, 1971) 204-23 and C.S. Evans, *Subjectivity and Religious Belief* (Grand Rapids, MI: W.B. Eerdmans Publishing Co., 1978).

15. These last three conditions may in reality all be different aspects of the same condition.

16. Dilman's argument here should make us rethink some of the things we standardly say about the relation of ethics and religion.

17. Part of the trouble here, and part of the reason for the persisting conviction that accounts such as Dilman's are reductionistic, is that the thrust of such talk, and its plain import, seems most certainly to be in setting out how religion is a distinctive moral orientation to life. It is not at all evident that, in such Wittgensteinian accounts, anything else is at issue. They seem to think that nothing else can coherently be said. The anti-metaphysical orientation is there, though—unlike the anti-metaphysical posturing of positivists—it is muted.

CHAPTER 12

On the Rationality of Radical
Theological Non-Naturalism*

I

IN MY *CONTEMPORARY CRITIQUES OF RELIGION* and in my *Skepticism*, I argue that non-anthropomorphic conceptions of God do not make sense. By this I mean that we do not have sound grounds for believing that the central truth-claims of Christianity are genuine truth-claims and that we do not have a religiously viable concept of God. I argue that this is so principally because of three interrelated features about God-talk. (1) While purporting to be factual assertions, central bits of God-talk, e.g., "God exists" and "God loves mankind", are not even in principle verifiable (confirmable or discon-firmable) in such a way that we can say what experienceable states of affairs would count for these putative assertions and against their denials, such that we could say what it would be like to have evidence which would make either their assertion or their denial more or less probably true. (2) Personal predicates, e.g., "loves", "creates", are at least seemingly essential in the use of God-talk, yet they suffer from such an attenuation of meaning in their employment in religious linguistic environments that it at least appears to be the case that we have in such environments unwittingly emptied these predicates of all intelligible meaning so that we do not under-stand what we are asserting or denying when we utter "God loves mankind" or "God created the heavens and the earth" and the like. (3) When we make well-formed assertions, it appears at least to be the case that a necessary condition for such well-formedness is that we should be able successfully to identify the subject of that putative statement so that we can understand what it is that we are talking about and thus understand that a genuine statement has actually been made. But, where God is con-ceived non-anthropomorphically, we have no even tolerably clear idea about how God, an infinite individual, occupying no particular place or existing at no particular time, and being utterly transcendent to the world, can be

*First published in *Religious Studies* 14 (1978).

identified. Indeed we have no coherent idea of what it would be like to identify him and this means we have no coherent idea of what it would be like for God even to be a person or an it. He cannot be picked out and identified in the way person and things can. Since this is so, we do not understand what it would be like to make statements in which "God" occurs as a subject because we have no coherent idea of *what* we are talking about such that we can say something about God. In a way that I have perhaps previously not stressed sufficiently, it is these three interrelated problems which, when taken together, provide us with our deepest perplexities about whether God-talk, admittedly mysterious, makes enough sense to be capable of making intelligible truth-claims. However, if we take any one of them in isolation from the others, the problems posed appear at least not to be so insuperable.

While I believe that non-anthropomorphic God-talk comes to grief in this respect, Terence Penelhum, by contrast, thinks it makes rough sense.[1] He accepts a similar division of the problems to the one I have made above and then argues that such religious utterances have an intelligible verification structure and that the problems of attenuation of predicates and identification can be met. He does not claim that we have verified religious claims and can thus conclude beyond reasonable doubt that they are true. He seems not to think that it is the proper business of a philosopher either to make or deny such truth-claims. What he does claim is that "there is no good reason to think that we could not, with a little ingenuity, think up some non-theistic statements which would serve, if true, to put some theistic conclusions beyond reasonable doubt" (RK 64). I shall be concerned here to take issue with this last claim.

Penelhum believes that we can well enough understand what it would be like for even fundamental religious claims to be true. So that is not, he would have us believe, the problem. The real problem is that we do not know, and are in no position to find out, whether they are true or even probably true. In a way that would make Wittgenstein, Malcolm, Brown, Phillips or Dilman shudder, vindicating one's faith for Penelhum comes to being in a position to see that it is verified and this means that someone must be "aware of the verificatory facts": that is have the evidence which would establish the belief (RK 86).

Because he believes that putative religious assertions have a verification structure, he is understandably impatient with a Braithwaite and a Hare who do not construe such putative assertions as assertions.[2] That seems to him both a desperate and an unnecessary move and, again understandably, he takes the approach of a Phillips, Holmer, Brown and Dilman as equally desperate when they deny that fundamental religious beliefs have or need either verification or any other kind of vindication or justification (RR 147-8).[3]

My most central thrust here will be to try to show that there is a genuine problem about the verification of religious beliefs and that Penelhum is mistaken in thinking that, with a little ingenuity, we can think up what would serve, if true, to verify fundamental religious claims. I should only add, by way of a final prefatory remark, that if I am in the main right on these large issues, both the "non-factualist" interpretations of religious discourse of a Braithwaite, Hare or Van Buren and the Wittgensteinian turn of a Phillips, Holmer, Brown or Dilman gain somewhat in attractiveness and, while perhaps still "desperate", they cannot reasonably be dismissed in the cavalier way Penelhum dismisses them.

II

Penelhum and I agree that most believers *believe* that they are making factual assertions when they say that God loves mankind or even that God exists, though we disagree about whether they actually succeed in making such assertions where they are not being thoroughly anthropomorphic (RR 126). We also agree that no believer who understood what he is saying believes that "the facts about the divine to which he thinks his assertions refer are comprehensible through and through," though we both also believe, as well, that "the incomprehensibility cannot be total or religious language would have no foothold whatever" (RR 126). We differ in that I think that the incomprehensibility of non-anthropomorphic religious utterances is so deep that these claims do not make sense and indeed fail to make genuine factual assertions, while Penelhum believes that this is not the case and that indeed they have a sufficient verification structure such that we do understand what must be the case for them to be true and what must be the case for them to be false. It is, he believes, only by the imposition, wittingly or unwittingly, of arbitrary empiricist dogmas that it even appears that this is not the case. As he puts it, "insofar as Flew's argument is merely a demand that religious assertions have to be falsifiable by reference to observable events in the world, the retort to it could simply be that this is an arbitrary standard of meaningfulness to adopt. Why must the believer be prepared to confine the assertions he makes about God within the limits of empirical criteria of significance?" (RR 124). A short answer is that by so restricting himself he knows the conditions under which he can rightly claim that an allegedly factual claim of his is true and under what conditions it is false. He has, that is, by such a restriction a reasonably firm understanding of the truth conditions of his talk. He will know what it would be like for his claims to be true or false. And this standard—I am tempted to argue—far from being an "arbitrary standard of meaningfulness" is a quite non-arbitrary standard of factual significance. That is, it provides us with a clue to whether our claims do actually have factual import: do actually make factual assertions and thus succeed in being factually meaningful.

However, for the nonce, we can put this issue aside, for Penelhum, like Hick, is confident that religious utterances are verifiable. Christians have eschatological expectations and we can describe eschatological predictions which, if things happen as predicted, would verify central claims of Christian theism (RR 137-9). The central empiricist challenge, Penelhum reminds us, is this:

> The essence of the 'falsification' criticism could be said to be that the believer seems prepared to accept any actual or imaginable state of affairs as compatible with his claims about God, so that it is impossible to know on what he would make these claims stand or fall. The essence of Hick's defense is to say that since the believer has certain expectations about a life after death that the unbeliever does not have, we can, by reference to these, say what would finally verify or falsify what he claims (RR 136).

Penelhum, as I just noted, believes that Hick has shown that Christian theism has a verification structure. Educated Christian believers and sceptics do not, here and now, disagree about what they expect to observe or in any way empirically detect. They do not, that is, disagree about the immediate facts. Such Christians, no more than sceptics, expect, here and now, their dying friends to be restored to life and health or epidemics to be miraculously halted. But they do have different all-inclusive worldviews and these differing all-inclusive worldviews involve different eschatological expectations. "The Christians' total view of the world contains essentially a belief in the ultimate triumph of God's purposes in the world, which will take the form, in part, of an afterlife for men who will live in union with God" (RR 136-7). If such a state of affairs comes to obtain, we will have verified the statements that God loves mankind and that God exists. If it does not obtain, we will have disconfirmed those claims.

Surely this gives us a sense of how Christian believers and sceptics have different world-pictures, different *Weltbilden*, but this does not show that the Christians' rather more ramified picture is not an incoherent or unintelligible picture. My problem is and remains that the concept of God—where "God" is construed non-anthropomorphically—is so problematic that we do not have any understanding of what we would have to experience in the hereafter Hick and Penelhum describe such that the probability of *either* the truth *or* the falsity of a putative factual statement such as "There will be a community of persons infused by grace over whom Jesus will return to reign as the Son of God" is seen to be one bit greater (RK 82). We have no idea at all of what observations we would have to make or, even in principle, could make which would make the assertion of that statement more probable than its denial. We cannot describe the observations we would have to make which would count for its truth and against the truth of its denial.

To reply by remarking that this is plainly false for we could observe Jesus on his throne and *thus* observe the Son of God is to be guilty of a *non sequitur* for "Jesus is the Son of God" is not a tautology and while we could indeed observe Jesus we would not thus have observed the Son of God and indeed we cannot—logically cannot—observe the Son of God.[4] In short, because of the theistic concepts ("the Son of God" and "grace") embedded in that utterance, there is no *directly* verifying, now or hereafter, such a putatively factual statement. That is, we no more understand what it would be like for "Jesus is the Son of God" or "There is a Son of God" to be true or false than we understand what it would be like for "There is a God" or "God loves mankind" to be true or false. And if we could directly verify the former statements, we could directly verify—would understand how to verify directly—the latter theistic statements as well and so would not need an eschatological verification structure to give sense—factual import—to our God-talk.

Some of Penelhum's remarks in *Problems of Religious Knowledge* could be construed as a response to my above argument. Penelhum is aware that Hick uses theistic statements in the stating of his eschatological predictions and in the setting out of statements which he believes would verify "God loves mankind" and "God exists". Recall, moreover, that a statement is a theistic one if and only if we cannot know its truth without knowing that God exists. And surely this is true of "the experience of a community of persons whose relationship to one another represents the sort of fulfillment of human personality indicated in the Gospels, and who experience communion with God as revealed in Christ" (RK 81-2). As if partially anticipating the sort of objection I would make, Penelhum goes on to claim that certain of Hick's crucial eschatological predictions could be "couched in non-theistic statements" which "have the same verificatory value." Penelhum then proceeds to produce some which he thinks will do the job. Instead of talking of a community of persons infused by grace over which Jesus will return to reign as the Son of God, we can, in what Penelhum takes to be non-theistic statements, confine ourselves to the following paraphrase:

> There will be a community of persons whose personalities are as they would be if they were infused by grace (in that they manifest love, guilelessness, self-sacrifice, understanding, purity of heart); that Jesus will rule over this community as the Son of God would (in a manner manifesting these same personality-traits plus a uniquely high degree of knowledge, authority, forgiveness); and that the members of this predicted community think and behave as they do at least in part because they consider themselves to be infused by grace, to be redeemed sinners, to be children of one God whose Son has returned to rule over his kingdom (RK 82).

Penelhum remarks that these are non-theistic statements and that "they could be known to be true by someone who did not know that God existed" (RK 82). However, what he does not note is that their factual import (their factual meaning or significance) would still not be understood by someone who did not understand what it would be like for "There is a community under the reign of the Son of God" to be either true or false. For if they *did not understand* that, they *could not understand* what it would be like to be in a community with Jesus where Jesus rules as the Son of God would, if there were a Son of God. For, if we do not understand what must obtain for it even to be probably true or probably false that the Son of God reigns and this is so because we do not understand *what* it is we are talking about in talking about the Son of God, then we *cannot* understand what it would be like to be in a community ruled by Jesus or anyone else which is ruled as it would be by the Son of God. If we cannot understand *what* we are talking about in talking about the Son of God, we cannot understand what it would be like to live in a community which was governed as if it were under his rule, if there actually were such a reality. Our understanding is blocked here, for we have no conception of such a reality. With it we draw a blank. It is like my asking you to imagine what it would be like if there were Irgligs when you have no idea what an Irglig is.

Again Penelhum partially anticipates this response. Speaking of his above paraphrase of Hick's predictions and his comments on it, remarked above, Penelhum in turn comments:

> It is natural to object that these predictions, even if non-theistic in the sense that someone could know them to be true without knowing that God existed, are theistic in another sense—that they could not be understood by someone who did not understand the claim that God exists, since they contain references to grace, redemption, and the Son of God. We might coin another technicality and say that any statement which cannot be understood by someone who does not understand the statement that God exists is a statement which 'contains theistic expressions'. Our discussion makes it seem very likely that any eschatological predictions which would be sufficient, if true, to verify the central claims of Christian theism, would be statements containing theistic expressions. But this is no objection to our claim that it is possible to state, in non-theistic statements, what post-mortem states of affairs would be sufficient to verify the central claims of Christian theism. It would only be an objection to a theory that was supposed to use the fact that such eschatological predictions can be made as a way of explaining the *meaning* of these central claims (RK 82-83).

However, this last remark made by Penelhum is just to the point, for I have been arguing that the only kind of verification which would meet what I have dubbed the empiricist challenge would have to have verifying statements which do *not* contain what Penelhum usefully calls "theistic expressions".[5] If our puzzle is to understand how "God exists" or "God loves mankind" could have *factual import*, could have the kind of meaning necessary for them to be *factual assertions*—the kind of assertive force Penelhum believes believers believe them to have—then so to understand them—that is to understand what it would be like for them to be true or false factual statements—we need to be able to do what Penelhum rightly, I believe, thinks that it is rather unlikely that we can do, namely to state in non-theistic terms what would actually verify (confirm or disconfirm) the central claim of Christian theism.

Penelhum is mistaken, however, in thinking that that is no objection to his own account and Hick's, for it is central to their accounts—and central to arguments about the rationality of theism—to be able to show that non-anthropomorphic Christian God-talk has factual import (i.e., factual meaning or factual significance) such that, contra Hare, Braithwaite, Van Buren and Miles, God-talk can be seen to have the kind of meaning that goes with making genuinely factual truth-claims. My argument, and Flew's and Ayer's as well, has been that *in that way* non-anthropomorphic God-talk is meaningless, i.e., we do not understand what it would be like for such God-talk to make true or false factual claims where such theistic conceptions are employed. Penelhum's disclaimers to the contrary notwithstanding, a central part of Hick's response to sceptical critiques such as Flew's is to try to show how God-talk has factual significance: how "God exists" and "God loves mankind" are genuine factual assertions and how, in response to Flew, it could be shown that there are certain coherently describable experiences which give factual content to those utterances and would be sufficient, were we actually to have them, to verify them. This is how, at least, Hepburn, Tooley and I—and I suspect a host of others—read Hick; and even if that surprisingly is not what Hick was up to and, as Penelhum makes plain, it is not what he is himself up to, still, if that challenge is not met, if that enterprise is not successfully engaged in, there is, to put it minimally, a serious question about whether these key bits of God-talk actually achieve the logical status of factual assertions.[6] But if that God-talk does not have that status, then it cannot be the case, as Hick and Penelhum believe, that "God exists" or "God loves mankind" or "Love is reality under the reign of Christ" are verifiable—eschatologically or otherwise—factual assertions. They have meaning all right, but, if they are not so verifiable, they do not have *the kind of meaning* Penelhum and Hick believe that believers think their talk has and they do not have the kind of meaning that they themselves believe is essential for the rationality of Christian belief.

Unless these doubts about the assertion status of God-talk can be resolved in a way supportive of traditionalist accounts, Penelhum is quite mistaken in claiming, as he rather vehemently does, that it would be irrational of the sceptic to continue to deny that God exists and God loves mankind had been verified—indeed conclusively verified—if he actually found himself in a post-mortem world face to face with Jesus in a community blissfully united and pure of heart which quite matter-of-coursely spoke of the reign of God. The sceptic could perfectly well understand (*a*) what it would be like to live in such happy togetherness, (*b*) for Jesus to be such a moral exemplar and (*c*) for the community to be such a through-and-through truly human society without understanding at all what was meant by "God" or "the Son of God" or without understanding what would make "the Son of God reigns over us" false or probably false. And, given the way factual assertions normally operate, he could in such a post-mortem state, reasonably ask the God-talk chaps what more they mean by "the Son of God reigns over us" than by "Jesus reigns over us" and it is far from evident that they could give a coherent answer.

III

Problems about the intelligibility of God-talk are complex and at least seemingly intractable. Penelhum and I agree that typical Christians and Jews *believe* that it is a fact that God exists and that they *think* that, when "God loves mankind" and "God shall raise the quick and the dead" occur in standard linguistic environments, factual assertions are being uttered. However, Penelhum also believes that these utterances not only are *believed* by such believers to have such a logical status, but that such utterances *actually do* have that logical status and have a verification structure very similar to the one Hick characterized. We do not know that these fundamental religious claims are true but we—believers and sceptics alike—know very well what at least conceivable experienceable states of affairs would, if they actually were to obtain, establish their truth or at least probable truth, i.e., verify them so that it would, in that circumstance, be irrational to deny them. Penelhum thinks the sceptic who would deny this—a chap he calls "*radical theological non-naturalist*"—is being arbitrary and irrational. By contrast, I do not believe any of these things, and, no doubt, by Penelhum's lights, I am, in so reacting, being irrational.

Penelhum characterizes a position like mine, and like Ayer's and Flew's as a *theological positivism* committed, as well, to *radical theological non-naturalism*. He believes, as I just remarked, that one is being arbitrary and irrational in sticking with either. It is quite possible that I am in some way badly confused about this matter, but I do not see that this is so nor that Penelhum has even given us any very plausible reasons for believing it to be so.

Let us see if we can untangle something of what is at issue here. A *theological positivist* holds that "theistic statements would, if meaningful, be verifiable in principle by reference to non-theistic ones, but that they are not" (RK 78). Penelhum holds (*a*) that that is an arbitrary criterion and (*b*), as we have already in effect seen in the beginning of the previous section, that even so that criterion can be satisfied by an account like Hick's of eschatological verification. To make contact with real targets, e.g., with Ayer, Carnap, Flew or myself, *theological positivism* should be reformulated as follows: theistic statements would, if factually meaningful, be at least confirmable in principle by reference to non-theistic ones fully characteriz-able in non-theistic terms, but they are not. The related thesis of *theological non-naturalism* is the view that "theistic statements cannot be proved from non-theistic ones" (RK 55). It has two forms, one, according to Penelhum, reasonable and the other irrational; *moderate theological non-naturalism* is, of course, the reasonable doctrine and *radical theological non-naturalism* the unreasonable, irrational doctrine. The difference between *moderate* and *radical theological non-naturalism* can be picked up readily, if we disam-biguate the modal term "cannot" in the above characterization of *theolog-ical non-naturalism*. A *moderate theological non-naturalist* is just denying that, as things stand, we can prove or verify or in any way establish that God exists or God loves mankind from knowing the truth of any non-theistic statement or statements. He doesn't deny that there are or at least very well might be certain non-theistic statements which would, if true, verify such theistic claims, but they just happen, as a matter of fact, not to be true or at least they are not known or reasonably believed to be true. A *radical theological non-naturalist*, by contrast, believes that non-theistic statements (expressible in non-theistic terms) that even could be conceived of, no matter how fanciful, would, if true, verify the existence or love of God. No matter how different things became from what they are, no matter how many terminal cancer patients inexplicably got well, no matter how often seas parted so the good guys could get through and no matter how often and conspicuously the stars rearranged themselves above Toronto to spell out "God", the *radical theological non-naturalist* would not take such occurrences as verifying that God exists or that any other theistic statement is true or probably true or even more probable than its denial (RK 58-9). He would, of course, be surprised and indeed utterly perplexed by such strange happenings especially if, after a bit, no scientific explanation was forthcoming of why they occurred. But that is an entirely different matter. It still does not help him to understand what is being claimed by those who talk of these occurrences as manifestations of God's will. He may well come to think, if such utter oddities came to pass, that there is something more in heaven and earth than was dreamt of in his philosophy, but this still does not give him an understanding of what is being talked about in speaking of God.

Traditional natural theology attempted to show, as Penelhum well remarks, "that in the face of certain natural facts which could be ascertained by someone who did not know that God exists, it is irrational to deny that he does exist" (RK 60). *Theological non-naturalists*, both radical and moderate, deny that there actually are any facts which would establish that claim of natural theology. But the *radical non-naturalist* goes on to claim that there could be none, "that nothing could make it irrational to refuse to accept any theistic conclusion if one does not have some knowledge of God already" (RK 60).[7] It is this position, along with *theological positivism*, which Penelhum regards as arbitrary and irrational.

Penelhum believes that the claim that he has described as a conceivable eschatological situation which, if it obtained, would unambiguously verify core theistic claims, can only be resisted by opting for either or both *theological positivism* or *radical theological non-naturalism*. We need now to follow out his argument that it is irrational to adopt either of these positions.

I shall consider first what he says about *radical theological non-naturalism*. To insist, Penelhum claims, upon denying that the eschatological situation he described would, if it obtained, verify Christian theism is a desperate irrational resort on the part of the sceptic. If we found ourselves, Penelhum maintains, mysteriously, after the death of our present bodies, in the presence of Jesus and among old friends who we had long since thought dead, and if we found there an egalitarian community united in love and sisterhood-cum-brotherhood with all sexist distinctions erased, and if we found, as well, a community where people were doing interesting and humanly satisfying things, we could not, rationally or reasonably, deny any longer that theism is true or even reasonably wonder whether it is true.[8]

That claim seems to me to be false. Not being able to make sense of "An infinite individual", "A pure spirit or pure Thou beyond the bounds of space and time" or an "Infinite being who created the world", we could accept all the above eschatological goings-on as a cluster of amazing and, presently at least, quite inexplicable but still perfectly natural facts, and still wonder—indeed rationally wonder—what all that had to do with that strange talk about God and about beings beyond the bounds of space and time and transcendent to the world. If that talk didn't make sense to us before, it would make no more sense after those experiences and we could readily wonder if perhaps the theistic expressions were after all just umbrella terms referring compendiously to such phenomena or we could reasonably wonder if perhaps they did mean something else in addition and wonder *what more* that was and what, even in principle, verifiable, non-verbal difference there was between the fellow who claimed that that was all we were talking about and the person who said that there was something more but could not, and indeed felt no need to try to, spell out the difference in terms of at least some conceivable experiential states of affairs.

The person who says things like the above need not at all be making the quite mistaken claim, "That one statement q can only suffice to verify another p, if it entails it . . ." (RK 83). But Penelhum and I have been concerned to argue—in my case in some detail—that it is "a mistake to claim that q can verify p only if q entails it." The "accumulation of facts of a certain kind may serve to verify a statement even though they do not entail it" (RK 68). But the radical theological non-naturalist is not at all committed here or elsewhere to talking of verification in terms of entailments. For him the God-talk in question seems at least to be nearly incomprehensibly problematic and he thinks he at least can understand the alleged verifying claims, when expressed in non-theistic language, perfectly well without making reference to such talk and, given those two factors, he sees no reason why we should say that even if the statements describing such possible, plainly experiential, states of affairs were to transpire he should regard this as verifying or even counting as evidence for the claim that there is a bodiless, infinite individual beyond the bounds of space and time.

So while radical theological non-naturalism may be irrational, Penelhum has not shown it to be irrational, arbitrary or even mistaken or even given us a good reason for believing that it is any of these things.

Does he fare any better with theological positivism? He thinks that no good grounds have been given for accepting the restrictions of even the weakest forms of positivism, but he also believes that if we do accept a weakened form of it in which non-theistic statements have at least some non-expungeable theistic expressions, key theistic claims can be shown to meet these positivist criteria of verifiability, but that this is not so for the stronger forms of theological positivism—the ones I have contended are the actual challengers—which do not allow that the allegedly verifying non-theistic statements can have any non-expungeable theistic expressions. Penelhum claims, as we have seen, that such positivism is irrational, not simply because it has a criterion for factual meaning (factual import) which is arbitrary but also because the demand that the non-theistic statements which serve to verify theistic claims be statements that do not contain theistic expressions "is a demand which cannot be met nor is it reasonable to expect it to be met" (RK 83).

I agree that it cannot be met; it was indeed one of the central points of my argument to show that it cannot be met. I also agree that it is not "reasonable to expect it to be met" (RK 83). But it is just the recognition of these two things which leads one—or should lead one—to the recognition that, if this is so, theistic utterances are not genuine factual truth-claims, with an empirical anchorage in virtue of which we could come to know whether they are true or false or in virtue of which they could be reasonably believed to be true or false. Because they lack these features, they are not genuine factual statements whose truth or falsity can be empirically ascertained or in any other way ascertained (if indeed there is any other way). Penelhum—strangely it seems to me—thinks, because these demands cannot be met and because it is unreasonable to expect them to be met, that these demands are therefore unreasonable, but that does not at all follow, for the point of these demands is just to show that they cannot be met, and because they cannot be met, that these key theistic utterances cannot have the logical status they are usually thought to have, i.e., they cannot be genuine factual statements whose truth or falsity can be ascertained. So it is not this feature of *theological positivism* which shows it to be irrational. What Penelhum must do, to make out his contention against *theological positivism*, is to return to a general position he shares with many philosophers—Copleston, Mavrodes and Plantinga among others—to wit, the position that such a general criterion of factual significance is arbitrary. But to do that is no longer, as he was doing above, to play Crombie's, Mitchell's and Hick's game of at least provisionally accepting such a criterion of factual significance and then proceeding to show that even key theistic utterances could meet it. Abandoning that way of meeting the empiricist challenge, he would then have to return to his arguments, made in *Religion and Rationality*, and discussed at the beginning of Section II of this chapter, that Flew's challenge is arbitrary if it simply amounts to insisting on the requirement that religious assertions to be factually significant must be falsifiable by reference to observable events in the world (RR 124). He would have to make good his claim that there is no good reason why the believer must "be prepared to confine the assertions he makes about God within the limits of empirical criteria of significance" (RR 124). And to do that he would, at the very least, have to meet the arguments I made against him at the beginning of Section II.[9]

NOTES

1.   Terence Penelhum, *Problems of Religious Knowledge* (London: Macmillan Press, 1971) and Terence Penelhum, *Religion and Rationality* (New York: Random House, 1971). All references to these two books will be made in the text. *Problems of Religious Knowledge* will be referred to as RK and *Religion and Rationality* as RR.

2.   R.B. Braithwaite, *An Empiricist's View of The Nature of Religious Belief* (London: Cambridge University Press, 1955) and R.M. Hare, "The Simple Believer," *Religion and Morality*, eds. Gene Outka and John P. Reeder, Jr. (Garden City, NY: Anchor Books, 1973) 393-427.

3.   D.Z. Phillips, *Faith and Philosophical Enquiry* (London: Routledge & Kegan Paul, 1970); Paul L. Holmer, "Atheism and Theism," *Lutheran World* XII (1963); Stuart Brown, *Religious Belief* (London: Open University Press, 1974); and Ilham Dilman, "Wisdom's Philosophy of Religion," *Canadian Journal of Philosophy* V.4 (1975): 473-522.

4.   This has been clearly and decisively argued by Ronald Hepburn in his *Christianity and Paradox* (London: C.A. Watts, 1958), chapters III and IV. John Hick, in his in many ways perceptive discussion of *Christianity and Paradox*, does nothing to unsettle that claim. See John Hick, "A philosopher criticizes theology," *The London Quarterly* XXI (1962): 103-10.

5.   See my *Contemporary Critiques of Religion* (London: Macmillan Press, 1971) and most particularly 28-30.

6.   Michael Tooley points out that Hick actually vacillates at times about whether he is trying to show the factual intelligibility of key strands of theistic discourse or whether

he is simply concerned to show how we can verify theistic claims. But there are repeated claims about the former and a realization of its central importance. In his inaugural lecture *Theology's Central Problem* (Birmingham: University of Birmingham Press, 1967), Hick makes it clear enough that he takes theology's central problem to be intimately linked with problems of meaning. He sees theology's central problem when viewed philosophically as "a problem concerning religious language" and he remarks that in "a sentence the issue is whether distinctively religious utterances are instances of the cognitive or of the non-cognitive uses of language" (1). (See as well page 15 of the same lecture.) He is concerned to show how religious utterances are cognitive by showing that they are factually meaningful because verifiable. This is a very central point in his "Theology and verification," *Theology Today* XII (1960): 12-31, and comes out definitely in his exchange with Binkley. See his remarks in the *Journal for the Scientific Study of Religion* II.1 (1962) and II.2 (1963). Michael Tooley's key remarks on this are in his "John Hick and the concept of eschatological verification," *Religious Studies* XII (1976): 177-99.

7.   Putting it just as Penelhum does in the above quotation obscures the force of radical theological non-naturalism. They say that it is not irrational to refuse any theistic conclusion until we have a sufficient understanding of God-talk such that we can understand what kind of truth claim if any is being made or presupposed in its characteristic use.

8.   I have accepted for the sake of this discussion the claim that talk of life after the death of our present bodies is coherent talk. In reality I would challenge that as I do in my "Logic, Incoherence and Religion," forthcoming, and in my "The Faces of Immortality," *Death and Afterlife*, ed. Steven Davis (London: Macmillan Press, 1988).

9.   If the general thrust of my arguments is well taken here, they would also tend to undermine, with only slight modifications, Basil Mitchell's criticisms of my account in his *The Justification of Religious Belief* (London: Macmillan Press, 1973) 7-20. I have further critically examined Penelhum's Christian revisionism in my "Radical Theological Non-Naturalism," *Sophia* XVIII.2 (1979): 1-6. This revisionism has been trenchantly criticized from a traditionalist point of view by Shabbir Akhtar in his *Reason and the Radical Crisis of Faith* (New York: Peter Lang, 1987) 135-206.

CHAPTER 13

Christian Empiricism*

. . . The transcendent God is bound always to be an idle element in our religious life.

R.M. Hare

Prolegomena

PHILOSOPHERS RATHER EASILY FALL INTO perplexity. They tend to have a cultivated incapacity to understand, even in those situations where in reality there may be no genuine perplexity. Sometimes even those perplexities—artificial as they are—still have a point, for, in some instances, even a partial sorting out of such perplexities will help us to better understand concepts which play central parts in our lives. Perplexities about religion sometimes have this aspect. They can, of course, be specimens of classical metaphysical worries. But they are seldom just that. I am inclined even to say that by definition, where the religious worry is genuine, they cannot just be that. Religious perplexities and an orientation toward or away from religion are intimately bound up with our conceptions of ourselves and of our life and our conception of how we should live our lives, and what attitudes we should take toward death, and how we should relate to our fellows. Religion is bound up, either negatively or positively, with our ultimate commitments. (This is not to say "God is what we are ultimately committed to.")[1] Our doubts and perplexities here are not just philosophers' perplexities but the doubts and perplexities of many who are struggling to make sense of their lives. God may be, in principle, an unobservable metaphysical reality, but God is not just a metaphysical reality.

It is hardly news that core religious conceptions—including core Jewish and Christian conceptions—are a scandal to the intellect. We are not only perplexed about whether we can know or reasonably believe that God exists, we are perplexed about the very coherence of God-talk.[2] Empiricism—in some form or other—is deeply embedded in our culture. It enters into the underlying, sometimes unwitting, assumptions of more

---

*First published in *The Journal of Religion* 61.2 (1981).

and more people in our culture. While it plainly has its philosophical difficulties, there are parts of it that are very persuasive indeed and would
seem to have become a part of critical and reflective common sense.[3]
Indeed, in that very broad sense, it might very well even be a part of the
framework of those contemporary philosophers who, under Chomsky's
influence, think of themselves as rationalists. Yet it is that very general
empiricist framework which has been one of the central sources of perplexities about religion and has engendered in many scepticism about religion.

What is striking, and what I want to examine here, is the claim made
by Braithwaite and Hare, both analytical philosophers who accept a tolerably
determinate empiricist framework, that religion can be made sense of and
Christianity can be consistently, coherently and, indeed, reasonably adhered
to or adopted even by someone who accepts a through and through empiricist orientation. Part I will be devoted to articulating the rationale of
Braithwaite's classic case for such a "Godless Christianity". Part II will
first consider Hare's much less familiar but more ramified and self-conscious
development of Braithwaite's case, and second it will raise, against the
background of Hare's self-conscious reactions, what I, at least, take to be
a cluster of critical questions and objections which remain, even after such
a Christian empiricism has been given a sympathetic hearing.

"Godless Christianity" in the Analytical Mode, I

A.

The kind of Christian empiricism developed by R.B.
Braithwaite and R.M. Hare I shall call, perhaps tendentiously, Godless
Christianity.[4] This view seems outrageous to many and this includes both
believers and nonbelievers alike. Yet it is clear enough that both Braithwaite
and Hare view themselves as sincere Christians trying to preserve what
they take to be essential to Christianity, in particular, and religion, in general,
in the face of what they regard as devastating logical objections to traditional
cosmological views of the world. They are also, as I remarked in the prole-
gomena, solidly in the broadly empiricist and analytical framework inherited
from Hume. If that framework is taken as normative for matters epistemological and methodological, and the concept of reasonableness is defined in
the terms utilized by this framework, then it may well be necessary—if
we are to make anything of religion at all—to characterize religion at least
roughly in the way Braithwaite and Hare do. Key religious utterances, ordinarily taken to be factual assertions, cannot be such assertions or be coherently treated as factual assertions. However, it is not unnatural to believe
that, if such an approach is necessary to make sense of religion, this constitutes a *reductio* of such an empiricist approach. Religion cannot be understood in those terms and still be seriously entertained.[5]

There is a steadfast resistance on Braithwaite's and Hare's part to such an attempted *reductio*. Braithwaite, whose general position I shall now lay out, has argued that there are "three classes of statement whose method of truth-value testing is in general outline clear . . ." (p. 129). They are (1) statements about particular matters of empirical fact, for example, "The coffee is cold"; (2) scientific hypotheses and other general empirical statements, for example, "Robins usually arrive in Ontario before they do in Nova Scotia"; and (3) logically necessary propositions of logic and mathematics, for example, "7 + 5 = 12".

Unfortunately, certain key religious propositions—that which is expressed by a religious utterance—do not fit into any of those three classifications. Yet, at least on a naïve view, we are inclined to believe that religious utterances in the declarative mood are either true or false. But if, as Braithwaite believes, the above is so, certain of them can be neither true nor false. Furthermore, if we agree that is so, are we then to conclude that they are meaningless and that religion rests on a mistake? But, if taken without qualification, that claim is itself—to put the matter rather minimally—paradoxical.

Braithwaite argues that this is not the conclusion we should draw. He points out that there are other types of utterance, which do not express verifiable propositions, but which are still plainly meaningful. His examples are moral utterances, for example, "You should show her more concern" or "She is too rigidly righteous." Such utterances are not statements of any of the above types, do not even appear to be empirically verifiable, and are used to guide conduct rather than, Braithwaite maintains, to describe conduct or merely to predict that so and so will be done. They are plainly meaningful, yet they do not fit the above paradigms of meaningful utterances. They are not, that is, verifiable and perhaps are not even truth bearing, yet they are plainly meaningful.

Braithwaite believes that the spirit of empiricism can still be maintained even though we must give up the verification principle as a general criterion of meaning. We can, while keeping in the spirit of empiricism, substitute for the verification principle the use principle, that is, the principle that "the meaning of any statement is given by the way in which it is used" (p. 133). Indeed the verification principle is just a specific and specialized application of the use principle. When we examine the actual use of factual statements, we find, Braithwaite claims, that they are all verifiable. Indeed on reflection and by an examination of their actual use, it should be evident that anything which would plainly and unequivocally count as a factual statement must have this property.

B.

Religious utterances do indeed plainly have a use in the language. The central philosophical task, as Braithwaite sees it vis-à-vis religion, is to explain and elucidate how religious propositions are used by people to express their religious convictions (p. 133). Their use is that of "being primarily declarations of adherence to a policy of action, declarations of commitment to a way of life" (p. 136). In this way they are modeled after a certain understanding of how moral utterances function, namely a theory which views them in a conative way, that is, as "expressing the intention of the asserter to act in a particular sort of way specified in the assertion" (p. 134). To find out the meaning of a religious utterance, Braithwaite claims, is to find out the intentions to act in a certain way which are embodied in them. Indeed, as Braithwaite puts it, "the primary use of religious assertions is to announce allegiance to a set of moral principles: without such allegiance there is no 'true religion'" (p. 138).

C.

It is important for Braithwaite to be able (a) to distinguish religious sentences from sentences which are merely moral, and (b) to distinguish between the religious claims of different religions. The most central difference, according to Braithwaite, between purely moral utterances and religious ones is that religion concerns essentially not only external but also internal behaviour. "Christianity requires not only that you should behave towards your neighbour as if you loved him as yourself," it requires, as well, that you love him as yourself; the "conversion involved in accepting a religion is a conversion, not only of the will, but of the heart" (p. 139). In a religious system, as distinct from a purely moral one, there is reference to a story as well as to a cluster of intentions.

It is important to recognize that the story or parable may or may not be believed by the believer to be true as a matter of empirical fact. He recognizes that the stories are composed of empirical statements, but, while the believer alludes to them and entertains them, he need not believe in their truth. The essential thing is that he has the story before him in the making of his commitments to act in one way or another. "To assert the whole set of assertions of the Christian religion is both to tell the Christian doctrine story and to confess allegiance to the Christian way of life" (p. 141). That he believes that the Christian stories are true is not, according to Braithwaite, the proper test for being a sound believing Christian. The proper test, rather, is whether he "proposes to live according to Christian moral principles and associates his intention with thinking of Christian stories" which he may or may not believe to be true, that is, believe to correspond to empirical fact.

D.

The above characterization sets out the core of Braithwaite's account of religion. There are, as commentators were quick to note, all sorts of tolerably evident objections, but, before we turn to some of them, let us consider a general objection that Braithwaite himself states and faces at the end of his essay.[6] It is the very natural objection

which contends that he has eviscerated religion of the claim to that objective
content which is essential to give it point.

> If a man's religion is all a matter of following the way of life he sets before himself
> and of strengthening his determination to follow it by imagining exemplary fairy-
> tales, it is purely subjective: his religion is all in terms of his own private ideas
> and of his own private imaginations. How can he even try to convert others to
> his religion if there is nothing objective to convert them to? How can he argue
> in its defense if there is no religious proposition which he believes, nothing which
> he takes to be the fundamental truth about the universe? And is it of any public
> interest what mental techniques he uses to bolster up his will? Discussion about
> religion must be more than the exchange of autobiographies. (p. 146)

Braithwaite responds by remarking that being social animals we
often do share convictions, but he also admits—what is also surely so—
that sometimes these convictions are very dissimilar. He then asks whether
there can be any reasonable interchange and argument pro and con between
their advocates when they so differ. Like Hare, Braithwaite believes that
decision—plain human commitment—is finally determinative here.[7] We
finally cannot establish or prove a set of moral principles. Instead we finally
must—logically must—simply subscribe to them or adopt them by a decision
of principle. But this does not, he points out, rule out the relevance of
ordinary empirical beliefs to those decisions. Though "an intention . . .
cannot be logically based upon anything except another intention," it does
not follow from that that our decisions, giving expression to our intentions,
cannot be made in the light of a reflection on, and taking to heart of, everything we know. In that way they can be reflective and amenable to
reason.[8] To call such intentions subjective or arbitrary is to misdescribe
their character. Religion can be a matter of following a way of life, rooted
ultimately in a personal decision of principle, and still be nonarbitrary and
nonsubjective for all of that.[9]

"Godless Christianity" in the
Analytical Mode, II

A.

R.M. Hare, nearly twenty years after Braithwaite's
lecture and the initial stirrings of the theology and falsification dispute,
returns in an interesting and distinctive way to that dispute. He has a view
of Braithwaite's essay shared by almost no one else. He heard the lecture
in 1955 and believed then, as he still believes, that it is "by far the best
thing on this subject (he) had ever heard or read" (p. 407). In view of
what have widely been held to be devastating objections to Braithwaite's
account, (a) what is it that Hare finds so right about this approach and
(b) how does he attempt to overcome those objections?

Generally, Hare thinks that many of the criticisms directed against religion are well taken and that religious belief, to remain a viable option for reflective and informed contemporary people, must be considerably reduced. The core of Christian belief, that which is really crucial to preserve, has very little to do, on Hare's view, with the cosmological claims which have seemed so baffling and unbelievable to so many people. There are, indeed, "lumps of orthodoxy that stick in the throats" of Braithwaite and Hare and—though they respond to them differently and more evasively— they stick in the throats of Tillich and the Bishop of Woolwich as well. It is these lumps, Hare argues, which need to be put aside as not essential to religion.

Hare tries to address himself, as he believes Braithwaite addressed himself, to "the quite genuine perplexities of those who want to call themselves Christians, and yet cannot bring themselves to believe what Christians are supposed to have to believe" (p. 393). He wants to articulate a conception of faith "which is defendable against the attacks of the philosophically well-armed atheist" (p. 394). Hare develops what he calls a version of Christian empiricism (p. 394). He believes that once the issues in the debate between belief and unbelief are seen clearly "nobody with any claim to rationality is going to say that he is a Christian," if to be a Christian is to "believe all the things that the orthodox say they believe and believe them literally . . ." (p. 395). The thing, Hare would have it, for a rational person to do is to articulate, or come to accept on someone else's articulation, a demythologized version of Christianity or Judaism rooted in an empiricist view of the world. Neither orthodox theologians nor atheists will like such a posing of the issues, but such a posing, Hare would have it, is the only nonevasive way to face the issues for a contemporary person who wants to make sense of his or her faith. He remarks that "Theologians have produced a succession of devices for concealing from Christians the starkness of the choice which, if the orthodox and the atheists are right, they have to make. Even the orthodox will often make use of these evasions if hard pressed. The reason why the vast majority of educated Christians are people who have evaded the issue is that those educated people who have not evaded it have ceased to be Christians. If there is no third alternative besides orthodoxy, strictly and clearly interpreted, and atheism, it is likely that most thinking people will choose the latter" (p. 395).

Hare is aware that there are pitfalls for the demythologizers: the determined and thorough Christian empiricists. The worry—indeed a very persistent worry—is that a form of Christianity or Judaism which squares with that account will be so eviscerated that we will come to have something which is, in substance, an atheism graced by a Christian or Jewish vocabulary.

Such a predicament—such an evisceration from "simple belief" to a kind of "sophisticated belief" through death by a thousand qualifications—raises, through the theology and falsification issue, what has come to be called Flew's challenge or, more appropriately, the empiricists' challenge.[10] It comes to this. For what is expressed by an utterance to constitute a genuine assertion which succeeds in making a real factual claim about the world—that is, an utterance that characterizes how the world is—something must count for its truth, and something must count against it. If an utterance denies nothing, if not even a possible state of affairs counts against it, then it also asserts nothing, that is, it makes no factual claim. This being so, perhaps the simplest way to find out whether an utterance actually succeeds in making a factual assertion is to find out whether it could be falsified or disconfirmed, whether any conceivable set of circumstances could show it to be false or probably false. With this test in mind, if we put the key religious utterances of contemporary religious people to such a test, they do not pass it. "An omnipotent and loving God exists" is so used by such people that it denies nothing and thus asserts nothing because whatever happens, or even conceivably could happen in any possible world, the believer will not give it up. No event or cluster of events which occurs or could occur will be accepted by him as something which would be evidence sufficient to make him give up his belief that there is such a God. His mind is firmly fixed. To test this, Flew's remarks take the form of a challenge to the believer: "What would have to occur or to have occurred to constitute for you a disproof of the love of, or the existence of God?"[11] If this question cannot be answered—the challenge runs—then we must conclude that the prima facie status of such religious utterances is not their actual status and that, in reality, they are not what they purport to be: namely grand cosmological (metaphysical), but still putatively factual, claims which are, in fact, true and thus are capable of being true or false. It is against the background of this challenge that we should understand Hare's dialectic and his remarks about the "simple believer." (It is important that the qualifier "putative" before "cosmological factual claims" be duly noted. The underlying assumption in such an empiricist challenge—an assumption which Braithwaite and Hare accept and an assumption which has been vigorously defended by empiricists—is that "an empirical factual statement" is a pleonasm. "Empirical" adds nothing to "factual". Where cosmological claims about "ultimate reality" do not meet that constraint, no clear contrasting conception can be given. But that is exactly what Flew's challenge was designed to smoke out. Throughout this essay, "cosmology" is used in its most typical sense, namely to refer to metaphysical claims about what has been called "ultimate reality".)

B.

Hare's "simple believer", after a series of encounters with atheists and "sophisticated believers", finds himself in the following bind. On the one hand, he does understand the old, literal ideas about God, where God is construed as an anthropomorphic being, but he has come to believe them to be false and, indeed, often fantastic. He understands them all right, or at the very least he has some inkling of what they are about, but they also seem to him to be falsifiable and, indeed, patently false claims. On the other hand, the ideas of the "sophisticated believer" seem to him so strange that it is hard to figure out what they mean and they seem, as well, far removed from "the God he used to worship" (p. 401). They seem, if we view them as some mysterious kind of allegedly factual beliefs, to be unfalsifiable or at least anomalous with respect to their falsification, but (and perhaps because of this) utterly problematic—anomalous with respect to their meaning. The suspicion thrust on him by a reflection on the empiricists' challenge is the suspicion that with sophisticated religious belief there really is not anything left which could be believed. The suspicion runs deep within him that, as a result of the "sophisticated believer's" qualifications, Christian and Jewish faith, so qualified, has become so insubstantial that it is hard to see what one is supposed to be defending (p. 402). The key religious utterances of sophisticated belief try to make genuine assertions concerning the nature of "ultimate reality", but fail. They do not succeed in asserting anything. Hare believes, in effect, to put the above point in a somewhat different way, that on his own grounds Flew has won out, but Hare also believes that there is something important in the faith of the "simple believer"— something he in part shares with such a believer—and he wants to strengthen that belief by freeing it from its philosophical muddles and by demythologizing it (p. 403).

It is Hare's conviction (a conviction he shares with Braithwaite) that it is not the holding of a set of factual or cosmological beliefs—being committed to a set of assertions in the narrow sense of that term—which centrally distinguishes a believer from a nonbeliever. Hare claims that, whatever putative assertions of such an order some believers might be committed to, they could be abandoned without their losing what is crucial to their faith. He stresses, in what by now is a well-known and nearly universally accepted move against positivistically oriented analyses, that there are many different kinds of intelligible utterance. Those used to make factual assertions are just one type of utterance among a myriad of very diverse types. Among the most important for the philosophy of religion are those expressive of "beliefs which are not beliefs in the truth of assertions, in the narrow sense, and which are fundamental to our whole life in this world, and still more in our doing anything like science" (p. 404).[12] Hare's non-religious example is the belief that, for whatever happens, there is some causal law to be discovered which would explain happenings of that sort. There is, he claims, no falsifying that claim. Yet it is a claim dear to the hearts of many scientists. Hare argues that it can meet the empiricists' challenge no more than many religious utterances. To believe it, to accept it, and to act in accordance with it is not, according to Hare, to believe in the truth of a factual assertion, yet it is to believe both groundlessly and reasonably. If we apply the empiricists' challenge and ask just what would have to happen to entitle the scientist to stop believing in that claim, the answer is, as in the case of sophisticated belief, nothing. Nothing would, or even could, falsify it.[13]

I do not think this example of Hare's really shows what he wants it to. I shall briefly indicate why I think this, but I do not want to lay much stress on this for (a) what I say here is too problematic to be so curtly argued; and (b) Hare could, perhaps, choose a happier example and convincingly support his general crucial point about the existence of special foundational beliefs or framework-beliefs. I shall, that is, briefly state my objections. But, after I have done that, I shall ignore them in order to continue the discussion along what I take to be more fruitful paths. In doing this, I shall treat Hare's case as if he had established what he had set out to establish.

As far as natural science is concerned, a central task, if not the central task, is to look for causes. So the scientist, as long as he keeps at his task, will continue to look for causes; but from this it does not follow that he believes, let alone that he must believe, that he will always find them, or that they always will be found if only the search is diligent enough and sufficiently protracted. He probably does believe that, but the crucial thing to see is that such a belief need not be part of what it is to believe in science or to be a scientist. Moreover and second, though he need not and probably does not hold that belief tentatively as a hypothesis and does not look to falsify it, yet it does not follow that it is not an empirical belief testable (weakly confirmable or infirmable) at least in principle.[14]

C.

It is not, however, implausible to argue that there are some beliefs, beliefs of a diverse sort, which have the status Hare characterizes. Indeed Wittgenstein, in *On Certainty*, and derivatively Malcolm have powerfully argued for just this. Hare mentions fundamental moral beliefs—beliefs of particular importance for his analysis of religious belief— as a further example. In a comment which reveals at least a partial rejection of scientism, Hare remarks that there "are whole fields of human conduct outside the laboratory where scientific belief does not give us the answers to the questions we are (or ought to be) asking. It does not give us answers, not because it is wrong, but because it does not apply in those fields" (p. 406). In a reaction which is just the opposite of Dewey's, Hare contends that morality is just such a field. "We cannot decide by experimental methods or by observation what we ought to do. That I ought to do this or that is another of those beliefs which I have to accept or reject (for what I do depends on this decision) . . ." (p. 406). Hare's decisionalism has been thoroughly criticized, but, for all of that, it is true that with respect to their truth capacity fundamental moral beliefs are very anomalous indeed.[15] It is not clear what their logical status is, but it is very questionable that they should be taken to be factual assertions true or false in the relatively unproblematic way in which such assertions are true or false.

However, while he thinks there is something to be salvaged in the faith of the "simple believer", Hare also believes much must be jettisoned as well. Indeed Hare rejects the very category of the supernatural as something beyond the possibility of rational belief for present-day educated people. He believes "that it is as impossible that a fully educated population should believe in the God of the orthodox as it is that the present day population of England or New England should believe in witchcraft" (p. 422). Like Braithwaite and Miles, Hare asks, and answers in the affirmative, the question of whether religion can do without the supernatural (p. 416). Christianity involves a commitment to a distinctive way of life, but does it also involve, and inexpungeably, a belief in the supernatural? Hare denies that it does. In asking whether belief in the supernatural is essential to Christianity, Hare claims that the key question is whether faith in the supernatural makes the Christian different, or whether this difference in behaviour and orientation to life is something that could be had by someone who did not believe in the supernatural? Hare thinks that it could be had by someone utterly without such cosmological beliefs. Thus, he claims, we can have a viable Christianity without any commitment to or belief in the supernatural.

D.

Hare sets out, in a candid and disarming way, an expansion of Braithwaite's account which he hopes will make such a Godless Christianity—to not mince words—a viable option for Christian believers (p. 414). In doing this, Hare develops what he calls a "minimum Braithwaitian position" and, after making certain clarifications and remarks designed to overcome certain predictable and natural misunderstandings, he considers how such a position "might meet the objections to it that would be made by an old-fashioned Christian believer, whether simple or sophisticated" (p. 408).

I shall first turn to some of the clarifications. It might be thought at first that Braithwaite and Hare are simply giving us to understand "that religious belief is a kind of moral belief or attitude" (p. 406). In religion one has "morals helped out by mythology" (p. 408). "A man", as Braithwaite tells, "is not . . . a professing Christian unless he both proposes to live according to Christian moral principles, and associates his intention with thinking of Christian stories; but he need not believe that the empirical propositions presented by the stories correspond to empirical fact" (p. 408). Hare, as we noted, is much enamoured of this account, but still he will not accept it just as it stands. The category "moral principles", particularly when identified with duties, is too narrow a category to play appropriately the role Braithwaite assigns to it. In the above quotation from Braithwaite, "way of life" should replace "moral principles". Moreover, and more important, "religion cannot be reduced to morality, even in an extended sense, unless we include also the faith that saves moral endeavour from futility" (p. 414).

This is a very important point for Hare, and it needs to be carefully explained and probed. Hare sees readily enough that we cannot reduce religion to agapeistic behaviour ritualistically decked out. Christianity involves love of neighbour, but it is not simply that. Among other things, we have the very central task on such an account of coming to understand what, with a rejection of the supernatural, love of God could come to. And to do that "we shall first have to explain in what sense, for Braithwaite, God can exist to be the object of love" (p. 409). After all, given its rejection of the supernatural, its nonreliance on anything like a Tillichian category of being, and given an emotive neutralization of "Godless", it is natural to call this Christian empiricism a Godless Christianity. Braithwaite and Hare do not call their Christian empiricism a Godless Christianity, but I am inclined to say that a rose by any other name would have as sweet a smell; for, after all, Hare does say that "the transcendent God is bound always to be an idle element in our religious life" (p. 424). So it seems evident that this is a Godless Christianity. Yet Hare does raise this question about God (p. 409). In trying to understand what could possibly be meant, on such an account, by the reality of God, it is crucial, he believes, to consider that in morality, besides duties and obligations, we have moral ideals. When we consider them and consider as well what it is to believe that what these ideals prescribe or proclaim will someday be achieved, we will come to understand, on Braithwaite's and Hare's account, what it is to believe in the existence of God. But this still seems to me to be an evasion, or at least misapprehension, involving a stipulative redefinition of "God".

However, before proceeding to assess this claim, we should develop Hare's account a bit. Not only "our moral attitudes" are involved in such a conception, "but all our wants, aspirations and ideals." Such things make up our total attitude toward life. It is such an attitude which Braithwaite and Hare denominate as religious belief (p. 409). What is being done, in an attempt in some way to obviate the empiricists' challenge, is to assimilate "statements of religious belief to a class of utterances which can be unfalsifiable without lacking content" (p. 410). This Hare and Braithwaite do by denying "that religious statements are any kind of factual assertion" (p. 410). Thus, even "There is a God" or "God exists" must not be construed as grand cosmological but still factual claims, but as expressions of certain, in a broad sense, moral ideals plus an expression of a conviction—in the form of an empirical belief—that they will be sustained (p. 410).

E.

There is a very natural objection to this that the orthodox Christian, but not only the orthodox Christian, will make. Hare is very aware of it and states it and tries to meet it. I shall first restate it and then consider the adequacy of Hare's response.

Surely (the response goes) religious assertions must be factual, for the Christian does not merely follow a way of life; he has, as well, the hope that this way of life is not vain or pointless. But such a hope would be pointless and futile if the world were not ordered in a certain way. The crucial thing, if we are to explicate Christian belief and not reduce it to something else, is to see that to be a Christian is not merely to be disposed to follow a certain way of life, it is also, and centrally, to believe that God is there to sustain one in this way of life (p. 410).

Hare recognizes that this is powerful and a natural objection but believes that he and Braithwaite "can go a long way to meet it." We need to recognize that Christians are "committed to certain factual assertions about the world, but that these are all empirical ones," open to the usual empirical tests. Christians will, for example, believe that it is reasonable to hope that the central aspirations, ideals, and wants, which in part constitute their religion, can be fulfilled. And this is an empirical belief which is weakly testable and is not devoid of content. It is very natural, for example, for Christians to believe "that the inanimate world is so ordered as not to make his endeavours pointless" (p. 411).

It is also important to stress that the key empirical beliefs that the Christian is committed to are typically "sufficiently indeterminate to escape refutation by single or even by quite numerous counterinstances" (p. 411). They are beliefs which contain "enough *ceteris-paribus* clauses to look after the counter-instances in all of which it will be claimed that other things were not after all equal" (p. 411). Such beliefs—and parallel things operate in science—are not given up because of a few bits of prima facie disconfirming evidence. Such evidence is treated as an anomaly.

The Christian's belief that moral endeavour and commitment are not pointless is not testable in an ordinary way, yet it still is about the world and is therefore factual and weakly confirmable and infirmable. We do not rule out the search for evidence concerning such a belief; we can specify something of what would count as evidence for or against such a belief. However, we do not expect this belief actually to be established by empirical investigation. Faith is required for the belief that moral endeavour is not futile as well as for the belief that all occurrences admit of a scientific explanation. But these beliefs are, nonetheless, both factual and weakly confirmable or infirmable (pp. 412-13). However, we should note that an abandonment of such beliefs would be very crucial for our beliefs about life, for the "abandonment of it would entail a radical change in our view about what the world is like" (p. 413).

Does this response actually meet the really crucial core of the orthodox Christian objection Hare considered? I am ambivalent about this, but I am inclined at least to believe that it does not. The conviction remains that in spite of what Hare has said about factual beliefs—and even factual beliefs of a rather extraordinary sort—he is still leaving out, and has no way to accommodate, given his epistemological beliefs and conceptions about meaning, what is most crucial to the Christian or Jew, namely, belief in God is not just the having of certain moral ideals or life ideals which are associated with stories (parables) and factual assertions of the sort Hare considers. Christianity or Judaism without God is a very strange thing indeed and—or so it seems—a pointless thing. But is it utterly pointless? There seems still to be room for what Hare calls "divine providence", namely the faith (trust) that it is possible that the ends of morality will be realized, that events will not massively and repeatedly frustrate the ends of morality. Faith in divine providence, on this account, is the trust that we can find moral policies—a set of moral prescriptions concerning how we are to live— which will not be futile. A moral man will want the ends of morality to be achieved; a Christian will trust that they will be achieved; that, most centrally, is what his faith consists in. But still, why talk of divine providence here? There seems to be no way of bringing God in on the Braithwaite-Hare account—no matter how minimal that account of God is kept. And yet a conception of God is at the heart of Christian and Jewish belief. Or is the belief that all is well and the thankfulness that that is so just what belief in God comes to? But then the secular humanist can be led gently into belief. Conversion is achieved by linguistic stipulation. Our conception of God is now so minimal that we have no conception of God at all.

Hare responds—rather weakly I believe—by saying that this "objection cannot be made clear until we have discovered what it would be like to bring God in" (p. 414). He takes this to mean the bringing in of the category of the supernatural, and this in turn he construes, not implausibly, to mean belief in the contranatural and/or transcendental; and he rejects both of these categories of belief. To commit oneself to either conception is, Hare continues, to commit oneself to what contemporary people with a reasonable scientific and philosophical education regard as absurdities. To have a reasonable, morally and humanly acceptable Christianity or Judaism, we must have a Christianity or Judaism without the supernatural. And—though Hare does not say this—this means, unless God is given a quite new sense, a Christianity or Judaism without God.

In effect, at the beginning of Braithwaite's essay, and explicitly in the last part of Hare's, arguments are given for rejecting the supernatural (pp. 414-27). They are reasonable arguments but not terribly developed or original. However, in recent times they have been considerably developed by Martin, Hepburn, Flew, Matson, Scriven and myself.[16] If our arguments are for the most part sound, then belief in God—as belief in the supernatural—is untenable.

Hare and Braithwaite (and Miles and van Buren as well) accept the central core of these arguments, yet they wish all the same to remain Christians. Their argument for sticking with a Godless Christianity is that (a) without it we either have absurd Christian belief or no Christian belief at all and (b) that a nonabsurd but Godless Christianity can still be maintained without departing too much in essentials from what Christians have always been centrally committed to. Can it?

F.

Can or should we have a Christianity or a Judaism without God? Hare sees the crux of this problem as being whether it is a belief in God which makes the believer different from other people (p. 417). He argues that it is not. It is not, he claims, over this problem that the really crucial differences emerge, though he does concede what should be evident, "that in abandoning the supernatural we should have to abandon some things which have been thought to be very central to traditional Christianity" (p. 417).

However, even if it is not belief in God which marks the most essential difference between the lives of Christians and sceptics, I am not at all sure that this is the relevant question to go with in asking whether Christianity or Judaism can or should get along without a belief in God. Suppose, ritualistic and purely verbal behaviour apart, that the most distinctive characteristic distinguishing a Christian from a religious sceptic (an atheist or an agnostic) is a pervasive love for humankind and a trust that in the deepest way nothing can harm him and that all is well no matter what happens. If this is the dividing line, it still is reasonable to respond that the only reasonable ground or rationale for such attitudes and such a conviction is a belief in God: a belief, whatever else it is, which either presupposes a cosmological belief or is itself a cosmological belief, namely, a belief that God exists. With that belief, such emotions and such convictions have a rationale, are intelligible; but without it they seem at least to be groundless and arbitrary. Given a certain belief in ultimate reality there is a sense in which one can coherently believe that a good person cannot be harmed no matter what happens; but, given a conception of a Godless universe, where values are simply universalizable decisions in principle, such a belief seems foolish indeed. Without such a cosmological background belief, without such metaphysical background beliefs, it is an arbitrary attitudinal posturing.

Suppose a present-day Kierkegaard were to respond that we must not look for justification or even for rationales for such fundamental beliefs. We use them in justifying almost everything else we do, but do not and cannot justify them. They are our yardstick in such domains, and we do not in turn have a yardstick for our yardstick. But while justification, no doubt, must come to an end, it is not something that can simply come to an end at any point. The religious attitudes I characterized have a point— have at least something like a rationale—with a belief in God, and they seem at least to be patently pointless and perhaps even not altogether rational without such a belief. Differences which appear to make deep differences between believer and sceptic make no reasonable or justifiable difference without belief in God, and this would seem to be a rather powerful argument for rejecting a Godless Christianity.

Hare might respond that, since contranatural and transcendent (transcendental) conceptions are not—for one reason or another—rationally believable, such a backing in mythology (God being for him a mythological concept) for such attitudes and convictions is not available, but that this does not matter for such attitudes are intrinsically desirable on their own or have their own sort of appeal.[17] But while this may be true of a love of humankind, it is also true that love of humankind by itself does not distinguish the sceptic from the Christian. The more distinctive notions that nothing can harm him and that all is well no matter what can only make sense if taken against the background of a belief in God. Without that belief they are without a rationale and, on reflection and on balance, they are not intrinsically desirable. They might even be undesirable.

G.

Let us come at our problem of the desirability of a Godless Christianity from another direction. Hare characterizes a "transcendental being" as a being whose "existence or non-existence makes no difference to observable phenomena" (p. 415). Now even if such a God is, in reality—as Hare believes—actually an idling conception, it does not follow that believers and sceptics do not react very differently to talk of God. Even if there is, in reality, no difference between claiming that God listens to prayers and directs events accordingly, and claiming it is just the case that such events take place, the effect of these different modes of speech is very different on many people. In this—that is, in terms of their effects on them—the concept is not idling at all, though one can make the normative claim, against the believer, that it should be once he recognizes that such transcendental beliefs involving the utilization of such a conception can, if Hare is right, make no intelligible truth-claim.

It is no doubt correct and important to say with Hare "a lot has changed about the Christian religion in the course of the centuries" and that, with an ever increasingly large educated and sophisticated population, it will change at an accelerated rate (p. 420). But it does not follow that it can change so deeply as to become a "Godless religion" and retain enough of a difference from an atheistic humanism to give point to Christian affirmations. What really is the point, with such beliefs and under such circumstances, in calling oneself a Christian or engaging in Christian practices? If Hare is right, a recognition of the autonomy of morals makes it clear that, even if the God of the orthodox exists, we could not ground morality in God or use such a conception to provide a ground for the commitment to morality.[18] But, more crucially for him, even if we could, there could not be such ground in or for morals because Hare defends a Christianity sans God. But what then is the point of such a Christian commitment?

Perhaps Hare could respond (in effect engaging in a replay of Kant) that even with such a Christianity, albeit Godless Christianity, we have hope that the ends of morality will not be frustrated, that our moral policies and moral practices will not be futile, that moral endeavour will not in the end be defeated, and that our "morality is not pointless" (p. 412). But, again, similar considerations such as those we have just considered hover into sight. Where our faith consisted, essentially but not exclusively, in the truth that there really is the transcendent God characterized in the Scriptures, such attitudes about the nonfrustration of the ends of morality have a plausibility. But with Hare's version of Christian faith they have no such plausibility.

To this, as we have seen in another context, Hare might in turn reply that just what in essence it is to have faith—to be the kind of Christian he recommends—is to have that trust in the achievement of the ends of morality (pp. 413-14). Having faith, for Hare, is just trusting, without grounds for that trust, that this will be the case. But where it is made, as it appears to be with Hare, without any appeal to evidence or reasons at all and, perhaps as a belief too persisted in, in spite of the evidence, trust in reality becomes hope or, perhaps better, fervent wish and belief is not opinion but commitment. But to have such wishes, and to take this to be faith, leads us all, as C.B. Martin once put it, gently into belief.[19] But now atheist and believer are no longer distinct and Christian belief has been thoroughly eviscerated.

H.

Hare might still respond that a Christian will be distinct from an atheist in that he will act on his wishes and his hopes. But it is very unclear what acting on such wishes or hopes comes to. The person with these hopes or wishes need not be an optimistic person at all. He might be very pessimistic indeed about what he expects. People with all sorts of differences in what they expect of their fellow humans and of "the world" might, quite equally, have those hopes and wishes. But, with different empirical beliefs, they would often act differently. Since this is so, it is entirely unclear what acting on such wishes or hopes would come to. So, if this is all we have to go on, we do not appear to have grounds for distinguishing the Christian from the religious sceptic.

Love of humankind and a rational hope—as distinct from a mere wish—that some day human ideals and aspirations will be realized can sit at least as well in a Marxist framework, or even a secular humanist framework (such as Dewey's), as it does in a Christian framework. Indeed, on either of those purely secular frameworks, the rational and unequivocal commitment to such conceptions is clearer. Why then Christianity? That many people grew up in those practices and beliefs—that they grew into frameworks—is not at all an adequate response in our circumstances. Nobody knows whether such human aspirations will in the long run, that is, within the life of humankind, prevail, but that does not at all lessen the desirability of tenacious and reflective efforts to bring about the conditions of their prevailing. But such commitments are logically and rationally independent of Christianity. Where there is a link it is purely historical and without logical or normative significance. There is no need here for Christianity, or for religion, or for anything like that. And to say that only that—that is, that particular set of normative commitments—is religion is to engage in an arbitrary and stipulative low-redefinition and to convert the nonreligious into the religious by stipulative fiat. There may be certain prescriptive principles which are essential to Christianity, but the ones that Hare has trotted out—which are very attractive normative principles that we would not on reflection wish to abandon—are not unique to Christianity, and there seems no need at all to continue running them under a Christian or even a religious flag. Indeed, to do so is to court confusion and misunderstanding (p. 425). The abandonment of Christianity need not lead to their abandonment, and Christianity does not add any rational underpinning to these moral commitments and aspirations.

It is surely fair enough to wish to give a reading to Christianity in which it turns out nonabsurd, and it is cheating to accept only a reading which makes it absurd. But it is also cheating to so eviscerate it—in seeking to make it intellectually and humanly respectable—that it undermines that which is distinctive about it and which enables it to hold out a hope that no secular humanism can match (p. 427).

NOTES

1.   Kai Nielsen, "Is God So Powerful That He Doesn't Even Have to Exist?" *Religious Experience and Truth*, ed. Sidney Hook (New York: New York University Press, 1961).

2.   I have tried to exhibit some of the reasons for this in my *Skepticism* (London: Macmillan, 1973), and in my *Contemporary Critiques of Religion* (London: Macmillan, 1971). I have more bluntly argued for it in my two essays—"In Defense of Atheism" and "Religion and Commitment"—reprinted in *Philosophy of Religion: Contemporary Perspectives*, ed. M.O. Schedler (New York: Macmillan, 1974). In my "Can Faith Validate God-Talk?" (*Theology Today* 20.2 [1963]: 158-73) and in my "Religious Perplexity and Faith" (*Crane Review* 8.1 [1965]: 1-17) I have argued that such problems cannot be avoided by an appeal to faith. There is no such short way with dissenters.

3.   I have tried to state what core empiricism is and distinguish it from logical empiricism in my "Is Empiricism an Ideology?" *Metaphilosophy* 3.4 (1972): 265-73.

4.   All page numbers cited in part I refer to Richard B. Braithwaite, "An Empiricist's View of the Nature of Religious Belief," *The Logic of God*, eds. Malcolm L. Diamond and Thomas V. Litzenburg, Jr. (Indianapolis: Bobbs-Merrill Co., 1975). Page numbers cited in part II refer to R.M. Hare, "The Simple Believer," *Religion and Morality*, eds. Gene Outka and John P. Reeder, Jr. (Garden City, NY: Anchor Books, 1973). Much earlier (1955), when the theology and falsification issue was first broached, Hare made a brief Braithwaitian sally into the debate. But he has come, and rightly, to regard that essay as confused. See *New Essays in Philosophical Theology*, eds. A. Flew and A. MacIntyre (New York: Macmillan, 1955) 99-103; see also in this vein R.M. Hare, "Religion and Morals," *Faith and Logic*, ed. Basil Mitchell (London: George Allen & Unwin, 1957). T.R. Miles and Paul van Buren have also developed arguments similar to those of Braithwaite's and Hare's. See T.R. Miles, *Religion and the Scientific Outlook* (London: Allen & Unwin, 1959) and "On Excluding the Supernatural," *Religious Studies* 1 (1966): 141-50; and Paul van Buren, *The Secular Meaning of the Gospel* (New York: Macmillan, 1963), *Theological Explorations* (New York: Collier-Macmillan, 1968), and *The Edges of Language* (New York: Macmillan, 1972).

5.   Terence Penelhum's reaction here is typical. See Terence Penelhum, *Religion and Rationality* (New York: Random House, 1971) 126-36.

6.   Keith Yandell, in his "Empiricism and Theism," expertly marshalls the standard objections to Braithwaite's account. But see, as well, his subsequent exchange with me. These essays are reprinted in *Philosophy and Religion*, ed. Keith E. Yandell (New York: McGraw-Hill Book Co., 1972).

7.   R.M. Hare, *The Language of Morals* (Oxford: Clarendon Press, 1952) 68-71. For some of the raw edges of this see my "Morality and Commitment," *Idealistic Studies* 7.1 (1977): 94-108.

8.   W.D. Falk, "Moral Perplexity," *Understanding Moral Philosophy*, ed. James Rachels (Encino, CA: Dickenson Publishing Co., 1976).

9.   See my essay referred to in note 7 and see W.K. Frankena, "Is Morality a Purely Personal Matter?" *Midwest Studies in Philosophy* 3 (1978): 122-32.

10.   See eds. Flew and MacIntyre and eds. Diamond and Litzenburg.

11.   A. Flew, "Theology and Falsification," in eds. Flew and MacIntyre 99.

12.   Compare here what Malcolm says about framework-beliefs and what Wittgenstein says about beliefs of the *Weltbild*: Norman Malcolm, *Thought and Knowledge* (Ithaca, NY: Cornell University Press, 1977) 193-216; Ludwig Wittgenstein, *On Certainty* (Oxford: Basil Blackwell, 1969), trans Denis Paul and G.E.M. Anscombe. I have discussed this in my "On the Rationality of Groundless Believing," *Idealistic Studies*, in press.

13.   It is surely understandable that people would so argue and this is perhaps the standard view, but for some considerations that would question whether it could meet the empiricists' challenge, see my "Is to Abandon Determinism to Withdraw from the Enterprise of Science?" *Philosophy and Phenomenological Research* 28.1 (1967): 117-21.

14.   See here Basil Mitchell's criticisms of Malcolm. Basil Mitchell, "Remarks," *Reason and Religion*, ed. Stuart C. Brown (Ithaca, NY: Cornell University Press, 1977).

15.   Hector-Neri Castaneda, "Imperatives, Decisions and 'Oughts': A Logico-Metaphysical Investigation," *Morality and the Language of Conduct*, eds. Hector-Neri Castaneda and George Nakhnikian (Detroit: Wayne State University Press, 1963). Less decisive but more readable criticisms occur in Philippa Foot, *Virtues and Vices* (Oxford: Basil Blackwell, 1978) and G. Warnock, *Contemporary Moral Philosophy* (New York: St. Martin's Press, 1967).

16.   C.B. Martin, *Religious Belief* (Ithaca, NY: Cornell University Press, 1959); Ronald Hepburn, *Christianity and Paradox* (London: C.A. Watts & Co., 1958); Antony Flew, *God and Philosophy* (London: Hutchinson & Co., 1966) and *The Presumption of Atheism* (New York: Barnes & Noble Books, 1976); Wallace Matson, *The Existence of God* (Ithaca, NY: Cornell University Press, 1965); and Michael Scriven, *Primary Philosophy* (New York: McGraw-Hill Book Co., 1966). See the differences from me in note 2. Three further atheist or agnostic accounts that should be noted here are Sidney Hook, *The Quest for Being* (New York: St. Martin's Press, 1961); Paul Edwards, "Difficulties in the Idea of God," *The Idea of God*, eds. Edward H. Madden *et al.* (Springfield, IL: Charles C. Thomas, 1968); and Walter Kaufmann, *Critique of Religion and Philosophy* (New York: Harper & Row, 1958) and *The Faith of a Heretic* (Garden City, NY: Anchor Books, 1963). The anthology *The Logic of God* cited in note 4 reprints some of the key sceptical essays, including some of mine not previously published in book form. Together these references set out, among the writings in English, the case made for unbelief by contemporary Anglo-American philosophers. That the argument has an important nineteenth-century ancestry can be seen from my "Agnosticism," *Dictionary of the History of Ideas*, ed. Philip P. Wiener, vol. 1 (New York: Charles Scribner's Sons, 1968).

17.   Given Hare's rejection of the philosophical category of intrinsic goodness, this is a rather unlikely turn for him to take. But, given readings such as those given by Georg von Wright or G.I. Lewis to such a conception, it is not implausible to believe that Hare is confused about this and that such a response is available to him.

18.   Hare means and I mean by the autonomy of morals that fundamental moral beliefs cannot be derived from factual beliefs or metaphysical beliefs. From the fact—if it is a fact—that God exists and that he commands certain things, nothing follows morally. It may well also be true, indeed it probably is, that to be moral one must, in some appropriate sense, be an autonomous person. But that plausible belief is not needed for the claim that one cannot ground morality in belief in God. Only the first, rather standard, claim about autonomy is required for that. I have argued the general claim about autonomy in my "Why There Is a Problem about Ethics," *Danish Yearbook of Philosophy* 15 (1978): 68-96 and in my "On Deriving an Ought from an Is," *Review of Metaphysics* 32.3 (1979): 487-514. I speak specifically to the problem about God and the autonomy of morals in my "God and the Good: Does Morality Need Religion?" *Theology Today* 21 (April 1964): 47-55 and in my *Ethics without God* (London: Pemberton Books, 1973).

19.   C.B. Martin, chapter 2.

CHAPTER 14

Talk of God and the Doctrine of Analogy*

If then we take the divine attributes one by one and ask whether each of them is to be found in God, we must reply that it is not there, at least as such and as a distinct reality, and since we can in no way conceive an essence which is nothing but an act of existing, we cannot in any way conceive what God is even with the help of such attributes. E. Gilson

The world requires as its cause a being totally transcending it in every respect; but how can we even affirm the existence of such a being, if our experience of the world gives us no words by which to define him? E.L. Mascall

I

THE CLASSICAL DOCTRINE OF ANALOGY HAS BEEN used to try to show how terms involved in God-talk have an appropriate meaning even if the key statements involving God-talk are not verifiable even in principle. Someone who (1) accepted the verifiability principle as a criterion for what is to count as *factually* meaningful and who (2) took the intent of the normal use of most indicative God-talk sentences to be to make factual statements, would assert that for "God loves his creatures" to be properly meaningful, we must show what implications for our experience would or at least in principle could count for or against its truth. Some defenders of the doctrine of analogy present an alternative account of the *meaning* of such utterances, an account which, if correct, would, for much of God-talk at least, supply an answer to the challenge that non-anthropomorphic God-talk is devoid of factual significance. I shall consider the merits of such views.

Father F. Copleston and Professor James F. Ross provide us with distinguished contemporary statements of such a position.[1] They both claim that where we are speaking of a transcendent and infinite being—the object of a religiously adequate God-talk—the terms predicated of this being must be used analogically if they are to have any meaning at all. We need such an analogical account to escape the following dilemma. If, on the one hand, the terms are used with the same meaning, say in respect to God and to man, then God becomes an anthropomorphic being. That is to say, if God's intelligence or love is like man's intelligence or love, then God becomes simply a kind of superman, a being that is a part of nature, and not an infinite, non-spatio-temporal being, transcendent to the world. Yet, on the other hand, if "intelligence" and "love" are said to have a completely different sense when applied to God, they lose all meaning

*First published in *The Thomist* XL.1 (1976).

for us. The meaning-content of terms such as "intelligence" and "loving" is determined by our experience of human beings, by our experience of human intelligence and love, "and if they are used in an entirely and completely different sense when predicated of God, they can have no meaning for us when they are used in this way."[2]

"Intelligence" as applied to dogs and men could have (I don't say it does have) a completely different sense and still "intelligence" could be intelligibly predicated of a dog's behaviour as well as a man's because we could ostensively teach how we used the term. But the case is different with God for we have not observed and cannot observe God—anything that could be observed, *ipso facto*, would not be God.[3] Since this is so we cannot discover by ostensive definition or ostensive teaching what it means to say God has intelligence or is loving. Thus if "intelligence" and "love" have a completely different meaning when applied to God, we can have no understanding at all of these predicates. If such key utterances as "God loves human beings" or "God's intelligence is manifest in his creation" are to have meaning, then "love" and "intelligence" must be used analogically: "that is to say, a term which is predicated of God and finite things must, when it is predicated of God, be used in a sense which is neither precisely the same as nor completely different from the sense in which it is predicated of finite things."[4] Terms like "love" and "intelligence" must be used in a "sense which is similar and dissimilar at the same time to the sense in which it is used when predicated of finite things."[5]

To put the matter in a slightly different way. For Aquinas and for other late medieval writers, who, as thoroughly as most contemporary writers, rejected any claim that there could be a *logically* necessary being or a purely conceptual identification of God, the problem of *meaning* was an acute one.[6] Our ordinary language with its pervasive empirical anchorage was accepted by these thinkers as being applicable to God. We must start from the language of common experience if we are to have any understanding of anything at all. But, as Ross puts it, Aquinas' problem then was this:

> How could he show that this language (all of the terms, expressions and employments of which are learned from human experience) can be applied, without such equivocation as would render invalid all argument, to God, an entity which is so different from the objects of experience as to be 'inexperience-able' in any of the ways common to ordinary human experience.[7]

It is claimed that it is just here—if our God-talk is to be shown to have an intelligible factual content—that we must develop a viable theory of analogical predication. Again, as Ross puts it, in a more technical rendering of Copleston's point:

> If the predicate terms in G-statements (statements with 'God' or a synonym as the subject) are *totally* equivocal with respect to the occurrences of the same predicate terms in E-statements (with any object of ordinary, direct or indirect experience as subject), then all arguments with an E-statement in the premises and a G-statement as the conclusion will be invalid, committing the fallacy of equiv-

ocation; and all G-statements will be meaningless because none of the human experience will count either as evidence for or as explications of those statements.[8]

But if our common terms here have a univocal meaning, we (Ross agrees with Copleston) fall into a gross anthropomorphism in which our statements about such an anthropomorphic deity are certainly literal enough but false or, as Copleston puts it, at least they commit their user to a concept of God that no one (presumably no "contemporary person") "would be seriously concerned to argue" for.[9] As Ross puts it "if the G-statement predicates are univocal with a representative set of instances of those predicates in E-statements, then our statements about God will be, in most cases, obviously false and, in the remainder, misleading."[10] We are back with the old problem: God-talk seems to be either without a proper meaning or, where it has an evident factual content, our first-order God-statements are simply false and embody religious concepts which are plainly religiously inadequate.[11] The analogy theory on such contemporary readings as Copleston's and Ross's is designed to bail us out here.

II

I shall begin by examining Copleston's account, for it is relatively straightforward and yet it attempts, taking into account the analytical or linguistic turn in philosophy, to break new ground. I shall then in section III examine Ross's "Analogy as a Rule of Meaning for Religious Language". Ross's essay is a complicated piece, full of stipulative definitions and a formidable jargon, but it does, though in an unnecessarily cumbersome way, attempt to come to grips with these crucial problems of meaning. I shall not examine E.L. Mascall's *Existence and Analogy* for two reasons: (1) it has already been extensively criticized and (2), as Ross points out, it does not really come to grips with the problems of *meaning*, for it treats analogy as a theory of inference rather than as a theory purporting to show how God-talk can have factual intelligibility.[12]

To say (1) "God is intelligent," (2) "God made men out of nothing," and (3) "God loves all human beings" is, according to Copleston, to use— when (1), (2) and/or (3) are vehicles for religiously adequate assertions— "intelligent", "made", and "loves" analogically. As we have noted, where our God-talk is not grossly anthropomorphic, all predications of God must be analogical. Where we have analogical predication as in (4) "James is intelligent," and (5) "Fido is intelligent," we must say that the terms predicated of the different subjects, for example James and Fido, are used in a sense which is neither precisely the same nor completely different. Yet this general remark, Copleston stresses, tells us very little. Moreover, to be told that "intelligent" is used analogically when applied to God is not yet to be told what *meaning* it does have or even how to determine what meaning it has.[13] To say that "intelligent" in (5) is used analogously to the way it is used in (4) is most certainly not to tell us how it is used. We still do not know what it means to say that Fido is intelligent. What behaviour traits are we referring to? What would Fido have to do not to be regarded as intelligent? As we have indicated with Fido and his canine brethren, we can resort to ostensive definition but with God no such thing is possible.

How then do we know how "intelligence" is used when applied to God? The negative way, though it is a natural way to proceed, will not do with (6), "God is intelligent," for we cannot intelligibly go on saying that God's intelligence is not like this or like that, if we cannot say *what* God's intelligence is. Every time I say that God's intelligence is unlike a characteristic of human intelligence, I whittle away more of its meaning. To intelligibly apply "intelligence" to God I must make, or be able to make, some *positive* affirmation such as "God is intelligent in an infinitely higher sense than human beings are." But this, Copleston is well aware, is still to say very little. Moreover, when asked to give "a positive account of this higher sense," I find myself, full circle, back to the way of negation. Furthermore, if I continue in the affirmative way I end in anthropomorphism.[14] A successful theory of analogical predication must combine those methods without falling into the pitfalls of either. As Copleston puts it, "to avoid anthropomorphism of a gross sort the mind takes the way of negation, departing from its starting point, namely human intelligence, while to avoid agnosticism it returns to its starting point."[15] We try here, in oscillating back and forth between anthropomorphism and agnosticism, in our predications concerning God, to hold together similarity and dissimilarity at the same time.[16]

This is indeed perplexing, but we must not forget that we are speaking, or trying to speak, of a mysterious being transcendent to the universe. We have, Copleston tells us, no direct apprehension of God.[17] God transcends our experience and thus he "cannot be positively and adequately described." This, he believes, should not lead to a rejection of God-talk as incoherent but simply to a recognition that our understanding of God—who after all is mysterious—is of necessity inadequate. Without the possibility of an adequate understanding of God, we must use analogy to have any understanding of God at all. This is simply one of the features "of our understanding of descriptive statements about God."[18] But, Copleston continues, that our concept of God is imperfect and can never be thoroughly purified of anthropomorphism does not mean that the very idea or concept of God is anthropomorphic; it only means that what Copleston calls the "*subjective meaning*" of "God is intelligent" or "God loves his creation" is inadequate and in part anthropomorphic. It does not mean that the *objective meaning* of these statements is inadequate.

Copleston's use of that tricky word "meaning" is rather unusual. By "subjective meaning" he means "the meaning-content which the term has or can have for the human mind."[19] By "objective meaning" he means "that which is actually referred to by the term in question (that is, the objective reality referred to). . ."[20] In the case of such key God-statements what is objectively referred to isn't at all anthropomorphic, but what our subjective meaning signifies is. It is this meaning that is inadequate, but not "necessarily false."

The distinction Copleston draws between "subjective meaning" and "objective meaning" most certainly seems to be crucial in his attempt to rehabilitate the appeal to analogy, but it unfortunately is not a coherent claim. We might intelligibly speak of the distinction between "subjective meaning" and "objective meaning," where the former referred to the meaning-content of a term as used on a given occasion or set of occasions by an individual or some group of people. This would make a nonvacuous contrast with "objective meaning," since the latter could be taken to refer to the meaning-content the terms would have if people were fully informed and took to heart the implications of the terms in question. But for Copleston "subjective meaning" includes any meaning-content the term or terms "can have for the human mind," the "objective meaning" of terms predicated of God is said to transcend our experience.[21] "It cannot be positively and adequately described."[22] But if the "can" and "cannot" here have a logical force, viz., if it is logically impossible to adequately grasp the objective meaning of these terms or even if it is some sort of "ontological impossibility," then there is no genuine contrast between "objective meaning" and "subjective meaning". We can have no understanding of this "objective meaning"; we can have no understanding of whether the "subjective meaning" adequately or inadequately characterizes that "objective reality" that the objective meaning adequately signifies. Any understanding at all of such matters that we humans can have—no matter how purified of anthropomorphic elements—is still subjective; the meaning we apply to predications of God is still necessarily and irredeemably "subjective meaning". Having no grasp of the "objective meaning," we can have no idea at all of whether our attempts to purify our "subjective meaning" succeed or fail. Indeed "purifying" actually has no use here, for we cannot know what would count as "purifying" the meaning of a term unless we had some grasp of the standard of perfection aimed at. How, in short, does subjective meaning A fall shorter of perfection than subjective meaning B? To know this we must have some understanding of the meaning-content of that which they fall short of, but if we have such a knowledge, then by definition it will not involve "objective meaning" but "subjective meaning". But again we do not know and cannot know how this stands in relation to A and B.

There is a further quite unrelated difficulty in Copleston's account. In trying to avoid agnosticism about our predications of God we try to "hold together similarity and dissimilarity at the same time."[23] To be an analogical predication of God and man, the terms in question must be used in a sense which is neither precisely the same nor completely different. But this characterization is ambiguous. Taken in one way it makes analogy the same as univocity; taken in another it makes analogy the same as equivocity. If, on the one hand, "James is intelligent" and "God is intelligent" have even one similarity, then it is the case (or so at least it would seem) that one property (characteristic) of intelligence when referred to man and God is the same. But this means (or so at least it would seem) that the term by which this property (characteristic) is signified is a univocal predication of man and God and that, after all, not all God-predicates are analogical. If this is true, then analogical predication is neither essential nor complete in our talk about God. Indeed even for analogical predications to be possible, there must be some univocal predications as well. Suppose, on the other hand, the "not precisely the same" rules out their having any common property or relation, then there can be no similarity since we cannot assert in what respect they are similar. If this is so, analogical predication really becomes the use of equivocal terms. Yet there seems at least to be no other way of intelligibly taking the terms being used so that in the different contexts they are used in a way which is neither precisely the same nor completely different. Thus Copleston has not been able to give us an intelligible account of analogical predication that would distinguish it from a univocal or equivocal use of predicates when applied to God and the world.

There is a further problem that Copleston should face which is directly related to the falsification issue. If his claim that "intelligent" (for example) is in a definite sense similar, when used of both God and man, then (given the correctness of the above argument) in both employments of "intelligent" the term must signify at least one common property or, if you will, a relation. But then, aside from being committed to claiming—inconsistently with his general thesis about analogical predication—that at least one predication of God is univocal, he also in effect commits himself to treating "God is intelligent" as a statement which can, at least in principle, be confirmed or disconfirmed, for if to be intelligent is to have property X and if property X is never manifested by God or if God does something inconsistent with ascribing X to him, then we have grounds—though surely nothing like conclusive grounds—for denying that God is intelligent and if he does manifest X we have grounds for asserting that "God is intelligent" is true. We have (if this is so) shown how such God-talk is verifiable by showing how evidence is relevant to the truth or falsity of "God is intelligent." The same, of course, applies to "God loves all human beings." But now these theological-metaphysical statements become what Copleston elsewhere has denied that they can be if they are to count as metaphysical statements, namely empirical assertions.[24]

This unintended implication of his account of analogical predication is surely unwelcome, for Copleston is committed to the view that such God-talk does not at central points consist in statements of empirical fact open to the usual procedures of confirmation and disconfirmation. Indeed Copleston seems anxious to meet, in some way, Flew's challenge about falsifiability. God-statements are taken by him to be factual statements, but they are alleged to be "factual metaphysical statements". Of these Copleston remarks: "I can hardly be said to know what is meant by a factual statement unless I am able to recognize that something at least is not asserted" and "unless I am able to recognize that something is excluded I do not know what is asserted."[25] But in his actual arguments concerning this, Copleston does not give us straightforward factual statements which could be used to confirm or disconfirm our theological statements. Rather, reasoning like what has been called a theological non-naturalist, his statements, used in confirmation and disconfirmation, have the same equivocal and controversial logical status as the statements to be confirmed or disconfirmed. He never breaks out of the religious network of statements; that is to say, in Ross's terminology, he gives us no E-statements to confirm his G-statements and so does not in reality meet Flew's challenge or give our G-statements their needed empirical anchorage.

That this is so can be seen from Copleston's own analysis of "God is intelligent" and "God loves all human beings." He asks us, in asking for the meaning of these statements, to consider why a person would make such statements. Consider "God is intelligent." A man who has the idea of an "existentially dependent world" naturally ascribes the order or system in the world to a creator. My "subjective meaning"—the only meaning I can have for "God is intelligent," on Copleston's account—is "There is a creator of the world who orders the world." But if one is puzzled over what (if anything) it could mean to assert or deny that God is intelligent, one is going to be equally puzzled about the statement, given as the "subjective meaning" or part of the "subjective meaning" of that statement. We do not have a statement that is plainly an empirical statement to give empirical anchorage to our G-statement. The same applies to "God loves all human beings."[26] Copleston remarks that if this statement or rather putative statement "is compatible with all other statements that one can mention and does not exclude even one of them," then it is devoid of factual significance. But it appears at least that it is so compatible, for no matter how many millions are put in the gas chambers, it is still said by the faithful that God loves his children. No matter what wars, plagues, sufferings of little children are brought up à la Dostoevsky, they are still taken, by the faithful, to be compatible with the truth of the statement "God loves all human beings." Given such linguistic behaviour, one is tempted to think that nothing is excluded in the statement and thus it appears to be devoid of factual content. But, Copleston avers, this impression is mistaken. Something is incompatible with it, only we have been looking for that something in the wrong direction, namely in the experiences of men. But the Christian theologian knows a factual statement with which it is incompatible, namely "God wills the eternal damnation and misery of all human beings." The truth of "God loves all men" is confirmed by "God offers all men through Christ the grace to attain eternal salvation." Knowing this latter statement to be true, we are justified in asserting "God loves all men." But here again Copleston is lifting himself up by his own bootstraps, for he is verifying religious statements by appealing to further religious statements without any of them getting the necessary empirical anchorage. The verifying statements are as problematic as the statements they are supposed to be verifying. In short, Flew's challenge concerning falsifiability is not met, for we have not been given any *empirically* identifiable state of affairs that is excluded by these statements. We do not have the anchorage in experience that Copleston so stresses as necessary for an understanding of God-talk.

In short, Copleston has not provided us with an answer to Flew's challenge: he has not shown us how experiential statements either verify or falsify "God loves all mankind" or "God is intelligent" or any G-statement at all and he has not given an intelligible account of analogy that would enable us to overcome the anthropomorphism of univocal predication or the impossibility of understanding what is meant by the predicates in God-talk if they are used equivocally when applied to God and the world. He has not shown us how it is that "we see through a glass darkly" for given Copleston's approach to the incomprehensible Godhead, we can never know whether, by self-consciously and sensitively using our analogical concepts, we purify or fail to purify our understanding of God, because we can have no idea at all of the "objective meaning" of such a concept.

III

Ross tries to state in contemporary terms what he takes to be the vital heart of Aquinas' theory of analogical predication. But while his statement is far more complicated than Copleston's, it is no more successful.

As has frequently been pointed out, "analogy" is itself an analogical term, that is to say, it has several meanings which are not unrelated: that is, they are partly similar and partly different. Moreover, "analogy" is a term of art for the scholastics. In speaking of analogy we speak of analogy of attribution, metaphor and analogy of proper proportionality. But, as Ross and others have argued, it is analogy of proper proportionality that is most crucial in considering the analogical relation between terms predicated of God and terms predicated of man and other "contingent natures". It is then to analogy of proper proportionality that we shall turn.

Ross escapes some of Copleston's confusions by arguing that "analogy of proper proportionality is the general form of language about God" and that it is improper to call this language inadequate "for no other language is *possible* given the Christian assumption that God is transcendent and different in kind from all other things."[27] "God", on this account, is "a shorthand for the definite description which would result from a combination of all the properties shown to be attributable to one unique being with some (psychologically prior) property such as 'First Cause' or 'Creator.' "[28] But the terms signifying these properties are all "analogous by proper proportionality with respect to psychologically prior instances of the same terms in ordinary experience describing statements."[29] In order to make sense of religious discourse, in order to explain how we have any understanding of the concept of God at all, we must give an intelligible account of analogy of proper proportionality and then show how it applies to God-talk.

What then are we talking about when we speak of analogy of proper proportionality? A proportion is the equality of two ratios, i.e., a is to b as c is to d. Ross gives several paradigms the least unfortunate of which is (a) Fido caused the barking and (b) Plato caused the murderous act.[30] Here "caused" is supposed to be such an analogical term. And in (a) and (b) we have an analogy of proper proportionality. Fido's causing the barking is as Plato's causing the murderous act. Where we have analogy of proper proportionality, we have statements of the form:

    1. (a) A is (or has) T
        (b) B is (or has) T

or:

    2. AT_x
        BT_y

where T is a term, namely a word capable of naming or applying to a thing or things, A and B are things, and x and y are properties, actions or events. No. 1 above, Ross argues, is reducible to no. 2.

We are asked initially to assume that in our paradigm "caused" is *not* being used univocally. Later Ross will attempt to show that this assumption is justified. Secondly, to have such an analogy there must be at least two instances of the property signified by "T". As Ross puts it, "the second condition states, briefly, that the two things denoted by the term 'T' must have the property signified by 'T' and that the first condition must still be preserved: that the term is equivocal."[31]

There is, as Ross recognizes, quite obviously a problem here. If "T" is equivocal, the properties would not be the same. But if the term "T" in its instances signified the same property, has the same meaning as or is equivalent in its instances, then, in its instances, it has the same intention (connotation). But if this is so, then either the term is, after all, univocal or the second condition is unsatisfiable.[32] The first and second characteristics of such analogical terms appear at least to clash and this casts doubt on the coherence of analogy by proper proportionality.

To make sense out of this conception of analogy, we must show how both characteristics of this type of analogy are jointly satisfiable. This is exactly what Aquinas, Ross tells us, sets out to do and in Ross's opinion he is successful. To do this Aquinas must show how a term can be "univocal in signification . . . while being equivocal in not conforming to the rule for univocity of intention."[33] That is in (a) "Fido caused the barking" and (b) "Plato caused the murderous act" we must show how "caused" in both cases signifies the same property, yet does not have exactly the same intention: does not in each case have the same conjunction of terms applicable to that to which each instance of "caused" is applicable. There must be some term which is applicable to that to which "caused" in (a) is applicable which is *not* applicable to that to which "caused" in (b) is applicable and yet "caused" in both occurrences must still signify the same property or set of properties. We must examine whether such a notion makes sense. It most certainly appears to be nonsensical. But, as Ross argues, appearances are not to be trusted here.

To understand how this might be done, we must attend to a distinction Aquinas makes and Ross stresses between the *res significata* and the *modus significandi* of a term. A necessary condition for having an analogy of proper proportionality is to have a ratio in which the *modus significandi* differs and the *res significata* is the same. In such a situation we have the requisite similarity in difference. We have a situation in which we have a univocal signification together with an equivocal intention of the terms in question.

To make anything of this we must understand Aquinas' distinctions here. The intention of a term specifies not only the property or properties signified by the term but the *way* it is signified. The former is the *res significata* of the term and the latter—the way it is signified—is the *modus significandi* of the term.[34] In considering our paradigms (a) and (b), if we take our allegedly analogical term "caused", we can speak of two instances of the term "caused" differing in their *modus significandi* in the sense that "caused" refers to *different* kinds of causality. (Ross also works out the same point for "knowledge".) The intention of "caused" is proportionally the same in (a) and (b) "but the mode in which the property is possessed makes entirely different the kinds of action which can be performed."[35] We have the foundation of analogy of proper proportionality in "the unequal and different in kind participation of different natures in the same property according to differing modes of being determined by their nature."[36]

The terms "knowing" and "causality" are indeed univocal or equivocal depending on their use *in sentences*. In (a) and (b) "caused" is not univocal even though we may form a meta-language term "caused" or "causality" which is neutral with respect to all the object-language senses of "caused". The object-language senses of "caused" are themselves equivocal. Given that the meta-language term "caused" is about language and is neutral in the respect mentioned, then it need not be univocal with respect to any object-language sense of "caused".[37] In the different kinds of causality, distinguishable in the different object-language uses of "caused", we have the basis for the difference (the analogues are partly different) and in the meta-language use of the term "caused" we have the basis for similarity (the analogues are partly similar). The neutral sense of "caused" is not on the same level as the different kinds of causality exhibited, in the different uses that "caused" has in different sentences in the object-language. The former is a metalinguistic notion which includes the other uses and signifies them all equally and alternatively.[38] It, as a metalinguistic term, is a predicate in sentences about predicates of sentences. This metalinguistic use of the term is univocal. But this does not make the object-language terms univocal. They are, in contrast, equivocal. It is here that we have an intelligible rationale for analogy of proper proportionality.

There is, however, a fundamental confusion in Ross's argument. Where "knowing" or "caused" (the analogous predicate in question) is a predicate about predicates, where it is a metalinguistic term, it is no longer "knowing" we are talking about but " 'knowing' ". Where we are actually talking about knowing or causing something—the object-language terms—we are not talking about linguistic expressions but about their meaning or use in object-language sentences. But where we are talking about the expression "knowing" or "causing" we are talking about language. "She is bald" makes sense; "She has three letters" does not. " 'She' is bald" is nonsense while " 'She' has three letters" is not. "Knowledge is difficult to obtain and Jane caused him to give up the quest" makes sense but "Knowledge has nine letters and caused has six letters" is nonsense. Again " 'Knowledge' is difficult to obtain and Jane 'caused' him

to give up the quest" is nonsense while " 'Knowledge' has nine letters
and 'caused' has six letters" is an intelligible metalinguistic sentence.

Ross thinks that he has found a univocal sense of "knowledge"
and "caused" and an equivocal sense of "knowledge" and "caused" and
that he has thus escaped a crucial difficulty about analogy of proper proportionality. But he has not at all, for he is not really talking about the same
verbal symbol, for, even on his own definition, we can only say that two
marks or sounds are the same verbal symbol when they have the "same
recognizable pattern." But "knowledge" and " 'knowledge' " are clearly
distinct. It is apparent we do not have the same verbal symbol or the same
expression, so we have no basis for univocity and thus none for analogy
of proper proportionality.

Let us assume, however, that somehow this difficulty has been sur-
mounted. Being analogous is a semantical property of a term and—someone
might possibly argue—I have mistakenly treated it as if it were a syntactical
property. This does not seem at all plausible to me, but let us assume
that my criticism can thus be put aside or that it can somehow be gone
around. (After all, Ross in his later "A New Theory of Analogy" has formulated a doctrine of analogy which is not vulnerable on *this* score.) Still,
even with these assumptions granted, is everything in order with Ross's
account?

When we apply this analysis to the concept of God, Ross's position
gives rise to exactly the same difficulty as Copleston's. In the *res significata*,
if analogous terms signify a common property or set of properties, as they
do, then the terms specifying that property or set of properties will be univocal and thus some univocal predications of God are possible. As Ross
shows, if there is to be an intelligible account of analogical predication,
the analogical terms have, through their *res significata*, a property or set
of properties in common. Thus there must be some univocal predication
possible concerning God if there is to be any analogical predication at all.
But the crucial point of Aquinas and the Neo-Thomists is that *all* predications of God are analogous. The fact that they are used in different modes
or in different contexts or with different intentions will not alter the fact
that, since they have a common term signifying (standing for) a common
property, it is the case that some univocal predication is possible. The terms
signifying those common properties must have been used univocally. In
neither of his essays has Ross escaped this difficulty.

That Ross (and, on his interpretation, Aquinas) is committed to such
a position can be seen from what he says about (c) "Fido knows his dog
house" and (d) "Plato knows philosophy." "Knows" in (c) and (d) is
supposed to be used analogously. But if we accept Aquinas' partial definition of "knowing", we have accepted a generic common feature of knowing,
a property that is common to and distinctive of all knowing. This feature
is, according to Aquinas, "the possession of the form of another as belonging
to another."[39] This is indeed but a partial and very obscure definition;
to fill out his definition Aquinas adds to the above quotation "according
to one's natural mode of possession." This last qualification presumably

gives us the difference which keeps the predication from actually being univocal. But it remains the case that, on the assumption (questionable in itself) that Aquinas' account of knowing is intelligible, it is true that on all uses of "knowing" there is a property that remains common to and distinctive of all these uses. That is to say, we could construct a predicate signifying the *res significata* of "knowing" that would be predicated of all cases of knowing. This would be a univocal predication.

Exactly the same thing would be true of the *res significata* of "God", if the predicates of "God" are to meet Ross's conditions for analogical predication. But to meet these conditions they must violate another supposed characteristic of predications of "God", namely that all such predications be analogical. *In short, for there to be analogical predication of a subject term some univocal predications must be possible.* Yet Aquinas and the Neo-Thomists will not allow that there can be any univocal predications of "God"; but then it is impossible for there to be any analogical predications either.

As a kind of postscript to this argument, it should be noted that Ross's account here clashes radically with Yves Simon's account of analogical predication. Ross is committed to the claim that in analogical predication the *res significata* picks out generic features common to all instances of a given analogical term. But Yves Simon's fundamental point is that such abstraction is impossible for analogical predication. Two important Thomistic accounts are in plain conflict with each other.

Even if my above arguments are mistaken and Ross has given an intelligible account of analogical predication, it will not work for what it is really crucial for, namely for "God". We, if it were correct, would never be in a position to understand the *modus significandi* of "God". As Aquinas, Copleston, Ross, Simon, and Thomists generally all stress, we can have no direct apprehension of God. We are limited to our own human ways of apprehending things. But the *modus significandi* of predicates applied to "God" is supposed to be distinguished by being according to God's distinctive mode of possession. But we finite creatures can have no understanding of that, so we can have no understanding of the *modus significandi* of the predicates applied to God. When Aquinas tells us that the nature of the thing denoted by the logical subject determines the modal elements of the intention of predicates which are applied to the subject, he cannot apply this to "God", for no direct apprehension of God is *possible* and if no direct apprehension is possible—if no use has even been given to "a direct apprehension" of God—then no indirect apprehension is possible either.

If it is replied that "knows" in "Fido knows his dog house" has the same logical features as "love" in "God loves all mankind," yet while "Fido knows his dog house" is plainly meaningful, it simply must be pointed out, against Ross, that "Fido knows his dog house" does not have all these logical features. It is not the case that there is "within the intention of the terms applied to animals . . . no term which specifies how the dog knows."[40] We can speak of conditioning, of memory, of seeing a familiar

object, of smelling and a host of other things. If we are prepared to use
"know" with respect to animals, we can bring in these definite characteristics, for this "mode of possession".

Let us again assume that all my previous criticisms of Ross's reconstruction of Aquinas have been in some way mistaken. Yet there are still
further difficulties in his account. Aquinas is claiming that a *necessary* condition for two terms being analogous by proper proportionality is that they
differ in their *modus significandi* but have the same in *res significata*. But
this is but a *necessary* condition, for the terms could still be equivocal.[41]
So far we have at best explained (1) "why certain terms cannot be used
of God and creatures univocally," and (2) "how a term can in two instances
signify the same property and yet be equivocal."[42] In short, we have at
best shown how the first two conditions for analogy of proper proportionality
are compatible. But there is a third condition, namely that there must be
a *proportional similarity* between what is denoted by the two putatively
analogous terms.

We must scrutinize this notion of "proportional similarity". There
is a similarity in what the terms in question stand for "if they are in some
respect identical but never numerically identical."[43] The respects, of
course, must be specifiable. "Proportion" for Aquinas is a synonym for
"relation". "Relation", for example, "to the left of" is a two or more place
predicate in object-language sentences. By "proportionality between A and
B," Aquinas means, according to Ross, that "there is a *similarity* in the
proportions (or relations) of A and B." Thus there is a "proportional similarity . . . between any two things, A and B, which have similar relations to
some property, event, or thing."[44] Thus for "caused" in (a) "Fido caused
the barking" and (b) "Plato caused the murderous act" to be analogous
by proper proportionality, they must have some common properties or relations.[45] Ross then significantly mentions that if we are to be able
adequately to establish a doctrine of analogy by proper proportionality,
we need some criterion to determine when in fact two things are proportionally similar.[46] We need in short "a criterion of similarity of relations"
and this in turn means that we must be able to say in what respect they
are similar and this, as Ross points out, means that they are in some respects
identical, though never numerically identical.[47] Recall that for Ross, as
for most followers of Aquinas, "God" is a shorthand substitute "for the
definite description which would result from a combination of all the properties shown to be attributable to one unique being with some 'psychologically
prior' property such as 'First Cause' or 'Creator'."[48] This means (gives
to understand) that there is at least a partial identity between God and
the world. But this most certainly seems to be a denial of God's transcendence. It seems, at least, to make it impossible to say what Thomists and
all orthodox Christians, Jews and Moslems want very much to say, namely
that God is transcendent to the world. (Note the initial quotations from
Gilson and Mascall.)

However, following J. Bochenski here, Ross sets out a criterion for
similarity of relations that might, if workable, mitigate somewhat this anthro-

pomorphism by making it innocuous. We can say that "Relation R is similar to relation R′" if (1) both are relations and (2) if they "have common formal properties with respect to either a formal or merely linguistic set of axioms, the latter not being explicitly formulated in ordinary language, or, they have a common property."[49] Yet, as Ross is quick to point out himself, there are plainly difficulties here. If we consider first whether there are common "formal properties, i.e., common syntactical and semantical properties," we face the difficulty that such an ideal language has not yet been worked out and that it "supposes a more extensive formalized language than seems practicable."[50] But, it seems to me that there is a far more crucial objection to this first alternative in setting out a criterion for similarity of relations, namely that in so talking about purely formal properties we are, in effect, talking about an ideal language or an uninterpreted calculus. To give it an interpretation so it would have some application to reality, including the putative reality of God, we would need to be able to specify some non-formal properties. Thus, the first alternative in effect reduces to the second and to specify non-formal properties would, in the case of talk of God, require the unwanted partial identification of God and the world. Indeed, we would have a univocal predication bobbing back up at us again, for we can, as Ross puts it, have a proportional similarity only if the terms are in some respect identical.[51] Ross operates (quite properly I believe) on the assumption that if x is similar to y, then there must be some respect in which x is similar to y. But this, given his reconstructions of Aquinas' account, in effect lays the foundation for the inescapability of some univocal predications of God. But it is exactly this conclusion that he and Thomists generally wish to avoid.

There is a further related difficulty in Ross's account similar to a difficulty we found in Copleston. His account would make a statement such as "God loves all men" open to Flew's challenge. That is, such statements would be empirically verifiable (confirmable or disconfirmable), for it is a question of empirical fact whether "loves" in "Nixon loves all Americans" and "loves" in "God loves all men" have a property in common. (That this is so is even more evident in Ross's "A New Theory of Analogy.") But, as Thomists argue in other contexts, such God-statements are not so verifiable.[52] But, if they accept this last criterion, of similarity of relations, they must treat such God-talk as open to empirical confirmation and disconfirmation. They want it both ways but they cannot consistently have it both ways.

Finally, even if we accept, as I argued we could not, common purely formal properties as adequate criteria for similarity, we still in a way are caught by Flew's challenge, for it is a fact whether there are or are not such formal properties. If we have no reason to say that there are, then we should say that it is probably false that "God loves all men" and the like are intelligible, i.e., do have their intended factual significance. At the very least, we should say that we had evidence that counted against the intelligibility of that claim. But the faithful are not at all willing to put their claims to such a test. In short, even if such a theory of analogy can be worked out for terms like "caused" and "knows", it does not work for God-talk. If no other language is possible, as Ross claims, if we are to talk literally and intelligibly about God, then it must certainly appear that we cannot talk literally and intelligibly about a non-anthropomorphic God, for such an account of analogical predication is thoroughly broken-backed.

IV

I have not claimed that generally speaking all theories of analogy have been shown to be unsatisfactory. I do not even claim that for the conception of analogy of proper proportionality. What I have shown, if at least most of my arguments are sound, is that two distinguished and influential accounts of analogical predication have crippling defects. Perhaps some account could, or even does, escape these difficulties; perhaps there is or could be a perspicuous account of analogical predication. I do not know of one, but it is well to remain agnostic on this score.

Finally, I should say something about a later and parallel effort by Ross, namely his "A New Theory of Analogy." There he deploys some of the techniques of structural linguistics and appeals to some of their findings. But, I shall argue, not with the result that he has shown how there is a formulation of the doctrine of analogy of proper proportionality that obviates the key difficulties I have found in his earlier and more extended account.

In his "A New Theory of Analogy," Ross shows what I have not been concerned to deny, that analogy is a pervasive feature of natural languages, that any predicative term can be used analogously and that analogy is a crucial "part of the expansion structure of . . . language."[53] Indeed it is the case that "many terms have varying meanings in different contexts and that the meanings of some pairs of the same-terms may be regarded as being derivative either from one another (*unus ad alterum*) or from some 'prior' use (or set of uses) of the same term (*multorum ad unum*) . . ."[54] Furthermore, I agree that competent native speakers can and do recognize, in practice at least, that "there are sets of same-term-occurrences which are, taken pair by pair, equivocal but which can be ordered as meaning derivatives . . ."[55] There are sets of same-term-occurrences which are in pairs equivocal which are regularity controlled and there are pairs which are not. Ross's example of the last for "fast" seems well taken. (Compare "He ran fast," "He observed the fast," "He stood fast" and "He considers her fast.") The various uses of "fast" here vis-à-vis each other seem at least to be regularity controlled, though it is difficult to be confident about this. (Is not "fast" in "He considers her fast" derivative from "fast" in "He ran fast"?) Now compare these uses of "fast" with the uses of "count" and "calculated" in the following: "Children count when taught to" and "Computers count when programmed to" and "In oppressing the dissidents the use of physical force was calculated" and in "In building the bridge the physical force of the spring floods was calculated." "Count" and "calculated" here are equivocal when just the same-term pairs are considered, but it is also the case that they differ from "fast" in being regularity controlled vis-à-vis each other. "Count" in "Computers count when programmed to" is derivative from "count" in "Children count when taught to" in a way that the different instances of "fast" cited above seem at least not to be derived. Similarly the first instance of "calculated" above is derivable from the second instance.

What Ross rightly stresses is that there are such analogy regularities built into the structure of our language. People with a grasp of the language readily understand derivative uses of terms; there are, legitimatizing them, meaning regularities within the corpus of our actual discourse and in mastering our language (English, Spanish, Swedish, etc.), we come to have an understanding of them.

However, the acceptance of all this is quite compatible with making the criticisms I have made of Copleston's and Ross's accounts of analogy, for they were giving a certain reading or account of "analogy" which would have a certain import for theology. They were not just establishing that there are analogical uses of language. My criticisms have been directed against their readings and against their attempted theological employment.

In his "new theory" Ross uses "count" and "calculated" to exhibit how analogy of proper proportionality works and indeed something which can quite naturally be extrapolated from semantic regularities in our natural languages. Consider the following:

(1)   Children count when taught to.
(2)   Computers count when programmed to.
(3)   The use of force by the police was calculated.
(4)   The force of the wind was calculated.

Here, with (1) and (2) and again with (3) and (4), we have relationships which are meant to exhibit analogies of proper proportionality. In (2) "count" is derivative from "count" in (1) and it differs in meaning from "count" in (1) in exactly the ways in which "computers" in (2) differs in semantic category from "children" in (1). That is to say, the meaning of "count" in (2) is derivative from its meaning in (1) and is altered "with respect to 'computers' in just the way the semantic categories of that term differ from those of 'children'."[56] It is "the difference-of-meaning by combinatorial contraction which corresponds to proportionality."[57] This enables us to understand the shift of meaning, while still carrying similarities, which sometimes obtain when there is a shift from one discourse environment to another.[58] The same considerations hold for "calculated" in (3) and (4).

In (1) and (2) and in (3) and (4) both pairs of terms differ in their respective pairings in their discourse environments and this is what in modern terms could be called their differences in *modus significandi*. But in both cases there is still a sameness in *res significata* for each. In simpler terms (or at least in a more familiar jargon) Ross's point could be put as follows: in both pairs respectively the property (set of properties) which the term signifies is present and indeed is the same property; i.e., both times "count" signifies the same property (set of properties), and both times "calculated" signifies the same property (set of properties), but in both cases respectively "the conditions of use of the term in two contexts . . . prohibit us from making all the same inferences of each occasion."[59] "Calculated" on both occasions of its use signifies the same property and "count" on both occasions of its use signifies the same property, but the entailments of "calculated" and "count" differ, showing that in each case the property is present in each subject in a different way.

However, as in his first account, there is in this very sameness in the *res significata* an implicit appeal to univocity. In (1) and (2) and (3) and (4) this can be seen. In spite of all the difference in discourse environment "count" in (1) and "count" in (2) both signify a reckoning up to find a sum or total. When we assert—talking about either or both what the computers did or the children did—"There was a reckoning up to find a sum," we can in that proposition say something which is significant and indeed sometimes even true. And there is also a predication here, but the predication "reckoning up to find a sum" here is univocal.[60]

The use of "calculated" in (3) and (4) might seem more helpful for Ross. In (3) "calculated" could be replaced by "deliberated" with little, if any, change in meaning. But no such substitution could be made in (4), yet "calculated" in (3) is derivative from "calculated" in (4). We move from "computed by figures" to "ascertained beforehand by exact reckoning" to "planned deliberately". And here "calculated" seems to have a family-resemblance rather than its being the case that there is any respect in which what they signify is similar. What, it is well to ask, is the characteristic in common signified by "calculated" in (3) and (4)? In both cases we are talking about something reckoned up according to plan. But do "reckoned up" and "according to plan" signify common properties or are they themselves family-resemblance terms?

Even allowing that the elusive conception of family-resemblance is well-enough fixed so as to exclude common characteristics between paired terms, both (3) and (4) would be false, if no expected result was ascertained. And it is implausible to claim that "result was ascertained" is so different in the two environments that there is no respect in which what they signify is similar. Moreover, as Ross acknowledges himself, where there is a similarity between two terms we must, for "similar" to be intelligible, be able to say in what respect they are similar. But then again we can see how univocal predication underlies analogical predication such that the very possibility of two terms being in an analogical relation of proper proportionality requires that we can make some univocal predications of what is referred to by these terms. And this brings with it the host of problems I discussed in the previous section.

In sum, Ross in two essays, one detailed and utilizing some of the techniques of modern logic and one more sketchy and using some of the techniques of structural linguistics, has sought to articulate a sound theory of analogy which will serve as crucial philosophical underpinning in making sense of our talk of God. I have argued that he has failed in both attempts, though in the latter he has made it quite evident that there are analogical uses of language and he has shown us something about these uses. But neither he nor Father Copleston have given us an account of analogy which will enable us to make sense of non-anthropomorphic God-talk.

NOTES

1. F.C. Copleston, *Contemporary Philosophy* (London: Burns and Oates, 1956) and James F. Ross, "Analogy as a Rule of Meaning for Religious Language," *International Philosophical Quarterly* 1 (1961): 468-502. In his later "A New Theory of Analogy," *Logical Analysis and Contemporary Theism*, ed. John Donnelly (New York: Fordham University Press, 1972), Ross uses work in structural linguistics to give the outline of a new theory of analogy which he believes to be compatible with the classical theory. His account there (where it applies to analogy of proper proportionality) is vulnerable to most of the criticisms I level at his earlier and more detailed account. I shall concentrate my discussion most extensively on his earlier and more detailed account, but I shall, in the final section, say something which applies particularly to the later account.

2. Copleston, *op. cit.* 93.

3. *Ibid.* 91.

4. *Ibid.* 94.

5. *Ibid.*

6. See here Terence Penelhum, *Religion and Rationality* (New York: Random House, 1971) 77-87, 121-62, 365-79.

7. Ross, *op. cit.* 470.

8. *Ibid.* 487-88.

9. Copleston, *op. cit.* 89.

10. Ross, *op. cit.* 498.

11. See here my "On Fixing the Reference Range of 'God'," *Religious Studies* II (October 1966); *Contemporary Critiques of Religion* (London: Macmillan Ltd., 1971); and *Skepticism* (London: Macmillan Ltd., 1972). For F.C. Copleston's account of this situation see his "Man, Transcendence and the Absence of God," *Thought* XLIII (1968): 24-38; "The Special Features of Contemporary Atheism," *Twentieth Century: An Australian Quarterly Review* 25 (Spring 1970): 5-15; and his reviews of Axel Hägerström's *Philosophy and Religion* and Richard Robinson's *An Atheist's Values*, *Heythrop Journal* 7 (1966) and 5 (1964), respectively.

12. Ross, *op. cit.* 469.

13. Copleston, *Contemporary Philosophy* 94.

14. Copleston, *Contemporary Philosophy* 94-95. See also his "Man, Transcendence and the Absence of God," *Thought* XLIII (1968): 24-38.

15. Copleston, *Contemporary Philosophy* 96-97.

16. *Ibid.* 97.

17. *Ibid.* 96-97.

18. *Ibid.* 97.

19. *Ibid.* 96.

20. *Ibid.*

21. *Ibid.*

22.   *Ibid.* 97.

23.   *Ibid.*

24.   This is very evident in his debate with A.J. Ayer. See A.J. Ayer and F.C. Copleston, "Logical Positivism: A Debate," *A Modern Introduction to Philosophy,* eds. A. Pap and P. Edwards, 2nd ed. (New York: Macmillan, 1967). In a later essay "Man, Transcendence and the Absence of God," *Thought* XLIII (1968), Copleston contends that while believers and non-believers have the same expectations in regard to events in the world, their interpretations of the world are different. (See page 37 of his text.)

25.   Copleston, *Contemporary Philosophy* 99.

26.   *Ibid.* 100.

27.   Ross, *op. cit.* 501-502.

28.   *Ibid.* 500.

29.   *Ibid.* 501.

30.   *Ibid.* 487.

31.   *Ibid.*

32.   *Ibid.*

33.   *Ibid.* 487.

34.   *Ibid.* 488.

35.   *Ibid.* 489.

36.   *Ibid.* 490.

37.   *Ibid.*

38.   *Ibid.* 491.

39.   *Ibid.*

40.   *Ibid.* 492.

41.   *Ibid.* 494.

42.   *Ibid.*

43.   *Ibid.* 495.

44.   *Ibid.*

45.   *Ibid.*

46.   *Ibid.* 496.

47.   *Ibid.* 495.

48.   *Ibid.* 470.

49.   *Ibid.* 496-97.

50.   *Ibid.* 497.

51.   *Ibid.* 495.

52.   See here M.J. Charlesworth, "Linguistic Analysis and Language About God," *International Philosophical Quarterly* 1 (1961): 139-67; Thomas Corbishley, S.J., "Theology and Falsification," *The University* 1 (1950-51); C.B. Daly, "The Knowableness of God," *Philosophical Studies* (Maynooth, Ireland) IX (1959): 90-137. I have critically examined their views in my "God, Necessity and Falsifiability," *Traces of God in a Secular Culture,* ed. George F. McLean (Staten Island, NY: Alba House, 1973). This is reprinted in chapter 2 of this book.

53.   Ross, "A New Theory of Analogy," *Logical Analysis and Contemporary Theism,* ed. John Donnelly (New York: Fordham University Press, 1972) 126.

54.   *Ibid.* 125.

55.   *Ibid.*

56.   *Ibid.* 139.

57.   *Ibid.*

58.   *Ibid.*

59.   Terence Penelhum, *op. cit.* 81. Penelhum generally in his discussion of analogy acknowledges his indebtedness to Ross.

60.   I simply use "predication" here in the standard way, characterized by Michael Durrant as follows: "An expression that gives us a proposition about something if we attach it to another expression that identifyingly refers to something which we are making the proposition about." See Michael Durrant, *The Logical Status of 'God'* (London: Macmillan Ltd., 1973) xiii-xiv.

CHAPTER 15

God and Coherence: On the Epistemological Foundations of Religious Belief*

I

THERE IS LITTLE INTEREST NOW IN SO-CALLED proofs for the existence of God. The salvoes fired against these classical arguments by Hume and Kant have been, though sometimes in rather rationally reconstructed forms, convincing to philosophers. There are those who would claim that some of these attempted proofs are useful in giving us a sense of deity but, a few scholastic philosophers apart, few would claim they give us a proof of, or even good evidence for, the existence of God.[1] The arguments for God's existence can, of course, given certain prima facie plausible assumptions about their intelligibility, be so stated that they are formally valid arguments, but a sound argument must in addition have reliable premises, and there is little inclination to take the premises in these arguments either as self-evident and substantive or as empirically confirmable or disconfirmable.[2]

The appeal to religious experience is not quite so dead, but even here, where the appeal is used to establish the existence of God as an objective supernatural fact, there is a shying away from it. "A felt utterly dependent or B had intimations of the numinous but there is no God" is not self-contradictory or even logically odd. The assumption that such feelings result from crucial childhood experiences and make no transcendent reference is a simpler hypothesis that does not seem to be at cross-purposes with the facts.

Many believers acknowledge both these points. Religious experience does not confirm divinity and God's existence cannot be demonstrated. Yet they remain believers and are not led down the primrose path to agnosticism or that fate worse than death, atheism. To understand that such rationalistic devices as we have been discussing will not work only

---

*First published in *Knowing Religiously*, ed. L.S. Rouner (Notre Dame, IN: University of Notre Dame Press, 1985).

makes room for the proper instrument of religious belief: faith. And Judaism and Christianity being what they are, this is just as it should be.

Alasdair MacIntyre, when he wrote *Difficulties in Christian Belief* and "The Logical Status of Religious Belief," was writing as a fideistic Christian.[3] In these two works he sets forth an argument of this general sort with considerable clarity and force. He points out that it is a theological requirement of Christianity that human beings be free to accept or reject God. If there were a proof for the existence of God that had geometrical rigour, it would be coercive for rational and informed people. If this were so, however, God's existence would *not* be something they could freely accept on trust and thus the belief in God available to us would not be the sort that was religiously appropriate. Such people could not freely accept or reject God. God, MacIntyre argues, "reveals himself in a way that depends on a response of trust which human beings are free to withhold."[4] The belief that there might be a rational demonstration of substantive religious claims, culminating in unquestionable conclusions following from unquestionable premises, clear to the light of reason, is a hangover from a thoroughly discredited rationalist metaphysics. It assumes, as Richard Rorty might put it, the worst sort of foundationalism.[5] Explicitly or implicitly, it models the structure of all reasoning on logico-mathematical reasoning, but while reasoning is often a form of calculation, a drawing of inferences, and weighting of various considerations, it is not characteristically deductive in form. There is no undeniable evidence for the existence of God, "but both in the works of nature and in that history of revelation which is the Bible," God "offers us opportunities for accepting or rejecting him."[6] But "to ask for proof," MacIntyre concludes, "is to put oneself outside the only attitude in which it is possible to confront God; and therefore to refuse to believe because one cannot have proofs is a simple missing of the point."[7] A God vindicated by geometrical demonstrations, MacIntyre claims, "just would not be the God of the Bible,"[8] for no such validation of credentials is attempted in the Gospels or even envisaged as a possibility. (Here MacIntyre echoes what Karl Barth put more profoundly.) MacIntyre repeats Kant's claim that to defend religion by such rationalistic arguments as we find in traditional philosophical theology is in effect to prepare the ground for unbelief. We should not look for such epistemological foundations for religious belief. Belief is achieved by conversion rather than by argument or investigation. We can only know God, fideists claim, "by trusting in what are taken to be the signs of his being in the world. And where we are unwilling to trust, no argument will take the place of trust. Belief cannot argue with unbelief, it can only preach to it."[9]

What we know about God, fideists claim, we do not and cannot learn from philosophy. All that the philosophers can hope to achieve is to clear up misconceptions about the nature of religious concepts and by so doing partly neutralize the acids of scepticism. Argument about whether or not to be a Jew or a Christian or to have any religious commitment at all is always finally *ad hominem*. When push comes to shove, all we can do in wrestling with such a question is to take a leap unto faith—a leap that we must take without any rational guarantee that our faith or any faith is or could be *the* true faith. Above all, we must recognize that philosophy itself cannot provide any adequate substitute for faith and it cannot, fideists claim, finally criticize, on logically relevant grounds, a religion accepted (as all religion should be accepted) solely on faith.

For Jews, Christians, or Moslems who so reason, belief in God does not and cannot rest on empirical or intellectual discoveries; "God created the heavens and the earth" is not a hypothesis that believers have confirmed and it is not a statement that is open to test and objective refutation. There are, these fideists claim, no proofs one way or another. We no more have a cosmological disproof of God's existence than we have a cosmological proof of God's existence. There may be signs, but they remain unalterably ambiguous; they are never rationally compelling. Belief and unbelief remain, some fideists claim, intellectually speaking, equally compelling. One must finally decide, finally wager, finally will, to believe or not to believe. The Jew or Christian is a person who in the last analysis must simply resolve to live his or her life as a person of faith. It is in this rather peculiar way that one can will to believe.[10]

Even after such an affirmation of faith, believers still do not come to know God with any certainty. In faith they find that *Deus revelatus* can be known only through faith. With such a revelation we are provided with a sure foundation for life, but even so, we remain without any intellectual assurance, for our feeling of certainty in our faith springs from our very trust. Our certainty here is in feeling; it is not that at last we have grasped the truth of our faith after an arduous intellectual voyage of discovery.

It is this very pervasive view, most evident in non-neanderthal Protestant Christianity, that I call *fideism*. It is the claim that religious belief cannot be based upon demonstrative knowledge, empirical investigation, or some set of rational principles uncovered by philosophical reflection, but rests solely on faith. There are neither metaphysical foundations nor epistemological foundations for religious belief. Religious knowledge is completely beyond the limits of finite human understanding. But all that notwithstanding, a fideist would argue, we are hounded by heaven; our very human condition drives us to faith if our lives are to have any meaning at all. Our wills are indeed free and we can, in our pride, turn from God, but if we do, we will in effect destroy ourselves by destroying all hope for a meaningful existence. Without faith, sensitive and nonevasive persons will be caught in the spite and self-laceration of a Dostoevskian underground person, but out of despair they will finally come to realize true helplessness. Despair will finally drive them to a leap of faith. Even though they are in the position of utter scepticism about the very possibility of religious knowledge, they will, to make some sense of their fragmented lives, be driven to a religious affirmation. An utterly secular world vision is just too bleak to be humanly acceptable. Reflective and passionate people who care about their own lives and the lives of others will be driven to a Kierkegaardian leap of faith even while in the grip of a sense that there is something absurd about believing in God. Scandal to the intellect or not, the believer will stick with it.

II

There is no doubt that this is a psychosocial reality for a not inconsiderable number of people. I want here to ask the normative and justificatory question—the epistemological question if you will—whether this need be or even should be so for any reflective and sensitive person of strong commitments who can also think clearly and live nonevasively.

I think a careful and dispassionate look at the facts, and a taking to heart of those facts, will give us good grounds for believing that this is not so. Our lives need not be without sense if we are not knights of faith committed to a belief in God. God or no God, there are things we can enjoy and find intrinsically good: the warmth of the summer sun coming down on me now as I write this, the rustle of the poplars in the clear northern air, a good meal with good companions, a life with people I love, and so on. There are many things of intrinsic or at least inherent value which are not at all dependent on the existence of God or belief in God or any kind of spiritual beings as Tylor might put it. To find these things of value we do not have to have any religious commitments or religious beliefs. And to prove, if that can be done, that what we reflectively value under conditions of undistorted communication is really of value is as much, or as little, of a problem for the believer as it is for the person without any religious belief at all.

But why commit yourself to moral ends, why care about the fate of others, particularly if they do not happen to be people who are close to you? It is natural enough to respond that we must do so because that is the right thing to do. Indifference to human suffering or human weal and woe is just evil. Anyone who is capable of moral response must recognize that, and whether you are capable of moral response or not does not depend, either causally or logically, on whether or not you were brought up in a God-fearing culture. Plenty of people who are utter atheists so respond with as much resoluteness as any believer.

To say that they must unwittingly be living off the cultural capital of their religious heritage is a claim that is without foundation. Even if those ideas originally got into the stream of their lives from a cultural endowment which was in origin religious, this would not establish their rationale or show why these people remained committed to them. The validity of our beliefs, and what justifies our holding them, does not depend on their origin.

There are deep puzzles about the foundations of moral belief. Indeed even foundationalist claims over questions of empirical knowledge seem to be in shambles.[11] To make foundationalist claims in moral epistemology is very chancy indeed. I am inclined to agree with Isaac Levi that to be an antifoundationalist is a virtue in a philosopher.[12] But, be that as it may, questions about the foundations of moral belief are equally problems, if indeed they are problems, for the believer as for the sceptic. To try to take a foundationalist turn with a divine command ethic runs into all the usual difficulties. Suppose fideists claim that they know with certainty what they ought to do, at least in many circumstances, for they know they ought always to do whatever God commands and usually God commands them what to do. But, for a starter, how does the fideist know, or how *can* she know, as Martin Buber once asked, that it is God telling her these things and not the devil? How can she know that it is God and not the promptings of her own objectivized id or superego?

Even suppose a person could in some way ascertain that there is a God and that it is God who is telling him to do these things, why does that make it something that he ought to do? That someone tells you to do something is not at all a sufficient reason for doing it. But in God's case, the fideist responds, we can know that we should do what God tells us to do because God is all-powerful and all-knowing. But an all-powerful being could still be evil and so could even a perfectly intelligent being who knew everything that could be known. And adding the two things together doesn't necessarily produce goodness either. Surely, if we know anything about the world at all, we know that evil can go with power and intelligence. And while it is plainly prudent to do what an all-powerful and all-knowing evil being commands, it does not establish that those commands are the *right* thing to do. Indeed we can have rather good grounds for believing that they are not, for such a being is the author of evil. We may, feeling the strains of commitment, have to make what Brecht would call our little adjustments, but this hardly makes that being's commands morally obligatory.

The believer will respond that this line of argument is silly because God is the Supreme Good. Asked, in turn, how she knows that, one can respond in a number of ways, none of which are satisfactory. One might say that we don't know that God is the Supreme Good but, as a fideist, one takes it as a given on trust. That is where one starts. But then the foundationalist quest has been given up. And, more importantly, since following God's commands is what she claims she ought to be doing, she has given us no reason to follow her there. People, particularly if we look at the matter cross-culturally and with different historical epochs in mind, can and do start from many places; there are innumerable givens. She has not shown, or even given the slightest inkling for believing, that her starting point is preferable to any other starting point. She has not justified her belief, either for herself or for others, or shown that it is not arbitrary.

Alternatively, a person might say that he knows that God is the Supreme Good or at least has good reason to believe that is so because it says so in the Bible and/or that this is a central teaching of the Christian tradition. But, it will in turn be asked, why take the Bible or any Scripture as the supreme guide or even as a guide for your life? If we consider the various cultures and sub-cultures around there are many alternative guides and alternative holy writs about. Why give the Christian one or indeed why give any one such pride of place, such deep authority over your moral life? If the answer is, in turn, because that is the way I was brought up, the reply should be: Why give such weight to that, why assume that gives you the true morality? People over cultural and historical time and space

have been socialized in a not inconsiderable number of ways, ways that
often conflict. Just to do, in such a circumstance, what you have been taught
to do is ethnocentric and arbitrary.

To say, instead, that you accept Christian writ and tradition because
it is really divinely inspired immediately prompts the question: But how
do you know, or *do* you know that? The faithful of every religion believe
that about their religion and tradition. To claim, in trying to escape relativism
here, that you have some sort of philosophical or rational grounding that
will prove that your particular holy scripture is so inspired, or that your
tradition is the embodiment of religious truth, is to go beyond anything
that fideists believe they have available to them and requires us to return
to the very shaky territory of rational or philosophical theology: the territory
the fideist, not without good reason, puts aside as rationalistic foolishness
or hubris.

The last tack of the believer that I shall consider in this context
is the response that it is true by definition that God is the Supreme Good.
She would not call anything God that she also did not take to be supremely
good. If there is a God then God is the Supreme Good. But, it needs to
be asked, how does she know that there is a God or a Supreme Good?
She cannot rightly respond that she must take that on faith, on pain of
life being revealed as senseless or morality as being absurd. For even if
we do not know that there is a Supreme Good we can still know many
things about what we ought to do and ought not to do. We can know, for
example, that kindness is good, that integrity is good, that a life without
agony is good, that cruelty and exploitation are evil, and the like. Here
we can perfectly well have knowledge without foundations.[13] To the sceptical question, How do we know these things are good? we can and should
reply that this, if it is a problem, is a common problem for believer and
sceptic alike. And if we cannot rely on such deeply considered judgments,
judgments held on reflection by both atheists and believers, we could not
even begin to know what the Supreme Good is. But the point that is most
germane here is that for these judgments to be available to us, for these
convictions to be our considered convictions, and for there to be convictions on which we can act, we need not know, or even have the faintest
inkling of, what the Supreme Good is. Morality does not crumble and life
does not become senseless if we are without an understanding of the
Supreme Good.

The believer might concede that and still say, But wouldn't it be
a very good thing indeed if we could have such knowledge? Yet here the
sceptical question returns. What is the Supreme Good? And why think
the religious believer has any better grip here than anyone else? if the
fideist responds: "If you really know what a bachelor is you will know
what an unmarried male is." The substantial questions are what, if anything,
is denoted by *God*, and what, if anything, is the Supreme Good; and why
should we believe that there is either a God or a Supreme Good to be
discovered? To be told that "God is the Supreme Good" is analytic or
true by definition does not help us at all in dealing with the substantive
questions that grip us in any quest for the Supreme Good. But, even more

fundamentally, we can have a robust sense of what morality requires of us, how we ought to live, even if we have no understanding at all of what the Supreme Good is or what God is. And Camus and Sartre to the contrary notwithstanding, we need not think our lives are without meaning even if we have no understanding at all of what the Supreme Good is or what God is. Indeed such things could be perfectly available to us, even if we denied that there is a Supreme Good or that God exists.

What has been neglected in the above discussion, for more important fish, is the claim that one might coherently claim to know that there is a Supreme Good and still deny that God exists. And this, also note, is perfectly compatible with "If God exists then God is the Supreme Good," though it is not, of course, compatible with "If there is a Supreme Good then God exists." But, compatibility aside, there is no good reason to believe that last proposition is true unless we mean "God is the Supreme Good" to be an identity statement. A believer, however, who takes "God is the Supreme Good" to be true by definition need not so read it, and indeed he shouldn't so read it on pain of making other things he wants to say about God nonsense. Remember that neither are all analytic propositions identity statements, nor all identity statements analytic.

III

So we have seen, if so far my arguments have been near to the mark, that we have no good reason to believe that God exists or that God is the Supreme Good, or even that there is a Supreme Good. We have also seen that there is no reason to conclude from this that morality crumbles or that life is meaningless.[14]

A fideist might respond that even if all of this were established there still would be another feature of our lives that would drive a reflective person to faith. Our lives are in myriads of ways unsatisfying and disillusioning. We often experience a defeat of our deepest hopes, the loss of people we very much love, horrible conflicts with those we love, debilitating illness, and the like. Moreover, sometimes we are people of extensive self-deception and of uncontrollable self-destructiveness or destructiveness. And the world we live in is a world of horrible conditions of degradation and exploitation, a world in which starvation and poverty are both rife and unnecessary and a world in which many people, again quite unnecessarily, are sunk in conditions of ignorance and without a reasonable control of the conditions of their own lives. Perhaps the world and our condition in the world is not as bleak as Pascal, Dostoevsky, Sartre, and Beckett have portrayed it, but it is very bleak indeed.

Against such a background the fideist could remark that a person with a good awareness of the above, who wishes to be a humane person, will hold out for herself and for others the Christian hope for immortality and eternal community with God. Like Kierkegaard, one might very well regard such a belief a scandal to the intellect and as something that has the worst sort of probability weight, but still, given the options, something for which we can rationally hope.

It isn't, as Pascal would put it, that we have everything to gain and nothing to lose. For perhaps we may lose our intellectual integrity by believing in something which at best seems plainly false and at worst is plainly incoherent, simply because we want or need to believe such things. Isn't it irrational to entertain such wishes for ourselves and for humankind generally? But need we, if we entertain such hopes, subvert our intellectual integrity if we continue to have such hopes in the face of an utterly unblinking awareness of the fact that a belief in immortality is such a scandal to the intellect? In what way must such a person be kidding herself? She sees the belief has no good warrant, indeed that it is an utterly fantastic, perhaps even an incoherent, belief. If she sees this clearly and still wishes or even hopes for immortality, how has she kidded herself? She doesn't somehow believe that after all it is really true or a little more likely than what the sceptic believes. Indeed, she agrees with the sceptic fully about the probabilities but continues to hope that in spite of everything she will survive the death of her present body and find eternal communion with God and other human beings. How is she being irrational or unreasonable in entertaining such a hope, if she has it under the conditions described above and does not let that hope divert her from making the life she has as meaningful as possible and from struggling to bring a world into being which is not as nasty as the world I have described? If this is her pattern of behaviour and her mindset, it does not seem fair to me to describe her as evasive, double-minded, or in any way irrational or even diminished in her reasonableness.

Shouldn't we all then hope or at least wish for immortality? Wouldn't we all, if we could behave decently, be with those we really care about, remain in good health, and continue to have good mental faculties, wish to live forever? Isn't it to be a spoil-sport and indeed to be a little bit irrational *not* to have such wishes?

Here it is best to speak personally. Wishes are one thing, hopes another. Hopes involve some conception of the possibility of what is hoped for. Wishes do not require anything that strong. When I think about it and articulate it to myself, I recognize that I do wish I could live forever under the conditions I have described above. However, this is not something I think about very often; nor do I think it should have any priority in my life. Such wishes do not count for much with me and do not translate into hopes. Why do they not count very much with me? Because they seem to me so plainly fanciful and, as well, very prone to produce self-deception. Moreover, they have a way of directing one's thoughts away from what is, humanly speaking, more important. There are so many other things to be wished for, hoped for, and indeed struggled for, that are vital and have some reasonable possibility of being achieved.

An analogy might help. I am a socialist living in a capitalist society which is not on the immediate threshold of a socialist transformation. I hope, I hope reasonably, for a socialist transformation in the next fifty to a hundred years—and indeed for one whose birth pangs will not be hellishly hard, though as a bettor I wouldn't bet on an easy birth. I think that such a transition is a reasonable possibility in the next fifty to a hundred years or perhaps even sooner. I often wonder if it is something I will see in my life and have sadly concluded that the chances are not very good; but I often hope, and I think not unreasonably, that after all I will be part of it and do my part in building it and making it flourish. That hope is frequently with me, given its importance to me and the likelihood of its achievement. But a hope that weighs much more with me is the hope, which I also judge to be a reasonable expectation, that in fifty to a hundred years' time we will not have blown ourselves to smithereens and we will have firmly made the transition to socialism. That, I judge, is not a quixotic ideal and is worth really struggling for, worth making a central part of my life. But I could understand a cultural pessimist who might, with a very different assessment of the possibilities, think of my hopes here as mere fanciful wishes. In the extreme case, he might see them, if he was very deeply pessimistic indeed, on a par with the Christian's wish for immortality. What we hope for, if we are reasonable and caring, is tied to what we think is really important and to what we think the empirical possibilities are.

Let me extend the parallel a little further. As I would fancifully wish to live forever, I would fancifully wish to wake up in the morning and miraculously find that a socialist transformation had bloodlessly and effortlessly taken place. We, the fancy goes, now live in a world free of war, in which capitalism and the authoritarian control of people no longer exists. People—everyone, everywhere—are at last free. They control their own lives in a world where there are no bosses and bossed, no exploitation or degradation, no sexism, no racism, no intolerance of human peculiarities, in a world of social equality in which we are all comrades together. The ideal, of course, means a lot to me. But the wish, the idle dream, that I might wake up tomorrow and find myself in that world means very little to me because it is so fanciful. It is like, in that respect, the wish for immortality. It is idle, utterly idle, and, if dwelt on, a distraction from the social realities of our lives, including the day-to-day concrete struggle to try to make something approximating that idle dream a social reality.

The wish to wake up tomorrow and find a dream of your life or world in place and the wish for immortality are rather parallel, except that the wish for immortality is perhaps incoherent or even a logical impossibility. For me neither wish counts for much—though I do not attempt to drive either out of my mind or reject either—for they are not tied to the real world where your fate and mine is indeed tied up. And it is to that world that an overriding importance should be attached, and where we will achieve our liberation, our human and moral majority, and our emancipation.

Late at night, perhaps after many drinks, we can wax sentimental about what it would be like if tomorrow the world were very different and immortality were really possible. I suspect it is all rather maudlin. Yet, I suppose, we could rather idly entertain all these things. But if we care about ourselves and care about our fellows there are things which are far more important that should engage our attention instead. Such idle wishes are not rejected; they are not to be driven out of our minds; they will just wither away as the demystification of the world gradually gains ascendancy and people gain greater social wealth, are better educated, and come to have more secure lives.

Fideists are bad psychologists if they think that all reflective atheists are tortured souls despairingly longing for the absolute or stoically fighting off Pascalian urges. The wish to live forever for many of us is idle, something we are concerned neither to accept nor to reject. It is not true that if we no longer entertain these wishes our lives will become meaningless, fragmented, emotionally crippled; it is not true that, given our atheistic intellectual convictions, our lives are something to be stoically endured with nihilism at the door. Fideists should not take their own personalities as humankind writ large, and they should not flatter themselves with the conceit that their response is the deepest, most human response to nonevasive reflection about our condition.

NOTES

1.   Austen Farrar, *Finite and Infinite* (Westminster: Dacre Press, 1943); and Austen Farrar, *Faith and Speculation* (New York: New York University Press, 1967) 131-55.

2.   Kai Nielsen, "Arguing about the Rationality of Religion," *Sophia* 12.3 (1973): 7-10; and Kai Nielsen, "A False Move in Reasoning about God," *Understanding* 4 (1975): 10-16.

3.   Alasdair MacIntyre, *Difficulties in Christian Belief* (London: SCM Press, 1956); and Alasdair MacIntyre, "The Logical Status of Religious Belief," in *Metaphysical Beliefs*, ed. Ronald W. Hepburn (London: SCM Press, 1957) 168-205.

4.   MacIntyre, "The Logical Status of Religious Belief" 175.

5.   Richard Rorty, *Philosophy and the Mirror of Nature* (Princeton, NJ: Princeton University Press, 1979). For how much of the positivist attack on metaphysics he would accept, see page 384.

6.   MacIntyre, "The Logical Status of Religious Belief" 180.

7.   *Ibid.*

8.   *Ibid.* 182.

9.   *Ibid.*

10.   Kai Nielsen, *Reason and Practice* (New York: Harper and Row, 1971) 204-25.

11.   Richard Rorty, *Consequences of Pragmatism* (Minneapolis: University of Minnesota Press, 1982); and *Philosophy and the Mirror of Nature*.

12.   Isaac Levi, "Escape from Boredom: Edification According to Rorty," *Canadian Journal of Philosophy* XI.4 (1981): 589-601.

13.   Kai Nielsen, "Grounding Rights and a Method of Reflective Equilibrium," *Inquiry: An Interdisciplinary Journal of Philosophy and the Social Sciences* 25 (September 1982): 277-306; Kai Nielsen, "On Needing a Moral Theory: Rationality, Considered Judgments, and the Grounding of Morality," *Metaphilosophy* 13.2 (1982): 97-116; and Kai Nielsen, "Considered Judgments Again," *Human Studies* 5 (1982): 109-18.

14.   Kai Nielsen, *Ethics without God* (Buffalo, NY: Prometheus Books, 1973); Kai Nielsen, "Linguistic Philosophy and 'The Meaning of Life'," *The Meaning of Life*, ed. E.D. Klemke (New York: Oxford University Press, 1981) 177-204.

CHAPTER 16

On the Viability of Atheism*

I

IN ARGUMENTS BETWEEN BELIEF AND UNBELIEF which are at all informed it is agreed by almost all parties that religious claims are paradoxical and that, if there is a God, he is indeed a very mysterious reality. The God of developed Judaism, Christianity, and Islam, whatever else that God is supposed to refer to, is supposed to refer to an Ultimate Mystery. God is supposed to be the Incomprehensible Other, the Ultimate Mystery whose mysterious reality is beyond all ordinary knowing. A God who was not such an ultimate mystery would not be the God of Judaism, Christianity, or Islam.

This alleged ultimate reality, at least in tolerably orthodox versions of these sister religions, is taken to be a personal creative reality in the form of an infinite and eternal individual who exists beyond the bounds of space and time, and who, without ceasing to be infinite, transcends the world. This is what, most essentially, "God" is taken to refer to in such religions. What in the essays in this book as well as in my *Philosophy and Atheism* and elsewhere I have probed is whether we have any good reasons at all for believing that there actually exists such a reality or whether it is even reasonable for us, standing where we are now and knowing what we know, to believe that such a reality could exist.[1]

I reject such a religious belief—the fundamental religious presupposition of these religions—because it seems to me that we have no good reason for believing that such a reality exists or indeed even could. It is not just that we cannot decide whether we can be justified in believing in such a reality and thus naturally gravitate toward agnosticism. Rather—or at least so I argue—the most reasonable thing for us to do is to reject such a belief because at best the probability that such a reality exists is of a very low order and at worst such a belief is so problematic as to justify

---

*Unpublished paper.

the claim that God, so conceived, connotes an illegitimate concept—an ersatz concept, if you will—that could never have an actual application because what we are saying in speaking of God is actually incoherent. Moreover, it seems to me that when we examine the matter carefully, we will come to see that the worst case scenario from the point of view of religious belief is also the more likely case.

Such a rejection is, of course, a form of atheism. And it is that atheism that I try carefully to characterize and defend in *Philosophy and Atheism*. I argue there, and in this volume as well, the strong thesis, some might even say the offensive thesis, that we cannot come to have a sufficient understanding of such perfectly orthodox talk of God such that the reality to which "God" purports to refer could be the object of a religious commitment that is both clear-headed and informed.

What I have sought to worry out and what seems to me to be plainly a central issue for a nonevasive consideration of religion, at least in cultures such as our own, is whether sufficient sense can be made of the key religious conceptions of the dominant religions of our culture to make belief in God a live option for a reflective and concerned human being possessing a reasonable scientific and philosophical understanding of the world we live in, or whether some form of atheism or agnosticism is the most nonevasive option for such a person. My argument has been that belief in God should no longer be a live option for us standing where we are and knowing what we know.

Suppose we say, in a properly orthodox manner, as Richard Swinburne does, that God is "a person without a body (i.e., a spirit), present everywhere, the creator and sustainer of the universe, able to do anything (i.e., omnipotent), knowing all things, perfectly good, a source of moral obligation, immutable, eternal, a necessary being, holy and worthy of worship."[2] What I call (perhaps tendentiously) *simple* atheism maintains either (a) that such a belief is false and that there is no such reality or (b) (more modestly) that there is no good evidence that there is such a reality and that the probability is so low that we will ever come up with evidence sufficient to make such a belief even plausible that we cannot, if we know that, be justified in believing in God. The simple atheist will then add, as a codicil, that we should in a society such as ours know such things, if we are informed. In a parallel way a simple believer will say either that we have enough evidence to be justified in believing in God or, as an alternative fideistic view, that, evidence or no evidence, we are justified in living by faith. We are justified, the simple believer claims, in taking belief in God to be a basic belief for which we do not seek evidence. And again, in a parallel manner, simple agnostics will say that we do not have evidence or more generally sufficient reasons here and now either to justify belief in God or to justify the belief that God does not exist or probably does not exist. So, in such a circumstance, the agnostic will say that the reasonable person should suspend any committing belief one way or the other; the reasonable person should neither accept religious beliefs nor reject them.

My argument is that, given a reasonable understanding of the development of Jewish, Christian, and Moslem belief systems, we should no longer, if we are so informed, be either a simple atheist, a simple agnostic or a simple believer. Such positions are no longer justified and the reasonable thing to do is to abandon them. Whatever may have been the case in the past when God was construed more anthropomorphically, the concept of God has become, since at least the Middle Ages, *problematic*, and the less anthropomorphic it has become the more problematic it has become.[3] Our perplexities are such concerning the concept of God that it is anything but clear that an utterance such as "God created man in his image and likeness" could be either true or false or reasonably be believed to be either true or false. The problematicity is at least conceptual. We do not understand what we are supposed to be asserting or denying when we assert or deny the existence of God. We do not understand what we are referring to when we speak of God. Many of the allegedly descriptive terms deployed in defining "God" are as elusive with respect to their denotation as "God". *Simple* believers, agnostics and atheists alike, do not face the logically prior question about the very legitimacy of the concept of God. The various conceptions extant in developed religions (religions which have ceased to be utterly anthropomorphic) are so problematic—or at least that is my claim—that it is anything but clear that we have a coherent concept of God such that that concept could have application.[4]

Contemporary atheists attuned to modernity, or for that matter postmodernity, and tolerably knowledgeable about philosophy and science will not be simple atheists and their counterparts will not be simple agnostics or simple believers. The central issue should not be whether it is true or probably true, or false or probably false, that God exists, or not yet determinable either way. The central issue should be whether a religiously adequate concept of God is sufficiently coherent that the central strands of religious belief can make legitimate truth-claims at all or, put differently, whether talk of God makes sense. (Or, to put it more accurately, though more pedantically, does it make the kind of sense that it must make for religious beliefs to be viable?) It is my contention that it does not.

This position is best understood as a form of atheism, though it is an atheism under a broader and more adequate construal than the traditional atheism of the simple atheist. On my construal, to be an atheist is to be someone who rejects belief in God for at least one of the following reasons (the specific reason will depend on how God is being conceived): (1) if an anthropomorphic God is what is at issue, the atheist rejects belief in God because it is false or probably false that there is such a God; (2) if what is at issue is a non-anthropomorphic God (the God of the major strands of Judaism, Christianity, and Islam), then the atheist rejects belief in God because, depending exactly on how such a God is conceptualized, the very concept of God is illegitimate because the concept of such a God is either cognitively meaningless, unintelligible, contradictory, incomprehensible or incoherent; (3) the atheist rejects belief in God (here we speak of the God portrayed by some modern or contemporary theologians or philosophers) because the concept of God in question is such that it merely masks an atheistic substance, e.g., "God" is just another name for love or a symbolic term for moral ideals. So, depending on how God is conceptualized, atheists reject God for different reasons, but, given the evolution of our religious belief systems, it is the range of conceptualization covered by (2) that requires the most serious attention and it is that cluster of conceptions which raises the issue of the coherence and hence the legitimacy of belief in God.[5]

Why should it be thought that non-anthropomorphic concepts of God, where they do not simply disguise an atheistic substance, are incoherent? "God", on these employments, is some sort of referring expression and so it is vital to ask about its referent. To whom or what does "God" refer? Is it a proper name, an abbreviated definite description, a distinctive descriptive predicate, or what? How could we come to be acquainted with, or otherwise come to know, what "God" stands for or characterizes? How do we—or do we—identify or indicate God? What are we talking about when we speak of God? *What* or *who* is this God we pray to, love, make sense of our lives in terms of, and the like? When we think seriously about these related questions, we will come to sense, or at least we should come to sense, how problematic our concept of God is.

Suppose we say, not implausibly, that "God" is an abbreviation for a definite description and we take Swinburne's orthodox definition of God, given above, as the spelling out of a definite description which will enable us to understand what our God-talk is about. However, if we are puzzled about what "God" refers to, we will also be puzzled about what "a person without a body" refers to, about what it is "to be the creator and sustainer of the universe", or "to be present everywhere" and (a), still be detectable and (b), be transcendent to the universe. And, to add insult to injury, how can something which is detectable be transcendent to the universe? Perhaps sense can be teased out of such notions or given to them, but, as they stand, they are just as problematic, or at the very least almost as problematic, as "God". It is certainly not unreasonable to wonder if these conceptions make any coherent sense and to wonder how it could be at all possible to identify the referents of such terms. It is very natural in such a context to come to wonder whether they can be more than empty phrases which for some people in some environments have great emotive force. Yet it is also the case that God is supposed to be the Ultimate Mystery, an at least partly incomprehensible reality. We are not to expect conceptions of God to be clear; a certain amount of incomprehensibility just goes with the mysterious sort of thing that we believe in when we believe in God. While it is true that we do not have to be unclear ourselves to portray unclarity, still a conceptualization of God that did not make it evident that we are talking about something which is in a way incomprehensible would not be a faithful portrayal of God. The person who demands certitude in religious domains just does not understand what religious risk is.

What is centrally at issue between sophisticated believers, atheists, and agnostics is whether the incomprehensibility of God is sufficiently constrained such that we can, in certain circumstances, have some inkling that our mysterious conceptions actually answer to a reality that would also be religiously appropriate (e.g., is not like the reality Feuerbach's God refers to), or whether the incomprehensibility is so total that the concept of God is illegitimate because incoherent, or whether we are not in a position

to know which it is or even to have good reasons for believing that it is
one or the other, and thus, if we would keep our integrity, we must remain
agnostics.[6]

Whichever way we go here, we are treating the concept of God as
problematic and regarding the logically prior question of the legitimacy
of the very concept of God as the central question to be dealt with before
we go on, if indeed after the examination of this prior question there will
be any reason to go on, to consider whether or not we can in some way
prove the existence of God, give evidence for his existence, or consider
whether we must assume God exists to make sense of our own existence.

I have attempted in this book, as I did in *Philosophy and Atheism*
as well, to come to grips with that prior question, and in doing so I argue
for the truth of atheism, namely in this context for the truth of the claim
that non-anthropomorphic conceptions of God are so problematic as to
be incoherent, though I am also concerned to show, against the fideist,
that we need not make a desperate Pascalian wager and, against all appearances of incoherence, try to affirm the existence of God so as to keep nihilism
at bay and, in so doing, give sense to our tangled lives and make sense
of a commitment to morality.

II

Let me now show in skeletal form some of the lines
of reflection and argument that led me to what for some no doubt is a
repugnant conclusion. Jews, Christians, and Moslems must believe that
God is not only a bodiless person, a conception whose intelligibility is far
from clear, but, as well, this extraordinary person that God is said to be
is also said to be an *infinite individual* who is everywhere and yet is also
utterly transcendent to the world while still standing to creatures in the
world in personal relations of caring and loving. Here we have a string
of words that, if we will think literally about what they are trying to say,
do not fit together so as to make sense. An individual cannot at one and
the same time both be utterly transcendent to the world and be an individual
in the world standing in personal relations of caring and loving. To so try
to conceptualize things is like saying that an individual is both utterly transcendent to the world and not transcendent to the world. "Infinite individual" is also nonsense. If something is an individual it is discrete and limited,
and if that individual is also a person, as God is said to be, that person
is only identifiable through having a body, but, even if that latter claim
were not true, an individual, as a discrete being, distinguishable from others
and distinct from others, can hardly be infinite, and to boot be everywhere.
If God is everywhere, if there is no place where God is not, then God cannot
be an individual, even an extraordinary individual, for as an individual,
or for that matter as a person, whatever we are referring to must be a
discrete and distinct reality. It cannot, if we are talking about an individual,
be an infinite or omnipresent reality. (To say the terms are not to be taken

literally takes us back to difficulties like those in the doctrine of analogical predication we discussed in Chapter 14.) Again, the religious believer is in effect saying that a given reality has both property p and property not-p. Moreover, even if we can somehow make sense of "infinite person" or "infinite individual", we do not have any understanding of what it would be like for something to be transcendent to the universe, the universe not being a name for a great big discrete thing but rather a label for all the distinct finite things and processes there are. But nothing could be transcendent to *all* the finite things and processes that there are, or at the very least we have no understanding of what this would be like. This becomes absurdly manifest when we come to see, as Axel Hägerström argued early in this century, that "finite thing" is a pleonasm.[7] We must, if we are struggling to see the world rightly in the teeth of centuries of religious talk, force ourselves to think literally.

If it is said, as no doubt it will be, that I am being too woodenly literal here, that I fail to see that these terms are being used in some metaphorical, symbolic or analogical way, it should be responded in turn that if this is so then we must still be able, at least in principle, to say in non-metaphorical, non-symbolic and non-analogical terms what they are metaphors of, symbols of and analogies to.[8] For these terms to function successfully in their non-literal ways, it must be at least in principle possible to do that. Non-literal meaning is parasitic on literal meaning. But then to be confident we have said anything coherent here, we must cash in the analogies, the symbolic expressions, and the metaphors, and state in literal terms what is being claimed without having reduced God-talk to: (a) something with an atheistic substance; or (b) to the sort of anthropomorphic talk where what is being claimed to be the case is not only plainly false, as in Zeus-talk, but is, as well, little more than a superstition; or (c) to using expressions in the reduction or the paraphrase which are either incoherent in ways similar to the ways exhibited above or are referring expressions where we have no way at all of knowing how either directly or indirectly to identify their referents. If the claim is to be able to identify a referent indirectly, then there can be, on pain of depriving "indirectly" of a non-vacuous contrast, no *logical* or *conceptual* ban on being able to identify the referent directly as well. Yet "God" is not the sort of term, in its non-anthropomorphic employments, whose referent can even in principle be detected directly. Anything that could be seen or in any way directly observed or noted or encountered—and thus anything that could be directly experienced—would not be the God of what Judaism, Christianity and Islam have long ago become. A directly observable God is an idol. There can be no literal standing or being in the presence of God.

This is a short way with dissent, a way that might not unreasonably prompt the response that perhaps some theologian or philosopher of religion might be able to give a construal of these problematic conceptions which would reveal that after all they could sustain a reading that would exhibit their legitimacy. Moreover, it would be a construal that would not claim their legitimacy at the expense of either, on the one hand, reducing them to anthropomorphic concepts whose matching truth-claims would be intelligible enough but plainly false, as in claims about Zeus's goings on, or, on the other, reducing them to such utterly secularized concepts (as in the work of Braithwaite, Hare, Dilman and Phillips) that they cannot succeed in being used to say anything that an atheist need deny. Indeed it would be dogmatic a priorism to deny that something like that may be possible.

What can be done is first to state what the problem is, as I have here. This comes to showing why God-talk is so problematic as to be at least arguably incoherent. That done, one should then proceed, as I have done in earlier chapters, and in a series of other books and articles as well, to consider *seriatim* the best attempts going to give a religiously appropriate and coherent reading to such notions.[9] If my arguments and arguments by others similarly motivated have been sound and the general challenge is sound, and if it can also be shown, as I and others have argued, that we do not need religious belief to make sense of our lives or to make sense of morality, then, if such arguments get repeated with similar results, it will become increasingly unlikely that the key concepts of Judaism, Christianity, and Islam are legitimate concepts capable of sustaining truth-claims. If something like that obtains, then the burden of proof clearly shifts to the believer to give us good reasons for believing that his very arcane and at least seemingly problematic claims make coherent sense.

The general situation vis-à-vis religion that I tried to portray is the following: now it is evident to at least most people who carefully investigate these matters that no one has been able to give a sound ontological proof or disproof of the existence of God; no cosmological or design-type arguments have been shown to be sound and no other attempts to infer the existence of God from either evident or not-so-evident empirical facts have worked.[10] In addition, it has become fairly evident to most philosophically literate people that it very much looks like it is the case, to put the matter cautiously, that the very idea (where we are being literal) of seeing God or directly knowing or encountering God is incoherent. Moreover, even if we assume coherence here, there seems at least to be no reason to believe that anyone has actually seen, directly known—as in knowledge by *acquaintance*—or actually encountered God. Given all these things, the prospects for a renewal of natural theology are, to put it minimally, very bleak indeed.

If arguments such as mine about the incoherence of God-talk are sound, we, of course, have a good *explanation* of the breakdown of the various projects for constructing a natural theology. If these concepts are really incoherent, we could hardly have valid, let alone sound, arguments for the existence of God, for valid arguments require intelligible premises, and if God-talk is incoherent it can hardly provide us with intelligible premises. However, even if my arguments are unsound or at least inconclusive, and such talk, or at least some of it, is not incoherent, philosophers such as J.L. Mackie, principally in his masterful *The Miracle of Theism*, assuming, mistakenly I believe, the coherence of God-talk, reveal the inadequacy of the whole range of the best attempts, in one way or another, to establish the existence of God, or show that religious belief is a plausible option for a philosophically and scientifically educated person in the twentieth century.

This throws the believer back on the rather desperate expedients of various forms of fideism. However, it is a necessary condition for the viability of religious belief erected on such deeply sceptical foundations that it show either, on the one hand, that the moral life is undermined, or at least our moral expectations are deeply damaged, if we abandon religious belief or, on the other hand, that without religious commitments we cannot make sense of our lives, or at least that our lives without a belief in God will be impoverished. But nothing like this has been established and, as I argue in *Philosophy and Atheism* (Chapter 9), in *Ethics Without God*, and in *God and the Grounding of Morality*, such claims most certainly appear to be false. There can be plenty of intact purposes *in* life, including coherent gestalts of such purposes, even if there is no purpose *to* life. Treating people as ends, seeing ourselves as comrades in a common kingdom of ends, working to alleviate the awful burden of human suffering, and struggling for a more extensive and equitable satisfaction of human needs are ideals which remain intact whether there is or isn't a God or the hope of human immortality. Morality and a sense of ourselves as living meaningful lives need not totter if there is no God or no belief in God.

III

I turn now to a detailed examination of some criticisms of my account.[11] Hendrik Hart, whose views I shall consider first, thinks that I take reason to be a kind of God and that my atheism is itself a religious affirmation. His discussion has the interesting strategy of trying to show that I have hoisted myself by my own petard, that the line of argument I take against belief in God can with perfect propriety be directed against what Hart takes to be my faith in reason. He does not seek to show that any of my specific arguments directed against the coherency, truth or the moral requiredness of religious belief are mistaken. Rather, he says that we all have our faiths, what in effect are our creedal systems, atheism as much as Judaism or Christianity. What we will regard as justified belief, or as what is morally required of us, or as what would constitute a meaningful life is determined by what Hart regards as our distinctive creedal perspectives.[12] These creedal "perspectives" are different and not infrequently incommensurable; it is rationalistic idolatry to think that there is, or even could be, some Archimedean point by virtue of which we can assess these various perspectives and ascertain which, if any, is "the true perspective".

I am not, perhaps not totally surprisingly, convinced of the soundness of Hart's arguments, or even that they have their target properly in focus. But before I turn to that I want first to observe that *if* Hart's criticisms are well taken and if these criticisms rest on his general perspective in the way he thinks they do, this in turn would in effect provide a devastating critique of Christianity, Islam and Judaism and indeed of all the historic religious belief systems. These belief systems all make claims to having "the ultimate truth". Hinduism, at least theoretically, is more hospitable to other religions than is Christianity, but even Hinduism lays claim to Ultimate Truth and Christianity proudly proclaims that Christ is *the* Truth and *the* Way. There is no historicist relativism of perspectives in the viewpoints and self-images of the historic religions. If our situation were what Hart takes it to be (something, he believes, my rationalism blinds me from acknowledging) the very self-images of the historic religions would be undermined, and scepticism over religion, if not atheism, would be firmly triumphant. No person, if Hart is correct, if she understood what she was saying and could be non-self-deceptive and non-evasive, could make any affirmation of Ultimate Truth. Her severe historicist perspectivism would constitute an unsaying of what she is saying.

What is to be accepted, given Hart's way of viewing things, is entirely dependent on one's perspective, and no one perspective with any objectivity (perhaps even with any coherency) can justifiably be said to be better than any other perspective.[13] Even assuming we can make sense of this, assuming self-referential paradoxes could be somehow overcome, and further assuming this historicist relativistic perspectivism could in some coherent sense be said to be true, this perspectivism would be the death knell of Judaism, Christianity and Islam, at least in anything like the forms we have come to know them. In fine, Hart's account has the key defects that I have sought in various places and in some detail, and I hope with a certain nuance, to pin on Wittgensteinian fideism.[14]

However, are Hart's criticisms sound? He takes me to be avowing and committing myself to what he calls a *rationalistic* atheism. And taking— he says—religion, any religion you like, to involve a belief in a transcendent spiritual being, I fail to see, suffering as I do from a kind of ethnocentrism about religion, my own commitment to reason or humanity to be itself religious and I do not recognize how I turn reason or humanity into divinities. This rationalistic atheism is for me, Hart claims, an ultimate position and as such, he claims, a religious position.

Since this is so, on *his* view of my view, Hart, as we have seen, claims that many of my objections to religion are also applicable to other ultimate positions, including my own. In my very commitment to reason, I deceive myself into seeing my position as rational rather than creedal. My very rationalism excludes the very possibility of religious truth, and it is a rationalism that I treat as being as unproblematic as a dogmatist such as Alvin Plantinga treats Christian belief.

Hart has not got my characterization of religion right. I make it clear in *Philosophy and Atheism* and elsewhere that a religion need not involve a belief in God, or several gods, or several spiritual beings. In *Philosophy and Atheism* I write: "we should beware of essentialist definitions of 'religion'. Theravada Buddhism, a religion of spiritual liberation, has no God or object of worship and devotion."[15] I go on to point out that while nirvana is a very different concept than God, it is like the concept of God in not being a naturalistic concept. But, notwithstanding that it does not refer to a transcendent spiritual being, Theravada Buddhism is just as much a religious belief system as Christianity. The above remarks were from the oldest essay in *Philosophy and Atheism* (1962) and this has been my account all along and it is not an account I have deviated from.

My commitment to reason, if it comes to that, does not, whatever else it may involve, involve any appeal to spiritual realities or to transcendental conceptions; it is thoroughly naturalistic, and thus, unlike the lesser vehicle, or so at least I would maintain, it is not a religious appeal. But this, admittedly, does not get to the heart of Hart's claim here about my rationalism, and presumably any rationalism, being implicitly religious. I shall return to this issue toward the end of my response to Hart.

I have never thought of myself as a rationalist, or of my atheism as being rationalistic. Certainly I am not a rationalist in the sense in which Spinoza and Leibnitz are rationalists and Locke and Hume are not, or in the sense in which McTaggert and Blanshard are rationalists and Russell and Ayer are not or, in the domain of moral and social philosophy, in the sense in which Sidgwick and Gewirth are rationalists and Rawls and MacIntyre are not. I have never thought that there were any substantive self-evident propositions, clear to the light of reason, or that there were any synthetic a priori truths, or that our belief systems, even when they were "true systems", even approximated a system of tightly knit internal relations. I am not wildly interested in ascribing -isms to myself, for they tend to be in one way or another misleading, but in the broad sense in which both Dewey and Quine are pragmatists I think of myself as a pragmatist and I think of that pragmatism in such a way that it involves the acceptance of (broadly conceived) both empiricism and realism. (Here again I think my views are like those of Dewey and Quine.) Beyond that, abandoning the attempt to articulate general philosophical frameworks for social theory, I have also come in recent years to think of myself as an analytical Marxist. I also, of course, take it that one can quite consistently be both an analytical Marxist and a pragmatist. I doubt if there is anything interesting which counts as philosophical knowledge but I do think that we can, perhaps in a reasonably systematic way, gain an understanding of how society works and what our options are in the contemporary world. But, since my salad days, I have always rejected the doctrines characteristic of rationalism, and there is, at least as far as I can see, nothing in my account of religion which commits me to such a doctrine.[16]

However, I think that Hart and I may be at cross purposes here. Hart uses "rationalism" in a very broad sense in which all the philosophers listed above, the empiricists as well as the rationalists, would be regarded as rationalists. For him the contrast between rationalists and nonrationalists would, I believe, be between Pascal, Hamann, Nietzsche, Kierkegaard, and Foucault on the nonrationalist side and Hume, Mill, Marx, Dewey, and Habermas on the rationalist side. Let me see if I can tease out what this broader sense of "rationalist" comes to, and with that see whether, and if so in what sense, my atheism is rationalist and whether, and if so in what sense, I make a religion of reason.

How does Hart conceive of rationalism and of rationalist atheism? (Presumably because of Nietzsche, Foucault and perhaps Feuerbach "rationalist atheism" is not pleonastic.) What, according to him, does my commitment to reason come to? Well, it comes to rejecting the supernatural and transcendent and accepting instead the authority of reason. But what is it to accept the authority of reason? Well, it comes to rejecting, as being incoherent or in some other ways illegitimate, any appeal to a "reality transcending what we empirically comprehend." It comes (a) to rejecting any claim to have access to a realm of truth or an order of facts which are even in principle empirically inaccessible, and (b) to rejecting any claim to such a "non-empirical realm of fact" as being conceptually incoherent. There is and can be no gnostic knowledge. (It seems to me, by the way, that *in this sense* both Nietzsche and Foucault, and most certainly Feuerbach, are also rationalists.)

Hart adds other things to his characterization of what he takes to be my rationalism which I would dispute (particularly his strange talk about "self-grounding"), but, if to accept the authority of reason is just to accept the above, I would happily plead guilty to accepting the authority of reason and thus *in that sense* to being a rationalist, *provided I am allowed to give a certain non-eccentric but still determinate reading to rejecting any appeal to a reality transcending what we can empirically comprehend.*[17] I would want to construe this after the fashion of the logical empiricists as being constrained by what it is *logically* possible empirically to detect and comprehend and not just as to what in fact we can observe or otherwise empirically detect, or as to what it is technically possible to observe or otherwise detect.[18] Without such a construal, we would be taken to be rejecting the belief that there really are, or even can be, photons or neutrinos since they in fact cannot be observed and such a denial of their reality I take, and have always taken, to be a *reductio.*[19] But I am not rejecting such de facto unobservables. What I am rejecting is any conception of there being any fact of the matter, any objects, relations or processes, that are not, even in principle, empirically accessible. I am rejecting any *logical* ban on their being observed. In that way for me, as for Axel Hägerström, all facts are empirical facts: "empirical facts" is pleonastic.[20]

Now, as not a few think, that may be too narrow a construal of "a fact of the matter" and of how we are to construe being able to determine what that is. Even if I am mistaken here, or if we cannot in any even reasonably decisive way determine whether or not I am mistaken, this doesn't turn such a belief on my part into a dogma or anything even remotely like a creedal statement. Whether it does or not depends entirely on how I hold it. If I hold it, as I in fact do, fallibilistically ready to abandon it in the face of rational considerations directed against it, then it cannot be a dogma with me. It may be a mistaken belief but it is not a dogma. In speaking of "rational considerations directed against it" I have in mind such things as: (1) claims that there are too many things we all, even on reflection, take to be facts which cannot be accommodated by that conception of the facts; and (2) various arguments against my conception, including alternative proposals about how to characterize the situation. If, after careful consideration, the alternatives are seen to have greater probity, I would, of course, then abandon my conception. I may very well not be able ahead of time to say what I would have to come to be convinced of to abandon the belief—after all it is a rather fundamental belief for me—but if I am open to discussion, argument and further inquiry concerning it and related beliefs, and if, in a fallibilistic spirit, I am prepared, depending on the force of the better argument in extended discourses about the matter, to abandon the belief on the basis of that further inquiry, argument, evidence and the like, then, given that is the way I hold the belief, it cannot be a dogma or a creedal matter for me.[21] But that is exactly how I hold the belief and there is nothing in my *Philosophy and Atheism* or in the present set of essays that gives to understand the contrary. And in so proceeding, I am presumably still appealing to the authority of reason. But there seems to me nothing wrong with that and nothing in the slightest religious about it. That is just how reasonable people, rationalists or nonrationalists, religious believers or nonreligious believers, should hold their beliefs. So there is nothing in the very idea of accepting the authority of reason which requires that there can be no appeal to facts which are not empirical facts. In that way there is nothing a prioristic about my approach. It is all a matter of what, appealing in this way to the authority of reason and carefully reasoning and investigating, we discover *or* conclude. And this means that I am indeed committed to sticking with what ultimately has the force of the more adequate deliberation when we human beings dispassionately and honestly deliberate together under conditions of openness and nondomination. If to be so committed is to be a rationalist then I gladly confess to being a rationalist, but that is a low-redefinition of a "rationalist". Instead, it just partially specifies what it is like to be a reasonable person who is not affected with hubris and is open to the voices and the views of others.

Hart might respond that right here in the spirit of modernity I have at a very deep level begged the question with the knight of faith. In fixing belief, I have, in the sense gestured at above, used the authority of reason. By contrast, in the domain of faith and morals at least, the knight of faith will use instead, in fixing belief, Divine Revelation. I cannot, relevantly and non-question-beggingly, use reason to judge Divine Revelation and we cannot, relevantly and non-question-beggingly, use Divine Revelation to judge reason. He has his perspective and I have mine. There is the perspective of rationalism and the perspective of faith and there is no neutral or mutually acceptable perspective or method that can be appealed to decide which has primacy when they conflict or at least appear to conflict. In this way my appeal to the authority of reason is like the appeal to a dogma and, given the determination and passion with which I appeal to it, it is, the claim goes, like a religious appeal.

I do not agree that we are caught in such irreconcilable conflicts such that we just have to leap as knights of faith. We are not caught in such incommensurables.[22] If there really were such a thing as Divine Revelation then we, of course, could use it to judge reason.[23] Knowing what human beings are and what God is, who are we to set our judgments against God's? That would be the height of irrationality and senseless rebellion. If reason seems to require *p*, but Revelation—a *genuine* revelation and not merely a *putative* revelation—requires *not-p*, then it cannot be the case that reason really requires *p*. Rather, we must have somewhere made a mistake in our reasoning in concluding that reason requires *p*.

If there is Divine Revelation it surely can rule reason.

However, I said, "*If* there is Divine Revelation". Whether we are persons of faith or what Hart calls rationalists, the facts are just there that, whether we like them or not, we can hardly miss if we know anything at all and do not avert our gaze. What I am principally referring to is the fact that anthropologically speaking there are, considering all the religions there are, simply thousands of *putative* Divine Revelations. Some may, in effect, say the same thing but most do not and not a few say what appear at least to be radically conflicting things. Where they say different things, as they at least frequently and indeed perhaps always do, at most one could be true, i.e., be more than a *putative* Divine Revelation, be instead a *genuine* Divine Revelation. Faced with that plethora of putative Divine Revelations often requiring radically different things, we cannot, barring a fideistic turn I will consider in a moment, reasonably (sensibly) just arbitrarily accept one of these putative revelations. In the Middle Ages we perhaps could have just plunked for one, for the range of choice was linked to a lesser awareness of what, given all humanity, the range of choice actually is, but by now we have lost our innocence: we just know too much to be able, without being irrational, to so plunk, *if*, Barth-like, all we are relying on is some putative Divine Revelation.

Hart has structured things in such a way that between his rationalist and his person of faith the choices are stark. But this is unrealistic and unjustified. I can show this best if I proceed indirectly. If the person uses the resources of the philosophy of religion, of natural theology, of an appeal to religious experience or an appeal to morality, to either justify his choice of one putative revelation rather than another or as devices for limiting the range of his choice, then he would in effect be appealing to the authority of reason and siding with what Hart called the rationalist. He must, to avoid "rationalism", take his putative revelation neat without any elaboration or defense beyond an explication of what revelation is and what that revelation is in particular. He cannot, without going beyond an appeal to revelation, say why his appeal is to a genuine revelation and the others are only appeals to putative revelations. But standing where we are now, knowing what we know, he cannot sensibly or reasonably just so take his putative revelation neat. There are just too many candidate revelations around to make such an appeal at all reasonable for anyone who is the least bit informed. Social anthropology has firmly blocked that revelationist route.

Hart might come back by remarking that, by invoking concepts of reasonability, and sensibly here, I have again rationalistically begged the question. But I think not. In speaking of what is reasonable and sensible I have not invoked any special conception of rationality from a rationalist or any other philosophical or scientific theory of rationality (assuming there is such an animal). I am appealing here, quite unexceptionably, to our ordinary and, if you will, somewhat loose use of "reasonable" and "sensible", captured in part in our dictionaries and employed, by believers and nonbelievers alike, in our stream of life.[24] The sense of "reasonable" and "sensible" is as much a property of the believer as the sceptic, including the atheist. I am inviting the person of faith to consider whether or not it would be reasonable for us moderns—after all, the contemporary, educated religious believer is also a modern—to appeal in such a single-minded way to what he takes to be Divine Revelation, given that our actual circumstances include most crucially the fact that there are a multitude of often conflicting candidate revelations. This, in effect, by a kind of method of challenge, is an invitation to believers, here particularly fideistic believers, to deliberate with secularists in a dispassionate manner about whether that is so.

A believer might think such an appeal to his putative divine revelation to be perfectly reasonable even in the circumstances I described. If so then we, using what certainly at least appears to be our common concept of reasonability, can in turn deliberate about that. Sometimes in certain practical and particularly pressing and unnerving contexts we run out of time or patience and we then must just act one way or another, sticking, so to speak, to our guns. But theoretically speaking there is no point where we just run out of anything that can possibly be said and we must just say: my spade is turned; or, here stand I; I can do no other.[25] We can in theory at least always step back and bracket for a time what we are at cross purposes about and search for a common ground from which we can deliberate and continue the dispute in a way such that, we at least can *hope*, will eventually break the deadlock. There is no a priori reason to believe we will invariably find such a common ground but there is plenty of empirical justification for thinking we will, if we are resolute enough in searching, particularly in a common culture, for shared beliefs from which we can deliberate. Wittgenstein was profoundly misleading when he said that justification must come to an end or it wouldn't be justification.[26] In a way that is so, but in the way at which I have just gestured it is not. Proof, of course, requires premises, but we can, using other premises, always challenge the premises used in the proof and, even if we get back to the rules of formation and transformation, if indeed there is anything like that in natural languages, we can always, in theory at least, challenge those rules and forge new rules and the like. This can, if there is any need for it, go on indefinitely, though, for those obsessed with Cartesian doubt, it can, as Peirce pressed home, also go on idly and pointlessly. (Philosophers have a real penchant for going on pointlessly.)[27] There is, however, no set place where we just must face each other with irreconcilable perspectives, like alternative geometries, where there is nothing more we can possibly say. This foundationalist picture is profoundly mistaken. The probing anti-foundationalist arguments of Dewey, Quine, Rorty and Davidson should have enabled us to set that old philosophical picture aside.

I mentioned a moment ago a turn the fideist could reasonably take to avoid this conclusion. It is a turn in effect powerfully taken in the past by Pascal, Hamann, Kierkegaard, and Dostoevsky (at least through some of his characters). Put without their powerful elaborations, the argument in kernel form comes to this: faced, without a belief in God, with the bleakness of life, the pressure of a Godless nihilism, the senselessness of life and the undermining of any kind of tolerable moral life, it is better to opt, however arbitrarily, however absurdly, for the claims of the putative revelation of Christianity than to live with such a black hole, to live in such a condition of utter hopelessness. With Christianity, or at least a belief in God, there is hope; with a purely secular view of the world there is none. So the reasonable person who cares about her life and the lives of others will opt for Christianity or some such religion even though she knows there is no rational warrant at all for accepting that belief system. She requires it to make sense of life—so life will not be just one damn thing after another until we die and rot—even though the leap of faith is cognitively speaking utterly arbitrary. For a caring person being reasonable requires such arbitrariness.

Leaving aside the very real question of why Christianity rather than one of the other historic faiths, it seems to me that this fideistic turn would have a very considerable force indeed if we really needed a belief in God to make sense of our lives or to justify the claims of morality. But it just is not the case that we have that need for belief in God, or so at least I have extensively argued.[28] Perhaps these arguments are defective and, beyond that not terribly surprising possibility, perhaps it is even true that such a secular humanist case, better put, cannot be sustained. But Hart, at least, does nothing to counter these arguments or to show that they rest on rationalistic excesses or unjustified assumptions. These arguments challenge the uncritical fideist assumption that we cannot have morality or an adequate sense of self without belief in God. Indeed that fideist assumption is not only challenged; it is also argued in some detail that key fideist beliefs deployed in support of that assumption are false. My argument here has not been countered and, unless and until it is, that fideistic turn will not have exposed an irrational or even an arbitrary or creedal core in what Hart takes to be my rationalism.

Hart says things about what he takes to be my view or theory of rationality which I find very puzzling. Indeed I hardly recognize them as my views and I fear that there we are so speaking past each other that I hardly know where to start. (That does not mean that there is no place to start, it just means that it is hard to find a common ground on which to begin the discussion.) I recognize, and indeed stress, that rationality is a very complicated concept subject to persuasive definition, ideological deformation and perhaps is what has been called an essentially contested concept.[29] I do not try to develop a ramified theory of rationality but try to stay as close to common sense as I can, and I remain resolutely eclectic between instrumental and noninstrumental conceptions of rationality. (I do not make the rather typical analytical assumption that the only rationality there is, is instrumental rationality.)[30] Hart thinks I make a god of reason and then treat reason wantonly, using it so broadly that it becomes simply a term of approval for anything I take to be good. Indeed he believes I use "rational" like many others use "good". "Reason, reasonable, and rational," he tells us, seem, on my usage, "to acquire the meaning of terms of approval for whatever is dear to Western people."[31] Like a good rationalist, I identify rationality, Hart would have it, with whatever I take to be deeply desirable and I "acknowledge the deepest meaning of all meaning to be rational meaning."[32]

I do nothing of the kind. (Or could it be that in some way I do not see the mote in my own eye?) For starters, I do not even understand what "rational meaning" means. Is it supposed to be contrasted with "irrational meaning"? But what is that? Words have meaning—that is, they have a use in a language—and this use, per se, is neither rational nor irrational. What I do, building on our public use of the terms, is try to say what rational beliefs are, what rational principles are, and what it would be like to be a fully rational person, stressing that this latter conception is a heuristic ideal and that this characterization of rationality, as indeed any good characterization, has a certain indeterminacy but certainly not such an indeterminacy that the term "rational" simply becomes a general term of approbation. Rational beliefs, I say unexceptionably, perhaps even platitudinously, "are typically beliefs that can withstand the scrutiny of people who are critical of their beliefs: that is to say, they are beliefs typically held open to refutation or modification by experience and/or by reflective examination."[33] They are beliefs which those holding them will hold in such a way that they will not brush aside an examination of their assumptions, implications and relations to other beliefs. Moreover, they are beliefs which their holders, knowing what, under the social circumstances they can be expected to know, will, relative to that knowledge, have good grounds for believing are free of inconsistencies, contradictions, or incoherences.[34] I also specify a number of rational principles of action, only some of which I will advert to here.[35] To act rationally is, *ceteris paribus*, to take the most efficient and effective means to achieve one's ends. Moreover, the ends which help form or are at least in accordance with a dispassionate and informed point of view, and which a person values higher than her other ends, are the ends to which, *ceteris paribus*, she should give priority. The *ceteris paribus* clauses are not just decorative here, for life is sufficiently complex that exceptional circumstances will sometimes arise when a rational belief will not have those features, or when acting rationally will not come to acting in accordance with those rational principles of action. When this is so will inescapably be a matter of reflective judgment.[36] There is no Benthamite or other formula which will relieve us from the making of those judgments. If we reflect carefully on this and if we are reasonably rational we will recognize that such indeterminacy is in fact not to be lamented. The principles mentioned above are a good subset of the principles of rationality and, like prima facie duties, they *always usually* hold. It is, that is, always the case that these principles, where applicable, usually hold in a way fully analogous to the way that for everyone all of the time it is the case that promises, *generally* speaking, are to be kept.

Fully rational people, keeping firmly in mind the *ceteris paribus* clauses, will have, under the above description, rational beliefs and rational principles of action. In addition, fully rational people will be enlightened and emancipated human beings. They will have achieved a firm sense of self-identity and adult autonomy (an autonomy which is compatible with a firm appreciation of human interdependence), will have a good understanding of human needs and will be liberated from the various illusions that fetter humankind.[37] None of us is, of course, a fully rational human being. It is plainly a heuristic ideal, and rationality does, equally plainly, admit of degrees. But it is an ideal that can be approximated and it is plainly a desirable thing that it be so approximated.

The various criteria for rational belief, rational principles of action and for being a fully rational person are in various ways indeterminate and context-dependent. However, it does not follow from this that they are vague or opaque, or just ideological slogans. Even "enlightenment" and "emancipation" cannot mean just anything. They are not mere hurrah words. Moreover, *pace* Hart, my usage of "rationality" is not a usage such that I can just use it as a general term of approbation or so that it becomes equivalent to whatever I would refer to as being good. Furthermore, again *pace* Hart, it is not something scientistic applying only to scientists and philosophers and not to poets or theologians or—perish the thought—to plain folks who are none of these things. Rational beliefs and rational principles of action are things that anyone can have. Whether we have them or not depends on how we behave. Being fully rational is, of course, very demanding indeed and, at least as things stand, few will even approximate it. But it is not a scientistic conception approximatable only by scientists and analytical philosophers. It is also not something which, Hart to the contrary notwithstanding, is self-grounding. Indeed, I am not even sure that I know what that means but, to the extent that I have some inkling, there is nothing "self-grounded" about my conception of rationality or my alleged rationalism.[38]

I have given a conceptualization of rationality that I hope, while being in accordance with our common concept of rationality, extends it in certain ways and makes it more determinate. To have a concept of rationality, or of anything else, it is necessary for there to be a term with a determinate use in a language (e.g., Dutch, French, English, German, Swahili). "Rationality" has a use in English. Building on that use, I tried to go some way in articulating what *we* take that rationality to be. Whether I have succeeded or not depends on whether my account squares with our public use of "rationality" and whether people on reflection will conclude that the extensions I have made help capture our sense—our public sense—of what rationality and reasonableness should come to. We want to know whether it matches people's considered judgments in wide reflective equilibrium about what rationality and reasonableness come to.

Have I, in effect, made reason into a kind of Divinity? I have treated being fully rational as a very desirable thing indeed, but I have plainly not made reason the sole good thing or the "ultimately good thing" and, indeed, to do so would surely be absurd. I think having a good time, experiencing love, being a caring considerate person, having something one very much wants to accomplish and sticking with the struggle to accomplish it, and (among other things) committing oneself to the moral point of view are all good things. But while I think reason *permits* these things I do not claim reason *requires* them. I have argued long and strenuously against moralists such as Kurt Baier, Alan Gewirth and David Gauthier, that rationality does not require morality, that in certain circumstances it is quite possible that a rational person could be a man of good morals without being a morally good man, i.e., a person could be rational, perhaps even through-and-through rational, without being a person of principle.[39] I have argued that if we are not caring persons we are going to fail as persons in very significant ways though that failure need not be a failure in rationality. (Person, as Rawls argues, is a moral category.)[40] I have even acknowledged, in discussing Pascal and Kierkegaard, that if it were the case that life would be meaningless without belief in God this would constitute a good reason for believing in God.[41] This is hardly the view of someone who thinks reason is the sole good, the sole intrinsic good, the ultimate good, or who treats reason as a god.

Hart believes that because I take rationality to be ultimate it must be for me a divinity. Moreover, he goes on to argue that "it is questionable whether an ultimately rational point of view can be rationally grounded without begging the question of its own grounding."[42] Because of these things, it is possible, he believes, to see my position as a religious position because "what makes a position religious is that it *ultimately* judges everything from that position, while never questioning that position without begging the question."[43]

There are, I believe, both multiple confusions here and unwitting misrepresentations, only some of which I will canvass. Why call a position religious simply because it ultimately judges everything from that position while never questioning that position without begging the question? Would it not be more appropriate to call such a position ideological or, alternatively, metaphysical or just more descriptively a comprehensively question-begging position? Perhaps all religions have that characteristic, but that fact, if it is a fact, does not justify the claim that what is perhaps a necessary condition is also a sufficient condition for something being a religion or even being religious. A materialist metaphysic or Freudian psychology may have that feature as well but it would be, to put it mildly, misleading to regard these holistic theories as religions or as being religious. Hobbes and Freud are not charismatic creators of new religions. The most that could justifiably be maintained is that such holistic theories have one of the features characteristic of a religion and they need not be what Jean-François Lyotard calls grand meta-narratives. Failing to consider the criticism I make of Paul Tillich for taking what *might* be another necessary condition—being ultimately concerned or being ultimate—to be a sufficient condition for a view's being a religious view, Hart himself makes a very similar mistake to that of Tillich.[44] Consider the matter this way. I am not sure that I know what it means to take rationality as ultimate, but, even assuming that a plausible reading can be given to that and even if I do somehow unwittingly take rationality to be ultimate, that in itself does not at all make a commitment to rationality a religious commitment or make reason a god. I do not believe that I do take rationality to be ultimate, but even if I did there would not be such a linkage as Hart alleges with being religious. To maintain that if you take something to be ultimate you must believe in God is a form of attempted conversion by stipulative redefinition. There are a number of belief systems that, prior to any attempt at a definition, we antecedently clearly recognize to be religious, namely the historic religions, East and West, and cosmological belief systems like those of the Dinka or the Neur. *Sometimes* with primitive societies, though not with the Dinka or Neur, we are going to be unsure whether what we have is simply a set of magical practices or whether it is as well a religion. In defining "religion" we want to see if we can catch features which are common to and distinctive of those practices and belief systems paradigmatically and commonly regarded as religions. This may not be easy to do. For a Westerner, for example, believing in God, or the gods, or in spiritual beings, is as natural a thing to fasten on as capturing what it is for a belief system to be religious, but it will not quite do as a characterization of religion for, as I mentioned earlier, it rules out—and this is a *reductio*—Theravada Buddhism as a religion since Theravada Buddhism does not commit its adherents to any belief in God at all but instead to a social structure sustaining practices aimed at spiritual liberation.[45] Theravada Buddhism has no concept of God or of worship, but it does have another non-naturalistic transcendental concept, namely nirvana. It is an alleged spiritual state in which those who are enlightened in a certain way achieve liberation from the endless series of rebirths of a life that is full of suffering. The goal of Buddhism, as much as that of Islam, is a spiritual one, namely, in Buddhism's case, to attain nirvana, a spiritual liberation. In this way, all religions, besides committing their faithful to some form of ultimate concern or to some form of ultimacy, also have some concept of the sacred or some concept of spiritual reality. These last two features are features which atheism, rationalistic or otherwise, does not have. Only by playing with words, by giving "low-redefinitions" of terms like "sacred" or "spiritual reality", can it be made even to seem otherwise.[46] It is like, in trying to define an MD, calling anyone who can perform first aid a doctor. Ultimate views may or may not be religious. Ultimacy may be a necessary condition for being religious but it is surely not a sufficient condition. However, that the belief system have a belief in spiritual realities or the sacred is clearly a less problematic candidate for a necessary condition for being religious or being a religion. Metaphysical views and perhaps other worldviews are indeed good candidates for ultimate views. But not all of them involve a belief in spiritual realities or the sacred. Moreover, "a religious worldview" is not a redundancy and a "nonreligious worldview" is not, as we use language, a contradiction. The same thing can be said for a metaphysical view. Plainly there are worldviews and metaphysical systems that do not involve any belief in God or the gods or engage in any positing of spiritual realities or sacred realities. Hart, in order to characterize my views as religious, departs radically from how we speak and think in characterizing what makes something a religion, but he has given us no good reason at all for following him in his stipulative departure. And while, in what he thinks is a too intellectualistic way, I do stress that religions are belief systems, I do not say or give to understand that they are *only* belief systems. Religion has very much to do with the *attitude* we take to life and with how we live or at least try to live. But I do not deny that or even underplay it. I am only concerned to assert, in this context, what is obvious anyway, namely that religions are necessarily also belief systems. Hart ignores this side of things. To be justified in calling my atheism a religious view he has to give us a justification for such a radical departure from how we think and speak. And that, to repeat, he has not done.

IV

                                    I turn now to Professor Béla Szabados's criticisms.[47] Strong, tendentious philosophical claims require, to have any reasonable force, strong arguments. My claim that belief in God is in our time irrational for a scientifically and philosophically sophisticated person is just such a strong and, to put it minimally, contentious claim. Indeed it is a claim to which not a few would take exception and some, no doubt, will find it offensive. Szabados does well to focus critical attention on that claim, for, if it is to be persuasive, it must be very well supported indeed. I do not know whether I have done anything more than make a start at providing that support or if such support can in fact be sustained. It surely would, to understate it, not be unreasonable to be wary of that claim. But, that to the contrary notwithstanding, it does seem to me, everything considered, the correct claim to make, so I will stick by my guns and, facing Szabados's objections, continue to argue, though with a full sense of my fallibility here, that such belief is irrational.

However, I should first make a disclaimer, for if my views here are misunderstood, as they might be by a careless reader or, more easily and more understandably, by someone who simply hears them, they could rightly be dismissed with contempt. I am not claiming that all or even most Jews, Christians or Moslems are irrational. That is just too grossly *parti pris* and too absurd to even be worth considering. Indeed, it would be a silly form of hubris, as if I were claiming I am more rational than Professor Hart or claiming that such paradigm Christian philosophers as John Hick, William Alston, Terence Penelhum or Hugo Meynell are irrational or less rational than I am. Anyone who knows them—and they are tokens of a familiar type—knows that such a claim is absurd. Béla Szabados does not, of course, think for a moment that I believe anything like that, but my plainly contentious claim might be confused with that absurd claim. So I make the disclaimer and append an explanation.

What I am claiming instead is that, if my analysis of the concept of God is on the whole well-taken and non-arcane, belief in God is irrational for a philosophically sophisticated and scientifically knowledgeable person in our cultural space, standing where we stand now in the Twentieth Century. I am *not* saying the religious believer is irrational—he may or may not be, just as the atheist may or may not be irrational; what I am saying is that, if the believer is a Twentieth Century person, with a good scientific and philosophical education, his or her belief in God is irrational if what

I say about God is so. It is the *belief* for such a person and not the *person* himself that I am claiming is irrational. And there is no hubris or exaggeration in that claim, though the claim may well be false or unproven (as Szabados believes) or perhaps even incoherent.

To claim that reasonable people can have some irrational beliefs should be little more than a commonplace. Indeed, if our criteria for a reasonable person are so strong that, if a person is properly said to be rational it could not be the case that he had any irrational beliefs, then the class of rational people would most probably be empty. Freud gives a partial explanation why, but, Freud or no Freud, it is as evident as can be that manifestly reasonable people not infrequently have a few irrational beliefs. My suit is not to convict the Christian of irrationality but to show that a key framework-belief of his is an irrational belief for him to hold if my analysis of the concept of God is non-arcane and near to the mark, and if he lives now in a society such as ours and has been educated in the way I have specified.

I will concede to Szabados, and acknowledge the importance in the context of my argument of making this very point, that the believer need not hold his belief in an irrational manner. What I will stand pat on is the claim that, if my arguments about the incoherence of non-anthropomorphic God-talk are sound and non-arcane then for a believer who could reasonably be expected to understand them, it would be irrational for her to believe in God. The crucial thing is not the propriety of my charge about irrationality but the soundness of my arguments about the incoherence of the concept of God. Moreover, I am not absurdly maintaining that believers' rationality or lack thereof in so believing depends on their having studied my views. Views bearing a family resemblance to mine are firmly fixed in the social space of our intellectual culture and are, as I see it, but a consistent drawing out of the implications of a current of thought which has been growing and developing from its inception in Enlightenment thought, including its response to the Counter-Enlightenment. Even Richard Rorty, a philosopher deeply influenced by the Counter-Enlightenment and by historicist modes of thought and fundamentally opposed to empiricist programs like those of Hume, Hägerström, Russell or Ayer, states unequivocally in his *Philosophy and the Mirror of Nature* that "the preservation of the values of the Enlightenment is our best hope," and that "the positivists were absolutely right in thinking it imperative to extirpate metaphysics when "metaphysics" means the attempt to give knowledge of what science cannot know."[48]

Szabados, like Hart, is perplexed and deeply sceptical about my account of rationality and its use in assessing religions as forms of life. He thinks, as does Hart, that I have not come within a country mile of showing that belief in God is irrational for critically educated people situated as we are now. Why and how does Szabados think I fail here? Unlike Hart he finds my account of rationality attractive, but he finds the application to which I put it in criticizing religion problematic, and he maintains that I do not recognize how problematic the concept of rationality is. Still, it is not that but my alleged failure properly to apply my own criteria of rationality to religion on which he fastens.

The principles of rational belief and rational action I adumbrate are, on my conception of things, universal and "we can use them to appraise institutions, practices and forms of life . . . ."[49] Judaism, Christianity and Islam are such forms of life and they are so appraised by me. My argument has been that when we appraise them in such terms they have little rational warrant.

I agree with Szabados, or rather he agrees with me, for I stressed just that point in *Philosophy and Atheism*, that the notions of rationality and irrationality are not pellucid or unproblematic and, given that, we should not throw caution to the winds in making sweeping claims about the irrationality of religious belief.[50] But, as he, in effect, also acknowledges with his remarks about my responses to anticipated objections, qualifications and the like, I am not so incautious. What he needs to do, to show that the problematicity of our concept of rationality is damaging to my case, is to show: (a) that my account of rationality is seriously defective or (what itself is a distinctive way of being defective) that it is ethnocentric in being (as Hart believes) just our modernizing Western account of rationality; and (b) that because of these inadequacies what I say about the irrationality of religious belief is skewed.[51] (It could be the case that (a) is true without it being the case that (b) is true.) But he claims none of these things and in fact makes no specific criticisms of my account of rationality.

What he actually does is something else and that something else, *if well taken*, would be a legitimate criticism of my account. He seeks to show that at least some religious believers and some religious beliefs can satisfy my various criteria of rationality, and that belief in God is among those beliefs. That is to say, given my own criteria of rationality, there is nothing irrational about the believers and the beliefs in the way I contend. And that claim, I admit, if true, would without doubt be damaging, indeed devastating, to my case. Given, Szabados argues, what I take rationality to be, there is no good reason for believing a reflective, religiously interested, scientifically aware and philosophically astute believer must be behaving irrationally in believing in God, or that this belief of his must be irrational.

The religious person's belief need not be internally inconsistent and he may be sensitive to relevant evidence, attend to it, recognize where it points and face its implications. Szabados believes that I, in effect, deny this, for in making my claims about the irrationality of religious belief, I just assume, Szabados further believes, that religious language is incoherent and that a rational believer must acknowledge this if he is philosophically sophisticated and attends to the argument. I do indeed largely assume that such religious beliefs are incoherent in the two essays in my *Philosophy and Atheism* Szabados discusses, which are, it is important to note in this context, the last two essays in that book, but in earlier essays in the same volume, namely "Does God Exist?", "Reason and Commitment" and, most centrally, "In Defense of Atheism," as well as in *Contemporary Critiques of Religion, An Introduction to the Philosophy of Religion* and in *Skepticism*, I do not assume but argue in some detail that central strands of the religious discourse of the developed religions of the West are incoherent. And in the essays in the present volume, I return repeatedly to that issue from a number of quite different angles. Perhaps my arguments are unsound or in some way question-begging or even themselves incoherent, but I do not just *assume* that religious talk and belief (including belief in God) is incoherent. Indeed, I stress, like Szabados, that religious discourse does *seem* to make sense, that religious people do not typically go around making *plainly* contradictory remarks, and that we do in a way understand some plain God-talk whatever may be the case for some kinds of theological talk (e.g., some of the talk of Tillich or Bultmann). But, to repeat, I argue in detail that central strands of God-talk—God-talk that claims, as Ninian Smart puts it, "the transcendent reference point"—make cosmological claims which, when we inspect them carefully, turn out *not* to make sense in the very specific sense in which they *purport* to make sense, for they actually fail to make anything that we on inspection would recognize to be a truth-claim while still purporting to make grand cosmological claims and while being taken by their adherents to be somehow making such claims.[52]

Some of my central arguments for this do indeed depend on a demarcated and very moderate and nuanced verificationism, but others do not, and the ones that do not are very prominent in a, perhaps *the*, central essay in *Philosophy and Atheism*, "In Defense of Atheism," in my book *Skepticism*, and in the first chapter of the present volume. Szabados does not even advert to these arguments, let alone refute them or even deflect them. Moreover, *pace* Szabados, not all forms of incoherence are contradictions or inconsistencies. "Procrastination drinks melancholy", "Alienation eludes being", "Being unfolds itself into utter transcendency" or "Being itself is the ground of being and meaning" do not say anything sufficiently clear to clearly count as being either contradictory or non-contradictory, yet they are surely good candidates for incoherences. I maintain that central strands of plain God-talk in our religious discourses are, though in a less evident way, similarly incoherent. I try, particularly in the first chapter of this book and again in *Philosophy and Atheism* and elsewhere, to exhibit specific ways in which certain very determinate strands of God-talk are incoherent, or at least have all the appearances of incoherence. Szabados no more than Hart has shown that appearances are deceiving here.

Some religious-talk may encourage paradox, and *perhaps* in some contexts rightly so, but sensible religious people, as Szabados well says, do not "revel in or encourage contradictions as such."[53] But, *pace* Szabados, I never argued or even suggested that they do. I argued instead that, in spite of what often is a firm determination on the part of their users to make sense, close inspection of central strands of, say, Christian religious discourse reveal incoherences that appear at least to be inescapable, to be part, as they used to say, of the very logic of religious discourse. Again, neither Szabados nor Hart does anything to show that I am mistaken here.

Szabados, like Hart, would in turn obliquely respond by saying that he does not see how it is possible, without begging the question, impartially to resolve issues concerning whether non-anthropomorphic God-talk is coherent, or whether it is irrational to believe in God. There is, he claims, no impartial, non-question-begging stance available to us here. I agree that burden of proof arguments are difficult to establish and that in fundamental philosophical disputes, if they are really pushed hard, it is difficult to avoid begging questions or assuming, often unwittingly, a problematic stance about the burden of proof. (I said it was difficult but I did not say it was impossible.)

With this in mind, let us try to see if I have begged the question with religious believers, or at least whether Szabados has given us good reason for believing I have. In attempting to show how I have begged the question Szabados seeks to show how a thoughtful philosophically and scientifically educated believer might continue to believe in God without lapsing into irrational belief. Such believers, he argues, might acknowledge that attempts to prove or establish the existence of God have all failed. In doing so they have on my own conception of rationality taken a rational stance; they, as Szabados put it, "have not ignored criticisms or objections but took them to heart."[54] Moreover, the unbeliever, as I stressed, cannot give an a priori proof that no proof of God's existence is possible. Of course, if the very concept of God is incoherent, then no proof of God's existence is possible but Szabados could perfectly rightly respond that arguments for incoherence also require premises and these premises could always be challenged—they are not all necessary truths—just as the premises used in that challenge could always in turn be challenged themselves and so on and on we can go without there being any a priori terminating point.

Because of these considerations and because of similar remarks about my rational principles of action, Szabados claims that fundamental arguments used in disputes between people like myself and reflective believers are question-begging. But if this is our criterion for stances being question-begging then all or at least almost all arguments are, and unavoidably so, question-begging, for, as I have just remarked, arguments require premises and premises can always be challenged. Even alleged claims to self-evidence and certainty, assuming (which is to assume a lot) they are substantive enough to support anything, can be challenged, and even if we get back to the rules of formation and transformation they in turn can always be challenged. There is no safe Cartesian harbour here.

In *that strong sense*, as Gilbert Ryle argued, there can be no proofs in philosophy or indeed anywhere else.[55] And it should be noted in this context, and with respect to the above, that there is nothing unusual in that respect about the dispute I have set up between the kind of atheist I am and the reflective believer. *In the sense Szabados gestures at*, the arguments made in the attempted resolution of any dispute, or at least almost any dispute, will be question-begging. Indeed they *can* hardly be anything else, and if that is so, then that is a *reductio* of Szabados's argument in effect depriving "question-begging argument" of a non-vacuous (significant) contrast and thus rendering it a claim without any force. One telltale evidence for this is that, on such a way of contending that arguments are question-begging, there is no need at all to examine the specific argument to maintain it is question-begging. The tides of metaphysical illusion are running high here.

Szabados rightly sees that for me the heart of the matter, in the dispute between belief and unbelief, is over belief in God. After all, if I thought it made sense to say that God exists, that God has a certain nature and that, in addition, it is reasonable to believe that he really does exist, I would not think there was any moral alternative to obeying his will. (That does not entail that anyone should accept a morality of Divine Commands.) But, since I reject those fundamental framework-beliefs, these other issues do not even come up for me.

Szabados, however, has not got my picture of what faith is right. Since I believe that belief in God is in most circumstances irrational for us (where "us" ranges over contemporary intellectuals in Western countries), I also believe that faith is in most circumstances irrational for us.[56] Szabados is right about that. But he is thoroughly off the mark about why I think faith is irrational and about what I think the knight of faith is like. The person who has faith in a Zeus-like God may be as Szabados characterizes the person of faith, and some of the more Neanderthal Christians may be such believers. But the reflective knight of faith—and certainly there are many such people—of developed forms of Christianity (mainstream Catholicism or Protestantism) is not someone who obstinately insists on believing something for which we do not now have adequate evidence or grounds, pigheadedly being certain of something that is really at best uncertain. (Recall here Kierkegaard's ironical parodies of Hegelianism. And do not confuse Pascal with Plantinga.) But that is not my picture of faith at all, though I agree that there is a kind of idolatrous belief that does have that kind of faith: treating God, as Kierkegaard quipped, as if he were some kind of great green bird. But this is an uninteresting, religiously insignificant religiosity which is little better than mere superstition. My picture of the knight of faith, and thus of faith, is that of a person with a full sense of the objective uncertainty of the object of worship, committing himself to what he acknowledges to be an incomprehensible ultimate mystery who in some sense is said to be, and thought by him to be, a person who is also an utterly spiritual being, who is as well an omnipotent, perfectly good, infinite individual who transcends the world, is beyond the bounds of space and time, and who still is encountered in a caring, saving relationship by the believer who, seeking salvation, will turn to him with purity of heart. The knight of faith is perfectly aware that such a conception is deeply problematic. His faith comes in trusting that this alleged utterly mysterious reality is indeed a reality, in trusting this alleged reality and in trusting that he and others can have sufficient understanding of this Incomprehensible Other to make faith possible, for, after all, we could not, no matter how much we might want to, have faith in anything of which we have no understanding at all.[57]

If God is utterly and totally incomprehensible we cannot have faith in God, for then we will have no understanding of *what* it is we are being asked to trust, or of *whom* or *what* we are to take on trust. "Having faith" presupposes some minimal belief *that*, just as "belief in" presupposes "belief that". And belief *that* in turn implies some understanding of what it is we are supposed to believe to be the case.[58] We can only believe something to be the case if we can understand to some extent at least what it is we are to believe is the case. But if God is said to be *utterly* incomprehensible, we cannot have faith in such an incomprehensible God for then we will have no understanding of what it is we are being asked to trust or of whom or what we are to take on trust. It would be like being asked to trust Urdink when we have no understanding of what "Urdink" means or refers to. We will not even know, if God is utterly incomprehensible, if the object of our discourse is a who or a what. It is, rather, a something we understand, not a what.

Szabados confuses my picture of faith with that of someone like Sidney Hook where the picture of religious faith comes to be something very like a picture of believers as stubborn people trusting that a system of rather wild speculative hypotheses might, after all, turn out to be true.[59] Faith is not (*pace* Hook) a matter of trustingly waiting for the evidence to come in. Recall Tillich's scornful remarks about not being interested in waiting around for a letter from the postman so that we could finally verify, or at least confirm, that God does really exist, or perhaps disconfirm it and abandon Christianity. (Kierkegaard's ironical remarks here are also important.) The believer cannot specify what would verify God's existence so that he could, either pigheadedly (to use Szabados's phrase) or otherwise, believe in something for which he did not yet have adequate grounds, like someone might pigheadedly believe that Santa might after all come down the chimney even though no reliable person has ever observed him doing it or seen him flying about in the sky on his sled. This is the great bird phenomenon that Kierkegaard rightly mocked.

The knight of faith of mainline Judaism, Christianity and Islam has no idea of how to identify his non-anthropomorphic God. He does not know what it would be like to specify the referent of "God", except intra-linguistically using terms whose referents are equally opaque, such as "infinite individual" or "omnipotent reality beyond the bounds of space and time".[60] The knight of faith, with fear and trembling, trusts that these opaque notions have just enough sense to make the religious life possible without requiring utterly irrational beliefs. (I do not speak here of the knight of faith who would voluntarily crucify his intellect.)[61]

My argument has been that when we clearly see what talk of God commits us to, we will come to see that such talk is incoherent. Zeus-talk, by contrast, is mere superstition, but a person need not be superstitious to believe in the God of Maimonides, Aquinas, Luther and Hamann. Such traditional God-talk is deep incoherence—deep because it reflects what something would have to be to be an adequate object of unqualified worship—but, deep or not, it is incoherence all the same.[62]

Szabados's central puzzlement about my views, to return again to the beginning, is about my account of rationality and its use in assessing religion as a form of life. I have maintained that for *us*, educated in the way we have been educated, belief in God is irrational. (Remember the restriction of "us" to critically educated people in modern industrial societies.) A belief is irrational on my account if the person holding it, on the one hand, either knows or, standing where he stands, can reasonably be expected to know that the belief is either inconsistent, unintelligible, incoherent or false. Or, on the other hand, the person has very good grounds for believing that that belief is either inconsistent, unintelligible, incoherent or false or that it is reasonable to expect, whether he has such grounds or not, that someone standing where he stands would have readily available to him such grounds. If the arguments I have made about the incoherence of non-anthropomorphic God-talk are non-arcane and sound or even very close to being on the mark, and if the truth-claims made by anthropomorphic God-talk are either patently false or are of such a low order of probability as to not even be creditable, as I have also argued, then, if these things are really so, for us (assuming we are philosophically and scientifically literate) belief in God is irrational on the quite unexceptional criteria of rationality I have adumbrated, criteria Hart admits square with our common-sense conceptions of rationality.

Such a claim is, of course, a complicated hypothetical. It rests centrally on the claims that such God-talk is incoherent, that anthropomorphic God-talk results in false or very probably false truth-claims, and that my account of rationality is approximately correct. None of these things may be true, though neither Szabados nor Hart even attempted to do anything to show that any of these central things in my account are mistaken. They simply dance around them. It is also the case that my arguments and claims here, true or false or incoherent, are not arcane. They can readily be grasped by anyone standing where we stand. If this is so and my arguments are sound or nearly so, then it is irrational for us to believe in God. (Remember the limitations of what the "us" ranges over.)

I am not saying (pace Szabados) that if one is a competent philosopher one must or even will assent to these claims. That would be stupid arrogance on my part. Rather I am arguing for, as specified and qualified, the incoherence of God-talk and then claiming that, *if* these arguments are near to their mark and non-arcane, it is irrational for someone, in a good position to know that, to believe in God. The voice of philosophy, if it is functioning at all according to its vocation, is not the voice of freely proclaiming thunderous truths or (for that matter) thunderous untruths or incoherences. It is rather that of *argument* or *reflective deliberation* (sometimes more of the one and sometimes more of the other) set in a *narrative* (in the ideal case a comprehensive narrative) aspiring to some approximation to a comprehensive truth, or a comprehensive cluster of truths, which, if such is ever to be had, will be had in forms of reflective intersubjective communication approximating the conditions Habermas characterizes for undistorted discourse.

NOTES

1. Kai Nielsen, *Philosophy and Atheism* (Buffalo, NY: Prometheus Books, 1985). See also my *Contemporary Critiques of Religion* (New York: Herder and Herder, 1971); *Skepticism* (New York: St. Martin's Press, 1973); and *An Introduction to the Philosophy of Religion* (London: The Macmillan Press, 1982).

2. Richard Swinburne, *The Coherence of Theism* (Oxford: The Clarendon Press, 1977) 110.

3. In the lengthy exchange between John Skorupski and Robin Horton these issues are brilliantly probed. Robin Horton, "A Definition of Religion and Its Uses," *The Journal of the Royal Anthropological Institute of Great Britain and Ireland* XC: 201-26; Robin Horton, "African Traditional Thought and Western Science," *Africa* 37 (1967): 131-71; John Skorupski, "Science and Traditional Religious Thought I and II," *Philosophy of the Social Sciences* 3 (1973): 209-30; Robin Horton, "Paradox and Explanation: A Reply to Mr. Skorupski I," *Philosophy of the Social Sciences* 3 (1973): 289-312; Robin Horton, "Levy-Bruhl, Durkheim and the Scientific Revolution," *Modes of Thought*, eds. R. Horton and R. Finnegan (London: Faber and Faber, 1973) 249-305; John Skorupski, "Comment on Professor Horton's 'Paradox and Explanation'," *Philosophy of the Social Sciences* 5.1 (1975): 63-70; and John Skorupski, *Symbol and Theory* (London: Cambridge University Press, 1976).

4. Antony Flew, "The Burden of Proof," *Knowing Religiously*, ed. Leroy S. Rouner (Notre Dame, IN: University of Notre Dame Press, 1985) 105-106, 112-14.

5. See the references to John Skorupski in note 3.

6. This is the kind of agnosticism Ronald Hepburn defends. See his "Agnosticism," *The Encyclopedia of Philosophy*, ed. Paul Edwards, vol. 1 (New York: The Macmillan Co., 1967) 56-59. See also my *Philosophy and Atheism* 55-75.

7. Axel Hägerström, *Philosophy and Religion*, trans. Robert T. Sandin (London: George Allen and Unwin Ltd., 1964) 175-305.

8. Paul Henle, ed., *Language, Thought and Culture* (Ann Arbor: The University of Michigan Press, 1958) 173-95.

9. See the references given in note 1 of this chapter.

10. This has been powerfully argued by J.L. Mackie, *The Miracle of Theism* (Oxford: Clarendon Press, 1982); Wallace Matson, *The Existence of God* (Ithaca, NY: Cornell University Press, 1965); Ronald Hepburn, *Christianity and Paradox* (London: Watts, 1958); Michael Scriven, *Primary Philosophy* (New York: McGraw Hill Co., 1966); and by various authors in the collection edited by Peter Angeles, *Critiques of God* (Buffalo, NY: Prometheus Press, 1976).

11. Hendrik Hart, "Kai Nielsen's *Philosophy and Atheism*" and Béla Szabados, "Religion and Irrationality," both in the symposium on my *Philosophy and Atheism* at the Canadian Philosophical Association Meetings, Winnipeg, Manitoba, 29 May 1986. The present chapter is a developed version of my response at that symposium. Hart's paper in a somewhat revised form has been published in *Philosophy and Theology* I.1 (1987): 334-46.

12. Hart takes it to be typical of creedal beliefs "both that they make the impression of being self-referentially incoherent from a rational-conceptual point of view and that they are held with great conviction." Creedal beliefs for him become religious beliefs "when their authority is ultimate and spiritual, when their role in life is destiny directing" (note 13). There seem to me to be a number of errors here. Most centrally in making all beliefs which are destiny-directing and ultimate into religious and spiritual beliefs, we confuse what could plausibly be maintained as a *necessary* condition for something being religious into a *sufficient* condition. That bit of conceptual legerdemain has the effect of making materialist and naturalistic worldviews into religious worldviews by stipulative redefinition. It is also at best misleading to speak of something appearing incoherent from a rational conceptual point of view with the implied suggestion that from some other point of view it could be coherent or at least appear coherent. What is involved here can be brought out by showing something of what is wrong with Hart's remarks about my alleged rationalism. Hart maintains that my "ultimate position" is my rationalism and this he construes as the belief—a belief he ascribes to me—that "truth can only be truth empirically accessible to reason and whatever is not thus rational is not true." I would not talk that way or con-

ceptualize things in that way. On a straightforward reading, it is false to say that that which is not thus rational is not true. That many poor people play the lotteries is true, that couples often fight over trivial things is also true; neither is rational. For something to be true it need not be rational; we need not understand why it occurs or have ascertained a rationale for it to be true. Thus in this straightforward way truth need not be accessible to reason. However, if something really is unintelligible or self-contradictory, it cannot be true. There can be no married bachelors, and if "Mulroney sleeps faster than Turner" is incoherent it cannot be true. It is, if it is incoherent, incoherent *sans phrase*. Moreover, it isn't from a point of view (rational or otherwise) the case that "Mulroney is Prime Minister of Canada" corresponds to the facts. It just corresponds to the facts period. Sometimes talking about something being true or false or coherent or incoherent from a perspective is itself incoherent.

13.   Hart, in a very unconvincing way, reminiscent of Peter Winch and D.Z. Phillips, denies that he is a relativist. (See his footnote 27.) He correctly avers, mistakenly thinking it enough to rid him of the charge that he is a relativist, that the fact that we "all have faith does not mean everybody's faith is equally good." However, if all claims are what they are because of the perspective they are taken from, if there are radically different perspectives, and if no one can make any non-perspectival claims (e.g. the atheist has his perspective, the Christian hers, the Hindu his and the Dinka hers), and there can be no Archimedean point, as Hart accepts, in virtue of which we can coherently argue that one of these perspectives is more adequate than another, then we are caught in a relativism. But this is exactly the position Hart is in. In fighting off rationality he has saddled himself with relativism.

14.   I have criticized Wittgensteinian fideism in a variety of forms and in a variety of ways and in a number of places: in chapters 6 through 11 of this book, in chapters 3, 4 and 5 of my *An Introduction to the Philosophy of Religion*, in chapter 5 of my *Contemporary Critiques of Religion*, in chapter 2 of my *Skepticism* and in chapter 10 of my *Philosophy and Atheism*.

15.   Kai Nielsen, *Philosophy and Atheism* 125.

16.   I have developed my more recent metaphilosophical views in the following articles: "Challenging Analytic Philosophy," *Free Inquiry* 4.4 (1984); "Rorty and the Self-Image of Philosophy," *International Studies in Philosophy* 18 (1986): 19-28; "How to be Sceptical about Philosophy," *Philosophy* 61.235 (1986): 83-93; "Scientism, Pragmatism and the Fate of Philosophy," *Inquiry* 29.3 (1986): 277-304; "Can there be Progress in Philosophy?" *Metaphilosophy* 18.1 (1987): 1-30; "Searching for an Emancipatory Perspective: Wide Reflective Equilibrium and the Hermeneutical Circle," *Anti-Foundationalism and Practical Reasoning*, ed. Evan Simpson (Edmonton: Academia Press, 1987); and "Reflective Equilibrium and the Transformation of Philosophy," *Metaphilosophy*, forthcoming.

17.   In claiming that rationality is self-grounding Hart acknowledges that his talk is strange. What he means in saying that rationality is self-grounding is that "when one believes that we ought only to believe what we have good grounds to believe, we have problems with the good grounds for this belief itself." (See his footnote 31.) But, as I make evident in my text, I do not for one moment think we either have, or need to have, good grounds for believing everything we believe or even should believe. Rather, as is particularly evident in chapter 9 but is made evident elsewhere in my writings as well, I believe that it is, reasonably and humanly speaking, perfectly inescapable that we will have many beliefs for which we do not have grounds. We, as I have put it again and again, reasonably believe things for which we do not have a reason. Hart unjustifiably imputes a rationalism to me in which I trust reason for its own sake as ground and not on grounds. I do not even remotely hold, and indeed do not even properly understand, the belief that rationality is our only ground for believing.

18.   Derek Parfit, in discussing personal identity, has recently shown the importance of that old positivist distinction without at all accepting positivism. Derek Parfit, *Reasons and Persons* (Oxford: Clarendon Press, 1984) 199-252.

19. This is a point that Hugo Meynell repeatedly misses in his criticisms of me and in his criticisms of verificationists. See Hugo Meynell, "Aspects of the Philosophy of Kai Nielsen," *Dialogue* XXV.1 (1986): 83-92. One general problem I have with Meynell's generous criticisms of me is with his belief that if we can spell out reasons for which a belief or set of beliefs is to be accepted we thereby commit ourselves to foundationalism. This seems to me plainly false. Dewey and Quine are paradigmatic anti-foundationalists, but they also, though fallibilists, are not sceptics and do not have problems about the very possibility of the justifying of beliefs and sets of beliefs. But I proceed in the same way. Meynell commends my appealing to considered judgments in wide reflective equilibrium as a promising method for showing how moral beliefs can be justified, but this method, taken from Quine and Goodman, is with its coherentism (*pace* Meynell) just the opposite of a foundationalist approach. See Meynell, 91-92, footnote 20.

20. Axel Hägerström, *op. cit.* 224-59.

21. Here, in general methodology, I follow Jürgen Habermas.

22. I extensively argue against such incommensurability claims in my "Scientism, Pragmatism and the Fate of Philosophy" 277-304.

23. Kai Nielsen, *Philosophy and Atheism* 145-57.

24. *Ibid.* 189-210. Kai Nielsen, "Principles of Rationality," *Philosophical Papers* III.2 (1974): 55-89; and Kai Nielsen, "The Embeddedness of Conceptual Relativism," *Dialogos* XI.29-30 (1977): 85-111.

25. Isaac Levi, "Escape from Boredom: Edification According to Rorty," *Canadian Journal of Philosophy* XI.4 (1981): 589-602; and Kai Nielsen, "Scientism, Pragmatism and the Fate of Philosophy" 277-304.

26. I followed him here too closely in my "On the Rationality of Groundless Believing." See chapter 9 of this book. For the necessary correction see *Philosophy and Atheism* 221-24 and my "Scientism, Pragmatism and the Fate of Philosophy" 277-304.

27. Hart tells us (footnote 21) that the religion of the Enlightenment is the belief that "rational grounding is the final authority in the grounding of our beliefs." He thinks of me and of Richard Rorty, and no doubt of many other modernists as well, as adherents to this faith. I have in the body of this chapter argued that that claim is false as far as it is a claim about religion. But what about rational authority being the final authority in the grounding of our beliefs? Even here there is a lot of sorting out to be done. In chapter 9 I argued, following Wittgenstein and Malcolm, that we have many groundless beliefs, indeed many more than we typically realize, and that there is nothing unreasonable about that. If, even after a diligent search, I cannot find my watch, I do not entertain, even as a possible wild hypothesis, that it might have just vanished into thin air. That is not something I would even think about at all or take as a possibility. That such things cannot happen may be for me a groundless belief. But it does not follow from that that it is an unreasonable belief. There are many things, I have repeatedly argued, we reasonably believe that we do not believe for a reason. What is more dicey is to claim that such a belief *could not possibly be rationally warranted* (come to be grounded) and that I could know that and still coherently claim that I know that unwarranted belief to be true or that I could reasonably assume its truth or acceptability. See Ernest Nagel, *Logic Without Metaphysics* (Glencoe, IL: The Free Press, 1956) 143-52. I should also remark here that, *pace* Hart, I do not claim anything to be the "only and final truth" or regard my own position as unproblematic. These things would not fit in with my pragmatist fallibilism or with my coherentist methodology of appealing to considered judgments in *wide* reflective equilibrium. See chapter 2 of my *Equality and Liberty* (Totowa, NJ: Rowman and Allanheld, 1985). My version of what is rational is, of course, like every other person's—just one version. Hart asks why accept it if it excludes religious faith as irrational? Well, if it is to be accepted as more than just my idiosyncratic version, it must be seen to square with how we use "rational," "reasonable," "rationality" and the like and with what reflective people, who are informed about these things, would accept after dispassionate and probing deliberation. It must, that is, meet Habermas's conditions for undistorted discourse. I throw it out as a hypothesis to be so tested. Surely

it will need to be refined and whether it has the force I believe it to have depends, if you will, on whether such ideas get a "democratic acceptance," though here the electorate must have proper qualifications. (*If* that is elitism make the most of it.) They must be aware, on all sides of the issue, what is at issue. It is what people would agree to under conditions of undistorted discourse that is vital. It is never a matter of simply tallying up the numbers.

28.   See my *God and the Grounding of Morality* (Ottawa, ON: University of Ottawa Press, forthcoming), my *Ethics Without God* (Buffalo, NY: Prometheus Books, 1973), my *Reason and Practice* (New York: Harper and Row, 1971) chapter 22, and my *Philosophy and Atheism* (Buffalo, NY: Prometheus Books, 1985) chapter 9.

29.   Kai Nielsen, "On Rationality and Essentially Contested Concepts," *Communication & Cognition* 16.3 (1983): 269-81; my "True Needs, Rationality and Emancipation," *Human Needs and Politics*, ed. R. Fitzgerald (Sydney, Australia: Pergamons' Publishers, 1977); and my "Is there an Emancipatory Rationality?" *Critica* VIII.24 (1976). In the context of talking about an emancipatory rationality, Hart's remarks about what he takes to be my views of rationality and my utopian emancipatory hopes should have a brief comment. Utopian hopes (*pace* Hart, note 23) need not at all be beliefs "whose scope transcends the empirical world." One utopian hope I have is the hope for a classless and genderless society. Whether such a hope will ever be realized or indeed can be realized is unclear, but we can say in perfectly empirical terms what it would be like for such a society to come into existence. Such a conception has what the logical empiricists used to call empirical meaning. It is not, like God, something which transcends the empirical world and does not admit of a purely empirical description. Moreover (again *pace* Hart), having utopian hopes does not show that my "belief in reason is not ultimately grounded in reason but rather in hope." I hope that certain things I judge to be desirable will come to obtain. But what I hope for is constrained by what I think is possible, and there reason does come in. But I do not tie my utopian hopes to what I take the most likely outcome to be. And what I take to be the most likely is not determined by what I most hope for. What is most *firmly* in accordance with reason may not be what is to be hoped for. It may very well be more likely than not that we will blow ourselves up in the next fifty years, but that surely is not the object of our utopian hopes.

30.   Here I think Jürgen Habermas's work has been very significant indeed. See particularly his *Theorie des kommunikativen Handelns*, Bands I & II (Frankfurt am Main, West Germany: Suhrkamp Verlag, 1981).

31.   Hart, *op. cit.* Note, particularly among his extensive substantive footnotes, footnotes 11 and 19.

32.   *Ibid.*

33.   Kai Nielsen, *Philosophy and Atheism* 192.

34.   *Ibid.*

35.   *Ibid.* 192-95. See also my "Principles of Rationality" 55-89 and my "The Embeddedness of Conceptual Relativism" 85-111.

36.   Kai Nielsen, *Philosophy and Atheism* 189-209.

37.   Kai Nielsen, "Reason and Sentiment: Skeptical Remarks about Reason and the 'Foundations of Morality'," *Rationality Today*, ed. Theodore F. Geraets (Ottawa, ON: University of Ottawa Press, 1979) 249-79. See also my "Distrusting Reason," *Ethics* 86.4 (1975) and the references in note 29.

38.   Hart, *op. cit.*, note 33 and my remarks in my notes 17, 26 and 29.

39.   Kai Nielsen, "Against Ethical Rationalism," *Gewirth's Ethical Rationalism*, ed. E. Regis (Chicago: University of Chicago Press, 1984); my "Must the Immoralist Act Contrary to Reason?" *Morality, Reason and Truth*, eds. David Copp and David Zimmerman (Totowa, NJ: Rowman and Allanheld, 1985) 212-27; my "Reason and Sentiment" and my "Why Should I be Moral Revisited," *American Philosophical Quarterly* 21.1 (1984): 81-92. Several of these essays have been reprinted in my *Why Be Moral?* (Buffalo, NY: Prometheus Press, 1989).

40.   John Rawls, "Justice as Fairness: Political not Metaphysical," *Philosophy and Public Affairs* 14.3 (1985).

41.   Kai Nielsen, "Linguistic Philosophy and 'The Meaning of Life'," *The Meaning of Life*, ed. E.D. Klemke (New York: Oxford University Press, 1981) 177-203 and my "Religious Perplexity and Faith," *Crane Review* VIII.1 (1965).

42.   Hart, *op. cit.*

43.   *Ibid.*

44.   Kai Nielsen, "Is God So Powerful that He Doesn't Even Have to Exist?" *Religious Experience and Truth*, ed. Sidney Hook (New York: New York University Press, 1961) 270-81.

45.   Ninian Smart, *A Dialogue of Religions* (London: SCM Press, 1960) and Ninian Smart, *Reasons and Faiths* (London: Routledge and Kegan Paul, 1958).

46.   On "low-redefinition" see Paul Edwards, *The Logic of Moral Discourse* (Glencoe, IL: The Free Press, 1955). This is also usefully related to what Charles Stevenson says about persuasive definitions. Charles Stevenson, *Ethics and Language* (New Haven: Yale University Press, 1944) 206-26.

47.   Béla Szabados, "Religion and Irrationality." I should also remark (again *pace* Hart) that there is nothing in my utopian hopes that is spiritual and transcendent. Of course, if through low-redefinitions, carrying us far from Christian orthodoxy, we simply mean, in talking about the spiritual and the transcendent, that which has to do with our future and our destiny, then I can, of course, be said to be concerned with the spiritual and the transcendent. All atheists by such a playing with words can be led gently to religious belief. But this, as Sidney Hook would put it, violates the ethics of words. When God is said to be transcendent and when God is said to be a spirit, what Christian orthodoxy or even near orthodoxy is trying to say is that God is beyond the world and God is not a material entity, a strange thing among things in the world, but is an infinite, non-spatial individual beyond the bounds of space and time. God is not even the world itself viewed in a certain way. To give the implicit low-redefinitions Hart gives is to take us back to either the errors of the reductionism of Braithwaite and Hare discussed in chapter 13, or to the errors of the more elusive reductionism of Phillips and Dilman discussed in chapters 6 through 11.

48.   Richard Rorty, *Philosophy and the Mirror of Nature* (Princeton, NJ: Princeton University Press, 1979) 335-36, 384.

49.   Szabados, *op. cit.*

50.   Kai Nielsen, *Philosophy and Atheism* 189-210.

51.   Clearly this is what Hart thinks but, as I have argued in earlier sections of this chapter, it is not something he has been able to show.

52.   Ninian Smart, "On Knowing What is Uncertain," *Knowing Religiously*, ed. L.S. Rouner (Notre Dame, IN: University of Notre Dame Press, 1985) 86.

53.   Szabados, *op. cit.*

54.   *Ibid.*

55.   Gilbert Ryle, *Collected Papers*, vol. II (London: Hutchinson and Co., 1971) 153-69, 194-211. See also F. Waismann, *How I See Philosophy* (London: Macmillan, 1968) 1-38.

56.   Hart is exercised about what "us" refers to, or my "we". He thinks my views here are elitist, showing scant respect for ordinary people. But just the reverse is the case. I do not say that many ordinary people believe irrationally in believing in God, or that intellectuals at other times and other places are irrational in believing in God. What we can rationally believe is in large measure a matter of what we are in a position to come to know, and that is in considerable measure a matter of time and circumstance, and good or bad fortune. Those of us who are relatively lucky can rightly say "And there by the grace of God go we."

57.   Kai Nielsen, "Can Faith Validate God-Talk?" *Theology Today* (July 1963). See also my "Faith and Authority," *The Southern Journal of Philosophy* 3 (Winter 1965) and my "Religious Perplexity and Faith," *Crane Review* VIII.1 (1965).

58.   Norman Malcolm tries to get around that but he fails. Norman Malcolm, "Is it a Religious Belief that 'God Exists'?" *Faith and Philosophers*, ed. John Hick (New York: St. Martin's Press, 1964) 103-109. See my critique of Malcolm in my "On Believing that God Exists," *Southern Journal of Philosophy* (September 1967).

59.   See the exchange (which among other things catches generational differences between contemporary secularists) between Sidney Hook and myself. Sidney Hook, *The Quest for Being* (New York: St. Martin's Press, 1961) parts 2 and 3 and the appendix; Kai Nielsen, "Religion and Naturalistic Humanism: Some Remarks on Hook's Critique of Religion," *Sidney Hook and the Contemporary World*, ed. Paul Kurtz (New York: John Day Co., 1968) 257-79; Kai Nielsen, "Secularism and Theology: Remarks on a Form of Naturalistic Humanism," *The Southern Journal of Philosophy* XIII (Spring 1975): 109-26; Sidney Hook, "For an Open-Minded Naturalism," *The Southern Journal of Philosophy* XIII (Spring 1975): 127-36; Kai Nielsen, *Philosophy and Atheism* 9-28.

60.   Kai Nielsen, *An Introduction to the Philosophy of Religion* 1-42 and Kai Nielsen, *Philosophy and Atheism* 9-31. See also Kai Nielsen, "On Speaking of God," *Analytical Philosophy of Religion in Canada*, ed. Mostafa Faghfoury (Ottawa, ON: University of Ottawa Press, 1982) 75-96.

61.   Kai Nielsen, "Religious Perplexity and Faith," *Crane Review* VIII.1 (1965).

62.   See chapters 2 and 3 of this book.

DATE DUE

OCT 2 1 1999			